Europe's Crisis of Legitimacy

Book Description

Europe's crisis of legitimacy stems from 'governing by rules and ruling by numbers' in the sovereign debt crisis, which played havoc with the eurozone economy while fueling political discontent. Using the lens of democratic theory, the book assesses the legitimacy of EU governing activities first in terms of their procedural quality ('throughput'), by charting EU actors' different pathways to legitimacy, and then evaluates their policy effectiveness ('output') and political responsiveness ('input'). In addition to an engaging and distinctive analysis of Eurozone crisis governance and its impact on democratic legitimacy, the book offers a number of theoretical insights into the broader question of the functioning of the EU, and international governance more generally. It concludes with proposals for how to remedy the EU's problems of legitimacy, reinvigorate its national democracies, and rethink its future.

Europe's Crisis of Legitimacy

Governing by Rules and Ruling by Numbers in the Eurozone

VIVIEN A. SCHMIDT

OXFORD
UNIVERSITY PRESS

Great Clarendon Street, Oxford, OX2 6DP,
United Kingdom

Oxford University Press is a department of the University of Oxford.
It furthers the University's objective of excellence in research, scholarship,
and education by publishing worldwide. Oxford is a registered trade mark of
Oxford University Press in the UK and in certain other countries

© Vivien A. Schmidt 2020

The moral rights of the author have been asserted

First Edition published in 2020

Impression: 4

Published in the United States of America by Oxford University Press
198 Madison Avenue, New York, NY 10016, United States of America

British Library Cataloguing in Publication Data
Data available

Library of Congress Control Number: 2020936533

ISBN 978-0-19-879705-0 (hbk.)
ISBN 978-0-19-879706-7 (pbk.)

Printed and bound in the UK by
CPI Group (UK) Ltd, Croydon, CR0 4YY

To my mother, Edith Kurzweil

Preface and Acknowledgements

Prior to the Covid-19 virus crisis, Europe's sovereign debt crisis had remained arguably the worst of the European Union 's many crises of the past decade. The health pandemic now rivals the Eurozone crisis in terms of its potentially crippling long term effects. But in this new context, there is all the more reason to look to and learn from the Eurozone crisis, which has not just been a crisis of economics or of politics but also of legitimacy. The EU took the wrong course in 2010 in responding to the Eurozone crisis. Rather than bold initiatives, EU actors ended up "governing by the rules and ruling by the numbers," with a focus on austerity and structural reform. As a result, the Eurozone suffered deteriorating economic performance while the politics became increasingly toxic, as mainstream parties declined and populist challenger parties prospered.

Fortunately, the story does not stop here. Having recognized that things had gone awfully wrong, European leaders and officials began to change Eurozone governance slowly and incrementally after the first couple of years, by reinterpreting the rules and recalibrating the numbers. But because EU actors reinterpreted the rules "by stealth," that is, without admitting it to citizens or even, often, to one another, legitimacy remained in question. Fundamental flaws were not fixed, as suboptimal rules continued to hamper economic growth while feeding populist discontents. And even though by 2015 most EU actors began to acknowledge their rules reinterpretations, the harm had been done.

This book identifies three components of legitimacy: "Output" legitimacy is related to policy effectiveness and performance, "input" to political representation and responsiveness, and "throughput" to the quality of the governance processes. In Europe's (euro) crisis of legitimacy, EU actors initially assumed that all they needed to do was to reinforce the rules (throughput) to guarantee good policy performance (output) and citizen acceptance (input), only to find that performance worsened along with citizens' attitudes. But subsequently, by reinterpreting the rules without admitting it, although (output) performance improved, perceptions of the quality of the (throughput) processes plummeted while the (input) politics continued to worsen.

The book seeks to deepen our understanding of a crisis that has threatened not just the economic and political stability of Europe but also the very project of European integration. What distinguishes this book from many others on the Eurozone crisis is that it uses the lens of democratic theory to examine the crisis from vantage points that analysts tend to deal with separately in different fields—political economy, politics, and governance—and at different levels—EU and national. The book concludes with suggestions on how to move beyond the crisis by continuing to deepen Eurozone integration while generating a more decentralized and democratized Eurozone governance. And because it appears at a time when a new Commission has recently taken over, with pledges to rethink the rules of the Eurozone while restarting growth and responding to citizen concerns, hopefully the book can make some modest contribution to its deliberations.

*   *   *   *   *

This book has its origins in a part-time, yearlong research fellowship on legitimacy in the Eurozone crisis at the Commission—specifically, the Directorate General for Economic and Financial Affairs (DG ECFIN)—in 2014–15. The time spent at DG ECFIN was extremely enlightening, and reinforced my sense of how important it is to understand institutions from the inside as much as from the outside. Special thanks go to Director-General Marco Buti as well as to many of his colleagues at the time, including especially Anne Bucher as well as Oskar Andruszkiewicz, Moreno Bertoldi, Pieter Bouwen, Stefan Ciobanu, Servass Deroose, Elena Flores, Antonio de Lecea, Outi Slotboom, Benedicta Marzinotto, Karl Pichelmann, Eric Ruscher, and Marcin Zogala.

The book builds on my final report for the DG ECFIN fellowship.[1] But it also relies on an extensive amount of work prior to that fellowship in which I developed my theoretical concepts of legitimacy on a senior research professorship at the Free University of Berlin, Otto Sühr Institute, in the Research College "The Transformative Power of Europe" (KFG), headed by Tanja Börzel and Thomas Risse (Jan–June 2010).[2] In Berlin I also examined the beginnings of the crisis.[3] I continued to work on the issues of ideas and communication in the crisis for an EU Commission Framework 7 project (GR:EEN), led by Richard Higgott.[4] I further benefited greatly from the collaborative Horizon 2020 grant ENLIGHTEN (2015–18), led by Len Seabrooke, focused on legitimacy in the Eurozone crisis. Under the auspices of this research project I developed the ideas about EU modes of governance;[5] elaborated on their application in the euro crisis with Amandine Crespy, Ramona Coman, and Frederick Ponjaert;[6] theorized about power and its uses and abuses in the crisis in collaboration with Martin Carstensen;[7] and worked on the general questions regarding the euro crisis with Len Seabrooke and Cornel Ban. Another senior research professorship at the Free University of Berlin, in the KFG of the Otto Sühr Institute (Jan–June 2017), enabled me to make further progress on the book, in particular on theorizing throughput legitimacy. Some of this came in collaboration with Matthew Wood, for a co-edited Symposium issue of the journal *Public Administration*.[8] Finally, my home institution, Boston University, was generous enough to make it possible for me to pursue my

---

[1] Schmidt 2015c; see also 2015a, 2016a.   [2] Schmidt 2013.   [3] Schmidt 2010b.
[4] Schmidt 2014.   [5] Schmidt 2018a.   [6] Coman et al. 2020.
[7] Carstensen and Schmidt 2016, 2018a, 2018b.   [8] Schmidt and Wood 2019.

research through sabbatical leaves in 2010, in spring 2017, and in spring 2018. I am grateful to all these generous patrons for having given me the time, place, and space to think, read, and ultimately write this book, as well as to all the collaborators on these many projects who provided inspiration along with immensely rewarding intellectual exchanges.

I owe a great deal to very many other people as well, to whom I apologize in advance for any inadvertent omissions. I conducted countless interviews and engaged in innumerable conversations with officials and concerned parties in Brussels and in national capitals, in private meetings and/or public conferences across Europe. Among the many individuals in and around EU institutions with whom I discussed the ins and outs of the Eurozone crisis, and from whom I learned a great deal, beyond those already mentioned, special thanks go to Joaquin Almunia, Lorenzo Bini Smaghi, Jim Cloos, Richard Corbett, Stefaan De Rynck, Anna Diamantopoulou, Kristalina Georgieva, Roberto Gualtieri, Emily O'Reilly, Aidan O'Sullivan, Jean-Claude Piris, Hannes Swoboda, Luuk Van Middelaar, Shahin Vallée, and Thomas Wieser. I am also grateful to the many Commission and Council officials interviewed in the context of the ENLIGHTEN grant who must remain anonymous. In addition, of the many close observers in think-tanks and academe and elsewhere with whom I spoke, special mention goes to Cinzia Alcide, Giuliano Amato, Carlo Bastasin, Richard Bellamy, Mark Blyth, Benjamin Braun, Furio Cerutti, Stefan Collignon, Roland Erne, Sergio Fabbrini, Maurizio Ferrera, Valeria Ferroni, Ulrike Guérot, Paolo Guerrieri, Leo Hoffmann-Axthelm, Erik Jones, Hans-Helmut Kotz, Sandra Kröger, Brigid Laffan, Deborah Mabbett, Matthias Matthijs, Marcello Messori, Stefano Micossi, Ashoka Mody, Giovanni Moro, Kalypso Nicolaïdis, Federico Lorenzo Pace, Romano Prodi, Stefano Sacchi, André Sapir, Waltraud Schelkle, Hans-Werner Sinn, Loukas Tsoukalis, Paul Tucker, and Pieter de Wilde.

Beyond this, I would like to thank many people for careful reading and advice on different parts of the manuscript at various phases, including Cornel Ban, Amandine Crespy, Ramona Coman, Carlo Bastasin, Ben Crum, Christian Kreuder-Sonnen, Manos Matsaganis, Wolfgang Merkel, Fritz Scharpf, Jonathan Zeitlin, and Michael Zürn. Beyond these, I thank all those who offered helpful comments on different aspects of the evolving book in the many workshops and conferences, and in particular the organizers and editors. These include Matthias Matthijs and Mark Blyth in the *Future of the Euro* book project, Brigid Laffan for the European University Institute (EUI) workshop on "Rethinking European integration," Piero Tortola and Lorenzo Vai for the Centro Studi sul Federalismo (CSF) and the Istituto Affari Internazionali (IAI) workshop on "Which Government for the EU?," Mark Pollack and Marieke Kleine for the Princeton and EUI workshops on "Liberal Intergovernmentalism at 25," Jonathan Zeitlin and Francesco Nicoli for the University of Amsterdam workshop on "Politicization," and Sergio Fabbrini for the LUISS University workshop on

"Differentiated integration." Moreover, for their invaluable comments at its final stages, I also thank participants in the book panel at the Council for European Studies: Jonathan Hopkin, Kalypso Nicolaïdis, Simona Piattoni, Ben Crum, Chris Bickerton, and Matthias Matthijs. All contributed immensely to the final product. Also deserving of thanks but by now too many to name are the graduate and undergraduate assistants I had over the years.

Finally, I must thank two members of my family. My brother Allen Kurzweil provided unfailing editorial advice and sympathy with the trials and tribulations of writing, which he himself knows only too well. My husband Jolyon Howorth, without whom this book would not have been possible, offered constant encouragement in addition to his many close readings of the manuscript at its many stages of (non-)completion and editorial suggestions. His patience was extraordinary, his sense of humor (almost) unfailing, and his emotional support unparalleled.

The book is dedicated to my mother, Edith Kurzweil, who passed away all too young at age 91 in February 2016. She was a wonderful role model, a great source of comfort, advice, and support, as well as a wonderful friend across my lifetime—and is sorely missed.

Contents

PART III   OUTPUT AND INPUT LEGITIMACY
IN THE EUROZONE CRISIS

List of Figures

List of Acronyms

AfD	Alternative for Germany
AGS	Annual Growth Survey
ALDE	Alliance of Liberals and Democrats for Europe (European Parliament)
AMR	Alert Mechanism Report
ANL	Independent Greeks
BB	Bundesbank
CDU	Christian Democratic Union (Germany)
CSDP	Common Security and Defense Policy
CSU	Christian Social Union (Germany)
CJEU	Court of Justice of the European Union
CME	Coordinated Market Economy
Council	European Council and/or Council of Ministers
CSR	Country-Specific Recommendation
DG ECFIN	Directorate General for Economic and Financial Affairs
DG EMPL	Directorate General for Employment, Social Affairs and Inclusion
ECB	European Central Bank
ECI	European Citizens Initiative
ECOFIN	Economic and Financial Affairs Council
ECON	Economic Affairs Committee of the European Parliament
EDIS	European Deposit Insurance Scheme
EDP	Excessive Deficit Procedure
EERP	European Economic Recovery Plan
EFB	European Fiscal Board
EFDD	Europe of Freedom and Democracy
EIP	Excessive Imbalance Procedure
EFSF	European Financial Stability Facility
EFSI	European Fund for Strategic Investment
EMF	European Monetary Fund
EMS	European Monetary System
EMU	European Monetary Union
EP	European Parliament
EPP	European People's Party
ESM	European Stability Mechanism
EU	European Union
ERM	Exchange Rate Mechanism
FDI	Foreign Direct Investment
FDP	Free Democratic Party (Germany)
FI	France Unbowed
FN	National Front (France)

FPÖ	Freedom Party (Austria)
GDP	Gross Domestic Product
IDP	In-Depth-Review
IMF	International Monetary Fund
IO	International Organization
LME	Liberal Market Economy
LOLR	Lender of Last Resort
LR	The Republicans (France)
LRM	The Republic on the Move (France)
LTRO	Long Term Refinancing Operation
MOU	Memorandum of Understanding
MIP	Macroeconomic Imbalance Procedure
MS5	Five Star Movement (Italy)
MTO	Medium Term Objectives
NEETs	Youth Not in Employment, Education, or Training
NGO	Non-Governmental Organization
NR	National Rally (France—formerly FN)
NRP	National Reform Program
OCA	Optimum Currency Area
OECD	Organization for Economic Cooperation and Development
OLAF	European Anti-Fraud Office
OMT	Open Monetary Transactions
QE	Quantitative Easing
PASOK	Panhellenic Socialist Movement (Greece)
PD	Democratic Party (Italy)
PEGIDA	Patriotic Europeans against the Islamization of the Occident (Germany)
PP	Conservative People's Party (Spain)
PS	Socialist Party (France)
PS	Socialist Party (Portugal)
PSOE	Spanish Social Democratic Party
PVV	Party for Freedom (Netherlands)
RQMV	Reverse Qualified Majority Voting
SGP	Stability and Growth Pact
SME	State-Influenced Market Economy
SPD	Social Democratic Party (Germany)
SRF	Single Resolution Fund
SRM	Single Resolution Mechanism
SSM	Single Supervisory Mechanism
TFEU	Treaty on the Foundation of the European Union
UKIP	United Kingdom Independence Party
VLTRO	Very Long Term Refinancing Operation

1

Introduction

Europe's Crisis of Legitimacy

The year 2010 was a difficult one for the European Union. This was the year when a relatively minor problem with the deficit of a rather small country with a GDP that represented little more than 2 percent of the European economy spiraled into a full-blown crisis of sovereign debt that became known as the Eurozone crisis. Had EU leaders only responded more quickly to reassure the markets that the EU would stand behind the sovereign debt of every one of its member states, the crisis might have been avoided. But because they delayed until the very last moment, and then backed into "solutions" that did little to resolve the underlying problems, the crisis went on and on. And as it continued, it quickly transformed itself from an economic crisis into a more general crisis of legitimacy, with the EU's governance thrown into question.

At the height of the Eurozone crisis, major decisions affecting millions of Europeans were taken behind closed doors by EU policymakers with little attempt to consult the people through the normal political channels—*and* the policies didn't work! The European economy suffered from slow growth, high unemployment, and rising inequality and poverty. It is not surprising that the politics in response became increasingly Euroskeptic and volatile, with citizens' loss of trust and confidence in EU and national authorities reflected in the frequent turnover of incumbent governments and the rise of extremist parties and populist movements.

By framing the crisis as one of public profligacy (rather than of private excess) and by diagnosing the causes as behavioral (member states not following the rules) rather than structural (linked to the euro's design), EU leaders found little need initially to fix the euro or to moderate the effects of the crisis. Instead, they chose to reinforce the rules enshrined in the Treaties, based on convergence criteria for countries' deficits, debt, and inflation rates. And they agreed to provide loan bailouts for countries under market pressure in exchange for rapid fiscal consolidation and "structural reforms" focused on deregulating labor markets and cutting social welfare costs. In the absence of any deeper political integration that could provide greater democratic representation and control over an ever expanding supranational governance, and in the face of major divisions among EU actors over what to do and how, the EU ended up "governing by the rules and ruling by the numbers" in the Eurozone.

Europe's Crisis of Legitimacy: Governing by Rules and Ruling by Numbers in the Eurozone. Vivien A. Schmidt, Oxford University Press (2020). © Vivien A. Schmidt.
DOI: 10.1093/oso/9780198797050.001.0001

The challenge for EU actors as the crisis continued unabated was how to get beyond the treaty rules to more workable ones in a context in which changing the rules is very difficult. The EU is unlike any national democracy, where policy change can be politically legitimated by elections that bring in a new government able to operationalize the "will of the people" and to govern in its name and on its behalf. The EU's governance system not only makes it hard for it to reach agreements that generate the best solutions; it makes it even harder to alter any decisions, however inadequate. This has not just been a question of institutional constraints, legal obstacles, political logics, or even diverging national economic interests. It has also been a question of how to build legitimacy for change in such a context.

The route initially chosen for change caused further problems of legitimacy. As EU actors became increasingly concerned about continued poor economic performance and growing political volatility, they began to reinterpret the rules and recalibrate the numbers "by stealth," that is, by proclaiming that they were sticking to the rules even as they were increasingly flexible in their application.[1] In efforts to fix the policies and calm the politics, they also began introducing policy innovations to solve some of the structural problems of the euro. But while both the rules reinterpretations and policy innovations did produce better results, the sub-optimal rules remained in place and the structural flaws of the Eurozone were not resolved. In consequence, economic growth remained anemic and public disenchantment grew. And although general acknowledgement of rules reinterpretations finally came in 2015, the damage had been done.

As a result, since the sovereign debt crisis began in 2010, the European Union has been in the throes not only of an economic crisis but also of a crisis of legitimacy related to problems of policy performance, political responsiveness, and procedural quality. While things may have gotten better as the crisis slowed and as EU actors have found innovative ways to ease the rules, thereby producing better results, much remains to be done.

Governing by Rules and Ruling by Numbers in the Eurozone

Whether the European Union is democratically legitimate has been a recurring question. If legitimacy can be understood not just as citizens' tacit acceptance of the EU's governing authority but equally in terms of its active approval of the EU's governing activity, then matters have never been as problematic as in the wake of the Eurozone's sovereign debt crisis. The challenges to legitimacy include the policies that have been largely ineffective in resolving the economic crisis, the

---

[1] Schmidt 2015a, 2016a.

politics that have become increasingly divisive and volatile, and the processes that began with highly restrictive rules and numbers but slowly shifted over time, without public acknowledgment until recently.

During the heat of the Eurozone crisis from 2010 to 2012, EU leaders in the European Council decided on a range of policies that sought above all to contain the conflagration. First, they rejected calls for greater social solidarity in the form of debt forgiveness or debt mutualization in favor of loan bailout funds with harsh terms for countries in danger of default, supervised by the "Troika" (made up of the International Monetary Fund, the European Central Bank, and the EU Commission). At the same time, through successive legislative packages and treaty agreements, they reinforced the rules of Eurozone governance by setting specific numerical targets for deficits and debts, with austerity and structural reform mandated for all those falling foul of the rules, and sanctions for those who failed repeatedly to reach the targets. Additionally, EU leaders agreed to enhanced budgetary oversight by Brussels officials over all member states through the "European Semester," meaning that the Commission was charged with vetting national governments' yearly budgets even prior to their being reviewed by national parliaments.

These governance policies failed to deal effectively with the problems of the European economy, raising questions about the EU's legitimacy when defined in terms of policy performance. Economic growth remained sluggish while deflation continued to threaten in a Europe characterized by increasing divergence between the export-rich surplus economies of Northern Europe and the rest.[2] Europe more generally was also facing a "humanitarian crisis," affected by rising poverty and inequality along with continuing high levels of unemployment, especially in Southern Europe, and in particular among youth.[3] Largely to blame for prolonging the economic crisis in the Eurozone periphery—as even the International Monetary Fund (IMF) and the OECD reported[4]—were the EU's demands for austerity along with "one size fits all" remedies to diverse national political economies with different institutional configurations and potential engines for growth.[5]

Citizens' disappointment with the EU's poor economic performance also fueled questions about the EU's political legitimacy, related to citizens' increasing dissatisfaction with and disaffection from EU and national politics. Citizens have come to perceive the EU as more and more remote (read technocratic) and national governments as less and less responsive to their concerns—often as a

---

[2] Blyth 2013; Hopkin 2015; Sandbu 2015; Tooze 2018; Mody 2018.
[3] See reports by the Council of Europe 2013, Caritas 2015; European Parliament 2015; see also Perez and Matsaganis 2017.
[4] IMF 2013; OECD 2016.
[5] Scharpf 2012a, 2014; Hall 2012; Baccaro and Pontusson 2016; Iversen and Soskice 2018.

result of EU policies and prescriptions.[6] National governments' dilemma—caught between the need to act responsibly by implementing unpopular EU policies and the need to be responsive to citizens' demands[7]—has translated into more and more volatile national politics. National elections have become increasingly unpredictable, as incumbent governments are regularly turned out of office while new anti-system parties with anti-euro and anti-EU messages get attention, votes, and more and more seats in parliaments.[8] Much of this is a function of the growth of Euroskepticism and the mounting strength of the populist extremes, but it also reflects the increasing divisions between winners and losers in the crisis, within the member states as well as between them.

Adding to these policy-based and politics-related challenges to EU legitimacy are the policymaking processes involved in the governing of the Eurozone by restrictive rules and numerical targets. Here, much of the problem has had to do with EU actors' implementation of "one size" rules that were a poor fit for most member states, and the fact that after an initial two-year period of harsh enforcement they eased the application of the rules without admitting it. Not acknowledging up front that the rules did not work meant that EU actors continued to operate under rules that were sub-optimal, and that constrained the range of possible solutions. Moreover, it left their actions open at any time to being contested as illegitimate because lacking in accountability or transparency. By the same token, however, not saying what they were doing gave EU actors the space necessary to reinterpret the rules incrementally to make them work somewhat better—while waiting for a time when they could gain agreement to legitimate changing the rules more formally. Even though by 2015 most EU actors had admitted that they were indeed reinterpreting the rules, it did little to change the dynamics of interaction among EU actors, which had become increasingly politicized over whether such reinterpretations were technically justified or normatively legitimate.

At the inception of the crisis, the Council became dominated by the "one size fits one" rules of intergovernmental negotiation that gave the most economically powerful member state (ie, Germany) outsized influence to impose its preferences. Subsequently, however, despite continued German predominance, the increasingly politicized dynamics of deliberation and contestation among the member states intermittently led to positive change. Along with innovative instruments of deeper integration such as banking union came acceptance of the need for growth (by 2012), flexibility (by 2014), and investment (in 2015). At the same time, however, the Council continued with the discourse of rules-based austerity (until 2013) and structural reform while imposing strict conditionality on member states forced into loan bailout programs. In consequence, the Council's intergovernmental rule

[6] Hobolt 2015; Kriesi and Grande 2015.   [7] Mair 2013.
[8] Bosco and Verney 2012; Mair 2013; Taggart and Szczerbiak 2013; Hopkin 2020.

can on the one hand be condemned as a (German) "dictatorship" imposing *diktats*[9] and on the other praised as a "deliberative body" driven in the crisis by the search for consensus.[10]

Similarly, the European Central Bank (ECB) at the beginning of the crisis continued to follow its own "one size fits none" rules of monetary policy.[11] While its inflation targeting policy further exacerbated the economic divergences among member states' economies, its repeated claims that it would not back member-state sovereign debt by acting as a "lender of last resort" through quantitative easing increasingly worried the markets. It was not until July 2012 that the ECB moved definitively from its "one size" rules to "whatever it takes," in the famous phrase of the ECB president Mario Draghi, which stopped market attacks dead in their tracks.[12] And only in 2015 did the ECB engage in full-scale quantitative easing. All the while, however, the ECB claimed to remain true to its Charter, hiding its reinterpretation "in plain view" as it switched from a discourse of "credibility" to "stability" in the medium term.[13] But in exchange for "saving the euro," the ECB pressed EU member states to be stricter with regard to the rules, by tightening their belts and reforming their economies, while it forced countries in trouble into conditionality programs. As a result, the ECB can be portrayed not only as the "hero" repeatedly rescuing the euro but also as the "ogre" pushing austerity and structural reform.

The EU Commission, much as the other actors, also initially applied its own "one size fits all" rules of budgetary austerity and structural reform to very different member-state economies. But after a couple of years, despite the fact that the EU Commission stuck to a harsh discourse of rigorous enforcement of the "one size" rules, it began to use its discretionary powers in the European Semester to become ever more flexible in applying the rules and calculating the numbers, with greater attention to social concerns. Only in 2015 did the newly appointed Commission admit that it had indeed been easing its application of the rules, but it insisted that it had the right to do so, as it established "rules" for its flexibility and further 'socialized' the European Semester. EU Commission officials therefore could not only be derided as "ayatollahs of austerity" intent on imposing austerity and structural reform but should equally be admired as "ministers of moderation" navigating between the Council and ECB as they (re)interpreted the rules for better results.[14]

As for the European Parliament (EP), it had almost "no size at all" when it came to setting policy for the Eurozone, before as well as at the start of the crisis.[15] Over time, however, the EP developed a growing presence, if not yet

---

[9] Eg, Fabbrini 2013; Schimmelfennig 2015a; Tsebelis 2016.   [10] Puetter 2014.
[11] Enderlein et al., 2012.   [12] Draghi 2012.   [13] Schmidt 2016a.
[14] I first used these catchphrases in presentations to the Directorate General for Economic and Financial Affairs (DG ECFIN) while on a part-time fellowship there in 2014–15—see Schmidt 2015c.
[15] Schmidt 2015a.

major influence, in Eurozone governance. That presence can be seen through its increasing involvement in both informal and formal legislative processes, its greater exercise of oversight over the main Eurozone actors, and those actors' concomitant recognition of the EP as the "go-to" body for legitimacy.[16] Hopes and fears therefore hinge on whether the EP will continue to be dismissed as little more than a "talking shop" in Eurozone governance or comes in time to exemplify more of an "equal partner" in a renewed set of governance processes for the Eurozone.[17]

What has become clear already over the course of the Eurozone crisis is that the challenge for EU institutional actors has been how to get beyond the original rules to more workable ones. This has not just been a question of overcoming the institutional architecture that makes formally changing the rules very difficult so long as there is significant disagreement among the member states about what to do and how to do it.[18] The challenges also involve the political divisions that have reinforced the institutional gridlock, given diverging national perceptions of the crisis that exert political pressures on EU member-state leaders.[19] The potential legal constraints that limit what they can do "constitutionally" (meaning in terms of the Treaties) represent additional obstacles.[20] And the very structure of the euro only further exacerbates the political divisions and the legal problems as it continues to produce increasing economic divergence among member states. Equally important, however, has been the question of how to build legitimacy for reinterpreting the rules—no easy task given the complexity of navigating the obstacle course constituted by the Eurozone's economic structure, the EU's political institutions, EU and national politics, and EU law.

Such problems of legitimacy have made the responses to the Eurozone crisis a test case for the future of the EU itself—on whether it will continue to deepen the integration project, and if so, how.

Democratic Legitimacy

The Eurozone crisis has a lot to tell us about the complications of democratic legitimacy in Europe or, more specifically, in the European Union. In the EU, even the most basic questions about democracy have no easy answers: Who really governs? In whose name? To what ends? These are the focus of unending debate among scholars in EU studies.[21] Some insist that member-state governments in the Council are in charge, bargaining or deliberating on the basis of national

---

[16] Hix and Hoyland 2013; Fasone 2014; Dinan 2014; Héritier et al. 2016; Kreilinger 2019.
[17] Hix and Hoyland 2013.   [18] See Scharpf 1999.   [19] Laffan 2014.
[20] See F. Fabbrini 2014.   [21] See discussion in Schmidt 2018a.

interests.[22] Others argue to the contrary that supranational actors in the Commission or the ECB are in control, designing and/or implementing initiatives in Europe's general interest.[23] And yet others suggest that the EP plays an increasingly influential role in representing European citizens' interests.[24]

More complicated still are questions about legitimacy in the EU: Does the EU benefit from the legitimacy required of any governing body, namely citizens' unquestioning acceptance of its authority? And if it does, is the EU's governing authority further legitimated by its governing activity, such that it provides for the public good, respects citizens' expressed will, and acts in ways considered just and fair? These questions lead to a whole set of more specific queries, including: Are the policies politically acceptable and appropriate? Do they reflect citizen needs and desires? Are the policies effective? Do they produce good results? Are the processes by which such policies are agreed and implemented carried out with efficacy? Are they also carried out in ways that are accountable, transparent, open, and inclusive? And who decides—technical actors, political actors, or the citizens?

Questioning whether the EU is democratically legitimate is not new. Long before the Eurozone crisis, political analysts disagreed as to whether the EU was or could be democratic and/or legitimate. While some analysts argued that the EU was indeed democratically legitimate,[25] others insisted to the contrary that it suffered from a democratic deficit at the EU and/or national levels.[26] Concerning the EU's responses to the Eurozone sovereign debt crisis, however, this division of opinion largely disappeared.[27]

Most analysts have found significant problems of democratic legitimacy. Some critics have faulted the deleterious outcomes of EU policies of austerity and structural reform, in particular for their impact on the political economies of peripheral member states.[28] Others have decried the lack of citizen political engagement in, let alone impact on, EU decision-making, and have worried about the concomitant rise in citizen disaffection accompanied by growing political volatility.[29] Yet others have blamed the poor quality of EU policy processes, with the increase in supranational

---

[22] For interest-based bargaining see Moravcsik 1998; Schimmelfennig 2015a, 2015b; for consensus seeking deliberation see Puetter 2014; Bickerton et al. 2015.

[23] Sandholtz and Stone-Sweet 1998; Bauer and Becker 2014; Becker et al. 2016; Dehousse 2016.

[24] Hix and Hoyland 2013; Héritier et al. 2016.

[25] For example, Caporaso and Tarrow 2008; Majone 1998; Moravcsik 2002.

[26] Follesdal 2006; Mair 2006; Schmidt 2006; Hix 2008; and even Majone 2009.

[27] See, eg, Blyth 2013; Bastasin 2015; Streeck (2013); Matthijs and Blyth 2015; Champeau et al. 2015; Cramme and Hobolt 2015; Legrain 2014; Peet and Laguardia 2014; Tsoukalis 2016; Varoufakis 2017.

[28] Scharpf 2012b, 2013, 2014; Blyth 2013; Höpner and Schäfer 2007; Armingeon, and Baccaro 2013; Mody 2018; Tooze 2018.

[29] See, eg, Kriesi et al. 2008; Mair 2006; van der Eijk and Franklin, 2007.

and intergovernmental rule to the detriment of the co-decision process and any significant involvement of the EP, let alone of national parliaments.[30]

These concerns about the impact of the Eurozone crisis on the legitimacy of EU policies, processes, and politics readily translate into concepts used by EU studies theorists who consider democratic legitimacy in the terms of political systems theory.[31] That theory originally identified two main legitimizing mechanisms for democracy, *output* and *input*, to which I have added a third, *throughput*.

Output legitimacy depends on the extent to which policy choices provide for the common good, and is predicated on those policies' effectiveness and performance. Input legitimacy depends instead on the extent to which policy choices reflect "the will of the people," which is predicated on citizens' engagement in representative processes and government responsiveness to citizens' concerns and demands.[32] Throughput legitimacy sits between the input and the output, in the "black box" of governance.[33] It depends on the procedural quality of the policymaking processes, including the efficacy of the policymaking, the accountability of the actors, the transparency of their actions, and their openness and inclusiveness with regard to civil society.[34]

Adding a procedural criterion to the mix is very useful. Throughput legitimacy enables us to consider not only the interaction effects among the different kinds of legitimizing criteria within throughput, for example between the efficacy of the processes and their transparency, or their accountability versus their inclusiveness. It also allows us to consider how throughput processes of governance interact with the political input into those processes or the policy output from the processes. Importantly, these three legitimizing mechanisms differ in their interactive relationships. Input and output can involve a trade-off whereby better output performance through effective policy outcomes can make up for little citizen participation or government responsiveness, and failed output can still be legitimated by extensive citizen input. Throughput, in contrast, offers no such trade-offs. If of good quality, governance processes disappear from view. If not, because policymaking appears incompetent, oppressive, biased, or corrupt, the governance processes can lose legitimacy not just on procedural grounds (throughput) but also because they may undermine perceptions of the legitimacy of the politics (input) and the policies (output).[35]

---

[30] Scharpf 2014a; Fabbrini 2013; Schmidt 2013; Crum and Curtin 2015.

[31] The systems approach is largely built on that of David Easton (1965), as updated by Scharpf 1999.

[32] Scharpf 1999, Ch. 1; 2012a.

[33] Schmidt 2013; see also Zürn 2000; Benz and Papadopoulos 2006. Note that Easton (1965) uses the term throughput, but limits it to administrative processes.

[34] See, eg, Scharpf 1988; Harlow and Rawlins 2007; Cini 2013; Héritier 2003; Coen and Richardson 2009; Greenwood 2007; Kröger 2008; Liebert and Trenz 2009.

[35] Schmidt 2013.

Using these three mechanisms of legitimation to analyze EU actors' initial "governing by rules and numbers" and their subsequent "rules-reinterpretation by stealth" suggests particularly interesting ways of stylizing our understanding of the Eurozone crisis. Put succinctly, it could be said that initially EU actors assumed that reinforcing rules-based governance (throughput) would ensure good policy results (output) even in the absence of citizens' political involvement (input). But as EU actors themselves soon recognized, however good the quality of rules-following (throughput), policy performance (output) did not improve as expected, while political volatility (input) rose in response. EU actors subsequently therefore began slowly to reinterpret the rules (throughput) in order to ensure better results (output) and to respond to the increasingly negative politics (input). But doing so "by stealth," by denying that they were bending if not breaking the rules, they risked further skewing the political input and tainting the policy output. To illustrate: when EU institutional actors ease the rules but continue to proclaim that they are imposing strict austerity and structural reform, Southern Europeans continue to feel oppressed even when accommodated, while Northern Europeans feel deceived regardless.

So why not tell the truth: that they were indeed reinterpreting the rules because the policies were not working? This is not so easy in a context characterized by differing perceptions of the causes of the crisis, conflicting ideas about how to govern the European economy, divergent preferences for courses of action, and differing normative orientations regarding the EU and what it is or should become.[36] Added to this are the institutional constraints, including the built-in constitutional and legal obstacles to action (especially the no-bailout clause) and the decision rules (in particular, unanimity) that make changing the Treaties almost impossible where member states disagree.

The political logics also matter. From the start, the opposing political positions of the member states made any win-win consensus very difficult to achieve. What needed to be done to solve the crisis was extremely unpopular with the voting publics of the core member states in Northern Europe—not only Germany but also the Netherlands, Austria, Finland, and even Latvia, where they saw themselves as having to foot the bill. At the same time, what was imposed on member states in the periphery in terms of austerity and structural reform was equally unpopular, and often seen as unjustly forcing the debtor countries to pay for the risky loans of creditor country bank. This has meant that Europe has been "trapped" by its deepening divisions between core and periphery, winners and losers, technocrats and populists, with the European project itself at risk as a result.[37]

---

[36] See, eg, Brunnermeier et al. 2016.   [37] Offe 2013.

Moreover, once EU leaders committed the Eurozone to rules-based numbers-targeting governance, that course became very difficult to reverse. In cases where sitting governments had imposed austerity and structural reform on their national constituencies, any turnabout in policy could have been seen as a tacit admission that their policies were failing or had been misguided in the first place. But even for newly elected governments intent on changing the policies, the question arose of how to do so when EU treaties committed them to honor all preceding agreements, and when EU institutional rules required unanimity for changing such agreements. Moreover, many EU leaders did not agree that the rules did not work, only that some member states had not properly implemented them. Ideology for some, legal obligations for most, along with political sunk costs for all meant that changing the rules would be very difficult in any event.

And then of course there is the difficulty of communicating to a public that consists of not just "the people" but also the markets. What EU leaders communicate can work at cross-purposes and has done, time and again, as they legitimated their own turnabouts in hyperbolic terms to their national constituencies, only to sow panic in the markets. A case in point is when Chancellor Merkel, having resisted a Greek bailout for months on the grounds that it was unnecessary while insisting that Germany would not take on the debts of others, justified her about-face in May 2010 by claiming that this was to "save the euro," at a time when the markets had never thought the euro at risk.[38]

All of these issues help explain why, once having decided to govern by rules and numbers at the beginning of the Eurozone crisis in 2010, it took a couple of years and the slowing of the crisis after July 2012 for any reinterpretation of the rules. But these reinterpretations remained largely surreptitious until late 2014 or early 2015, when EU actors became more open about them, including seeking to legitimate them to other EU actors and the public at large. Thereafter, such reinterpretations continued to be debated and contested, in large measure because there continued to be little agreement on how to govern the Eurozone, despite incremental progress in a number of areas. In other words, institutional reforms based on normative principles of legitimacy—that followed more accountable and inclusive procedures to produce better outcomes likely to meet with greater citizen approval—came up against the continuing empirical realities of divided publics and EU actors at odds.

EU Actors' Different Pathways to Legitimacy

In all of this, there have been significant differences among EU actors in their pathways to legitimacy and their problems in achieving it. Among such actors, it

---

[38] Schmidt 2014.

is useful to distinguish in particular between the "political" actors in the Council and the European Parliament and the "technical" actors in the ECB and the Commission.

Among political actors, both the Council and the EP tend to assume that they retain legitimacy through their (input) representation of the citizens—the member-state leaders in the Council indirectly via national elections, the members of the EP directly via European parliamentary elections. In actual fact, the Council is far from a (input-legitimate) representative forum while the EP is only minimally representative. Not only do the Council's intergovernmental decisions generally go beyond any individual member state's national aggregation of interests, but most member states' parliaments also lack the information and competences to hold their governments to account. At best, the Council may establish a kind of (throughput-legitimate) mutual accountability as a deliberative body in intergovernmental decision-making or with the EP and Commission in co-decision making. At the same time, the EP serves as a weak representative forum, not only due to low citizen electoral turnout and awareness but also because it has no formal remit to hold the Council to account, in particular in Eurozone governance.

As for technical actors, the ECB tends to conceive of its legitimacy as gained primarily from the (output) effectiveness of its policy performance, although it also claims quality (throughput) procedures through its formal accountability to the EP. But the output legitimacy of the ECB was far from guaranteed in the first two years of the Eurozone crisis, given the poor results, and remained problematic for the program countries throughout the crisis. Moreover, with regard to throughput legitimacy, ECB formal accountability remains weak with regard to the EP and non-existent for the Council (although it has lately developed informal channels of accountability), at the same time that, for reasons of efficacy, ECB transparency is limited. In contrast, the Commission tends to consider that it maintains legitimacy via the (throughput) quality of its governance processes, including its efficacy in administering the rules, its double accountability to input-legitimate actors—encompassing both the Council and the EP—and the transparency, openness, and inclusiveness of its interface with citizens. But such procedural legitimacy was also in short supply in the Eurozone crisis. (Throughput) accountability and transparency were jeopardized by the Commission's discourse denying its increasing flexibility between 2012 and 2015, while (output) policy effectiveness was undermined by the sub-optimal rules, however flexibly applied over time.

With such different pathways to and problems with legitimacy, it follows that when confronted by rapidly changing events, failing solutions, and constraining institutions, EU actors have looked in different places for innovative ideas to solve the crisis as well as to build legitimacy for their policy responses. Whereas technical actors look mainly toward the expert networks and epistemic communities with which to engage in the search for ideas as well as legitimacy, political actors look more toward their national constituencies for legitimacy, even if they turn to the experts for the technical ideas on crisis responses.

Institutional configurations of power and circuits of influence also matter for legitimacy. In the case of technical actors, the ECB has the autonomy to (re)interpret the rules set out in its Charter so long as it can build a sense of agreement about what to do via an epistemic community of banking and economic experts. Any such agreements can help the ECB to persuade its own member-state governing board members of the economic validity of its reinterpretations—although often it will also need to persuade powerful Council members of the reinterpretation's appropriateness (not to mention legal validity), as well as the EP in its quarterly encounters. But the ECB also needs to speak convincingly to the markets and the people of the (output) effectiveness and (throughput) efficacy of its decisions. The Commission has much less margin for maneuver because the rules it devises and administers have to be agreed by the Council (with the EP in certain instances), and it has much less capacity to exercise voice. That said, within the limits of the rules, the Commission does have room for maneuver with regard to its (re)interpretation of the rules, as already noted.

Compared to technical actors, political actors such as the Council and the EP may be in a better position in principle to change the rules since, as legislators, they make the rules. In practice, however, the EP has little sway in Eurozone governance, in particular in contrast to the Council, which can impose its decisions. The Council has exercised tremendous power and influence during the Eurozone crisis—although some member states have been more "equal" than others in this context (Germany in particular). That said, member states in both the Council and EP have been boxed in by diverging preferences—in particular between "creditor" and "debtor" countries—and caught in a "politics of constraint" that is very difficult to reverse.[39]

Timing has been equally important, in particular between the "fast-burning" phase of the crisis from 2010 to 2012 and the phase thereafter, once it had moved to a slow burn.[40] During the peak period of the crisis, EU actors had to respond quickly as market attacks threatened the very existence of the euro, and pushed one member state after the other into a loan bailout package. For political actors in the Council, the fast-burning crisis demanded quick action and led to much improvisation, mainly based on pre-existing ideas of rules-based governance and bailout regimes.[41] New ideas would have had to have come from the technical actors who, given the unanticipated and unprecedented nature of the crisis, had

---

[39] Laffan 2014.

[40] On the logics of fast-burning versus slow-burning crises see: Tsingou 2014; Seabrooke and Tsingou 2016, 2018.

[41] Van Middelaar 2019.

little to offer other than reviving the old ideas. The quandary for the EU in the midst of the Eurozone crisis is that technical actors are more likely to innovate in slow-burning crises, when they have time to reflect and consult, and political actors in the fast-burning one, under pressure for results—so long as technical actors have prepared the ground. But when they have not, new ideas may have to wait until the next flare-up of the crisis—or be incrementally layered on "by stealth."

Finally, power is also central to any understanding of crisis responses. The bases of power and influence have changed over the course of the crisis for all the institutional actors, and with it views about who can legitimately exercise power and influence by deciding on the policies and processes of the Eurozone. What kind of power, however, is in question: Is it coercive, based on bargaining among member states with unequal influence; institutional, resulting from the embedding of previous decisions in policies and practices; or ideational and discursive, with persuasion the key to changing power and influence?[42] And who wields such power? Analysts disagree. Those convinced that member-state leaders in the European Council are in charge depict such actors as either engaged in coercive processes of hard bargaining, in particular Germany,[43] or deliberative processes of consensus seeking.[44] Those who insist instead that supranational actors in the Commission and ECB are in control emphasize either their institutional powers of enforcement[45] or their ideational role in policy design and discretionary oversight.[46] And finally, those who see the European Parliament as an increasingly important actor base this on its growing institutional and/or discursive influence.[47]

Rather than taking sides, I argue that EU actors have all gained in power and influence, but in different ways and differently over time. EU governance has become not only increasingly interactive but also more politicized in a system in which power may be exercised through persuasion as well as through coercion or institutional predominance. Such politicization has sources not only "at the top," at the EU level, in the increasing contestation as well as cooperation among EU institutional actors all vying for power and influence; but also at the national level, subject to an increasing politicization "at the bottom," which has in turn had "bottom up" effects on EU-level interactions.[48]

This suggests first of all that my 2006 catchphrase characterizing the EU level, as consisting of "policy *without* politics," based on the tendency to apolitical and/ or technocratic decision-making, no longer fully describes EU governance, which

---

[42] Carstensen and Schmidt 2016, 2018a.   [43] Schimmelfennig 2015a; Tsebelis 2016.
[44] Puetter 2012, 2014; Bickerton et al. 2015; Fabbrini 2015, 2016.
[45] Ioannou et al. 2015; Kassim et al. 2013; Jones et al. 2015.
[46] Bauer and Becker 2014; Becker et al., 2016; Dehousse 2016; Epstein and Rhodes 2016.
[47] Hix and Hoyland 2013; Fasone 2014; Dinan 2014; Héritier et al. 2016.
[48] Schmidt 2018a, 2019a.

has increasingly become "policy *with* politics" in crisis areas. The question here is whether this new politically charged dynamic of EU governance is beneficial—because more political deliberation and contestation helps generate greater EU responsiveness and transparency. Or is such a dynamic problematic—because politicization makes it more difficult to produce effective policies while at the same time negatively affecting national citizens' perceptions of the EU's political responsiveness, procedural accountability, and policy performance? The answer is that both are happening simultaneously.

This new, more politically charged EU governance has also had an impact on member-state democracies. The enhanced intergovernmental authority of the Council,[49] combined with the increased supranational control of the technocracy, including the ECB and the Commission,[50] and even the creeping empowerment of the EP,[51] have in different ways reduced the political autonomy of member-state democracies. In fact, the very existence of the EU as a system of supranational governance above the nation-state alters the democratic properties of national institutions, along with their claims to legitimacy. Because more and more policies traditionally decided politically at the national level are now decided at the EU level, mainstream parties have had increasing difficulty in mediating between their responsibilities to govern (by the EU rules) and their need to be responsive to their electorates.[52] National citizens often no longer feel that their political input matters. The resulting malaise has in turn fueled the rise of anti-system parties given to populist extremism and Euroskepticism,[53] as their leaders decry mainstream elites' failures to tell the "truth" about the encroachments of the EU or to defend national interests (as they conceive them). As a result, the national-level "politics *without* policy" that I had metaphorically identified in 2006 has only worsened.[54] We now increasingly see "politics *against* policy" in contentious areas such as the euro, or even "politics *against* polity," as in the case of Brexit.

One final point: while reinterpreting the rules "by stealth" may over time have diminished rigidities in the application of the rules to the "normal" countries subject to the budgetary oversight of the European Semester, thereby ameliorating certain aspects of legitimacy, it did nothing for "program" countries under conditionality. These include Greece, Ireland, Portugal, and Cyprus, which were subject to the technocratic rule of the Troika (IMF, ECB, and Commission), later called the 'institutions' (with the addition of the European Stability Mechanism).[55] A similar logic applies to the Central Eastern European countries, including Latvia, Hungary, and Romania, subject to IMF and Commission rule in the aftermath of the financial crisis of 2008.[56] The problems of democratic legitimacy for program

---

[49] Fabbrini 2013, 2015; Puetter 2014; Bickerton et al. 2015.
[50] Dehousse 2015; Bauer and Becker 2014; Becker et al. 2016.
[51] Héritier et al., 2016; Dinan 2015.
[52] Mair 2013.   [53] Hopkin 2020.   [54] Schmidt 2006.
[55] Sapir et al. 2014; Varoufakis 2016.   [56] Lütz and Kranke 2014; Ban 2017.

countries have been exponentially greater than for normal non-program countries subject to EU rules. The Greek crisis is the worst-case example of what may happen when the rules have been reinforced rather than reinterpreted.[57]

A Note on Methodological Approach

Explaining the Eurozone's progressive reinterpretation of the rules in terms of a disjunction between discourse and action demands not only a normative theory to define legitimacy but also a methodological theory to explain institutional change.[58] For the latter, I turn to the analytic framework of discursive institutionalism, which I developed over the past two decades to remind political scientists of the importance of ideas and discourse in political analysis.[59] Discursive institutionalism focuses on the substantive content of ideas and the interactive processes of discourse in institutional context.[60] By considering agents' ideas about what to do and their discursive legitimation of what they do as they coordinate with one another and communicate to the public, discursive institutionalism can help explain the dynamics of change (and continuity) in the Eurozone crisis over time.

In discursive institutionalism, ideas may take a variety of forms, such as frames, narratives, stories, collective memories, and myths; they may be supported by different kinds of arguments, whether cognitive or normative; and they may come at different levels of generality, including policies, programs, and philosophies. In the Eurozone crisis, for example, the framing of the crisis as one of public debt combined with deep philosophies of ordoliberalism and neoliberalism to produce a policy program of austerity and structural reform. In Germany, the storyline evoking excessive debt in support for that program was reinforced by cautionary morality tales, such as Merkel's evocation of the Schwabian housewife who knows that she has to tighten her belt in tough times. And it was underpinned by collective memories, most significantly the 1923 inflation that demanded wheelbarrows of money to pay for a loaf of bread rather than the 1931 deflation and high unemployment that brought in Hitler. In invoking such ideas, moreover, agents may use different kinds of legitimating arguments. Such arguments are most likely to make reference to cognitive knowledge focused on (social) scientific studies and expert opinion explaining, say, the benefits of fiscal consolidation. Additionally, they are likely to make appeal to normative values, such the moral duty of paying one's debts. But they may instead draw on authority, based on tradition, law, or institutional position, such as the legal obligation of member states to follow the

---

[57] Featherstone 2016.   [58] See discussion in Schmidt 2016a.
[59] Eg, Schmidt 2002, 2006, 2008, 2010a.   [60] Schmidt 2008, 2010a.

rules.[61] Or they may make reference to prudential concerns, as in the example again of the Schwabian housewife.[62]

The discursive interactions through which such ideas and legitimating discourses are articulated generally occur in both the policy sphere, in which technical and political actors coordinate on policy construction, and in the political sphere, in which political actors and increasingly also technical actors communicate with the public about the nature, scope, and legitimacy of the policies.[63] In the "coordinative" discourse, "epistemic communities" may be key to the generation of new policies,[64] as in the case of the loose network of central bankers and finance experts supporting the ECB's increasingly non-standard monetary policies. Alternatively, policies may be constructed by "advocacy coalitions,"[65] such as the pro-austerity "Brussels–Frankfurt" consensus. Or "policy entrepreneurs" may be the driving force in the adoption of new ideas,[66] such as the Commission in its push for the European Semester and the ECB in its push for banking union. More generally, EU actors' failure to develop a positive blueprint for Eurozone crisis resolution reflects their failures in discursive policy coordination.

In the communicative discourse, the interactions are equally varied. "Political entrepreneurs" may attempt to form mass public opinion,[67] most notably EU leaders seeking to explain and legitimate the loan bailout packages and austerity policies in response to the crisis. At the same time, the media, interest groups, and social movements, along with ordinary citizens, are all involved in processes of discussion, deliberation, and contestation of such policies, albeit largely split between Northern and Southern Europe. In the Eurozone crisis, the increasing cacophony of voices expressing opposing messages at national and EU levels has often worked at cross-purposes, making it difficult for any one EU actor to speak to other such actors, the markets, and "the people" at one and the same time. For example, communication about new policy initiatives that calm the global markets can easily inflame the national publics of Northern Europe while comforting Southern Europe, or vice-versa.

Although other analytic frameworks used in the explanation of the Eurozone crisis go a long way toward explaining the crisis response, discursive institutionalism provides a necessary complement. Rational choice institutionalism focuses on the interest-based logics of the EU's sub-optimal incentive structures and member states' divided preferences, which led to hard bargaining games in which the "creditors" transferred all the costs to the "debtors."[68] Historical

---

[61] As in two of Weber's (1946) underlying bases for authority—see Chapter 2.

[62] For a similar range of categories, see Van Leeuwen 2007; p. 91; see also Van Leeuwen and Wodak 1999.

[63] For more detail, see Schmidt 2008.   [64] Haas 1992.   [65] Sabatier 1993.

[66] Kingdon 1984.   [67] Zaller 1992.

[68] Scharpf 2012a; Schimmelfennig 2015a; Tsebelis 2016; Copelovitch et al. 2016; Frieden and Walter 2017.

institutionalism concentrates on the path dependencies of or incremental changes to formal rules and institutional regularities during the crisis,[69] and on the ways in which EU actors have continuously "failed forward."[70] Sociological institutionalism centers on the cultural frames, ideologies, and worldviews that defined EU and national actors' different conceptions of the crisis.[71] And structural political economy delineates the structural power of political economic arrangements, including pressures brought on from the crisis of democratic capitalism,[72] or by the transnational European capitalist class.[73] But only discursive institutionalism can set EU action in full institutional context. It enables one to use the results of these other approaches as background information even as it helps to explain the dynamics of change through the (re)defining of interests, the (re)shaping of institutions, and the (re)framing of culture.[74]

Institutional context here therefore needs to be understood not only as the (cultural) frames, (historical) institutions, (rationalist) incentives, or (structural) forces within which agents may find themselves, but also as the "meaning" context for their ideas and the discursive "forums" in which actors articulate their ideas.[75] Using discursive institutionalism, we can show that different EU actors may follow different pathways not only because of their different institutional settings, their perceived clash of interests, or their cultural blinders but also because of their different constructions of meaning and the different communities of interlocutors with whom they engage in coordinative discourses of policy construction and communicative discourses of political legitimation.

Discursive institutionalism is also useful as a way of considering the relationship between power and legitimacy.[76] In traditional understandings of power, actors may have coercive power as a result of their material resources and institutional positions; institutions themselves can constitute powerful path-dependent constraints on action; and capitalist forces have the power to structure the overall environment.[77] Legitimacy is largely absent from such analyses. But power in the context of legitimacy, or legitimate power, requires more than imposing a course of action, following a set of established rules, or being subject to structural forces. Any legitimate authority—even if coercive, institutional, or structural—requires legitimation. And this demands a different kind of power: the power of ideas and discourse. Processes of legitimation are matters of ideational construction and discursive persuasion not only about what is the legitimate exercise of power but often even about what constitutes legitimate (or illegitimate) coercive,

---

[69] Gocaj and Meunier 2013; Verdun 2015; Salines et al. 2012; Jones et al. 2015.
[70] Jones et al. 2015.   [71] Howarth and Rommerskirchen 2013.   [72] Streeck 2013.
[73] Apeldoorn 2013.   [74] Schmidt 2008, 2012, 2016a.
[75] Toulmin 1958; Schmidt 2012a.
[76] For further elaboration, see Carstensen and Schmidt 2018a, 2018b.
[77] Eg, Barnett and Duvall 2005: 43, 49; Dahl 1968.

institutional, or structural power.[78] Ideational construction and discursive persuasion can serve to legitimize the exercise of power (even when coercive, institutional, or structural), by explaining why it may be acceptable and appropriate in terms of output performance, input politics, and/or throughput procedures. EU actors have not just wielded power or exerted influence; they at the same time have been acutely aware of the need for legitimacy as they exercise power, and have generally sought to legitimize their power and influence to one another and to the public.[79]

Beyond this, discursive institutionalism, used in conjunction with EU systems concepts of legitimacy, serves as a bridge between normative and empirical approaches in EU studies. While the normative approach is derived from philosophical principles that define the expected criteria a democratic political system would need to fulfill to be considered legitimate, the empirical one is derived from more pragmatic questions that evaluate the extent to which a given democratic political system is considered legitimate.[80] In making its case, the book combines normative theories about legitimacy focused on the norms, principles, and criteria of evaluation regarding public action with empirical descriptions of the legitimacy beliefs of citizens and evaluations of public actors' discourses of legitimation. In so doing, the book engages in a continuing dialogue about the nature of legitimacy during the Eurozone crisis. It analyzes what EU actors 'ought to have done' while evaluating 'what they did' according to normative principles; investigates how they themselves legitimated what they did empirically according their own principled views and pragmatic considerations; and describes empirically how citizens perceived the legitimacy of those actions. This can sometimes make for a complex assessment of legitimacy, given questions regarding which normative principles of legitimacy apply at which level, and whose empirical ideas about legitimacy count.

The best illustration of the complexities involved in assessing legitimacy is arguably the third Greek bailout in 2015. Normatively, the bailout program's legitimacy is questionable, given EU actors' continued imposition of austerity measures in largely unaccountable, secretive negotiations that produced negative economic outcomes while ignoring the will of the Greek people. But empirically, everyone claimed legitimacy: The newly elected Syriza government demanded renegotiation of the program and an end to austerity in order to be politically

---

[78] See Carstensen and Schmidt 2016, 2018a, 2018b.

[79] Such ideational and discursive power can be further specified as coming in three forms: coercive power *over* ideas and discourse, where actors may impose their ideas on others through their discourse, like it or not; institutional or structural power *in* ideas and discourse, when certain ideas may predominate by being embedded in the rules or by being embodied in discourse that structures thought; and persuasive power *through* ideas and discourse, which is the main focus of this discursive institutionalist inquiry into legitimacy in the EU and the Eurozone crisis. See Carstensen and Schmidt 2016, 2018a.

[80] See, e.g., Habermas 1996; Thompson 2008; Mansbridge 2015, pp. 32–33.

responsive to citizens' expressed wishes, while protesting the lack of procedural accountability in negotiations for a program deleterious to an already devastated Greek economy. In contrast, the finance ministers in the Eurogroup, led by Germany, and supported by the ECB and Council leaders, refused to renegotiate on the procedural/legal grounds that the previous government had signed the memorandum of understanding for the program, that they themselves were also democratically elected, and that their main concern was the health of the Eurozone economy as a whole, which demanded following the pre-established rules. The outcome, in which Greece had no choice but to accept Eurozone actors' demands, demonstrates that coercive power, with or without legitimacy, wins over legitimacy without power—which is metaphorically like a gin-and-tonic without the gin. But the drama itself, which was closely followed across Europe, only further drove the rise of Euroskeptic populism, suggesting that this kind of naked exercise of coercive power, of gin without the tonic of legitimacy, is highly problematic for any kind of polity, by serving to undermine trust in governing authority.

Conclusion

This book seeks to show how important it is to bring together the many different ways in which scholars and policy analysts have explained the Eurozone crisis and political actors and citizens have perceived it. To do so, the book considers the crisis from the vantage point of different disciplines and fields, including macro, micro, and socioeconomics, international and comparative political economy, international relations, comparative politics, sociology, and history as well as of course democratic theory. Different analytic frameworks also provide distinctive insights, whether rational choice institutionalism, historical institutionalism, sociological institutionalism, or my own discursive institutionalism. The book builds on all of these approaches, but privileges discursive institutionalism because it is able to use the results of the other institutionalisms productively while providing a bridge to issues of legitimacy. Moreover, by considering three very broad normative conceptualizations of legitimacy related to performance, politics, and procedures, I am equally able to examine the empirical impact of the crisis on the EU's political economy, politics, and governance. As such, using the lens of legitimacy makes for a book that offers an all-inclusive exploration of the causes and consequences of the Eurozone crisis.

This book begins in Part I with the theoretical conceptualization of legitimacy in the EU. Chapter 2 explores questions of democracy and legitimacy in the EU, defines the three legitimizing mechanisms of output, input, and throughput, and then examines the five main criteria for throughput legitimation—efficacy, accountability (both generally and in the EU), transparency, and inclusiveness and openness. Chapter 3 discusses the dilemmas of the EU's "split-level" legitimacy, where output and throughput operate primarily at the EU level, input at the national. It then describes the politicization of EU governance at the bottom, from the bottom up, and at the top, ending with the question: Is politicization a good thing or a bad thing?

Part II focuses on throughput legitimacy in Eurozone governance. This comes first not because it is the most important legitimizing mechanism in any democracy—much the contrary, as we have already discussed—but because it is key to understanding why the crisis response went so wrong, leading to bad output performance and increasingly volatile input politics. The first of the five chapters in this part, Chapter 4, provides an overview of the Eurozone crisis, beginning with a brief discussion of its historical sources, followed by the economic ideas and institutional innovations that came during the fast-burning phase of the crisis, and ending with the benefits and drawbacks of the rules reinterpretations that came afterwards. The subsequent four chapters discuss EU actors' different pathways to legitimacy. They all begin with an analysis of the nature of EU actors' particular sources of power and grounds for procedural legitimacy followed by a discussion of the Janus-faced public perceptions of their Eurozone governance. In Chapter 5 these perceptions divide between views of the Council as unaccountable (German) dictatorship or mutually accountable deliberative body (in the shadow of Germany)—except for the program countries, subject to either harsh dictatorship or deliberative authoritarianism. In Chapter 6, they are split between views of the ECB as the hero saving the euro or an ogre imposing austerity and railroading countries into programs. In Chapter 7, they alternate between views of the Commission as ayatollahs of austerity or ministers of moderation. And in Chapter 8, they vacillate between seeing the European Parliament as talking shop or a potential equal partner.

Part III concerns output and input legitimacy. In a first draft of this book, the chapters on these two legitimating mechanisms came first, on the assumption that it was best to begin with the poor policy outcomes and the disastrous political consequences in order to demonstrate how problematic were the governance processes. But by the time I was finishing the book, economic historians and political analysts had already told these parts of the story, often with great narrative panache in long tomes.[81] In contrast, analyses detailing the governance processes remained for the most part fragmented, as the domain of scholars

---

[81] See, for example, Mark Blyth's *Austerity* (2013); Carlo Bastasin's *Saving Europe* (2013, 2015); Martin Sandbu's *Europe's Orphan* (2014); Markus Brunnemeier, Harold James, and Jean-Pierre Landau's *The Euro and the Battle of Ideas* (2016); Adam Tooze's *Crash* (2018); Ashoka Mody's *Eurotragedy* (2018); and Jean Quatremer's *Il Faut Achever l'Euro* (2019).

concerned with different EU actors and/or member states.[82] I also realized that putting output and input after throughput is arguably even more convincing a demonstration of the dangers of governing by the rules and ruling by the numbers. Placed in this order, we can see that Eurozone governance processes were a legitimacy risk not only on their own throughput terms—because perceived to be incompetent, biased, unfair, or oppressive—but also in terms of their negative effects on output policy and input politics.

In Part III, Chapter 9 examines the Eurozone's policy effectiveness and performance. It starts with analyses of the macroeconomic impact of the crisis misframing and misdiagnosis, along with the wrong chosen remedies and the lack of adequate solutions. The chapter then follows with a discussion of the excessive socioeconomic costs of austerity and the perversity of EU-led structural reforms. Chapter 10 explores the political impact of Eurozone governance. It first details citizens' rising Euroskepticism against a background of declining trust, fueled by economic and social as well as political sources of discontent. It next considers the EU's growing political polarization and party realignments in the shadow of populism. Finally the chapter charts the decline of mainstream parties in the periphery as well as the core, followed by the rise of populist extremes on the right, on the left, and in what I call the radical center.

In the Conclusion, after briefly setting the Eurozone crisis in international context, the book asks how the EU may move forward, reforming Eurozone governance while resolving the EU's (euro) crisis of legitimacy in ways that ensures greater input, output, and throughput legitimacy. To do so, it recommends a more differentiated and decentralized Eurozone governance in a more differentially integrated and democratized EU.

---

[82] For a notable early exception, see Philippe Legrain's *European Spring* (2014). For especially readable accounts of particular actors, see Luuk Van Middelaar's *Alarums & Excursions* (2019) for a positive take on the Council, and Yanis Varoufakis' *Adults in the Room* (2017) for a very negative take.

PART I

CONCEPTUALIZING LEGITIMACY IN THE EU

2

Conceptualizing Legitimacy

Input, Output, and Throughput

Is the European Union democratic? Is it legitimate? Answers to these questions prior to the Eurozone crisis divided rather evenly between those who thought the EU democratically legitimate and those who instead argued that the EU suffered from an increasing democratic deficit.[1] Since the inception of the crisis, however, most analysts have found the EU wanting in legitimacy because of its governing activities, whether in terms of the policies, the politics, or the processes.[2] In the language of EU democratic systems theorists, this translates into concerns about the EU's output legitimacy, focused on policy effectiveness and performance; the EU's input legitimacy, centered on citizens' political representation and governing elites' responsiveness; and the EU's throughput legitimacy, concentrated on the quality of the governance processes, including their efficacy, accountability, transparency, inclusiveness, and openness to interest consultation.

Throughput legitimacy covers everything that goes on in the "black box" of governance, as it processes the input demands "*by* the people" to produce the policy outputs "*for* the people." It is a necessary accompaniment to output and input legitimacy, by ensuring people's trust that the rules are being applied fairly, in the spirit as much as the letter of the law, in ways that are responsive to citizens' input demands while ensuring the best possible policy outputs. But the relationship of throughput legitimacy to the other legitimizing mechanisms differs from the interrelationship of input politics and output policies, where more of one or the other may be sufficient to ensure the public's sense of legitimacy. Even the highest quality of governance procedures, however throughput legitimate, cannot make up for problems with either input or output legitimacy. Good governance (throughput), in other words, cannot make up for failures to respond to citizens' expressed demands (input) or to produce effective outcomes (output). Worse, bad governance resulting from incompetence, corruption, bias, or exclusion can be disastrous for all three kinds of legitimacy, by precipitating a public loss of trust or

---

[1] See, for example, Williams 1991; Beetham and Lord 1998; Majone 1998; Scharpf 1999; Moravcsik 2002; Lord 2004; Follesdal 2006; Hix 2006; Schmidt 2006.

[2] Scharpf 2012a, 2012b, 2014; Schmidt 2009a, 2013, 2016a; Tsoukalis 2016; Nicolaïdis 2013; Nicolaïdis and Watson 2016.

Europe's Crisis of Legitimacy: Governing by Rules and Ruling by Numbers in the Eurozone. Vivien A. Schmidt, Oxford University Press (2020). © Vivien A. Schmidt.
DOI: 10.1093/oso/9780198797050.001.0001

perception of illegality in the governance processes and contaminating perceptions of the legitimacy of the politics (input) and the policies (output).

This chapter begins by asking how to conceptualize democracy and legitimacy in the EU. It then defines the three concepts at the center of this book's analysis of legitimacy, output, input, and throughput, along with their interaction effects. It follows this with an in-depth look at how to conceptualize throughput legitimacy, by examining in turn each of its five criteria of evaluation.

Democracy and Legitimacy

Democracy and legitimacy are not equivalent terms. Simply defined, democracy refers to a specific form of government and legitimacy to whether a government of any form is accepted by its citizens as having the authority to govern. Legitimacy may exist without democracy, but democracy cannot exist without legitimacy, since it is by definition based on citizen consent. Liberal democracy comes with additional requirements, however, including—at a minimum—free and fair elections, active citizen participation in political and civic life, protection of all citizens' human rights, and adherence to the rule of law.[3] Another expectation is that the citizens in a democracy see themselves as constituting a *demos*, that is, they have a sense of belonging together as a self-governing people. Legitimacy in a liberal democracy, moreover, ordinarily further depends on a government's ability to satisfy citizens' interests and concerns as well as to serve community needs and values.[4] Democratic legitimacy, putting the two terms together, can therefore be characterized as a state of affairs in which an elected government is accepted as legitimate by its citizens because it governs effectively while responding to their expressed preferences in ways that benefit the public interest and are in keeping with common values.

This particular definition of democratic legitimacy puts its primary emphasis on citizen acceptance of what a government does. But this in turn depends upon a prior kind of legitimacy based on acceptance of what that government is, as a rule-based authority and guarantor of political order. At this deeper level, following Max Weber's definition, legitimacy depends on citizens' acceptance of a set of governing arrangements as morally authoritative, such that they will voluntarily comply with government acts even when these go against their own interests and desires.[5] Any such authority, as Weber further specified, could have its origins in custom and tradition, result from charismatic leadership, or be based on legal-rational reasoning.[6] In political philosophy, this last form of authoritative legitimacy had its earliest and most dramatic expression in Socrates' decision to accept

---

[3] See, eg, Diamond and Morlino 2016.
[4] Henceforth, references to democracy and legitimacy should be understood as referring to liberal democracy.
[5] Weber 1978—See discussions in, eg, Scharpf 1999; Cerutti 2008; Schmidt 2013.
[6] Weber 1946.

his death sentence and drink the hemlock rather than flee, as proposed by his friend Crito. Although he considered the decision wrong, he explained that he felt that he had to abide by it because he regarded the laws, government, rules, and procedures by which he was convicted as legitimate, having implicitly accepted them by staying in Athens and benefiting by all it had to offer (rather than leaving when reaching adulthood).[7] Much of modern philosophy, beginning with Hobbes and culminating with Locke, was concerned with establishing the grounds for such legitimacy, with acceptance of the authority of a political order as the *sine qua non* of mankind's exit from the state of nature.

This kind of legitimacy, linked to acceptance of political institutions as having moral authority, has been mainly situated at the level of the nation-state, and linked to notions of national sovereignty and community. The question is whether it can be equally valid for any kind of supranational authority.[8] In the case of the EU, I would argue, this sort of authoritative legitimacy has been established slowly and incrementally over the course of the EU's integration process. As sovereignty became increasingly pooled[9] and nation-states became "member states,"[10] the EU's authoritative legitimacy was incrementally accepted (at least in principle) at the EU level in policy area after policy area and institution after institution by national governments, national courts, and by implication European citizens. The customs union was followed by the Single Market, Schengen, and European Monetary Union (EMU); the Court of Justice of the European Union (CJEU) gained formal (legal) supremacy and direct effect; the European Central Bank (ECB) was given control over money, monetary policy, and lately the banks; and the Commission increased its supranational powers of policy formulation, implementation, regulation, and oversight in areas such as international trade negotiation, financial markets, and recently EMU via the European Semester.

While the basic Weberian conditions for the EU's authoritative legitimacy could therefore be said to have been met, given citizens' tacit acceptance of the EU as mediated by their morally authoritative governments, the question remains as to whether this incremental development of the EU fulfills the more demanding conditions of democratic legitimacy listed above, based on its governing activity. This is not easy to establish.

The EU is not itself a "democracy" in the conventional sense, since it lacks many of the expected features, including a democratically elected government. But its member states are democracies with elected governments, the EU operates according to democratic values and principles, and the EU's own morally authoritative (Weberian) legitimacy has been built up over time in policy area after policy area. Moreover, we cannot really talk about the EU as apart from its member

---

[7] Crito 51c–52e; see also use in Andeweg and Aarts 2017.
[8] See the extensive debate in international relations theory on the nature of institutional authority and its relationship to legitimacy, eg, Hurd 2007, 60–1; Lake 2007, 56; and discussion in Tallberg and Zürn 2019.
[9] Keohane and Hoffmann 1991.   [10] Bickerton 2012.

states other than semantically, since the EU *is* its member states. And its member states meet the standards of democratic legitimacy outlined earlier (though question marks are now raised for Hungary and Poland). Additionally, EU institutional actors have themselves all sought to enhance EU-level legitimacy in their own ways. But be this as it may, the EU still confronts major challenges with regard to democratic legitimacy that are inherent to its national/supranational institutional setup.

The greatest problem for the EU and its member states is that deeper European integration—even prior to the Eurozone crisis—has taken its toll on member states' national democracies, as decision-making in more and more policy areas has moved up to the EU level while politics remains national. Citizens vote for national governments that promise to carry out their expressed preferences but which may instead take actions that reflect not those national preferences but their supranational responsibilities under EU agreements that may not meet with citizens' approval—and may even not work. This has especially been an issue during the Eurozone crisis, in which the greatly accelerated pace of European integration has intensified questions regarding whether the EU is sufficiently legitimate, let alone democratic. Importantly, even if citizens' use of the euro in their everyday practices suggests that they have tacitly accepted its authoritative legitimacy as a currency,[11] they have increasingly politically contested the legitimacy of euro-related policies and processes.

So how do we determine legitimacy in the EU? Beyond the basic question of the legitimacy of the EU as a governing authority, we need to consider two further questions related to the EU's governing activities: who decides what is legitimate, and according to which criteria? We begin here with the question of who decides—for which there are no easy answers, only more questions, in particular in the case of the EU.

Ordinarily, one's immediate response to the question of who decides would be to say that just as citizens' consent establishes governing authority, so citizens' opinions determine the legitimacy of governing activities. But this only begs the question. Citizens may indeed decide, but on whose advice, in which ways, and on what grounds? The increasingly complex nature of governance has led political actors to rely more and more on technical experts to propose as well as to assess policy success, in particular in the supranational sphere. So is legitimacy a matter for the experts, basing their judgments on (social) scientific criteria of evaluation, in discussion with other experts in networks, advocacy coalitions, and epistemic communities? Or is it the case that political agents actually decide, as the elected representatives of the people who translate the technical matters into terms intelligible to the citizenry while connecting these to the normative values

---

[11] McNamara 2015a.

of the polity? But perhaps the politicians instead take their cues directly from the citizens themselves? And if the citizens are the final arbiters of legitimacy, which responses count: tacit support or active contestation, as expressed through the ballot box, through the media, or via opinion polls?

Does this then mean that legitimacy is solely a question of citizens' empirical beliefs about what works, fits with their values, and meets their expressed demands? Is it instead enough to have technical agents with superior knowledge about what really works and political agents who can persuade citizens that they are meeting their concerns? Or do independent observers equally have something to say, by assessing legitimacy through universal and/or community-based normative standards?

The problem is that citizens can be wrong about what is good for them, and so can the experts, while political leaders may be misguided and yet provide convincing arguments for policies that do not work, do not respond to citizen concerns, and are not in the common interest. And what if policies violate principles of liberal democracy—as in Poland and Hungary, where majorities have voted for governments that are dismantling some of the most basic institutions of liberal democracy and thereby risk becoming "illiberal (non) democracies"? Worse, what if the policies violate universal principles of human rights, decency, and dignity?[12]

This leads us to a final comment: legitimacy is always "constructed," as a matter of discussion, deliberation, and contestation, and not just among citizens, politicians, and experts. There is also an important role to be played by independent observers and critics with reasoned arguments who consider things from a certain distance, in comparison with other polities and times. Political philosophers over the ages, along with social thinkers, policy analysts, political activists, and civic-minded citizens, as dissident voices from "the people," have provided such arguments, speaking "truth to power" by invoking universal rights and community norms regarding what is legitimate and what is not.[13] In sum, any empirical judgments about legitimacy, whether by citizens, politicians, or experts, cannot come to the exclusion of normative standards of evaluation tied to principles concerning democratic freedom, social justice, and human rights, or of the considerations of independent critics and activists from the vantage point of history and philosophy. By the same token, however, reforms and suggestions that meet normative criteria for legitimacy may not meet with popular approval or at least gain

---

[12] The classic example is Nazi Germany, where the citizens were persuaded by Hitler and the "experts" of the necessity and appropriateness of the regime's policies. But note that even here, the Nazis themselves may have been concerned about the limits of what their own citizens might accept with regard to the "Final Solution," and thus did not communicate to the public (let alone seek to legitimate) what they meant by it, although it was explicit in the coordinative discussions among government and military officials. See eg, Roseman 2002; Browning 2004.

[13] Thanks to Sascha Kneip and Wolgang Merkel for having raised this issue in a presentation of an earlier version of this chapter at the WZB, Berlin, June 21, 2017. See also Merkel 2019.

widespread acceptance, and thus butt up against empirical considerations based on public perceptions of what is legitimate.

Who decides what constitutes legitimate governing activity, thus, cannot be answered without also considering the normative standards and empirical judgments by which to establish legitimacy. Our next task is therefore to consider which criteria to use in assessing legitimacy.

Assessing Legitimacy

There are many different theoretical approaches to democratic legitimacy. These generally run the gamut from normative theories that define the expected criteria which a democratic political system would need to fulfill to be considered legitimate to empirical theories that evaluate the extent to which a given democratic political system is considered legitimate. The normative approaches tend to be deductive and often derived from philosophical principles concerned with the public good, political equality, justice, fairness, identity, public discourse, and deliberation.[14] Such approaches normally set up a range of criteria or standards of evaluation by which to assess public action. The empirical approaches tend to be more inductive and derived from pragmatic questions about such things as citizen support for the political system, elite and mass perceptions of economic performance, political responsiveness to citizen concerns, and administrative accountability as evidenced in opinion polls, voting, and public discourse.[15] Empirical investigation often focuses on citizens' beliefs about legitimacy and on community-based evaluations of public action, as well as on the ways in which institutional authorities' actions are legitimated and contested in ways that shape such beliefs.[16]

The approach to EU legitimacy herein combines the normative and the empirical by building on a set of concepts that are normative in their criteria for legitimacy but serve at the same time as useful categories for empirical investigation.[17] Normative considerations naturally infuse empirical investigations. The two are impossible to disentangle, in particular because empirical perceptions are generally influenced by normative principles and standards about what ideally to expect. Moreover, because such principles are generally rooted in "beliefs, narratives, and conceptual language shared by, and among, dominants and subordinates,"[18]

---

[14] Eg, Beetham and Lord 1998; Bellamy and Weale 2015; Habermas 2001; Mansbridge 2015.

[15] Eg, Schmitt and Thomassen 1999; Koopmans and Statham 2010; Hobolt 2015; van der Brug and De Vrees 2016; Ham et al, 2017; Anderweg and Aarts 2017.

[16] See Tallberg and Zürn 2019 and Kneip and Merkel 2018 for extensive discussion of the empirical evaluation of legitimacy beliefs in global governance.

[17] See also Beetham 2013; Sternberg 2015.   [18] Sternberg 2015, p. 617.

claims to legitimacy are also a matter of contestation.[19] This leads us to ask how (Weberian) legitimacy, as public consent to governing authority, is reinforced, or *legitimated*. And for legitimation, it is useful to consider how different kinds of governing activity can serve to support, or undermine, perceptions of governing authority.

Defining Output, Input, *and* Throughput Legitimacy

We turn for normative definitions of legitimacy to the language and concepts most often used in the EU studies literature,[20] which is found in the political systems theory that builds on the terms of David Easton,[21] as updated and elaborated in particular by Fritz W. Scharpf.[22] This approach focuses on two legitimizing mechanisms: "output" and "input." Output legitimacy describes acceptance of the coercive powers of government so long as their exercise is seen to serve the common good of the polity and is constrained by the norms of the community. Input legitimacy represents the exercise of collective self-government so as to ensure government responsiveness to people's preferences, as shaped through political debate in a common public space and political competition in institutions that ensure political officials' accountability via general elections.[23] These definitions of legitimacy pick up on Abraham Lincoln's famous dictum about democracy requiring government *by* the people (political participation), *of* the people (citizen representation), and *for* the people (governing effectiveness), with input legitimacy represented by government *by* and *of* the people and output legitimacy by government *for* the people.

Missing has been a systems concept that would separate out the processes that absorb the input and generate the output, notionally situated in a neglected "black box" of governance. I have proposed to label these legitimizing processes, consistent with the language of systems theory, as *"throughput."*[24] This fits well with Easton's political systems theory, since Easton himself uses the term throughput, although he limits it to administrative processes.[25] My concept of throughput not only encompasses the internal processes and practices of EU governance but also adds a fourth preposition to Lincoln's three: interest intermediation *with* the people.[26] Throughput legitimacy is dependent upon the quality of the policymaking

---

[19] Rittberger and Schroeder 2016, p. 581.
[20] I use the term legitimacy here for clarity of presentation. But it is important to note that I use it to cover both legitimation and legitimacy, that is, the mechanisms (or processes) of legitimation that serve to create and/or enhance legitimacy, and the legitimacy that results from the use of such legitimizing mechanisms and processes. For further elaboration on the different uses of the terms, see Kneip and Merkel 2018; Tallberg and Zürn 2019.
[21] Easton 1965.   [22] Scharpf 1970, 1999.   [23] Scharpf 1970, 1999, 2014.
[24] Schmidt 2013; see also Zürn 2000; Benz and Papadopoulos 2006; Bekkers and Edwards 2007.
[25] Easton 1965.   [26] See Schmidt 2006.

processes, including the efficacy of the decision-making,[27] the accountability of those engaged in making the decisions,[28] the transparency of the information,[29] and the processes' inclusiveness and openness to consultation with the interest groups of "civil society."[30]

All three of these legitimizing mechanisms have deep foundations in political history and philosophy. Output legitimacy takes us back not just to Lincoln's famous phrase about the need to "govern *for* the people" but to ancient philosophers (eg, Plato and Aristotle) as well as modern philosophers (eg, Hobbes and Locke) whose focus, long before modern democracy, was on the duties and obligations of rulers to govern wisely and well for the good of their people. But even once democracy as a political system was firmly ensconced, with citizens' political representation (input) the added criterion for legitimacy, output legitimacy retained its importance. This is because citizens' sense of legitimacy, even if now dependent upon expressing their voice (input), remains equally contingent on having their needs and desires fulfilled by governing authorities whose policies solve problems and produce good results that serve not just their individual interests but those of the polity as a whole (output).[31] The good of the people, meaning the "big" goals of output legitimacy, have always been linked to such things as ensuring peace and security, promoting economic prosperity and social wellbeing, guaranteeing political stability and social rights, and building common identity and greater democracy.

Output legitimacy is therefore not simply a question of meeting citizens' immediate desires or demands, but rather entails that the good of the polity is also achieved. This means that output legitimacy is to be judged on the basis of whether policies effectively fulfill the major purposes for which people live together in polities. It is therefore about the long-term survival and flourishing of a polity as much as the short-term meeting of needs. It follows therefrom that any empirical assessment of output legitimacy would need to evaluate the effectiveness of the governing authority's policies in solving the polity's problems and such policies' performance in terms of economic and social outcomes. Given the technical nature of many such assessments, determining legitimacy has often been considered to be as much a matter for the technical experts as for the political leaders or "the people," and increasingly so in recent years under the influence of neoliberal principles and programs.

Input legitimacy has an equally long pedigree. It can take us back to Athenian democracy or the Roman republic, although it has its greatest elaboration in the work of John Locke and John Stuart Mill or, in another tradition, Jean-Jacques

---

[27] Scharpf 1988.   [28] Harlow and Rawlings 2007; Cini 2013; Crum and Curtin 2015.
[29] Héritier 2003.
[30] Eg, Coen 2007; Coen and Richardson 2009; Greenwood 2007; Smismans 2003; Kröger 2008; Liebert and Trenz 2009.
[31] See Scharpf 1999.

Rousseau. Hannah Pitkin's classical definition of political representation puts it as "acting in the interest of the represented in a manner responsive to them."[32] Input legitimacy is at the very basis of liberal democratic systems of representation, and contains expectations related to the principles and practices of political participation and representation, such as free, fair, and open elections, with citizens guaranteed an equal opportunity to vote; freedom of expression and freedom of the press; the ability to organize freely as political parties and field candidates for election; majority rule, with respect for minority rights; and much more.

But representation can be understood in two mutually reinforcing ways, in keeping with Abraham Lincoln's conceptualization. Government *of* the people assumes that the citizens are represented by people like themselves, that is, citizens rather than, say, monarchs, oligarchs, dictators, or foreign colonial powers. Government *by* the people presupposes that citizens elect their leaders and that public officials govern in their name while expressing their will. What expressing the will of the people exactly means, however, has been subject to long-standing debate, in particular in light of the dual nature of the role of representatives. Do elected officials represent "the people" by following the people's expressed preferences (one way of interpreting government *by* the people) or by doing what they think is right under the circumstances (a way of interpreting government *of* the people)?

The first interpretation links representation to the expression of political will, generally through elections. This runs the risk, as Nadia Urbinati points out, of too closely relating political legitimacy to the correspondence between what was promised and what gets decided, and thus eliminates the judgment component of democratic representation.[33] The second interpretation points instead to how closely tied output legitimacy is to input legitimacy, suggesting that the political representative has a choice between being responsive (for input legitimacy) or responsible (for output legitimacy). But as Peter Mair has argued, this choice has become a major source of tension today. As a result of globalization and Europeanization, political representatives find themselves increasingly torn between their desire to be responsive to the citizens, by fulfilling their electoral promises and citizens' changing expectations (eg, as expressed in referenda), and the need to govern responsibly by honoring supranational commitments.[34]

Output legitimacy is thus tied to input legitimacy as part of a feedback loop that enables citizens to sanction governments that they deem to have failed to perform responsibly and/or in ways that meet their needs, fit with their values, and respond to their wishes, as expressed in the previous election cycle.[35]

---

[32] Pitkin 1967, p. 209.   [33] Urbinati 2006.   [34] Mair 2013.
[35] This should be distinguished from procedural accountability, discussed under throughput legitimacy, in which officials (elected or unelected) are expected to give account for their governance processes to specialized forums, political or technical.

Good performance is naturally most likely to ensure citizen confidence while bad or ineffective performance generates distrust or low citizen confidence.[36] That said, good performance alone does not guarantee legitimacy if citizens do not feel that the regime is sufficiently responsive to their expressed desires.[37] This points to the dangers of the second interpretation of political representation, when political representatives do what they decide is right despite or even against the will of the people, such that output legitimacy trumps input legitimacy. A further problem concerns how to determine which legitimizing mechanism, output or input, is to be preferred to ensure the proper functioning of democracy. For some EU scholars, input legitimacy through democratic voting and other forms of participation is the *sine qua non* of democratic governance.[38] Others have tended to see the insulation of decision-making by technical bodies from politics as legitimate so long as it produces good results, in particular where the policies are distributive in nature.[39]

Throughput legitimacy also has deep historical roots. Efficacy in the performance of public officials' ruling functions and accountability in terms of public actors giving account and/or being held to account for their actions in public forums are traceable all the way back to Confucius and forward through Hegel's *Philosophy of Right* and Max Weber's legal-rational authority, and on to the vast public administration literature focused on these issues. Accountability is also historically rooted in the practice of bookkeeping and the discipline of accounting.[40] Transparency in the provision of information by public officials was a major concern of Jeremy Bentham and Jean-Jacques Rousseau, while "transparent management" has been central to good governance, coming into general usage in the 1990s.[41] In contrast, inclusiveness and openness in decision-making are often considered in the context of pluralist theories of interest intermediation, and find greatest support from American democratic theorists such as David Truman and Robert Dahl. Pluralist theory serves as added justification for my decision to add a fourth preposition to Abraham Lincoln's original three, such that governing *with* the people can be seen to make up for the limits of government "*by, of,* and *for* the people."[42] The theory of "associative democracy" even sees this as another form of democracy in its own right, as well as a corrective to representative democracy.[43] More recently, "deliberative democracy" has been seen as a major procedural remedy to problems related to both input and output legitimacy. This may involve improving the quality of citizen participation via deliberative forums, such as citizen juries, issues forums, and deliberative polls,[44] or introducing more deliberation in expert arenas, including independent commissions, regulatory

---

[36] Newton and Norris 2000, p. 61.   [37] McEvoy 2016.   [38] Eg, Follesdal and Hix 2006.
[39] Majone 1996; Moravcsik 2002; Scharpf 1999.
[40] See Bovens et al. 2014b.   [41] Hood 2010, p. 990.   [42] Schmidt 2006, p. 35.
[43] Cohen and Rogers 1992; Hirst 1994.
[44] Mansbridge 1983; Bohman 1996; Goodin and Dryzek 2006.

authorities, and watchdog organizations.[45] In Eurozone governance, such deliberation has been a major feature of the European Semester process, as in the case of the wide range of expert economic committees that discuss the country-specific reports (CSRs).[46]

Underpinning the five evaluative criteria of throughput legitimacy are other requirements, including the "hard" criterion of legality and the "soft" criterion of trust. Relevant actors generally need to be perceived to act legally within the rules and to inspire trust in those with whom they engage, such that they are believed to act with integrity and without bias so as to ensure equal and open access in governance while meeting expected ethical and moral standards as well as legal ones.[47] Fairness, meaning enforcing the rules in such a way as to apply equally and appropriately to all, and doing this in a way so as to be seen to be fair, is also a key component, and another defining attribute of legitimacy.[48] As a result, central to throughput legitimacy are expectations about the qualities necessary to policymakers, which can be summarized by such buzzwords as trustworthiness, integrity, fairness, impartiality, and credibility. Competence, of course, is also a requirement, linked to efficacy; respecting citizens' democratic prerogatives, for example by not being oppressive or biased in applying the rules, is related to accountability; and not being restrictive or closed to organized interests and citizen involvement in the decision-making process (where possible) connects to inclusiveness and openness.

In brief, output is a performance criterion for legitimacy, which expects responsible governing *for* the people to generate effective policies with appropriate outcomes. Input is a political criterion for legitimacy, which requires responsive governing *by* and *of* the people focused on satisfying citizens' concerns as expressed in a common arena. And throughput is a procedural criterion for legitimacy, which demands efficacious governing *with* the people through processes that are accountable, transparent, inclusive, and open to interest intermediation. These three democratic legitimizing mechanisms are seamlessly interconnected, as well as sometimes difficult to separate at the boundaries.

Differentiating Throughput from Output and Input

Taking account of the quality of the governance processes, and not only the effectiveness of the outcomes and the involvement of the citizenry, is important for

---

[45] Sabel and Zeitlin 2010; Rosanvallon 2011. Pierre Rosanvallon argues that the wide range of activities associated with procedural legitimacy—including the expansion in recent decades of independent commissions, NGOs, regulatory authorities, and watchdogs, along with an expanded role for the courts—represents new sources of legitimacy which can be seen to serve democratic values of impartiality, reflexivity, and proximity, by finding new spaces for minorities, the particular, and the local.
[46] Zeitlin and Vanhercke 2014, 2018; Maricut and Puetter 2017; Coman 2019b.
[47] See eg, Levi 1998, p. 88; Offe 1999.   [48] Franck 1995.

evaluating EU legitimacy. Adding throughput to the systemic mix of criteria for legitimacy is useful because it enables us to separate out issues regarding the procedural legitimacy of the governance processes from the performance legitimacy of the policies they may produce, as well as from the political legitimacy of the representative politics by which those policies were generated. At the same time, bringing the different elements involved in assessing procedural quality under the single rubric of throughput legitimacy enables us to theorize their interaction effects even as it allows us to consider how the more general categories of input or output legitimacy relate to throughput legitimacy. Moreover, by shining the spotlight on the procedural aspects of legitimacy, throughput focuses attention not only on the quality of the processes but also on the qualities expected of the agents engaged in policymaking, such as trustworthiness, fairness, integrity, credibility, impartiality, competence, and more.

Curiously enough, there has been little theorization of the "throughput" legitimacy of EU governance processes taken as a whole. The only exception has been a cluster of scholars mainly in Germany and bordering countries who have for the most part defined throughput as a question of procedural legitimacy involving the quality of decision-making.[49] Such scholars have often examined this in terms of governance beyond the state[50] or private governance.[51] Most leave out explicit discussion of interest-group participation,[52] or include it as part of "input" to representative institutions.

Theoretical approaches to output and input legitimacy have sometimes mixed the governance processes (throughput) either with the policy outcomes (output)—in particular those focused on non-majoritarian institutions[53] and legal institutions[54]—or political representation (input)—especially those concerned with interest-group intermediation.[55] And some continue to do so, challenging the necessity of any conceptualization of throughput legitimacy either on the grounds that it is already included in the terms of input and output or because they fear that it will be normatively accepted as a substitute for input legitimacy.[56] Admittedly, the boundaries between mechanisms may be a bit fuzzy. But as analytic categories, the legitimizing mechanisms are distinct.

The overlap between output and throughput occurs, say, when regulators and central bankers efficiently generate policies with good economic outcomes, or between input and throughput, when interest groups speak "in the name of the people" as they lobby EU institutions. But there is no guarantee that the efficacy

---

[49] See, eg, Zürn 2000; Benz and Papadopoulos 2006; Eriksen 2006, pp. 262–3; Dingwerth 2007; Holzhacker 2007; Risse and Kleine 2007; Bekkers and Edwards 2007; Wimmel 2009. For an in-depth discussion of the differences, see Steffek 2019.

[50] Eg, Zürn 1998.   [51] Eg, Dingwerth 2007.

[52] Eg, Risse and Kleine 2007; but see Bekkers and Edwards 2007.

[53] Eg, Majone 1993; Moravcsik 2002.   [54] Harlow 2016—but see critique in Fossum 2016.

[55] Eg, Kohler-Koch 2010.   [56] Eg, Bellamy 2010; Steffek 2015, 2019.

of regulators or central bankers is linked to policy performance, good or bad, let alone whether they were accountable or transparent. Nor is there any certainty that interest groups are actually representing "the people" as opposed to special interests. But whether or not they do (as an issue of input legitimacy), this does not capture the (throughput) ways in which interest articulation has become an integral part of the processes of EU governance,[57] in particular when assessing how their presence helps ensure the openness and accessibility of EU institutions and, thereby, the overall fairness and inclusiveness of the process.

This said, it is important to note that certain terms are common to both input and throughput legitimacy. With the concept of accountability for elected officials, for example, we need to be careful to differentiate between political actors being "held accountable" by citizens through elections (input legitimacy) and by their reason-giving in public forums (throughput legitimacy).[58] Representation and accountability are different things, even though, as Christopher Lord and Johannes Pollak suggest, they are closely interconnected through "communicating tubes."[59] Ben Crum and Dierdre Curtin explain the difference as one in which accountability in public forums is "the *ex post* complement to the *ex ante* mechanisms of democratic election or authorization through which executive actors are initially appointed." In other words, accountability in the throughput sense comes after input-legitimate elections, and applies to the ways in which elected officials are expected to justify their exercise of power in public forums, most often parliamentary, with the understanding that they will be judged on the basis of whether that exercise serves the popular constituency.[60]

Similarly, interest-group involvement in decision-making also requires careful distinction between citizen activities that serve the function of political representation (input) versus ones that serve a function of procedural openness and inclusion (throughput). Interest groups are engaged in processes of representation when they organize grassroots letter-writing campaigns, bring busloads of farmers to national capitals or Brussels to protest a new bill, organize demonstrations of mothers for peace, and represent "civil society," meaning citizens, in public interest-related activities meant to influence elected officials. They are involved in procedural inclusiveness and openness when they become part of an elaborate interest intermediation process focused on policymaking, in which they lobby political and technical officials, testify in committee meetings and parliamentary hearings, provide informational evidence to administrative functionaries, and serve as counterweights to one another as they seek to influence policy formulation and implementation.

---

[57] See Smismans 2003; Kohler-Koch 2007; Kroger 2008; Liebert and Trenz 2009.
[58] Cashore 2002; Borowiak 2011; Crum and Curtin 2015; Wood 2015.
[59] Lord and Pollak 2010.
[60] Crum and Curtin 2015, pp. 64–6; see also Bovens and Curtin 2016.

Throughput, understood as the procedural quality of policymaking processes, plays a special role in EU conceptualizations of legitimacy. It has long been one of the central ways in which EU institutional players have sought to counter claims about the poverty of the EU's input legitimacy and to reinforce claims to its output legitimacy.[61] In so doing, such actors have operated under the assumption that high-quality throughput may serve as a kind of *"cordon sanitaire"* for the EU, ensuring the trustworthiness of the processes and serving, thereby, as a kind of reinforcement or, better, reassurance, of the legitimacy of EU-level output and attention to input.[62] This assumption is problematic.

Input politics and output policy can be seen to involve trade-offs with regard to democratic legitimacy, in which more of the one may be seen to make up for less of the other.[63] While weak citizen input may appear to be offset by good policy output, a lot of citizen input may legitimate a policy even if it is ineffective. This is a relationship of interdependence, where actors must continuously (re)construct how their actions and policies speak to both input and output concerns, in order to decide what constitute legitimate trade-offs.[64] That said, bad policy performance in the absence of citizen participation will not only undermine output legitimacy, it may also have negative effects on input legitimacy, were citizens to see their political representatives as unresponsive to their needs because they have implemented policies that do not work. This was certainly the case in the Eurozone crisis.

Throughput does not interact with output and input in the same way. High-quality throughput cannot compensate for either bad policy output or minimal input participation. In contrast, bad throughput—consisting of oppressive, incompetent, corrupt, or biased governance practices—is likely to undermine public perceptions of the legitimacy of EU governance. It can even throw input and output into question by seeming to undermine representative politics or contaminate policy solutions. An emblematic case is the scandal involving the Santer Commission, when charges of nepotism and abusive contracting led to its resignation in 1999. This was not just a major blow to perceptions of the EU Commission's underlying trustworthiness, accountability, or transparency (throughput). It served to obscure the Santer Commission's notable achievements (output), such as Enlargement, while giving Euroskeptics ammunition for their claims about the EU's democratic deficit (input).[65]

---

[61] Héritier 1999.   [62] Schmidt 2013.
[63] Eg, Katz and Wessels 1999; Torres 2006. We might also question whether there really is a trade-off between input and output, since both are likely necessary to ensure robust legitimacy in a democracy, even if one may help compensate for an absence of the other. Another issue is whether it is actually possible to separate input and output—on this see Sternberg 2015.
[64] Sternberg 2015.   [65] Schmidt 2013.

Throughput legitimacy, in short, cannot make up for a lack of input or output legitimacy.[66] Nonetheless, quality throughput certainly serves as a complement to policy output and political input in any democratic system. As an analytic category, moreover, throughput enables us to explore more fully the legitimizing benefits as well as the delegitimizing drawbacks of policymaking processes that translate political input into policy output. It is particularly valuable in contexts of supranational governance such as the EU, where input politics is at many stages removed from policymaking, and thus diffuse, while the output policy results may be uncertain for some time, and in any case subject to interpretation.

In the Eurozone crisis, throughput legitimacy enables us to assess the quality of the policymaking processes through which EU actors have formulated and implemented policies, centered first on governing by rules and ruling by numbers and subsequently on reinterpreting the rules and recalibrating the numbers by stealth. Output legitimacy at the same time allows us to focus on the policies that are embodied in the rules, to evaluate the effectiveness and performance of austerity and structural reform policies along with the ideas behind them and the discourse supporting them. And finally, input legitimacy points us to the complicated politics that have followed from the policies and policymaking processes in the EU.

Evaluating Throughput Legitimacy

The processes encompassed by throughput legitimacy involve all aspects of governance, including policy formulation and policy implementation, policy coordination and policy evaluation, interest intermediation and consultation, rulemaking and rule adjudication, standard-setting and harmonization, legal assessment and judicial review, and so on. For the EU specifically, throughput legitimacy naturally applies to all of its different modes of governance, including the intergovernmental mode of the Council, the supranational mode of the Commission and the ECB, and the co-decision mode in which the EP is also a major player with the Council and Commission. While the question of "who governs" is a consideration in assessing EU actors' input legitimacy, "how they govern" is a question for throughput legitimacy, which in turn naturally also leads to the question of "how effective the governance is" for output legitimacy.

Of the five criteria for the evaluation of throughput legitimacy, while efficacy is primarily a technical standard of evaluation, focused on the efficiency of policymaking, the remaining four constitute normative criteria, including standards by which to assess the accountability of the policymakers and the transparency, inclusiveness, and openness of the processes. But whether technical or normative, all five criteria are significant not only with regard to how they are applied to

---

[66] See discussion in Steffek 2019 on throughput as a subordinate category.

governance processes but also in terms of how they may complement or contradict one another so as to enhance or reduce overall throughput legitimacy. Ordinarily, we expect good governance to involve efficient processes of decision-making by highly accountable public officials who provide full information (transparency) to forums that are equally accessible to all (inclusiveness and openness).[67] But just as in input legitimacy, where responsiveness and responsibility may be at odds, so it is with throughput legitimacy. For example, efficacy can trump accountability, by leaving insufficient time for forums of review; transparency can undermine efficiency by slowing decision-making; and it can be at odds with accountability where public actors require secrecy in order to be able to reach politically sensitive agreements, which may in turn also preclude inclusiveness and openness.

Efficacy

Efficacy is the criterion that finds the least amount of scholarly discussion with regard to legitimacy. It refers mainly to engaging in decision-making and proceeding with policy implementation in an efficient manner. Buzzwords include such phrases as "streamlining operations" or modernizing practices. As such, it is more of a technical criterion than a normative one, the standards of which are generally laid out in administrative guidelines and management studies about what constitutes, say, efficient governance or competent management. For example, efficacy has been the main justification for contemporary technocratic innovations of governance such as "new public management" (NPM), which applies private sector techniques to the public sector.[68] But although therefore not a normative standard like the other criteria of throughput, efficacy is nonetheless a necessary component of throughput. It has long been linked to considerations of the legitimacy of rulers, as a function of rulers' competence to rule. And although it could be said that the presence of efficacy does not necessarily legitimate a ruling authority, failures of efficacy related to incompetence and inefficiency in governance are often linked to processes of delegitimization—as, for example, in Max Weber's third definition of authority as legal-rational.[69]

Throughput efficacy has in consequence most often been conflated with output effectiveness. But there is a difference between processes that are carried out with efficacy, that is, in an efficient and competent manner, and policies that are effective, that is, that work. Although it is generally likely that efficacy in creating and administering policies will have a positive impact on their effectiveness, even

---

[67] See discussion in Crum and Curtin 2015.

[68] NPM sought to introduce efficiency into public management by splitting large bureaucracies into small units, introducing competition between public agencies, and possibly even bringing in private firms to provide public services. See, eg, Pollitt and Boukaert 2011.

[69] Weber 1946.

processes that are inefficacious because of long-drawn-out decision-making or poorly administered implementation can nonetheless produce good policy outcomes if the policies themselves prove effective. The inverse is also true— that however efficient the administrative processes, the resulting policies can prove ineffective, with bad results. Efficacy, then, is mainly about processing the job well, meaning proceeding in a competent and efficient manner, whatever the outcomes.

Efficacy has been one of the principal concerns of EU institutional actors, as they have sought to enhance the governance processes through which input politics is transformed into output policies. This has involved seeking to improve the operating efficiency of the EU's many different modes of governance. For example, the co-decision mode, often known as the Community Method (which includes the European Commission, the Council, and the EP), has been made to function more efficiently through fast-track legislation via early agreements (which went from 28 percent in 1999–2004 to 80 percent in 2004–9). But this comes at the expense of transparency and accountability as well as to the detriment of input legitimacy, due to the short-circuiting of parliamentary debate and the exclusion of the views of smaller party groupings in the inter-institutional meetings (called "trilogues") among a handful of individuals representing the EP (mainly larger party groupings), the Council, and the Commission.[70]

In supranational governance as well, the EU has focused on improvements in efficacy. Periodic proclamations by the Commission that it will seek to cut red tape and streamline operations are instances of this, along with promises to simplify the procedures of the European Semester. Impact assessments have since 2003 been another way of evaluating efficacy while trying to reinforce it by tying it to other procedural principles such as inclusiveness—although this has more often been more successful internally, through coordination across administrative units, than externally, by bringing in experts or being open to stakeholders and civil society.[71] Moreover, EU Commission failures of oversight with regard to member-state transposition and implementation of EU directives also raise problems of throughput efficacy, in particular with regard to whether and when the Commission engages in the different stages of infraction proceedings against the member states.[72] These problems also affected the European Semester, which the Commission sought to address by revamping the Semester to emphasize enhanced "ownership" by national actors and civil society. But this, too, yielded limited results.[73]

Intergovernmental governance by the Council has also frequently been criticized for its lack of efficacy. The unanimity rule for treaties, which allows any member state to veto any agreement, can lead to delays, dilution, or deadlock, along with

---

[70] Héritier and Reh 2012; Dehousse 2011b.   [71] Bozzini and Smismans 2016.
[72] Börzel 2001; Batory 2016.   [73] Vanheuverzwijn and Crespy 2018.

sub-optimal outcomes.[74] Although there are certainly good reasons related to input legitimacy to keep the unanimity rule (because it ensures that member states can safeguard national preferences), unanimity often frustrates goals and values related to output legitimacy—plus it is highly inefficient. Equally problematic is that once any agreement is reached, it becomes almost impossible to change, given the likelihood that at least one or more member states would oppose changing the agreement. As a result of this "joint decision trap," a policy once agreed remains even when it no longer serves the interests of the community and of many member states.[75]

Modalities of Accountability

Accountability is arguably the most important aspect of throughput legitimacy, at least if judged by the attention paid to it. It has been defined in myriad ways, often depending upon the disciplinary angle as well as the actor in focus.[76] But stripped down to its core conceptualization, accountability can be defined as public officials giving account of and being held to account for their actions in public forums that have the authority to judge their behavior such that the officials can face consequences for their actions, including the (potential) imposition of rewards or sanctions in cases of eventual misconduct.[77] Accountability also assumes that public officials have the autonomy and discretion to carry out their duties, which can be used or misused.[78] Integrity is generally cited as another key prerequisite of accountability.[79] The other normative procedural criteria of throughput legitimacy are often also attached to accountability, with public officials expected to provide full disclosure and information about their actions (transparency) and to discuss or deliberate about that information in forums that are fully accessible to civil society (inclusiveness and openness).[80] Moreover, where accountability is seen as a virtue of public officials and not just as an evaluative political or administrative mechanism, as Mark Bovens and collaborators note, it comes with a set of standards of conduct for good governance, including willingness to act in a transparent, fair, compliant, and equitable way. Accountability deficits or "bad" governance instead manifest themselves in "unresponsive, opaque, irresponsible, and ineffective" behavior.[81]

---

[74] Schmidt 2009a, pp. 28–32.   [75] Scharpf 1988.
[76] See, eg, Bovens 2010; Bovens et al. 2014a; Keohane and Grant 2005.
[77] Bovens 2010, pp. 946–8; Bovens et al. 2014b.   [78] March and Olsen 1995, p. 152.
[79] Transparency International (2015), for example, looks at integrity safeguards in law and in practice, in order to assess whether the behaviours and actions of civil servants are consistent with their own institution's external and internal legal frameworks meant to serve as barriers to corruption. See Ban and Seabrooke 2017.
[80] Crum and Curtin 2015.   [81] Bovens 2010; Bovens et al. 2014b.

Accountability is most often discussed in terms of the administrative activities of technical actors in non-majoritarian institutions, delegated agencies, and governmental administrations. But it also applies to political actors in majoritarian institutions engaged in the processes of decision-making. Both kinds of actors are expected to give account to and to be held to account in accountability forums, with technical actors accountable to both technical and political forums on an ongoing basis, political actors mainly to the political. As Giandomenico Majone specifies, because "majoritarian standards" of (input) legitimacy are not appropriate for independent regulators, "accountability" requires a "multi-pronged system of controls" including such mechanisms as clear and narrow specification of objectives, political oversight, requirements for hearings and reporting duties, judicial review, professionalism, and peer review, along with transparency and participation.[82]

Technical accountability forums consist of specialized bodies of administrative or technical expertise generally made up of administrative bodies and regulators, such as courts of audit, ombudsmen, inspectorates, regulatory agencies, and judicial bodies of various sorts.[83] In addition to these formal administrative forums are the often more informal but equally important professional ones, consisting of networks of experts who can provide "objective"—meaning (social) scientific—assessments of the quality of technical actors' activities (throughput) as well as of the effective performance of the resulting policies (output).[84] In technical forums, the "giving of accounts" generally comes in the form of highly specialized arguments that make reference to mathematical calculations, economic formulations, socioeconomic impact assessments, macroeconomic charts and graphs, and the like. This is the daily bread of civil servants, whether in the ECB, the Commission, or other regulatory bodies.

Political accountability forums include specially designated or generally elected political bodies acting in a representative capacity for the citizenry at large. These are ordinarily parliamentary bodies not only expected to "take account" of the quality of political as well as technical actors' (throughput) activities but also charged with evaluating the effectiveness of the resulting policies (output legitimacy), along with their ability to respond to citizens' concerns, resonate with citizen values, and promote the common good (input legitimacy). In political forums, political and technical actors' "giving of accounts" generally includes not only cognitive arguments focused on making policies comprehensible but also normative arguments that seek to show that the policies are not just morally acceptable and appropriate for the community but equally promote the public's wellbeing and benefit.[85] For technical actors in particular, the normative arguments

---

[82] Majone 1998. Although Majone himself places such procedural accountability under the rubric of output legitimacy, we find it useful here to separate it out as part of throughput legitimacy.
[83] Bovens et al. 2014b, p. 11.   [84] Seabrooke 2014.   [85] Cashore 2002; Wood 2015.

are expected to speak to the "social purpose" of the policies,[86] with a kind of macro-thinking that stiches together compatible cognitive and normative ideas so as to communicate a vision of the good and desirable system derived from past experience.[87]

EU Accountability

The EU, as is to be expected, has both kinds of accountability forums. But while EU technical actors like the Commission and the ECB are engaged with political as well as technical forums at the EU level, the most powerful EU political actor, the Council, is subject to very little scrutiny from any EU forum when in inter-governmental mode. The only outside bodies in a position to judge the Council's accountability are the CJEU, which has strong powers in a narrow sphere to rule on the constitutionality of Council action; the EU Ombudsman, which has weak powers in a wide sphere (and therefore generally focuses on transparency); and the EP, which has hardly any powers at all.

Unlike at the national level, where parliaments largely serve as forums of accountability for national executives, the EP has little such authority with regard to the Council. The Council's *de jure* accountability to the EP is weak, covering mainly information, since the EP has little or no power to ensure debate and little corrective capacity. In consequence, the Council has no formal EU-level forum that can both hold it to account and to which it has to give account. This would not be a problem were accountability predicated solely on the (input-legitimate) linkages between member-state leaders and their national parliaments or public opinion more generally.[88] But this logic fails to deal with the fact that in practice very few national parliaments (with the notable exception of some Northern European legislatures) are able to hold their national executives to account in Council decision-making.[89]

That said, even if national parliaments were able to hold their executives to account, this would not be sufficient to guarantee the Council's EU-level accountability. Most collective EU-level decisions go beyond the aggregation of member-state governments' individual interests in ways that cannot be adequately assessed by any individual national parliament on strictly national accountability grounds because of Council negotiations in which member states generally reconsider their initial interest-based calculations, and make concessions that do not necessarily conform to interest-maximizing bargains.[90] In other words, Council deliberation effectively weakens or eliminates the direct accountability

---

[86] Ruggie 1982—see discussion in Baker 2018.   [87] Baker 2018.
[88] See discussion in Chapter 5 on the Council.   [89] Auel 2007; Crum 2017; Kreilinger 2019.
[90] See discussion in Crum and Curtin 2015, pp. 78–9; see also Puetter 2012; Bickerton et al. 2015.

link between a government's decision in the Council and its national parliament, at the same time that there is no public body to judge the Council's accountability at the EU level.

We would avoid this problem only if, following theories of deliberative democracy,[91] especially when applied to EU governance,[92] we were to argue that the Council can achieve a kind of mutual accountability as a deliberative body, with its members holding one another accountable for their decisions. But this requires that deliberation meet certain standards, in particular that it proceed without major inequalities in the exercise of power or voice, or at least that these are balanced out in such a way that member states do not feel unduly disadvantaged.[93] In many domains, this may actually be the case. It remains in question with regard to Council decision-making during the Eurozone crisis not only because of the predominance of only one or two powerful member-state governments in the European Council but also because of the lack of any formal accountability for the Eurogroup of finance ministers in the Troika.[94]

In contrast with intergovernmental decision-making, the co-decision mode of governance, where the Council, EP, and Commission are all involved in policy-making, could very well be seen as throughput legitimate in terms of mutual accountability. But even here, the internal process of Council decision-making is not accountable to any specific forum, with little or no information on Council members' internal positions. The EP on the contrary is publicly accountable in the sense that it sets out its positions for all to see. However, in the fast-track discussions, here too the compromises among actors are not visible. Only the Commission may appear to be fully accountable in this process, since it has to develop the initiatives on which the Council and EP deliberate, with the double accountability forum of the Council—its administrative master—and the EP—its "political" master following the *Spitzenkandidat* election of 2014, in which the head of the victorious political majority was appointed President of the Commission.

In the supranational mode of governance, the Commission has also become much more accountable to the EP over time, as the EP gained increasing powers to vet candidates for Commissioner, to confirm the Commission as "fit for purpose," and even to reject individual candidates and/or impeach the Commission as a whole.[95] Such accountability takes various forms, including producing reports and collecting data on their own performance and responding to the

---

[91] See eg, Bohman 1996; Dryzek and Niemeyer 2008; Parkinson and Mansbridge 2012.

[92] Puetter 2014; Bickerton et al. 2015.

[93] A full list of such standards, following Mansbridge 2015, p. 36, includes respect, absence of coercive power, search for consensus, attention to rational and emotional considerations, orientation toward the common good, equal participation or access to political influence, inclusiveness, accountability to constituents, publicity and transparency, and sincerity in matters of importance.

[94] Joerges 2014; Kreuzer-Sonnen 2017a, 2017b; Braun and Hübner 2019; see discussion in Chapter 5 on the Council.

[95] Corbett et al. 2014.

demands of committees of the EP as well as, for that matter, the Council. This is what Bovens and colleagues call the "real world" of accountability in the EU.[96]

Moreover, not only do Commission officials pay attention to the epistemic community of experts in their various fields of endeavor, they also have to render accounts and/or be held to account in a number of other forums, including the CJEU, the European Anti-Fraud Office (OLAF), the European Court of Auditors, and the European Ombudsman.[97] Most of these bodies have strong enforcement powers backed up by law. In contrast, the Ombudsman has the "softest" of powers. This was illustrated in the Commission's unsatisfactory response to ethical concerns raised about the "revolving door" through which former Commission President Barroso moved (too) quickly into a top position at Goldman Sachs, and about the procedurally questionable way in which the Commission appointed its Secretary General.[98]

The ECB is also accountable in technical and political forums, but less so than the Commission. Its main accountability is arguably the informal, technical one constituted by the epistemic community of economists, banking experts, and other central bankers. But the ECB is also formally accountable to the EP, as the forum in which it is charged to explain its actions and to hear the concerns of MEPs.[99] That said, by mandate the ECB does not have to listen, and it cannot be sanctioned by the EP, making the EP a very weak accountability forum indeed. The ECB's charter-based independence also enables it to ignore other EU actors' attempts to hold it to account if it so chooses. This includes the Council, in particular in its first years, when ECB heads focused on ensuring their "credibility." But the ECB's ability to deflect accountability demands were also in evidence when ECB President Draghi refused the EU Ombudsman's recommendation to suspend his membership in the Group of 30 so as to avoid any appearance that the Bank's independence was compromised.[100]

Accountability is not just about rendering accounts to specialized or political forums via cognitive and normative arguments, however. It is also about making them public. For political actors, accountability in the "court of public opinion" is a *sine qua non* of their public life, with elections the ultimate sanction. But it is relatively new for EU technical actors, who only in recent years have become increasingly aware of the need to legitimate their policies to the more general public, and not just internally to the "principals" to whom they are accountable as "agents." In this context, technical actors tend to be focused on building public understanding and trust in their work in order to reinforce their authority, to achieve "credible commitments," and to ensure that the policy is accepted by the

[96] Bovens et al. 2010.   [97] Crum and Curtin 2015.
[98] O'Reilly 2018.   [99] See Draghi's 2015 speech to the EP.
[100] O'Reilly 2018. The Group of 30 is a private Washington-based club whose members included global banks such as Goldman Sachs, JP Morgan, and UBS, which are directly or indirectly supervised by the ECB.

public as appropriate and justified.[101] In consequence, they have recognized the need to develop communicative strategies on a daily basis in this "mediatized" age.[102]

As a result of this, the media can also be seen to function as a kind of public accountability forum, with agencies giving account to the media even as the media give account of those agencies' regulatory activities to the public.[103] This arguably works best for technical agencies speaking on specialized issues—such as when the Directorate of Competition announced a state aid ruling that sanctioned Ireland's special tax regime for Apple, or set high fines for the internet giant Google on competition grounds. But it may not work as well for the EU Commission on general questions because there is no EU-wide media to which to give public account, while national media may take nationally colored views. The paradox is that the Commission's increasing attention to internal accountability has not solved "the problems of rendering accounts externally,"[104] which leaves the EU invisible to the public, remote, and seemingly unaccountable.[105] But this is also where transparency comes in.

Transparency

Transparency has long been seen as a key accompaniment to accountability in EU governance—as matching parts producing good governance only when in combination, or even as "Siamese twins."[106] Transparency refers here to the availability of provisions ensuring that citizens and political representatives have access to information about governance processes and that decisions as well as decision-making processes in formal institutions are public.[107] This applies not only to technical actors in EU supranational institutions but also to political actors such as the Council.[108] As Maarten Hillebrandt and colleagues put it, transparency refers to "rules enabling the public to monitor processes taking place in a public body" and comprises such aspects as wide access to documents all the time, by any feasible and accessible means, with few exceptions that are interpreted restrictively.[109] In practice, this means checking on how well the public can examine the integrity and accountability of the EU actor itself as well as of the functioning of inter-institutional oversight relations.[110]

The underlying assumption related to transparency is that information can empower citizens to hold public officials accountable for their actions and performance, with the goal of improving public services or reducing corruption and clientelism. But transparency can equally have a regulatory function, by serving

[101] Cashore 2002; Schillemans 2011; Wood 2015.   [102] Hajer 2012.
[103] Bovens 2007; Maggetti 2012.   [104] Wille 2010, pp. 84–5.   [105] Schmidt 2013.
[106] Hood 2010.   [107] Héritier 2003.   [108] Novak 2013.
[109] Hillebrandt et al. 2014.   [110] Eg, Braun 2017, Ban and Seabrooke 2017.

to tame undue private power, with public officials mandating public disclosures about private companies' products and practices such that citizens have the requisite information to press for corporate social responsibility and performance.[111] In the EU, both senses of transparency are operative, since EU officials seek to make their own actions and publications more transparent while demanding the same of all entities that do business in the EU.

Transparency also serves to ensure that the public knows not only that political and technical actors follow ethical standards but also that they are doing what they say they are doing, such that their discourse can be measured against their actions. As such, transparency has been seen as a key component of any free society, related to citizens' right to know and governments' obligation to share information about all aspects of public life. It sits at the very heart of how citizens hold their public officials accountable, and thus is closely linked to accountability. In transnational democracy, moreover, transparency can equally be seen as a component of citizen empowerment.[112] That said, it is important to remember that transparency is no substitute for accountability, since although accounts may be given and discussion may follow, nothing may subsequently happen.[113]

The Commission has attempted to ensure general transparency by providing increasing access to the mountains of EU documents and materials for media and interest groups as well as to the general public through the internet and the development of e-government—although the massive volume of EU-generated information has also led to information overload and thus, perversely, less transparency.[114] But access to information, however great, does not ensure that citizens will automatically gain insight and knowledge about the proceedings. And more information is not always better, since it is easier to lose any sense of what is important and what is not.

Even though transparency has been an increasing focus of EU actors more generally, there are many instances of a lack of transparency, in particular from delegated agencies and administrations. For example, the European Stability Mechanism (ESM), which acts as a lender of last resort in conjunction with the ECB, argues that if it made the reasons for its investment decisions public, the markets would be the greatest beneficiaries, to the disadvantage of the member state receiving ESM support.[115] In this case, considerations of output legitimacy—meaning good performance—appear to win out over the search for throughput legitimacy via transparency, although accountability to the ESM's "principals" is also in play.

The EU's political actors have also been resistant to transparency. Most notably, the Council has resisted making available information on meetings with lobbyists on legal grounds, claiming that Council meetings are a matter of national

---

[111] Kosack and Fung 2014.   [112] Smith 2012.   [113] Papadopoulos 2010, p. 1034.
[114] Héritier 2003.   [115] Ban and Seabrooke 2017.

competence. Similarly, the EP long dragged its feet on limiting meetings of MEPs to registered lobbyists, claiming that such meetings were a legal requirement of their mandate.[116] It established a voluntary registration scheme and code of conduct for lobbyists only in 2011.[117] Lack of transparency, in this last case, is perversely linked to inclusiveness and openness, to the possible detriment of integrity while leaving open the possibility of bias or even corruption. The rules changed only at the end of January 2019, when MEPs agreed that rapporteurs, shadow rapporteurs, or committee chairs involved in the preparation of specific legislative acts would need to publish on the EP website their scheduled meetings with representatives of organizations that might stand to benefit or lose from the proposed legislation.[118]

Transparency can also clash with efficacy, in particular in negotiation settings.[119] In Council meetings, for example, secrecy, meaning a lack of transparency, has been touted as ensuring greater efficacy—by helping member-state officials clinch agreements that would not be possible if national publics knew about their officials' specific compromises—and enables fruitful side deals.[120] But as such, as EU Ombudsman Emily O'Reilly reported, it leaves its decisions in a "black hole"— whether in intergovernmental or co-decision modes of governance—because it fails to inform the public on member-state positions.[121] Such secrecy may make the Council not just less accountable but also less efficient, contrary to assumptions. Recent scholarship by Sara Hageman and Fabio Franchino finds that increased Council transparency through the publication of legislative records actually facilitates decision-making by increasing credibility and thereby lowering risks of negotiation failure.[122] That said, greater transparency could simply displace the locus of deal-making. In the EP, for example, where public debate is mandated in the co-decision process, negotiations often end up taking place over lunch or in the corridors, to the detriment of accountability as well as transparency.[123]

For the trade-off between transparency and other legitimizing criteria, then, much depends upon the reasons for the secrecy, and whether it is necessary in order to ensure against worse consequences, or instead is used to hide problematic decisions. In the Eurozone crisis, as Christian Kreuder-Sonnen argues, there is a difference between secrecy as crisis management, intended to avoid further deterioration of the situation, and secrecy as crisis exploitation, where those in authority benefit from opacity to adopt policies that would otherwise not have been possible.[124] An example of defensive crisis management could be seen

---

[116] Freund 2017.   [117] Cini 2013.
[118] http://www.europarl.europa.eu/news/en/headlines/eu-affairs/20190124STO24226/transparency-key-meps-to-declare-meetings-with-lobbyists
[119] See, eg, Stasavage 2004.   [120] Naurin 2007.   [121] O'Reilly 2018.
[122] Hagemann and Franchino 2016.   [123] Novak 2010, 2013.
[124] Kreuder-Sonnen 2018b. For more detail, see discussions of the Eurogroup in Chapter 12 on the Council.

in the ECB's coming ever closer to a lender of last resort (LOLR) as it sought to "save the euro."[125] An example of crisis exploitation is best illustrated by the Eurogroup in the various Greek bailout negotiations, where Eurogroup finance ministers' ability to act in secrecy enabled them to wrest much more out of Greece than they would have been able to had they had to make their positions public.[126]

The more general problem with this latter kind of 'emergency politics', as Jonathan White calls it, is not just that it is unaccountable in procedural terms. It may also be profoundly anti (liberal) democratic in political terms. White argues that EU actors' exercise of emergency powers, generally rationalized away as necessary haste under exceptional circumstances in response to existential threat, delegitimizes dissent on decisions of lasting importance while undercutting public debate.[127] In addition to the Eurogroup's Greek bailout decisions, examples include EU leaders' agreement to establish technocratic oversight of national budgets via the European Semester; EU leaders' interference in national politics, as exemplified by their 2011 push to remove the Berlusconi government and their 2012 insistence that the Papandreou government withdraw its proposed referendum; and pressures by EU actors and the markets on eurozone members in trouble to engage in welfare state retrenchment.[128]

Inclusiveness and Openness

Transparency as well as accountability can also be linked to the final two criteria of throughput legitimacy: openness and inclusiveness. Openness means that the political and technical actors involved in creating and/or implementing policies are willing to engage with any and all of those members of the public—mainly organized in groups of citizens, but also and increasingly individuals via online consultation—desirous of having a say with regard to such policies. Inclusiveness means that public officials are open to all such groups, and bring them in in such a way as to ensure balance and fairness in their representation.

In the EU, where input legitimacy is largely situated at the national level, interest groups play a vital role in ensuring that citizens' national-level political input is translated via throughput processes into EU-level output. This is what Sandra Kröger calls the "two-level mechanism" in which determining the quality of EU governance processes requires establishing whether EU level groups "have a reliable link to their domestic constituencies, without which they are likely to feel less bound to the related inputs, making it more likely that the input will not

---

[125] Kreuder-Sonnen 2018b, 2019b; see also Braun 2017.
[126] Kreuder-Sonnen 2018b, 2019b. For more detail, see discussions of the Eurogroup in Chapter 12 on the Council.
[127] White 2015, pp. 300–301.   [128] White 2015, pp. 304–8.

come out as "uncorrupted output."[129] This means that to be fully throughput legitimate, interest groups not only need barrierless access as part of pluralist processes of interest intermediation but also need to remain closely linked to their membership in order to ensure that they represent their members' views with efficacy and accountability, to those members' satisfaction.

Problems with regard to inclusiveness and openness come from the nature of pluralist interest intermediation. These include unequal access, differentials in power and influence, corruption related to the trading of favors, clientelistic politics, lack of accountability, and the dangers of agency "capture" by special interests (as elaborated, for example, by James Q. Wilson).[130]

The EU has its own version of pluralism.[131] In the EU, governance *with* the people through pluralist-type consultation comes mainly through co-decision-making, and was initially focused primarily on the technical agents of the Commission. This has changed with the increasing powers of the EP in co-decision, as lobbying MEPs has become a veritable growth industry.[132] Moreover, rather than competition among interests, following the norm of the United States, the Commission has fostered cooperation in a consensus-based policy formulation process.[133] In the EU, the rules of the game demand that participants gain and maintain credibility as trusted actors providing accurate technical information.[134] Trust-based beneficiaries include not just business and public interest groups but even social movements, which in recent years have been able to exercise informal influence.[135]

The EU has deliberately encouraged such pluralism as a way of counterbalancing the paucity of governance *by* or *of* the people through interest-based governance *with* the people. But it took a while for such interest-based "functional representation" to be seen as an additional form of democratic legitimization in the EU,[136] as a way of making up for the weakness of electorally based legitimacy.[137] This is at least in part because the Commission, starting with its *White Paper on Governance* in 2000, made increasing efforts over the years to ensure that policymaking became "more inclusive and accountable" to "civil society"—in the definition of which it included business interests. The Commission used this term in order to make it also appear as if it was improving political (input) legitimacy through procedural (throughput) means,[138] even though this was really mainly about generating better (output) results.[139] That said, the Commission made significant progress in righting the balance in access and influence among organized

[129] Kröger 2018.   [130] Wilson 1980; see also Bianculli et al. 2014.
[131] Schmidt 2006, ch. 3.
[132] Eg, Coen and Katsaitis 2015; Rasmussen 2015; Coen and Richardson 2009.
[133] See Schmidt 2006, pp. 104–8.   [134] Coen 2007; Coen and Richardson 2009.
[135] Della Porta 2009; Crespy 2010.
[136] See Smismans 2003; Lord and Beetham 2001; Greenwood 2007.
[137] Héritier 1999; Magnette 2003; Ruzza and Della Sala 2007.
[138] Smismans 2003; Schmidt 2013; see also discussion in Parker 2018.
[139] See Crespy 2010.

interests representing business versus those representing unions or public inter-est organizations,[140] sometimes even creating groups from under-represented interests (eg, of women and consumers) at the EU level. More generally, by funding civil society organizations that voice the concerns of excluded or under-represented groups, Rosa Sanchez Salgado finds that the Commission has helped build characteristics of associative democracy into its interest intermedia-tion processes.[141]

But even though the EU's throughput legitimacy judged in terms of normative standards of inclusiveness and openness have certainly increased over the years, how much influence this has enabled public interest groups to wield empirically remains debatable.[142] The difficulties of transnational mobilization only add to the problem.[143] For the most part, business interests continue to exert great influence,[144] even if recent empirical studies suggest that their actual success in determining legislative outcomes may be more limited than previously thought.[145] Moreover, the interest groups of some countries are more present than those of others in the intermediation process.[146] As for the umbrella interest groups that bring a wide variety of member groups together under a single organization, the results vary greatly. In a study of three different EU-level umbrella groups and their national members in Germany and the UK, Kröger found that the agri-cultural umbrella scored high on both counts with its domestic members, the environmental umbrella much lower, and the anti-poverty umbrella—itself set up by the Commission to ensure inclusiveness—lowest.[147] This suggests that the Commission's best intentioned efforts to enhance the inclusiveness and openness of interest intermediation "top down," by establishing EU-level umbrella groups for the less represented domestic groups, is not enough to guarantee high-quality throughput legitimacy 'from the bottom up'. But it is nevertheless important, and has certainly enhanced the access and influence of civil society organizations, in particular where the EP is also involved.

The EP provides yet another route in to citizens, including to public interest groups and social movements that find themselves with little Commission or Council access. But here, too, private interests and experts often have greater weight. The problem, as David Coen and Alex Katsaitis explain, is that while the EP is very open to "outsider" public interest groups in its formal hearings, primarily to demonstrate its democratic credentials, such hearings generally only formalize information and expert advice already received informally from "insider" groups such as specific EU-level associations, companies, NGOs, and think tanks in par-ticular. This tends to have a simultaneous effect of both establishing an image of

---

[140] Greenwood 2007; Pianta 2013.   [141] Sanchez Salgado 2014.
[142] Kröger 2008; Kamlage and Nanz 2017.   [143] Imig and Tarrow 2001; Della Porta 2009.
[144] Eising 2007; Dür and Mateo 2012; Kohler-Koch and Quittkat 2013.
[145] Dür et al. 2019.   [146] Dür and Mateo 2012; Kohler-Koch and Quittkat 2013.
[147] Kröger 2018.

inclusiveness while at the same time depoliticizing the process, as actors without the requisite "expertise" are crowded out of committee hearings.[148]

And yet, the EP does provide access that some groups would not have otherwise, in particular in the case of social movements. As Amandine Crespy and Louisa Parks have argued, social movements opposed to EU initiatives have sometimes been highly effective in stopping EU legislation where they have been able to connect with MEPs in the parliamentary opposition. But this is mainly where the EP already had a significant role to play, as in the cases of ACTA (the Anti-Counterfeiting Trade Agreement) and the Bolkestein Services Directive. Where the EP has had little role to play, in the financial and Eurozone crises, protest movements have had little purchase on decisions—even where they may have had high public salience, as in the cases of the "*indignados*" and Occupy protests against austerity and inequality.[149]

Eurozone economic governance during the crisis has posed special problems with regard to openness and inclusiveness, in particular for organized labor in light of the European Semester, which empowered the European Commission to prescribe labor market policies and sanction non-complying governments. In the highly critical view of one observer, Roland Erne, this new EU governance regime followed the logic of multinational corporations, which control their notionally autonomous local subsidiaries through whipsawing tactics and coercive comparisons based on performance indicators. This, he argues, has led to a situation in which the EU, rather than dealing with the conflicts between business and labor at the supranational level through inclusive negotiation, "nationalizes social conflicts" through country-specific recommendations, corrective action plans, and sanctions that push deflation and labor market deregulation.[150] For Erne, in other words, in the Euro regime, national "authoritarian" imposition in the case of countries in conditionality programs replaces EU-level inclusiveness with regard to labor.

Ensuring inclusiveness and openness is thus not always easy, and often easily thwarted. But where it does exist, it can have positive spillover effects on other aspects of throughput legitimacy. For one, ensuring greater openness to interest participation serves to improve transparency, mainly through the provision of more information on rules and procedures as well as through procedural requirements for active participation by a broad range of stakeholders in regulatory decision-making.[151] Inclusiveness and openness also improve accountability, by promoting deliberative procedures that are designed to ensure that citizens' community power is adequately channeled in societal and administrative decision-making.[152] Recent innovations in these areas have fostered a more

---

[148] Coen and Katsaitis 2019.   [149] Crespy and Parks 2017.
[150] Erne 2015.   [151] Sabel and Zeitlin 2010, pp. 18–20.
[152] Bekkers and Edwards, 2007, p. 53; see also Joerges and Neyer 1997.

dynamic accountability, by shifting away from older forms of governance focused on rules compliance to consensus-focused intermediation through peer reviews in forums, networked agencies, councils of regulators, and the open method of coordination.[153] But however much such new deliberative forms of governance may serve to normatively enhance throughput legitimacy, they may not always be empirically as inclusive or as open as they may seem on the surface, as Owen Parker argues, given that EU actors determine the (continuing neoliberal) agenda and who is brought into the deliberative forums.[154]

Finally, greater inclusiveness has also enhanced accountability through ad hoc deliberative moments such as the Constitutional Convention,[155] although there is some question as to whether it actually lived up to its promise;[156] and by instances of informal supranational "discursive representation."[157] This is when INGOs such as Greenpeace or significant personalities such as Habermas articulate a discourse about what the EU ought to do that has an impact, albeit somewhat vague, on policymakers and their deliberative processes. Moreover, institutionalized processes such as the European Citizens' Initiative (ECI) or even the Early Warning Mechanism (whereby national parliaments can signal their opposition to Commission initiatives for new EU laws) are meant to ensure greater openness to citizens either directly or through their parliaments. That said, these initiatives have largely failed in their intent. In the case of the ECI, the Commission has rejected almost all petitions on procedural grounds (eg, insufficient signatures, outside the Commission's mandate)—including the 2014 petition against TTIP and CETA that had garnered 3.28 million signatories, in a decision the General Court of the European Union itself condemned in May 2017.

Conclusion

This chapter began with definitions of democracy and legitimacy. It then concentrated on the legitimacy of the EU's governing activities on the assumption that the EU has over time slowly acquired legitimacy as a governing authority in policy area after policy area. Both forms of legitimacy are naturally interconnected, since legitimacy is a matter of discursive construction and contestation, such that public perceptions of a governing body's activities can negatively or positively affect perceptions of its governing authority.

The chapter also set out to show that the concept of throughput legitimacy is a useful and necessary accompaniment to output and input legitimacy, but not a substitute for either. Enhancing the procedural quality of policymaking serves to reinforce people's trust that the rules are being following fairly, in the spirit as

---

[153] See, eg, Sabel and Zeitlin 2010, pp. 12–17.   [154] Parker 2018.
[155] Risse and Kleine 2007.   [156] Crum 2012.   [157] Dryzek and Niemeyer 2008.

much as the letter of the law, in ways that are responsive to citizens' input demands while ensuring the best possible policy outputs. Perceptions of illegality or unfairness that can lead to a loss of trust serve to endanger the EU's throughput legitimacy and, in turn, its input and/or output legitimacy. But good governance (throughput) cannot make up for failures to respond to citizens' expressed demands (input) or to produce effective outcomes (output). The overall question with regard to the EU's throughput legitimacy, in the end, is whether it ensures the seamless flow of input to output as part of a governing system that acts both responsively (input) and responsibly in ways that produce good outcomes (output) efficaciously via accountable and transparent processes that are also inclusive and open (throughput). And when it does operate seamlessly, throughput legitimacy serves as an invaluable complement to the other two forms of legitimacy, in many instances enhancing citizens' political input by providing another way for them to be heard whilst ensuring better policy output

As we will see in subsequent chapters, EU actors' throughput legitimacy largely depends upon changing ideas about what to do to ensure procedural quality while responding to public perceptions of any deterioration in policy performance and political responsiveness. It is also the case that EU actors often turn to throughput legitimacy because it is the one type of legitimacy that they can most influence on their own. For output legitimacy, the EU is generally dependent on member-state implementation, while input legitimacy and its associated politics is similarly primarily situated at the national level, as we will see in the next chapter. This is why, before we look more closely at EU actors' different pathways to throughput legitimacy in Part II, we turn to the challenges to EU governance arising from the complications of the EU's institutional context. In the next chapter, we look more closely at the EU—first at its split-level legitimacy, where output and throughput legitimacy are found mainly at the EU level while input legitimacy is at the national level, and then at the EU's increasing politicization at the bottom, from the bottom up, and at the top.

3

Split-Level Legitimacy and Politicization in EU Governance

The nature of the EU system further complicates questions of democracy and legitimacy for the EU and its member states, since the legitimizing mechanisms of output, input, and throughput are largely divided between EU and national levels. Because the EU lacks the political legitimacy (input) of a directly elected government, supported by a *demos* in which citizens share a sense of identity and common purpose,[1] its legitimacy has long rested primarily on the effective performance of the policies (output) and the quality of the processes (throughput) at the EU level. In contrast, the national level has mainly been concerned with political (input) legitimacy, as the locus of national elections and the focus of national identity and sovereignty. Even though over time the EU has developed a thin European cultural identity and a European sense of peoples-hood, or *demoi*, this has done little to reduce the split between EU-level policy and processes and national-level politics.

While such split-level legitimacy may have seemed of little importance initially, it has become more and more problematic over time, as citizens have become increasingly critical of the effectiveness of the policies, the quality of the governance processes, and their own inability to exercise voice, let alone vote on EU decisions and decision-making. Such dissatisfaction has led to a heightened politicization of EU governance, as issues that had previously been considered apolitical became political, as matters for contestation or deliberation in collective decision-making.

Politicization here is defined as the process through which European integration has become the subject of public discussion, debate, and contestation. Such discussion may concern the legitimacy of the EU's governing authority—that is, the EU's very right to exist, along with its impact on national sovereignty and identity—as much as the legitimacy of the EU's governing activities—judged on the basis of their policy effectiveness (output), political responsiveness (input), and procedural quality (throughput). Over time, the EU's authority and/or activities have become increasingly contested, with a rapid escalation in the polarization of

---

[1] Weiler 1996, 2001; Grimm 1995; Zürn 2000.

Europe's Crisis of Legitimacy: Governing by Rules and Ruling by Numbers in the Eurozone. Vivien A. Schmidt, Oxford University Press (2020). © Vivien A. Schmidt.
DOI: 10.1093/oso/9780198797050.001.0001

debates in the context of the EU's recent crises, including not only the Eurozone crisis but also the refugee crisis and Brexit.[2]

Such politicization has multiple manifestations. There is a politics that exists purely at the national level, putting pressure on mainstream national party politics through the increase in citizen dissatisfaction and the rise of anti-system, populist parties. There is a politics that moves from the bottom up, through the nationally influenced politicization of EU governance, which has especially affected the Council. And there is also a politics that exists solely at the top, with the increasingly politicized dynamics of interaction in EU governance, as all EU actors engage in struggles for power and authority as well as legitimacy for their governing activities.

The result is that at the national level, citizens who had long seemed unconcerned about the "politics *without* policy" engendered by increasing European integration have become more and more politicized with regard to the EU and its impact. This has fueled the rise of Euroskepticism on the back of populism, which has made for national "politics *against* policy" in the more contentious areas. At the EU level, such national politicization has been one source of the increasingly charged political dynamics of interaction that has moved the EU from "policy *without* politics" to more and more "policy *with* politics." But EU-level politicization also results from intra and inter-institutional political conflicts among EU actors over policy ideas, as much as over who should wield power and influence.

EU governance has in consequence become much more complicated, and much more contested in terms of all three of the legitimizing mechanisms discussed in Chapter 2. In this chapter, we examine these issues in greater detail, beginning with a discussion of EU legitimacy. In addition to discussing the split between EU-level policies and processes and national-level politics, we briefly explore for each of the three categories how the EU has built legitimacy over time and the challenges it has faced in recent years, in particular as a result of the Eurozone crisis. The chapter then discusses the ways in which politicization has affected EU governance at the bottom, from the bottom up, and at the top, ending with the question of whether politicization is a good thing or a bad thing.

Split-Level Legitimacy in the EU

In any national polity, the flow from one legitimizing mechanism to the next generally appears straightforward, with the system depicted as moving from citizen input through procedural throughput in the "black box" of governance to policy

---

[2] Eg, Falkner 2017; Börzel and Risse 2018; Caporaso 2018; Schimmelfennig 2018.

performance, and back to citizen input through feedback mechanisms. The EU's governance system is more complex. With regard to input, citizens vote for national governments that indirectly represent them in the Council and for candidates for the European Parliament (EP) that are intended to directly represent them. Concerning throughput, national governments in the Council engage in policymaking either on their own in the intergovernmental mode of governance or in tandem with the Commission and the EP in the joint-decision mode. At the same time, supranational actors mandated by the Council (and sometimes the EP) such as the Commission, the European Central Bank (ECB), or the European Stability Mechanism (ESM) additionally engage in policymaking (throughput) in the supranational mode of governance. All of these then generate the output that citizens may approve or sanction in a feedback loop to national-level input. As a result, while the activities of the Council and the EP are at the intersection of input and throughput legitimacy, the Commission and the ECB are at the intersection of throughput and output legitimacy. As Figure 3.1 illustrates, the boundaries between input, output, and throughput legitimacy overlap, and therefore need to be considered carefully so as to determine where institutional actors may be concerned with one or the other, or both but in different ways.

Depicted as a system, one might assume a functionalist equilibrium in which inputs flow seamlessly via throughputs into outputs and then back into inputs, and that dysfunctional pressures are defused as the system continually adjusts (as in "homeostatic" equilibrium). But this fails to deal with the fragmented nature of EU "democracy," in which output and throughput appear mainly at the EU level and input at the national. Nor does it take into account the impact of European integration on the national level, as EU-driven policies and processes increasingly substitute for national ones while nationally based politics becomes more and more politicized in response. What is more, a systemic view that assumes any kind of homeostatic (or self-adjusting) equilibrium also overlooks how growing national politicization could unsettle the EU-level system in a self-undermining way, especially once the successive crises hit, beginning with the Euro crisis.

But this is not to suggest that the EU or its member states are therefore necessarily doomed to illegitimacy. Much the contrary: the EU has been remarkable in its ability to build legitimacy into its governance system. But this has not been easy, and the current crises represent challenges to much of what the EU has already attained in terms of legitimacy. To demonstrate this, we need to shift from what is already a systems theory "lite," without assumptions about systemic equilibria or pre-determined goals, to more historical and interpretive modes of analysis.

EU Output Legitimacy

European integration has since its beginnings sought to have an enhancing effect on Europe and its member-state democracies through the output legitimacy that

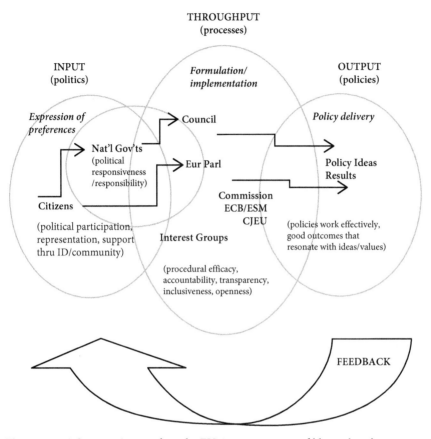

Figure 3.1. A Systems Approach to the EU: input, output, *and* 'throughput'
Source: Adaptation and revision of Schmidt 2013

was to flow from its "big goals" to serve the European public interest. In addition to meeting its initial commitments to peace and prosperity, the EU has generated policies to address problems that national governments could not resolve effectively on their own in an increasingly globalized world. Integration has enabled the comparatively small countries of Europe to stand together as a supranational region, thereby giving them international scale and scope. It has equally helped them to stand up to the challenges of economic globalization in an increasingly interdependent and competitive world economic system, by regionalizing their economies through a single market and a common currency while giving them extra heft as a regional power and economic authority in the international arena.[3] Non-material and symbolic aspirations have been equally important, such as building a common sense of European identity to underpin deepening EU integration (via such symbols as the European flag, the anthem, and the common

---

[3] Schmidt 2002.

currency), or projecting Europe's "normative power" in its neighborhood as well as in the world.[4] More recently, as part of the Europe 2020 goals and the European Pillar of Social Rights, the EU has promised to promote growth and employment, combat climate change and shift to renewable energy, reduce poverty and inequality, and enhance social rights and public services.[5] In short, the EU's policy performance can be seen as a success over the long haul, even if its more recent track record in confronting its many crises or meeting the Europe 2020 goals has been disappointing.

For some scholars, many elements of the EU's output legitimacy have been enough to offset its problems of input legitimacy. Some analysts have cited the virtues of the EU's non-majoritarian institutions and independent regulators in producing effective policies,[6] others the benefits of the checks and balances in the EU's multiple veto system to ensure appropriate outcomes,[7] and yet others the community-enhancing performance of EU policies—including most notably the Single Market, the single currency, and the wide range of guaranteed citizen rights.[8] But however good such policy output may have appeared to be, this line of reasoning makes three questionable assumptions.

First, to assume that policy outcomes are necessarily legitimate simply because they are produced by independent regulators fails to acknowledge the difference between non-majoritarian institutions at the national level and those at the EU level. National-level non-majoritarian institutions operate in the "shadow of politics," as the institutional delegates of political actors who have the capacity not only to create them and appoint their officials but also to alter them and their decisions if they so choose. EU-level non-majoritarian institutions have no such political control, given the absence of an EU "government" that could force the issue, while the decision rules make it difficult for political actors to alter non-majoritarian decisions.[9] Second, to assert that EU policies cannot be bad solely because the system features multiple vetoes overlooks the dangers of gridlock in the EU's "joint-decision trap"[10] while presupposing that checks and balances are inherently democratically legitimate. The latter may be true for compound federal systems such as Germany or the United States, but not for simpler unitary states like France and the United Kingdom, where such checks could be seen as thwarting majoritarian expressions of the popular will.[11] Third, to insist that all such policies intrinsically serve the general interest ignores the fact that EU policies have become increasingly contested, as they clash with different member

---

[4] Manners 2002.

[5] http://ec.europa.eu/europe2020/europe-2020-in-a-nutshell/index_en.htm; https://ec.europa.eu/commission/priorities/deeper-and-fairer-economic-and-monetary-union/european-pillar-social-rights/european-pillar-social-rights-20-principles_en

[6] Majone 1998.   [7] Moravcsik 2002.

[8] Caporaso and Tarrow 2008; Menon and Weatherill 2008.

[9] Scharpf 2010, 2012b; Schmidt 2013.   [10] Scharpf 1988; Falkner 2011.

[11] Schmidt 2006, ch. 2.

states' national norms and values. Think about the Commission's initial services directive, which sparked massive protests in France (focused on the "Polish plumber");[12] the CJEU's decisions in the Laval and Viking cases, which curtailed national unions' right to strike in the name of the free movement of labor;[13] not to mention the Eurozone crisis policies.

Moreover, when considering the Eurozone crisis in particular, output legitimacy remains in question because of the lack of effectiveness of the policies focused on austerity and structural reform, which generated comparatively weak macroeconomic performance and poor socioeconomic outcomes. With regard to (lack of) policy effectiveness in particular, we can point to the (mis)framing of the crisis as one of public rather than private debt, the (mis)diagnosis of the problems as resulting from member-state behavior rather than the structure of the euro, the (wrong) choice of remedies via austerity policies and structural reform, and the (inadequate) solutions that failed to innovate, whether through Eurobonds, a European Monetary Fund, quantitative easing (which came only after five years of crisis), or others.[14] And for policy outcomes, the problems for output legitimacy stem from the poor economic performance in the Eurozone since the beginning of the sovereign debt crisis, with unemployment, poverty, and inequality on the rise.[15] Here, it is important to emphasize that the very assumptions underlying the policies—about what ensures fiscal stability and economic growth—failed to take into account differences in national varieties of capitalism and growth models.[16] The "one size fits all" model of structural reforms actually fit none of the countries in trouble. And the creditor versus debtor logic of the 'solutions' harmed the latter to the benefit of the former.

EU Throughput Legitimacy

Much as with output legitimacy, throughput legitimacy has also improved over the course of time. EU governance began with an intergovernmental process in which member-state leaders in the Council took decisions behind closed doors through hard bargaining, served by a Commission "secretariat," joined by a consultative parliamentary assembly, and accompanied by a European court.[17] Slowly but surely, all such institutional bodies increased their procedural legitimacy along with their policymaking powers. For example, Council decision-making gained in efficacy, as policy area after policy area became subject to qualified majority voting, and in mutual accountability, as deliberative consensus-seeking

---

[12] Crespy 2012.   [13] Höpner and Schäfer 2007.
[14] See discussion in Chapter 9 on output legitimacy.
[15] See, eg, Blyth 2013; Sandbu 2015; Mody 2018; Tooze 2018.
[16] Scharpf 2012a; Johnston and Regan 2016; Hall 2018.   [17] Hoffmann 1966.

increasingly came to be the *modus operandi*.[18] Moreover, as the original parliamentary assembly turned into the European Parliament, its growing legislative powers of oversight as well as of co-decision—where the EP engages with the Council and the Commission in extensive legislative deliberation and contestation—made for better general accountability as well as transparency in policymaking. In addition, as the Commission expanded its supranational powers of policy formulation and implementation, it continued to be accountable to the Council and increasingly the EP. At the same time, the Commission sought to improve its own efficacy by streamlining operations, its transparency by increasing public access to information, and its inclusiveness and openness by augmenting civil society access. The EU has thus made great strides with regard to its procedural legitimacy, even if there is much room for improvement in all areas, as already detailed in the previous chapter.

The biggest problems with regard to throughput legitimacy are the most recent ones, resulting from the major backsliding in the Eurozone crisis. As already noted in the introduction, throughput legitimacy became particularly salient because of the focus by European leaders on Eurozone "governing by the rules and ruling by the numbers" in the sovereign debt crisis. The initial actions involved in reinforcing rules-based, numbers-targeting governance raised legitimacy problems not only in throughput terms—regarding its efficacy, accountability, transparency, inclusiveness, and openness—but also in terms of their negative effects on output performance and input responsiveness.[19] The subsequent attempts to improve output policy performance and thereby to calm national input politics, by reinterpreting the rules "by stealth," only added to the problems of throughput legitimacy, even if they somewhat alleviated those related to output and input legitimacy.

As we shall see in greater detail in Part II, the Council has come in for criticism as a result of its return to intergovernmental decision-making, dominated by Germany and other "creditor" countries, while sidelining the EP and turning the Commission into a secretariat. That criticism focuses on the inefficacy of EU governance, largely because of the Council's incompetence in crisis management and its lack of accountability and transparency in decision-making along with its perceived bias against "debtor" countries.[20] The Commission has equally been under attack, whether for its inflexibility in the European Semester between 2010 and 2012—especially by Southern European countries—or subsequently for its failure to enforce the rules more rigorously—in particular by Northern European

---

[18] Puetter 2014.

[19] There is a substantial literature on the dysfunctionality of using any such targets. Although generally claimed to reinforce public trust, their usage leads for the most part to a lack of trust and greater public skepticism, in particular for unrealistic targets. See Boswell 2018.

[20] Eg, Fabbrini 2013; Matthijs and Blyth 2015.

countries.[21] In the interim, although the EP did gain increased powers as an accountability forum, questions remain as to its real influence in the Eurozone crisis.[22] Arguably most in question have been the institutions constituting the Troika (the IMF, ECB, Commission, and later the 'institutions' with the ESM), in which the EP plays no role, and which have been faulted for their lack of accountability and transparency as well as their impact on democracy in program countries. As Christian Joerges has persuasively argued, at the height of the crisis such institutions were about as far from representative democracy as one can go, and more like authoritarian imposition when it came to decisions about the deficit reductions and structural reforms required for countries in trouble in exchange for bail-out funds.[23]

When EU institutional actors slowly and incrementally over time began reinterpreting the rules "by stealth," they certainly improved output policy performance. But at the same time they split the input politics, in particular between North and South, while they raised major questions about the throughput processes. Transparency was undermined by key actors hiding the fact that they were reinterpreting the rules and with it accountability to the "principals," that is, the Council, even if efficacy may have benefited by the increasing discretion of EU actors in applying the rules flexibly. The lack of clear guidelines for administrative discretion and flexibility, moreover, raises questions of both accountability and transparency, while the absence of political actors "taking account" of technical actors' decisions raised questions for its input legitimacy. Finally, all of this jeopardized the values of trust and legality that underpin the throughput governance processes, without which EU actors have great difficulty moving forward.

EU Input Legitimacy

But whatever the positive trajectory of the EU's output performance and throughput qualities (leaving aside the current crises for the moment), it has continued to confront major problems with regard to political input. Part of the problem stems from the tension between responsibility and responsiveness. The pressures to be responsible affect not only the sitting governments that agreed to the supranational policies but also the opposition parties that may have campaigned against the very policies that they will then be expected to implement when they gain office, even against "the will of the people." The result is what Brigid Laffan has termed a "step-change" in member states' commitment to responsible government, to the detriment of responsive government, leading to a "politics of constrained choice."[24] In the Eurozone crisis in particular, politicians have generally faced a

---

[21] Schmidt 2015a, 2016a.   [22] Fromage 2018.
[23] Joerges 2014. See also Kreuder-Sonnen 2018a, 2018b.   [24] Laffan 2014.

Hobson's choice between alienating their citizens or incurring sanctions by EU institutions and the punishment of the markets.

European integration, simply by its very existence, has served to undermine national democratic practices associated with political legitimacy. As decision-making in policy area after policy area has moved up to the EU level, European integration has increasingly encroached on issues at the very heart of national sovereignty and identity. Money and monetary policy, economic organization and labor markets, defense and security, borders and immigration, public services, and even welfare guarantees have all increasingly come under EU policies or prescriptions and proscriptions. The problem for national democracies is not so much that EU policies have encroached on national ones, however, but that citizens have had little direct say over these matters, let alone engaged in EU-wide debates about the policies. And without a fully developed EU "government" similar to that of national democracies, EU citizens are unable to aggregate their concerns and demands in such a way as to express their will directly at the EU level.

Although member-state leaders in the Council have long claimed for themselves the greatest political (input) legitimacy, based on their indirect representation of their national citizens, the Council is not a representative forum. It is rather a bargaining or deliberative arena in which member-state leaders represent their countries' interests and their citizens' concerns while acting with a degree of independence generally impossible within their own national arenas. National parliaments often do not even know their governments' positions in Council meetings ahead of time (the exceptions are mainly in Northern Europe), let alone exercise requisite oversight.[25]

In contrast, the EP is indeed a representative arena, in particular as the EP's growing governance powers and responsibilities have also improved its capacity to represent EU citizens. But it is still only marginally representative, given the high rate of voter abstention, the low level of citizen awareness or engagement with the EU, and the second-order status of its elections, in which national political concerns tend to dominate political debate and national electorates use the elections to punish or reward incumbent governments.[26] A question often raised with regard to the EP up until the 2019 election was: How input legitimate is a parliament in which declining percentages of the electorate participate—only 42.54 percent in 2014—and for which, among those voting, close to a quarter went for extremist parties? Note that at that time the low turnout came despite the "*Spitzenkandidat*" initiative that was at its *apogee* in 2014, when EP parties ran separate candidates for Commission President in EU-wide campaigns and held televised debates centered on European issues.[27] Moreover, even though the

[25] Auel 2007; Crum 2017; Kreilinger 2019.
[26] Franklin, and van der Eijk 2007; Mair 2006; Hix 2008; Boomgaarden and de Vreese 2016.
[27] Hobolt 2014; Dinan 2015.

numbers went up in 2019 to slightly more than 50 percent, on the back of the increasing politicization of the EU, the increase in Euroskeptic MEPs further jeopardizes the EP's ability to govern efficiently (throughput) and effectively (output) in a politically (input) legitimate manner.

As for the non-majoritarian institutions such as the ECB and the Commission, they generally have significant autonomy without any significant democratic control from the classic "democratic circuit" of parliamentary oversight.[28] In the EU, there is very little of the horizontal dialogue between officials of non-majoritarian institutions and their input-legitimate counterparts in majoritarian institutions. Instead the dialogue is more vertical and hierarchical between supranational authorities and national agents, thereby ensuring that EU-level officials are much more insulated from the demands and/or oversight of majoritarian institutions than their formally independent national-level counterparts.[29] With regard to the ECB, beyond appointing its head, the Council has no formal control over the body; nor do its member-state leaders over their national central banks, whose heads are on the ECB governing board. And although the ECB is formally accountable to the EP, this only means that it has to explain its actions, respond to questions in its four yearly mandated meetings, and listen to comments; it need not heed MEPs' advice. Although the Commission is certainly more open to dialogue with both the Council and the EP, given its accountability to both institutions, it also has many domains in which it is formally independent, such as in competition and trade policy as well as in its many oversight functions.

This is not to suggest that the answer for the EU is therefore to establish a "government" in the traditional (nation-state) sense. Any such government would neither be feasible nor particularly democratic. The reasons why have been discussed and debated at length since the 1990s. For those who have seen little hope for EU democracy, the problems include the lack of a European "*demos*"—a sense of common citizenship, or an EU-wide identity.[30] As Michael Zürn insisted at the height of the debates in 2000, democratic self-governance is "only possible within the framework of a *demos*," which means that there is no possibility for a political community beyond the modern nation-state.[31] Many scholars add to this the absence of any European public sphere characterized by a common European language, a European media, or a European public opinion that would allow for (input-legitimizing) communication and deliberation about political preferences,[32] let alone EU-level intermediary political structures through which to mobilize, aggregate, and represent public preferences and opinions.[33] But is democracy really limited to longstanding definitions focused on the nation-state?

[28] Héritier and Lehmkuhl 2011, pp. 138–9.
[29] See discussion in Scharpf 2012b, pp. 19–20.
[30] Most notably, Weiler 1995; Grimm 1997; Zürn 2000.
[31] Zürn 2000, p. 191.   [32] Habermas 1996; Grimm 1995; Weiler 1999.
[33] DeVreese 2007; Mair and Thomassen 2011; Mair 2013.

EU Legitimacy and Its Relationship to Identity

In recent years, scholars have taken a more positive view of the potential for EU-level democracy and legitimacy. Thomas Risse contends that although there may not be one public sphere, overlapping public spheres have developed across the EU in which national publics have become increasingly sensitized to the concerns of other member states.[34] Kalypso Nicolaïdis argues that although the EU may not have one *demos*, or people, it has many "*demoi*," or "peoples," capable of constituting a EU "*demoicracy*."[35] And Kathleen McNamara suggests that a thin common European identity has grown out of the very banality of the EU's socially constructed authority. Even if they may not feel European, people are living and breathing "European-ness," with their understandings of the EU deeply grounded in the reality of everyday life (eg, using euros to buy food and necessities, visa-free travel, carrying a EU driver's license).[36]

The question remains as to whether the building of a European identity, whether based on the unconscious acceptance of everyday practices, a sense of "peoples-hood," or the discursive interactions of overlapping public spheres, is sufficient to ensure the legitimacy of the EU, either in terms of its (input/output/throughput) governing activities or its (Weberian) governing authority.[37] Identity depends on the development of people's shared sense of constituting a political community whereas legitimacy relates to people's sense that the political institutions of such a community along with the decisions emanating from those institutions conform to accepted standards while providing for the common good. At the national level, processes that build citizen identity are almost impossible to separate out from the processes that build legitimate authority and legitimating activity.[38] But in the EU's split-level system, although these two processes of building identity and legitimacy are generally linked, they may not always reinforce one another.

It may be possible to build a European identity without enhancing the EU's legitimacy. The euro is a case in point. Since the crisis, large numbers of citizens in Eurozone countries have questioned the legitimacy of Eurozone governing activities even as they have continued to accept its governing authority, by engaging in the everyday practices of using the euro and leaving unquestioned their countries' membership in EMU. But a growing minority of such citizens have equally questioned the EU's governing authority, and have voted for anti-euro extremist parties promising to leave the euro, or even the European Union.

---

[34] Risse 2010, 2015; DeVreese 2007; see also Trenz and Eder 2004.
[35] Nicolaïdis, 2003, 2013; Nicolaïdis and Watson 2016; see also Cheneval and Schimmelfennig, 2013.
[36] McNamara 2015a.   [37] See Schmidt 2017c for a fuller discussion of the question.
[38] Schmidt 2006; Lucarelli et al. 2010.

This complex interaction between identity and legitimacy means that even though identity may continue in the midst of the Eurozone and other crises, legitimacy has been at risk. The risks to legitimacy have been particularly apparent in the growing loss of trust in the EU,[39] in the increasing polarization of views on the EU, in the continuing nationalization of debates, or even in the "parallelization of national public spheres" during the Eurozone crisis, in which the main voices heard across public spheres have been those of the more powerful member-state leaders, German in particular.[40] In other words, while citizens' increasing engagement in EU cultural practices and their growing sense of identity means that they may passively accept EU governing authority and implicitly give it legitimacy in their daily lives, they may still actively question the EU not only on grounds of output legitimacy—if they feel that the policies do not work—and throughput legitimacy—because they find that governance lacks accountability and transparency—but also on grounds of input legitimacy—because they think that the political practices do not enable them to have significant impact on decisions. Thus, even though we may agree that a European identity is under construction, EU legitimacy continues to be in question.

The Politicization of EU Governance

The growing presence of the EU in citizens' lives, as they develop a thin identity and sense of being part of a European *demoi*, coupled with increasing dissatisfaction with EU policies and processes, in particular since the EU's recent crises, has meant that EU governance has also become a political focus of concern. Having started life as largely apolitical and technocratic, with output and throughput the main criteria for legitimacy, the EU has become more and more politicized at the bottom, in the increasingly volatile national politics that has weakened mainstream parties and empowered populists; from the bottom up, as national politics has increasingly influenced EU actors in the most contested areas; and at the top, where EU actors have been developing an increasingly political dynamics of interaction. All of this is all the more interesting in light of the fact that the EU had for a very long time largely managed to depoliticize its governance processes.

Depoliticization in EU Governance

In the early years, the main legitimacy assumed possible for the EU was "output" legitimacy, based on good economic performance—whether by serving national

---

[39] Hobolt 2015.   [40] Kriesi and Grande 2015.

interests,[41] satisfying domestic constituencies,[42] or providing beneficial policies for all.[43] The guiding principles for such legitimacy were first economically liberal and then neoliberal, as the EU moved from a liberal program focused on freeing up markets via policies such as the reduction of tariff and then non-tariff barriers in the postwar era to a neoliberal program beginning in the 1980s that pushed for even greater market opening via financial liberalization and business deregulation while reducing the power of labor and cutting the welfare state.[44]

Neoliberalism also influenced the increasing emphasis on throughput legitimacy as an accompaniment to output legitimacy, under the assumption that the quality of the governance processes would improve were they to be moved from the administrative state—directly under the authority of governments—to the regulatory state, with governing authority conferred on independent "non-majoritarian" (ie, not elected by citizen majorities) bodies.[45] The shift itself was predicated on the belief that while mandates would still be set by political officials, technical officials would best be able to produce effective policies because they would provide non-partisan administrative stewardship that would inspire trust while ensuring against corruption and clientelist practices.[46] Neoliberalism thus favored technocratic "governance" carried out by independent regulatory bodies in place of political government administered by state bureaucracies.[47] And it held a jaundiced view of politics as subject to rent-seeking politicians and bureaucrats who lacked the requisite integrity and/or competence to produce policies that really worked. As such, output legitimacy for neoliberals was seen as a substitute for input legitimacy, which would not be necessary so long as effective policies produced good performance.

Neoliberalism has also been part and parcel of the growing supranationalization of decision-making in an era of globalization, where governments have exchanged national autonomy for shared supranational authority in order to regain control over the forces they themselves unleashed through national policies of liberalization and deregulation.[48] This supranationalization has been particularly acute for the EU. The main difference between most advanced industrialized countries and EU member states is that other countries retain a certain modicum of autonomy and control over the forces of globalization. Their politically elected governments are able to choose to accept, to contest, or even not to implement policies of which they (or their citizens) disapprove. EU member states, having pooled their sovereignty by giving up autonomy and control for the EU's shared authority, cannot do this as readily, given the role of EU technocratic

[41] Keohane and Hoffmann 1991.   [42] Moravcsik 1998.
[43] Haas 1958; Sandholtz and Stone Sweet 1998; Stone Sweet et al. 2001.
[44] See, eg, Schmidt and Thatcher 2013.
[45] Eg, Majone 1996, 2001; Genschel and Jachtenfuchs 2014.
[46] Thatcher 2013; Schmidt and Thatcher 2013.   [47] Majone 1998.
[48] Schmidt 2002; de Wilde and Zürn 2012; Schmidt and Thatcher 2013; Zürn 2019.

institutions in enforcing the rules through EU Commission oversight, CJEU opinions, and the national courts that generally uphold CJEU opinions.[49]

The result has been the depoliticization of increasing numbers of policy domains, as responsibility has been taken out of the hands of political officials embedded in party government and put into those of technical experts ensconced in technocratic governance.[50] Such depoliticization was seen as the way of ensuring better government *for* the people without significant effects on government *by* and *of* the people. The danger here comes when or if technocratic governance is seen to predominate, such that "the people" no longer feel that they are the co-authors of decision-making but rather believe that non-elected officials make the (unpopular) decisions. In such circumstances, citizens may feel that they are subject to government *over* the people—which is fundamentally delegitimizing.[51] And indeed, since the Eurozone crisis, followed by the EU's many other crises, technocratic governance has increasingly been accused of bringing about the impoverishment of democracy,[52] with reactions against it epitomized by populist outcries against the "experts."

In short, the EU initially favored technocratic throughput over popular input to produce optimal output. The depoliticization resulting from this emphasis on output and throughput legitimacy to the detriment of input legitimacy is at the basis of what I metaphorically described in my book *Democracy in Europe*, published in 2006, as the EU level's "policy *without* politics" and the national level's concomitant "politics *without* policy."[53] As more and more policies have moved up to the EU level for apolitical decision-making, the national political realm has been deprived of those substantive issues for political debate and decision. The first major revolt against this loss of input politics could be seen as the defeat of the referendum on the Constitutional Treaty in 2005, even as output legitimacy remained largely intact given a booming economy. But with the financial crisis followed by the Eurozone crisis, the precipitous loss of output legitimacy had further feedback effects on input legitimacy.

Politicization "At the Bottom": Growing Politics *against* Policy

In the early years of the EU, the lack of input legitimacy was not seen as a very big problem. So long as citizens perceived EU policies as working (making for output legitimacy), or did not pay much attention to them (whether they worked or not), the absence of input legitimacy was not considered to be detrimental to the EU.

---

[49] Schmidt 2018a.

[50] Ferguson 1990; Habermas 1996; Majone 2001; Flinders 2008; Fawcett and Marsh 2014; Wood 2015.

[51] Thanks to Ben Crum for this insight.   [52] Caramani 2017.   [53] Schmidt 2006.

This is what made for the "permissive consensus" of the early years of the EU, which neo-functionalist scholars argued had allowed EU actors to deepen integration without much public scrutiny or concern.[54] Positive outcomes seemed to ensure that there was a trade-off, with output legitimacy making up for the lack of input legitimacy.

But even before the EU's multiple crises, it was clear that the EU's policies and processes were becoming increasingly politically contested, and the EU a more and more salient issue for national politics.[55] The "sleeping giant" of EU-related party divisions and Euroskepticism was finally awakening.[56] Analysts worried about the growing importance of crosscutting cleavages at the national level between traditional political divisions based on adherence to right/left political parties and newer identity-related divisions separating citizens whose vision of Europe was more open, universalist, liberal, and cosmopolitan from those with more closed, communitarian, xenophobic, and nationalist (or even EU-regionalist) orientations.[57] Such cleavages have meant that the socioeconomic divides between the winners and losers of European integration related to the redistributive consequences of the Single Market and the Eurozone crisis have now been joined by growing cultural divides. These manifest themselves in acceptance or opposition to migration, whether with respect to the principle of "free movement of people" for EU citizens or to political asylum for third country nationals (TNCs).[58] In many countries this combination has upended traditional party politics, with anti-system challenger parties often mixing xenophobic anti-migration messages typical of the extreme right with support for the welfare state long characteristic of the left.[59]

The causes of such politicization are many, with sources in socioeconomic and sociocultural concerns as much as purely political ones. The socioeconomic sources of politicization include anger at policies seen to have created growing unemployment and poverty along with rising inequalities, with many people "left behind" by globalization and Europeanization.[60] The sociocultural sources encompass worries about the loss of social status[61] and/or about the changing "faces" of the nation as a result of migration.[62] The political concerns are reflected

---

[54] Lindberg and Scheingold 1970.
[55] De Wilde and Zürn 2012; Hurrelmann et al. 2015; Zürn 2016; Kriesi 2016; Hutter et al. 2016.
[56] Franklin and Van der Eijk 2007.
[57] Scholars have variously defined these structuring cleavages as "GAL-TAN" (Hooghe et al. 2002), "integration-demarcation" (Kriesi et al. 2008), "universalism-communitarianism" (Bornschier 2010), "cosmopolitanism-communitarianism" (Zürn and de Wilde 2016), "cosmopolitanism-parochialism" (de Vries 2017), or more simply "transnational cleavage" (Hooghe and Marks 2018). But whatever the specific label, they describe largely the same phenomenon.
[58] Hooghe and Marks 2018.   [59] Hopkin 2019.
[60] See, eg, Prosser 2017; Rodrik 2018; Hopkin 2019.
[61] See, eg, Inglehart and Norris 2017; Gidron and Hall 2017.
[62] See, eg, Hochschild and Mollenkopf 2009.

in people's sense of a loss of control in the face of deepening European integration where responsibility increasingly trumps responsiveness.

In all of this, the EU has gained increasing salience in public debates, in particular as a scapegoat. It has been blamed as a conduit for globalization via the Single Market's liberalizing initiatives or as a contributor to migration via Schengen's open borders and the Single Market's free movement of peoples. The EU's recent crises have only added fuel to the fire, generating divisions in national electorates as to the EU's "solutions"—North–South divides in the Eurozone crisis;[63] East–West in the migration crisis as well as the "rule of law" crisis.[64] It is little wonder that in order to express their dissatisfaction, electorates have more and more frequently voted to turn out incumbent governments, to vote down EU-related referenda whenever they have had the chance,[65] and to vote for the populist extremes.

Populist parties have given voice to citizens' economic, social, and political discontent through the "mobilization of resentment."[66] Changes in the "supply side" of populism have brought in new leaders with new messages conveyed through the new social media as well as the old. Such populist parties, whether on the extremes of the left or the right, are generally characterized by a "thin ideology" that distinguishes them from the traditional hard right or left parties with clearly defined ideologies.[67] Their leaders tend to claim that they are the sole representatives of "the people" against corrupt elites and unfair institutions. They contest institutionalized expertise and mainstream parties' policies while promising radical changes mostly at the expense of details about how such change will take place—at least while out of power.[68] And in power, they represent threats to liberal democracy.[69] In short, whether on the right or the left, all such parties tend to excoriate political elites for the policies that they claim do not work (making for output illegitimacy), the processes that they insist are corrupt and unaccountable (ensuring throughput illegitimacy), and the politics that they maintain are unrepresentative (entailing input illegitimacy).

But despite the fact that parties on the political extremes of the left and the right may use similar kinds of anti-EU, anti-elite rhetoric, they diverge on both substantive policies and principles with regard to European integration. While the Euroskepticism of radical left-wing parties is more economically driven, founded on their defense of welfare state arrangements and their opposition to ongoing market liberalization, the Euroskepticism of radical right-wing parties is more sociocultural, coming from their perception of European integration as a threat to national sovereignty and cultural homogeneity. Moreover, whereas

---

[63] Schmidt 2014; Matthijs and Blyth 2015.
[64] Börzel and Risse 2018; Hutter and Kriesi 2019.   [65] Schimmelfennig 2019.
[66] Bonikowski 2017.   [67] Mudde and Kaltwasser 2012.
[68] See, eg, Taggart 2000; Mudde 2017a; Müller 2016; Judis 2016.   [69] Pappas 2019.

radical right parties reject in principle anything in the EU that goes beyond basic economic cooperation, radical left-wing Euroskeptic parties critique the EU's current practices, but often not European integration as such.[70] In policy terms, this means that while the extreme right long opposed such things as EU-related migration and the euro (until very recently), the extreme left contested the marketization of welfare services.[71] National contexts also make a difference, with the differential impact of globalization and Europeanization important factors in explaining the victory of left-wing versus right-wing extremes. Shocks related to trade, finance, and foreign investment generally provide an opening to left-wing populists, whereas those related to immigration and refugees offer right-wing populists the advantage.[72]

While these various kinds of politicization at the bottom have been building over time, the multiple crises can themselves be seen as having acted as triggers for a sea change in anti-system attitudes, as expressed in party elections. Eurobarometer polls (EB 2007–18) show that trust in national governments and EU governance dropped precipitously after 2007, along with the positive image of the EU, as the financial crisis was followed by the Eurozone crisis and later the migration crisis.[73] This loss of trust helps explain why populist parties' anti-system messages about self-serving, corrupt elites may have resonated, as they have mustered growing public support for views that contest EU authority and activities in increasingly polarized public debates.[74]

Note, however, that such feelings (and the realities) of disenfranchisement are not only due to the EU.[75] While in Europe, Brexit was probably the acme of the EU's populist revolt—at least until the Italian election of March 2018, when Euroskeptics won a governing majority—Trump's election in the United States was fueled by very much the same sentiments. Moreover, although the populist revolt seemed to come on very suddenly, it had been in gestation for a while. People's disenchantment with politics has been growing at least since the beginning of the 2000s, when Colin Crouch called the problem "post-democracy," Chantal Mouffe named it "the political," and Colin Hay asked "why do people hate politics?"[76] Party politics itself is partially to blame for the problem, going all the way back to the 1960s. "Catch-all parties," with their un-ideological or even anti-ideological "politics of compromise, adjustment, negotiation, bargaining" carried out by pragmatic political professionals, alienated voters,[77] while "cartel parties" used the resources of the state to maintain themselves in power against the rise of alternatives.[78] But citizens' rejection of technocracy, which has

---

[70] De Vries and Edwards 2009; Hooghe et al. 2002; March and Rommerskirchen 2012; see discussion in van Elsas et al. 2016.
[71] Crespy 2016.   [72] Rodrik 2018.   [73] Debomey 2016; Hobolt 2015.
[74] Kriesi 2014, 2016; Hobolt 2015; Mudde 2017b.   [75] See, eg, Zürn et al., 2012.
[76] See, eg, Crouch 2004; Mouffe 2005; Hay 2007.   [77] Dahl 1965, pp. 21–2.
[78] Katz and Mair 1995; see discussions in Zürn 2019 and Hopkin 2019, Ch. 2.

increasingly encroached on all aspects of "the political" by taking more and more issues outside the realm of political debate and decision-making, constitutes a crucial added element.[79]

Taken as a whole, such politicization at the bottom suggests a revision of my earlier characterization of the EU. At the national level, the EU has now moved from national "politics *without* policy" to national "politics *against* (EU) policy" in the most contested areas—or even "politics *against* polity" in the most extreme cases, where citizens vote for parties opposed to staying in the EU, or even vote to exit the EU, as in the case of the United Kingdom.

Politicization from the Bottom Up: EU Actors' Increasing Policy *with* Politics

Politicization at the bottom has had a major bottom-up impact on EU governance. It is at the basis of what post-functionalist scholars have called the new "constraining dissensus," which ever since the Maastricht Treaty has ensured that decision-making on European integration increasingly "entered the contentious world of party competition, elections, and referendums."[80] And with this growing awareness of the EU on the part of citizens has come greater attention by EU-level actors to national citizens' responses to their actions. All now seek to communicate and legitimate their actions to the wider public on an ongoing basis, keenly aware of the political importance of public perceptions.

In the Council, politicization can be seen in the growing influence of public opinion and electoral politics on member-state leaders' positions,[81] with relations among member states increasingly contentious, and agreements over difficult issues harder to broker. Even if partisan politics per se remains largely absent in the interrelationships among member-state leaders, the politics of nationally partisan governments has infected Council decisions. Individual governments have increasingly sought to impose their preferences through threatened (or actual) vetoes of impending legislation—as was often the case with the UK pre-Brexit—and through refusal to agree to and/or implement legislation. This has been the case with governments in Central and Eastern Europe on aspects of refugee and migration policy as well as rule of law. At the same time, coalitions of member states have forced through agreements reflecting mainly their own preferences, whether as the result of coercive threats[82] or deliberative persuasion.[83] A case in

---

[79] Caramani 2017.
[80] Hooghe and Marks 2009, p. 7; see also Hooghe and Marx 2018; Franklin et al. 1994; Dunphy 2004.
[81] Eg, Schimmelfennig 2015a.   [82] See, eg, Schimmelfennig 2015a.
[83] Puetter 2012.

point is the Eurozone, with its restrictive budgetary policies and structural reforms that were pushed by a Northern European alliance led by Germany.[84]

In the EP, bottom-up politicization has arrived first and foremost in the form of the larger presence of populist representatives elected in the 2009 elections, with more in the 2014 elections,[85] and even more in the 2019 elections. Even though their actual presence has had minimal impact on EP policies (so far), it has given populists a EU platform from which to speak to their national constituencies. Moreover, it has left the EP with a thinning center. In 2009 and 2014, this forced the remaining majority of center-right and center-left parties to continue with their longstanding "grand coalition" approach to decision-making. In 2019, the grand coalition is likely to require even more parties, including the liberals (now Renew Europe) and the Greens, as a result of the losses of the center-left S&D (Socialists and Democrats) and the center-right EPP (European People's Party). As part of grand coalition politics, the EP has long focused on the politics of the public interest. But the EP's growing sensitivity to the political concerns of citizens has meant that it has increasingly made public pronouncements on the political issues of the day, often accompanied by scathing critiques of the Council, the ECB, and the Commission through EP hearings and in commissioned reports.[86] Day-to-day partisan politics is also very present in the EP. This was most apparent in the center-right EPP shielding against censure one of its more extremist national party constituent members, the Hungarian extreme right party Fidesz, headed by the increasingly anti-democratic Prime Minister Victor Orbán. Only just before the 2019 EP elections was the party suspended.

Although non-majoritarian supranational actors such as the Commission, the ECB, the ESM (European Stability Mechanism), and other regulatory agencies have not experienced the same degree of politicization as the majoritarian institutions of the EU, bottom-up politics has nonetheless exerted its influence. That influence can be seen mainly in the ways in which the Commission, the ECB, and the growing array of regulatory bodies have all become keenly aware of the political importance of public perceptions. Supranational actors have increasingly sought to appear (input) responsive to the public on politically salient issues so as to improve citizens' views of their (output) performance.[87] In certain cases, they have also become more sensitized to their own country's attitudes toward the EU, in particular with regard to Euroskepticism. In the Commission, for example, while national background remains a key factor in explaining the attitudes and beliefs of EU officials,[88] more "fluid" national factors help account for change in Commission officials' conceptions of their institutional role, mainly from promoting more supranational policymaking toward favoring more subsidiarity.[89]

---

[84] Blyth 2013; Crum 2013; Schimmelfennig 2015a.   [85] Treib 2014.
[86] Héritier et al. 2016.   [87] Hartlapp et al. 2014, pp. 229–30; Rauh 2016.
[88] Hooghe 2005, 2012.   [89] Bes 2016.

Concerns about national-level politicization have also led EU officials to become increasingly intent on communicating with the public directly—to inform the citizens of EU actions as well as to legitimate those actions.[90] An early example of this was the Commission's "Plan D for Democracy, Dialogue, and Debate," launched in 2005 following the failure of the Constitutional Treaty, which sought to introduce democratic consultation into EU decision-making to improve input legitimacy.[91] But the ECB has perhaps been the most effective of supranational communicators. It honed its message carefully to make certain to persuade citizens and the markets alike that it was always acting within its mandate, even as its interpretation of that mandate shifted radically over time from a very narrow interpretation—never a lender of last resort, with limited possibility for monetary expansion[92]—to an increasingly expansive one—including open monetary transactions in 2012 and quantitative easing beginning in 2015.[93]

Politicization "At the Top": Policy *with* Politics in EU Actors' Dynamics of Interaction

Politicization is not only at the bottom or from the bottom up, however. It is equally at the top. As integration has deepened, the interrelationships among major EU-level actors—Council, Commission, ECB, and European Parliament—have become more political in every way, with longstanding relations of cooperation now riven in many domains by greater contestation.[94] Such contestation may certainly be connected to the national pressures. But it also concerns political struggles for power and influence among the various EU-level actors. Although such struggles have always been present to some extent, they have sharpened in the recent crises, with hard bargaining more pronounced[95] and productive consensus more difficult to achieve.[96] Such struggles are ideational—regarding which political-economic ideas about what to do prevail—as much as institutional—involving which actor gets to do what—and coercive—concerning who imposes the costs of the decision on whom.[97]

EU-level politicization, it should be said, is not a new phenomenon, since politics has always been present in the EU. Cases in point include power struggles between the Council and the Commission—one of the earliest most famously being the "empty chair" crisis of 1966—and the clash of ideas about how to govern the EU economy,[98] which EU actors have long sought to defuse through

---

[90] Biegón 2013.   [91] See http://europa.eu/rapid/press-release_IP-05-1272_en.htm
[92] Blyth 2013.   [93] Schmidt 2016.
[94] See discussion in Schmidt 2018a, 2019a.   [95] Schimmelfennig 2015a.
[96] Hodson and Puetter 2018.   [97] Carstensen and Schmidt 2016, 2018a.
[98] Brunnemeier et al. 2016.

strategies of depoliticization.[99] But today these struggles have become more pronounced, and more clearly political. The politics is particularly manifest in the greater pressure from majoritarian bodies, both the Council and the EP, on non-majoritarian institutions such as the Commission and the ECB to do their bidding. But it is also evident in the ways in which non-majoritarian actors respond—in some cases by attempting to deflect majoritarian attacks, in others by seeking to bring majoritarian actors onto their side.

Such political battles are not only about power, however; they are also about legitimacy. Battles are fought not just over who is in charge of decision-making but also over who acts with the power of legitimate authority, which policies are legitimate, and on what grounds.[100] What used to be presented as purely technical and therefore impartial decision-making is now increasingly contested politically, as political.[101] Such battles are manifest in the increasingly intense internal debates on policy construction, not only about what to do but also about who should decide. Those debates now also spill out from the corridors of power into the political sphere, as policymakers communicate their views publicly, addressing not only fellow policymakers but also European citizens more generally as they seek to explain and legitimate their actions.[102] EU actors now join in public discourse, deliberation, and contestation about what should be (or is) done, who should do it, and why—much more so than in the past, when the main voices heard were those of the member-state leaders. This politics "at the top," together with the "bottom-up" politics, therefore suggests that the EU's seeming "policy *without* politics" at the supranational level has now been replaced by "policy *with* politics" in the EU's more contentious areas.

Most scholars focused on EU governance today do acknowledge this politicization. But their individualized focus on the Council, the Commission, or the EP, as they depict the increasingly intense battles for power and influence among these EU institutional actors, means they tend to overlook the EU's political dynamics of interaction as whole.[103] It is therefore useful to lay out the different points of view on EU governance, to see how the theories demonstrate the increasingly politicized stances taken by each of these actors with regard to their fellows.

First, however, brief definitions of the different theoretical approaches are in order. While the "intergovernmentalists" assume that the EU's intergovernmental leaders in the Council are in charge, the "supranationalists" insist instead that the EU's supranational actors exercise control, while what we shall call the "parliamentarists" consider the EP to be increasingly influential.[104] Complicating such

---

[99] Fawcett and Marsh 2014; Caramani 2017.   [100] Crum and Curtin 2015; Schmidt 2018a.
[101] Caramani 2017.   [102] Schmidt 2014, 2018; Carstensen and Schmidt 2018a.
[103] For more in-depth discussion see Schmidt 2018a, 2019a.
[104] See discussion in Schmidt 2018a.

divisions over which EU actor exercises significant power and influence have been crosscutting differences among such scholars over how EU actors exercise power, whether through coercive, institutional, or ideational and deliberative means. Briefly stated, while the traditional intergovernmentalists see member-state governments in the Council as exercising coercive power through rationalist processes of hard bargaining focused on their geopolitical or socioeconomic interests,[105] the self-styled "new" intergovernmentalists view those same actors as engaged in constructivist processes of deliberative persuasion in pursuit of consensual agreements.[106] Moreover, whereas the traditional supranationalists see the Commission and other regulatory bodies as exercising institutional power via dynamics of functional spillover and bureaucratic entrepreneurialism,[107] the self-styled "new" supranationalists instead conceive of supranational actors' power in terms of ideational innovation and consensus-seeking deliberation.[108] The only thing the new and older intergovernmentalists and supranationalists have in common is that they largely ignore the role of the EP, and see the co-decision process as the great loser in recent years. For the parliamentarists, old and new, this is a mistake, since although the EP continues to have little coercive power in comparison to intergovernmental or supranational actors, it has wielded increasing institutional power—if only informally, by tactically using its legislative competences—as well as ideational power, in particular by becoming the "go-to" body for legitimacy.[109]

Traditional intergovernmentalist scholars whose approaches theorize hard bargaining in the Council tend to reinforce post-functionalists' negative (bottom-up) views of the consequences of national-level politicization. Recent illustrations center on how such politicization led to the hard-bargaining games of chicken in the Greek crisis, pitting German Finance Minister Wolfgang Schäuble against Greek Finance Minister Yanis Varoufakis.[110] Scholars who add an institutionally oriented, neo-functionalist component to this approach make a similar point by describing the dynamics of "failing forward" through which intergovernmental bargaining in the Eurozone crisis has led time and again to incomplete agreements and failed reforms that soon require new intergovernmental bargains.[111]

Self-described "new intergovernmentalist" scholars who see consensus-seeking deliberation rather than hard bargaining as the Council's mode of governance argue instead that politicization has not so much constrained integration as pushed EU member-state leaders to govern differently. Since the Maastricht

---

[105] Hoffmann 1966; Moravcsik 1993.   [106] Puetter 2014; Bickerton et al. 2015.
[107] Sandholtz and Stone Sweet 1998; Ioannou et al. 2015.
[108] Bauer and Becker 2014; Dehousse 2016; Epstein and Rhodes 2016.
[109] Hix and Hoyland 2013; Fasone 2014; Dinan 2015; Héritier et al. 2016; see discussion in Schmidt 2018a.
[110] Schimmelfennig 2015a; Tsebelis 2016; Varoufakis 2017.   [111] Jones et al. 2015.

Treaty, they contend, member-state leaders have not only decided more in the European Council but have also created de novo supranational bodies like the ECB and other regulatory agencies outside the main EU institutions in order to contain, if not reduce, Commission powers.[112] This has involved not only keeping the Commission out of those bodies but also putting the member states *qua* member states *in*, for instance by ensuring their representation on the governing boards, as in the cases of the ECB and the European Stability Mechanism.[113] The implication here is that in response to the bottom-up pressures of national-level politicization, member-state leaders sought to reassert their political authority to initiate and control any new integrating activities.

But at the same time that these new intergovernmentalists find the Council in a political struggle with the Commission to take back control, they also acknowledge that national-level (bottom-up) politicization has taken its toll. Thus, Dermot Hodson and Uwe Puetter argue that although EU member-state leaders have continued to deepen integration, they have done so at the risk of producing a "destructive dissensus." This is because consensus-seeking in the Council leads mainstream member state leaders to accommodate extreme right populist challenger governments to the detriment of EU norms and values, as in the cases of Hungary in the migration crisis and Hungary along with Poland on rule of law.[114] We could add that a similar dynamic has been operative with regard to quashing extreme left governments to the detriment of national democratic norms, as in the case of the Syriza government on the third Greek bailout.[115]

Intergovernmentalist approaches to EU integration, then, both traditional and new, lead us to see two kinds of politicization at the top. The first involves political struggles over who is in charge, as member states in the Council seek to retain power for themselves while disempowering traditional supranational institutions to the benefit of new ones. The second is about political struggles over what to do in the midst of crises, as the member states may end up brokering sub-optimal solutions (in the Eurozone) or reaching flawed normative consensus (in the migration crisis). What all such approaches hold in common is that they see intergovernmental actors as the central players in EU governance, and supranational actors as secondary or even bit players in the crisis dramas.

Scholars who take a supranationalist approach generally dispute (old and new) intergovernmentalists' views of the Council as having won the political battle for power and authority. They argue instead that although the Council may remain "in charge" of decision-making, in particular in crisis moments, supranational EU actors have become more "in control" in a number of domains as a result of their institutional or ideational power.[116] For traditional supranationalists, the

---

[112] Bickerton et al. 2015; Puetter 2012, 2014; Fabbrini 2016.
[113] Hodson 2015.   [114] Hodson and Puetter 2019.   [115] Vasilopoulou 2018.
[116] Schmidt 2018a.

Council's deliberate decision to create de novo bodies so as not to increase the Commission's powers simply enabled a wider range of EU supranational actors—the ECB, the ESM, and other de novo bodies—to gain even greater institutional powers of enforcement than in the past, which they then could use to deepen integration via neo-functionalist processes.[117] And of course, these supranationalists can also point to the massive increase in the Commission's own powers during the sovereign debt crisis, if only with regard to its oversight responsibilities in the European Semester, and to the fact that Commission powers suffered no erosion in the migration crisis even as new EU de novo agencies were established.[118] The new European agencies set up in response to the Eurozone and migration crises were after all established in areas where the Commission's own powers were previously weak and served to enhance its objectives and/or provided an additional means of rule-making, information and enforcement.[119] Supranational (non-majoritarian) actors more generally were empowered by Council action, even if the Commission was not the direct beneficiary.

Self-described "new" supranationalists further argue that these same supranational actors have, ironically, through the exercise of ideational power, developed and proposed to intergovernmental leaders the policy initiatives they themselves have then been charged to enforce—including the European Semester by the Commission and Banking Union by the ECB.[120] In this latter instance, scholars have shown that the ECB has not only become more politically strategic but also more politically interactive "at the top," in particular by opening up dialogue with the more powerful governments to gain tacit agreement for politically sensitive departures from orthodox monetary policy[121]—most notably just prior to ECB President Draghi's announcement that he would do "whatever it takes" to save the euro.[122]

Scholars concerned with the EP also see it as an increasingly significant political actor in the inter-institutional political dynamics "at the top." Although no "parliamentarist" would argue that the EP is either in charge or in control in any domain, such scholars do point to the strategies through which MEPs have sought to gain increasing political influence in EU decision-making.[123] Importantly, politics comes in through the EP's role in co-decision processes via "trilogues" with the Council and Commission, in which the EP has increasingly pushed its own political agenda.[124] But even in areas where the EP has had little remit, it has successfully been engaged in "integration by stealth" in efforts to extend its power beyond the provisions of the Lisbon Treaty.[125] Moreover, the EP's successful election push on the *Spitzenkandidat* in 2014, in which it insisted that the leader of

---

[117] Ioannou et al. 2015; Schmidt 2018a.
[118] Scipioni 2018.   [119] Peterson 2015.   [120] Bauer and Becker 2014; Dehousse 2016.
[121] Schmidt 2016a.   [122] Spiegel 2014.   [123] See discussion in Schmidt 2018a.
[124] Roederer-Rynning and Greenwood 2015; Héritier et al. 2016.
[125] Meissner and Schoeller 2019.

the majority party be named President of the Commission, constituted a "win" for the EP over the Council, at the same time that it served to create a direct "political" link between the EP and the Commission.[126] Importantly, even though the *Spitzenkandidat* procedure was abrogated in the 2019 selection of the Commission President, with a return to the Council's traditional horse-trading, the political link between the EP and the Commission was, if anything, reinforced in efforts to mollify the EP. Finally, even where the EP is completely left out of the decision-making process, it can still play a role, whether as the EU actor to which other EU actors go to demonstrate their accountability or through its increasingly vocal critiques of other EU actors' actions.[127]

Only very recently have scholars started to combine such different theoretical approaches in analyses of the political dynamics of interaction among EU actors. For example, Tanja Boerzel and Thomas Risse contend that politicization had differential consequences as a result of the Council's varied governance strategies in recent crises. In the Eurozone crisis, they argue, deeper integration was accompanied by depoliticization through the reinforcement of the rules to be administered by the Commission in the European Semester. In contrast, the migration crisis was characterized by continued politicization, and the impossibility of any depoliticization strategy, or of integrating solutions.[128] Frank Schimmelfennig takes a different tack, contending that institutional and material path-dependencies shaped responses, with domestic politicization and intergovernmental conflict overridden in the Euro crisis by transnational interdependence (via euro membership and the financial markets) and supranational capacities (of the ECB and the Commission), neither of which existed in the migration crisis.[129] Finally, Nielsen and Smeets have argued that rather than constraining environment or contestation among EU actors, it is the multi-agent collaboration of all such actors that better explains the processes of deepening integration, as in the case of the creation of the EU's banking union.[130]

What comes out of this overview of theoretical approaches to EU governance is that all EU actors are much more engaged with one another through cooperative and/or contestational interactions in political struggles for coercive or institutional power and ideational influence, in particular in response to recent crises. It is not just that the Commission or the ECB may supply the ideas that the Council then decides upon, which may result in greater enhancement of supranational actors' ability to act autonomously or with discretionary authority. It is also that the member states—inside or outside the Council—may raise political objections or threaten legal action in order to constrain such supranational actors' autonomous or discretionary action. And supranational actors are therefore more political in considering how intergovernmental actors might respond to their

---

[126] Dinan 2015.   [127] Eg, Héritier et al. 2016.   [128] Boerzel and Risse 2018.
[129] Schimmelfennig 2018.   [130] Nielsen and Smeets 2018.

initiatives, anticipating possible objections and/or consulting prior to action in order to gain preliminary agreement. Moreover, both intergovernmental and supranational actors are increasingly aware of the EP, with its growing demands for attention on grounds of political legitimacy.

Is Politicization a Good Thing or a Bad Thing?

The jury is still out as to whether the new EU "policy *with* politics" has positive or negative effects on EU legitimacy. The main question is whether politicization is a good thing or a bad thing for EU governance. For the most part, this question has long divided scholars concerned about EU integration. On the one side have been analysts focused primarily on input legitimacy who have argued that politicization is a good thing, necessary for European integration to be accepted by national publics.[131] On the other side have been those centered on output legitimacy who see politicization as a bad thing, making it difficult for the EU to produce effective policies because of conflicting preferences, or even to agree on the benefits of the outcomes.[132] By now, however, asking whether politicization is a good thing or a bad thing is beside the point because, like it or not, it is a "thing," and here to stay.[133]

In the Eurozone crisis, if we were to focus solely on the substance of Eurozone debates, we could argue that the mutual accusations among EU actors are politically delegitimizing in a top-down sense—leading arguably to more EU-related "politics *against* policy." But if instead we were to pay more attention to the discursive processes through which such contestation takes place, we could see a glimmer of hope.

EU governance, so long apolitical and technocratic, as "policy *without* politics," where disagreements were treated in private and deals remained behind closed doors, has changed. Discussions are more politically charged among EU actors, with differences debated in public. And all such actors seek to communicate so as to legitimate their positions directly to the citizens as well as to one another. Such greater EU-level public deliberation and debate, however contentious, is in and of itself politically (input) legitimizing. Recent scholarship has found that politicization of EU policy processes, in particular where civil society mobilizes in ways that increase media attention, ensures greater public and policy responsiveness.[134] For citizens, moreover, the back and forth of political contestation, as political

---

[131] Eg, Hix and Follesdal 2006; Zürn 2006; Hix and Hoyland 2015.
[132] Majone 2009; Scharpf 1999.
[133] Kriesi 2016; De Wilde and Zürn 2012; Hooghe and Marks 2009.
[134] De Bruycker 2019.

actors challenge one another's view, looks a lot more like what goes on in national democracies, with compromise generally the outcome.

But can the EU level's new "policy *with* politics," with its more politically charged interactions, provide a response to national-level politicization? Not really. While the EU level may gain in political salience and input legitimacy, it cannot resolve the problems of political legitimacy at the national level. Much the contrary: so long as the negative discourse among EU actors persists, it may further fuel the Euroskeptic populist extremes, in particular if the EU's multiple crises continue without resolution. The problem is only exacerbated where member-state leaders use their communications strategically as opening gambits in negotiations, not to inform the citizens but to raise the stakes with other EU member states, even when they do not necessarily believe in what they are saying. The problem here is that although this may be good negotiating strategy, it is "bad news for European democracy," as Anna Sauerbrey noted when commenting on the German "game" of poker during the third Greek bailout, which made for a "broken conversation" between leaders and voters.[135] It was also bad news for Greece, which was dealt a bad hand.

Even were the EU's many crises to be resolved, however, politicization at the bottom would still be a problem. This is because citizens' "politics *against* (EU-related) policy" also has national causes, and addressing them would require national leaders willing and able to be responsive to citizens' nationally generated concerns. This means engaging in domestic reforms that address the socioeconomic and sociocultural sources of citizen discontent rather than making the EU the scapegoat. It also calls for more positive discourse about the EU that acknowledges its problems without forgetting its benefits. This is a tall order indeed at a time of politicization at the bottom and from the bottom up, which also ensures even more politicization at the top.

Conclusion

The overall question with regard to the legitimacy of the EU's governing activities in the end, then, is whether it allows for active citizen representation through a governance system that acts both responsively (input) and responsibly in ways that produce good outcomes (output) efficaciously via accountable and transparent processes that are also inclusive and open (throughput). The split-level nature of the system complicates this significantly, as does the increasing politicization of decision-making at all levels in the EU.

---

[135] Anna Sauerbrey, "European Political Poker," *International New York Times*, August 10, 2015 http://www.nytimes.com/2015/08/10/opinion/anna-sauerbrey-european-political-poker.html?_r=0

The Eurozone crisis has not only exacerbated the national politicization *at the bottom*, fueling the rise of populist challenger parties. It has equally increased the pressure from the *bottom up* on EU actors, who have become increasingly concerned about public perceptions of the legitimacy of their governing authority and activities. But politicization has also had an impact purely *at the top*, with the growing politicization of EU actors' inter-institutional dynamics making also for changes in interrelationships of power and legitimacy. At the inception of the crisis, the Council accrued greater power for itself while claiming to be the most politically legitimate authority. But its interactions were highly politicized, with a lopsided exercise of power as creditor countries with Germany in the lead called the shots, to the detriment in particular of debtor countries. During this time, the Commission and the EP seemed to lose power and even legitimacy whereas the ECB, left on its own to "save the euro," gained both in power and legitimacy even as its interactions with other EU actors became increasingly (informally) politicized.

Over time, in particular as the crisis slowed, politicization at the top increased as EU actors struggled with one another over the application of the rules in ways that could be seen as more legitimizing. Interactions within the Council as well as between the Council and the Commission involved greater internal contestation among member-state leaders and more testy relations with the Commission, in particular once the latter sought to introduce greater flexibility in the interpretation of the rules. Relations between the Council and the ECB also took a turn for the worse in the case of certain member-state actors, most notably German, who objected to the increasingly unconventional actions of the ECB. At the same time, the EP began to assert itself more and more, with increasing opposition to the harshest of Eurozone rules-based policies, as it also lent legitimizing support to the Commission.

In the following chapters, we explore in detail how these issues played themselves out in the context of the Eurozone crisis. In Part II, focused on throughput legitimacy, we begin with a general discussion of EU governance in the Eurozone crisis, as EU actors initially doubled down on the rules with increasingly restrictive numbers, after which we assess each EU actor in turn from the vantage point of their throughput legitimacy—beginning with the Council, followed by the ECB, the Commission, and finally the EP. In Part III, we consider the effects of such governance processes: first in terms of the output legitimacy of the resulting policies, by considering their effectiveness and performance, and then in terms of input legitimacy, by exploring the political responses to the Eurozone crisis.

PART II

THROUGHPUT LEGITIMACY IN THE EUROZONE CRISIS

4

Governing by Rules and Ruling by Numbers in the Eurozone Crisis

In early May 2010, the European Union took a major step toward deeper economic union when the member states agreed first to a major loan bailout worth €110 billion to save Greece from sovereign debt default, and then to a massive three-year €750 billion loan guarantee mechanism (the European Financial Stability Facility—EFSF) designed to stop the contagion from Greece infecting other weaker economies and fatally undermining the euro. In exchange for such unprecedented EU-level financial commitments, countries in need of bailouts were to accept harsh programs of austerity and to commit themselves to major structural reforms; at the same time, all member states were to agree to slash their budgets in order to bring down deficits and pay down public debt. In conjunction with this, the European Central Bank (ECB) started buying euro-denominated government debt to help stabilize the markets, while making clear that it would not act as a lender of last resort (LOLR), meaning it would not buy member-state sovereign debt at will to stop market attacks.

EU leaders assumed that such general belt-tightening would reassure the markets as to the soundness of the Eurozone economy as a whole, while the loan bailout funds would "shock and awe" the financial markets into stopping their attacks on vulnerable member states.[1] The markets were not impressed. They very quickly decided that austerity was a problem for growth, and were not convinced that the EU would stand by the euro. They therefore continued to subject the Eurozone to a rollercoaster ride of market speculation for the next two years, until the ECB finally declared that it did indeed stand behind member-state debt. But in the interim, first Greece, then Ireland, followed by Portugal and later Cyprus, gained protection from the markets by formally entering the "conditionality" of bailout programs overseen by the "Troika" (made up of the IMF, the ECB, and the Commission), while Spain and Italy engaged in "informal conditionality," self-administering the bitter medicine to avoid having to enter formal programs.[2]

Instead of reaching agreement on any genuine solutions to the Eurozone crisis, member-state leaders concentrated their policy efforts on "governing by rules and

---

[1] "Shock and awe" was the term used by many analysts to describe the program. See, eg, *Financial Times* May 10, 2010.

[2] On informal conditionality, see Sacchi 2015; Pavolini et al. 2015; Perez and Matsaganis 2017.

Europe's Crisis of Legitimacy: Governing by Rules and Ruling by Numbers in the Eurozone. Vivien A. Schmidt, Oxford University Press (2020). © Vivien A. Schmidt.
DOI: 10.1093/oso/9780198797050.001.0001

ruling by numbers," that is, by reinforcing fiscal discipline through more restrictive rules with more stringent numbers on deficit and debt. The rules of the Stability and Growth Pact (SGP) were reinforced by successive legislative packages such as the "Six-Pack" and the "Two-Pack," which established oversight procedures for all member states along with sanctions in cases of non-compliance, and by treaty agreements such as the "Fiscal Compact," which required member states to constitutionalize a balanced budget rule. At the same time, member states agreed to allow the European statistics agency, Eurostat, to review their accounts and the Commission to vet their annual budgets through the new "European Semester." Only in 2012 did the EU add a banking union to deal with the problems of the banks, followed in 2013 by a bigger, permanent bailout mechanism, the European Stability Mechanism (ESM), to replace the temporary European Financial Stability Facility (EFSF), at a time when EU actors were also finalizing the last of the legislative and treaty-based initiatives to reinforce Eurozone rules. But despite these institutional innovations, Economic and Monetary Union (EMU) continued to be at risk in the absence of further substantial risk-sharing mechanisms—whether in the form of sufficient firepower for a financial backstop in case of bank failures, individual deposit insurance, or common debt issuances—let alone redistributive mechanisms, such as cyclical adjustment funds or unemployment insurance.

The reason for the failure to put the "E" in EMU, meaning an economic union to back up its monetary union, takes us back to the early history of EMU and to the compromises that launched monetary union without economic union, as well as to the very different rationales countries had for becoming members of the single currency. Each member state had compelling reasons to join but very different ideas about what EMU would be and do, why it was necessary and appropriate to join, and how much sovereignty and control could or should be ceded to any new Eurozone governance. Naturally, none anticipated the consequences of euro membership in terms of reductions in national sovereignty and control in the wake of the Eurozone crisis, let alone the impacts—for better or for worse—on their very different national economies. But their different ideas about EMU, along with their very different economic vulnerabilities, made for difficulties with regard to coming to agreement on quick resolution to the crisis.

Significantly, however, the initial rules-based initiatives that at first served as little more than band-aids for a potentially fatal wound were followed by a range of actions that at least served to cauterize the wound, and to begin the healing process as the crisis slowed. This is when EU member-state leaders in the Council began moderating their approach to crisis management in attempts to get better results, adding growth to the agenda in 2012, flexibility in 2014, and then investment in 2015 with the inauguration of the so-called Juncker fund, given this name after the new Commission President and officially called the European Fund for Strategic Investment (EFSI). At the same time, the EU Commission slowly introduced increasing flexibility into its application of the highly complex and seemingly rigid rules along with greater consideration of social issues. Across the entire period, moreover, the ECB's bond-buying programs slowly became bigger and bolder, in particular following Mario Draghi's announcement that he would do "whatever it takes" to save the euro in 2012, and especially with the introduction of quantitative easing in 2015.

To develop these arguments, in what follows we begin with a discussion of the sources of the Eurozone crisis, including the policy ideas, discourse, and decisions that established Europe's economic and monetary union. These are illustrated through the cases of Germany and France, necessary because of their key roles in creating EMU, and Italy, emblematic because of its herculean efforts to join. We then turn to the Eurozone policies themselves, focusing on the policies that were institutionalized and operationalized along with the accompanying ideas and discourse of EU member-state leaders and EU officials in the run-up to the crisis and in the initial phase of the crisis. We end with a brief consideration of issues related to the EU's throughput legitimacy as EU actors began reinterpreting the rules "by stealth" in efforts to respond to deteriorating performance and increasing political volatility.

Sources of the Eurozone Crisis

Ideas favoring a single currency start early. There is even mention of it in the Treaty of Rome. Periodic commissioned reports considering the viability of a single currency and the possible modalities followed, culminating in two reports. The stillborn Werner report of 1970, which proposed much deeper integration than the Maastricht Treaty would establish twenty years later, required national public budgets to be decided at the Community level, including "the overall volume, the size of balances and the modes of financing as well as their use."[3] The equally unsuccessful MacDougall report of 1977 argued that a monetary union would demand a Community budget of approximately 5 to 7 per cent of gross domestic product (GDP) to absorb economic shocks and allow for a minimum degree of income convergence.[4] For many, a single currency was in line with the big (output) goals of European integration more generally, to ensure peace and prosperity through "ever closer union." This was certainly the federalist dream. For others, in a world still divided between the liberal democracies of the West and the communist dictatorships to the East, a common currency would further consolidate market liberalism against communist state-managed economies. But even anti-federal pragmatists were convinced that for the Single Market to be complete, a single currency was a *sine qua non*. This was supported by the Commission-sponsored Cecchini report of

[3] Werner 1970, p. 12.   [4] MacDougall 1977.

1988, which highlighted how much would be saved for the Single Market in currency transaction costs if a single currency were to replace national currencies. The Commission itself, as Nicolas Jabko argues, provided further political rationale for European Monetary Union by time and again invoking "the market" as a "talisman" to promote the idea of EMU as a solution to the perceived problems of globalization.[5] Moreover, an epistemic community of central bankers, economists, and finance ministry officials across Europe had developed a common language and framework of analysis about the necessity and appropriateness of a common currency based on the German model.[6] This was embraced by European officials in the Commission, put down on paper in the Delors report of 1989,[7] and ultimately taken up by member-state political leaders in the European Council, with EMU ultimately hailed as "the most ambitious experiment in the international monetary and exchange rate cooperation of the post-Bretton Woods era."[8] Notably, there was no significant debate on the political implications of such fiscal integration. The unspoken assumption was that the transfer of such powers to the EU level would come with an expansion of the EU's budget along with the reinforcement of the powers of the Commission and involvement of the European Parliament.[9]

But nothing would have been possible without key players willing to commit their countries to monetary union—in particular the two "essential" countries, Germany and France. Germany was concerned mainly with unification, so compromised with France, which was intent on getting out from under German dominance in monetary affairs in the European Monetary System (EMS). As for Italy, the inclusion of which ensured that EMU membership would not be limited to already convergent countries, it was mainly focused on not being left behind by all the other member states, as a matter of pride as well as practicality.

Trials and Tribulations in the Run-Up to the Maastricht Treaty

The Maastricht Treaty, negotiated in 1991 and signed in 1992, established the numbers-based criteria for membership in EMU. By this time, any significant increase in the EU budget such as that proposed by the MacDougall report was seen as politically unrealistic. Although there was some discussion of a "rainy day" fund to deal with asymmetric shocks and the Delors report included a recommendation to use the EU budget flexibly, only the latter was included in the Maastricht Treaty—but in such watered-down form so as to prove unusable. The only "solidarity" was the Cohesion Fund, created to promote convergence by supporting the poorer countries' efforts to qualify for EMU.

---

[5] Jabko 2006, pp. 150–4.   [6] McNamara 1998; Verdun 1999.   [7] Delors 1989.
[8] Buiter et al. 1998, p. 1.   [9] Rubio 2015.

The main focus now was to guarantee euro members' fiscal discipline through a combination of market discipline underpinned by the "no bailout clause" in the Treaty and rules for fiscal discipline.[10] The agreed rules set a budget deficit of no more than 3 percent of GDP, a public debt approaching 60 percent of GDP, and an inflation rate no more than 2 percentage points higher than the lowest rate among member states, and in any case at or below 3 percent. Moreover, to qualify to join the single currency, member states not only had to meet the Maastricht criteria; they also had to have been members of the Exchange Rate Mechanism (ERM) of the EMS for two years. So the race was on for the member states, which had to qualify by the initially set date of 1997, and in the end by 1999. In 1997 the Stability and Growth Pact (SGP) was added, to ensure that member states continued to abide by the Maastricht criteria once they had joined EMU, by facilitating fiscal monitoring of member-state compliance by the European Commission and the Council of Ministers.[11]

The route to monetary union was fraught with difficulty. Not only did most prospective members have to institute austerity measures that generally sought to reduce public spending, in particular on the welfare state, in order to meet the criteria. Market speculation against monetary union began as soon as the ink was dry on member-state signatures on the Treaty, sparking two monetary crises that involved major runs on European currencies. The first in September 1992 pushed a number of countries out of the ERM of the EMS, including Italy and Britain, the latter of which—having suffered the biggest single loss in monetary history, of around 3 trillion pounds—left, never to return. The second monetary crisis in August 1993 nearly destroyed the EMS altogether, and forced the widening of the band of fluctuation allowed within the ERM.

Neither major events nor expert opinion dissuaded EU leaders from continuing their pursuit of monetary integration. The fall of the Berlin Wall, with the end of the Soviet Union and its satellite states, eliminated one important reason for establishing a single currency. But this did not deter EU leaders. Nor did the public pleas of world-renowned economists (most European, many based in the United States, such as Nobel Prize winner Franco Modigliani and Olivier Blanchard, later Chief Economist at the IMF), who pushed EU leaders to give up pursuit of a project that the economists argued would bring disaster and was no longer necessary. But politically, there was no going back, given the sunk costs of the previous decade, with the turn toward monetarism, the move to the independence of central banks, and the economic belt-tightening and market-leaning reforms that came at great political cost, all done in the name of Europe and a future

---

[10] Rubio 2015; Schelkle 2017.

[11] The SGP set up both a "preventive arm" to strengthen "the surveillance of budgetary positions and the surveillance and coordination of economic policies" and a "dissuasive arm" focused on "speeding up and clarifying the implementation of the excessive deficit procedure."

common currency. Moreover, the attacks on member-state currencies after the signing of the Maastricht Treaty only increased leaders' resolve to see monetary integration through to the end. France was even more determined than ever, having managed to stay in the ERM by a thread thanks to German Bundesbank help in the 2003 attack. Italy, pushed out of the ERM in 1992, was equally determined to get back in. At the same time, Spain and others, also under assault in the 1992/3 attacks, were all the more intent on qualifying for EMU membership.

German Ideas and Discourse on Monetary Integration

Each country had its own specific reasons for pursuing membership, though. In the immediate moment of treaty negotiation, German Chancellor Helmut Kohl saw EMU as the inescapable bargain in negotiations with President François Mitterrand to gain agreement for German unification as well as a strengthening of the EU. The Germans had wanted at best a small monetary union, in which economic convergence would precede monetary union. By contrast, the French assumed that once monetary union occurred, economic convergence would follow. The Germans capitulated on this, but not on another French desire, which was to have a *gouvernement économique*, which would reinforce the political side of Eurozone governance as a counterbalance to central bank independence.[12] Instead, Kohl—at the insistence of the Bundesbank, which had lost its battle to entirely block the single currency—pushed for a monetary union in which the ECB would be modeled on the Bundesbank, but even more independent to guard against French meddling.[13] Its mandate, moreover, would be based on German ordoliberal principles of rules-based stability focused on fighting inflation. The dual mandate of central banks such as the US Federal Reserve to consider unemployment along with inflation was not considered. Moreover, because German policymakers, together with Dutch allies, feared the 'moral hazard' of countries incurring high debt once the common currency eliminated risk premia and currency devaluation, they sought to write fiscal restraint into the rules while limiting fiscal risk-sharing.[14]

As a result, the EU ended up with the restrictive numbers-based qualifications for membership that actually made Eurozone governance much more inflexible than German economic governance, and a European central bank more independent than the Bundesbank to set monetary policy, with a primary focus on fighting inflation. The requirements for membership, demanding that prospective members meet the very high bar set in terms of deficits and debt, were ostensibly made to ensure that the new currency would be as strong and stable as the currency

---

[12] Howarth 2007.   [13] McNamara 1998; Dyson and Featherstone 1999.
[14] Schelkle 2017, pp. 138–9.

Germany would be giving up. But they were also an attempt to make certain that weaker, less fiscally disciplined member states—mainly in Southern Europe, and Italy in particular[15]—would not qualify—not to mention Greece, the accession of which was not even imaginable at the time.

Kohl's insistence on establishing a strong European currency was also meant to convince German citizens, who were largely dead set against losing the Deutschmark, to accept the euro. The Deutschmark was the closest thing Germany has had to a symbol of national sovereignty, as well as a sign of economic strength and stability. Giving up the Deutschmark in favor of the euro was therefore seen as acceptable only if the replacement currency would have the same strength as well as the same symbolic value that it had in Germany, as a guarantor of stability. But Germans were not convinced that this would be the case. Warnings from academics and the media came fast and furious during the run-up to EMU, while the public opinion polls were negative at the time of the overwhelming Bundestag vote in favor.[16] In efforts to convince the public as well as fellow politicians, in the 1991 Maastricht ratification debate in the Bundestag Kohl invoked the "big" goals of European integration by claiming that "the united Germany wants no return to the Europe of yesterday," and intoned that "Germany is our fatherland" and "Europe our future."[17] Eurobarometer polls on citizens' support for the euro in the mid to late 1990s show that the Germans were significantly less supportive than the French and especially the Italians in the beginning, with a low of 32 percent in favor in spring 1997, by contrast with France's 56 percent and Italy's 74 percent. They joined the majority view only in 2002, when the currency started circulating, at which point German approval ratings climbed to the level of France, at 67 percent.[18]

French Ideas and Discourse on Monetary Integration

President Mitterrand and the French had a very different perspective on EMU from Chancellor Kohl and the Germans. They saw the move to a single currency, with its own independent central bank, as a way out from under the dominance of the German Bundesbank in the EMS, in which the Bundesbank set rates in response to German macroeconomic indicators (which was after all its mandate), often to the detriment of the other member states. During the inflationary pressures sparked by German unification, for example, in the absence of government policies to counteract this, the Bundesbank raised interest rates, which worked to dampen inflation in Germany but at the same time pushed France into recession.

---

[15] Mody 2018, pp. 116–121.   [16] Thiel and Schröder 1998, p. 115.
[17] *Bulletin* 1991, pp. 72–3, cited in Banchoff 1999, p. 192—see discussion in Schmidt 2006, p. 205.
[18] See Schmidt 2006, p. 207.

More generally, though, the French wanted a common currency because in the EMS the franc was consistently adversely affected by dollar instability, since investors regularly moved to the mark when the dollar weakened, and vice versa. Although French officials fought hard for their idea of a *"gouvernance économique,"* they went along with numbers-based rules. Adherence to the rather strict Maastricht convergence criteria was seen to serve as a clear message to the markets about the stability and investment-worthiness of EMU-linked European economies generally, and of France specifically.[19]

But while French elites were united in favor of monetary integration, French public opinion was divided. This came out most clearly in the results of the referendum on the Maastricht Treaty, which passed by the thinnest of margins (50.8 percent to 49.2 percent). In France, however, concerns at the time were less about the economics than the impact on French sovereignty and identity. Therefore, even before the famous televised debate that pitted French President Mitterrand against a prime defender of French sovereignty, Philippe Séguin, Mitterrand had engaged in a legitimating discourse to the public that referred to the past, invoking the need to avoid "the risk of reversion to the destructive rivalries of the past"; to the present, pointing to France's "eminent vocation to play a determinant role in Europe"; and to the future, insisting that "France is our fatherland, but Europe is our future."[20] In the debate itself, in response to Séguin's contention that to ratify the Maastricht Treaty was to give up national sovereignty and democracy for an undesirable federal system in which French interests would be subordinated to those of foreign interests, Mitterrand argued that "neither national sovereignty nor democracy would be jeopardized; there was no necessary transition to a desired (for Mitterrand) federal system; and neither French interests nor French preferences were in any danger of foreign domination."[21] In addition, he argued that France would have a seat on the board of the ECB, whereas it had no real say in the EMS.

The economic objections to monetary integration came later, by the mid to late 1990s, when the *franc fort* policies, linked to austerity, entailed cuts in pensions and other social policies. Some complained about the virtual taboo among mainstream parties regarding criticism of EMU, characterized as a *"pensée unique."*[22] But public dissatisfaction with monetary integration mainly came to the surface in the 1997 snap election, which brought the Socialists to government. This is when new Prime Minister Jospin pushed for a renegotiation of the then entitled Stability Pact in the name of growth, and got in exchange no more than a name change, to the Stability "and Growth" Pact.

---

[19] Schmidt 2002, pp. 80–1.
[20] *Politique Étrangère* December 1991: 151–2, February 1992: 164, June 1992: 122—cited in Banchoff 1999.
[21] "Dialogue" 1992—see discussion in Schmidt 2006, pp. 182–3.   [22] See, eg, Todd 1998.

Italian Ideas and Discourse on Monetary Integration

Prime Minister Prodi and the Italians had other reasons for pursuing member-ship: to remain full members of the club of which they were founding members; as a matter of national pride; and as a way to reform the country. Italy was one of a number of countries that suffered from the "paradox of weakness,"[23] along with Belgium and Greece, in which political elites used the EU in their communicative discourse to the public as the compelling external constraint, the "*vincolo esterno*" for the Italians, to overcome resistance to reform.[24]

For Italy, getting back into the ERM (which it managed by 1996) and then join-ing EMU became a major rallying point for the reform of the country's public finances and welfare system. Technical experts—in particular those in and around the Bank of Italy and the Treasury—crafted the macroeconomic discourse based on sound monetary policy that pushed state and societal actors alike to accept the austerity budgets, the one-off EU tax, and the labor and pension reforms deemed necessary to enable the country to accede to European Monetary Union.[25] Political leaders communicated all of this to the citizens in a discourse that argued that government instability combined with in-built permeability to interests impeded internally led structural readjustment, and that therefore the *vincolo esterno*— the external constraint or, better, "opportunity"—represented by EU pressure was necessary and appropriate for promoting reform.[26] The "tax for Europe," more-over, as the "price of the last ticket to Europe," appealed to national solidarity and pride, while messages like "either Europe or death" served to add passion and emotion.[27] As Prime Minister Romano Prodi explained at the time, "Nobody would have hidden his or her shame and frustration if our country had been excluded from the euro zone."[28] These discourses, added to the Italian postwar foreign policy goal of not being marginalized in Europe, served as powerful argu-ments for reform, enhancing the government's efforts to get the unions to agree to pension reforms and the public to accept the EMU tax.[29] The newspapers rein-forced this, as in the headline in *La Repubblica*: "The Twelve ask us for tears and blood."[30] Equally important was the blow to national pride if Italy, as one of the founding members of the EU, were not to be able to join the single currency— and Spain were![31] Prodi himself, in a 2011 interview, mentioned many of the above reasons, adding that France also played a major role in ensuring Italy's membership. He cited Chirac in a press conference saying, in response to a query assuming that Italy would not be part of the euro, that "there is no Europe without Italy."[32]

---

[23] Grande 1996.   [24] Dyson and Featherstone 1996.
[25] See discussion in Schmidt 2006, p. 149.   [26] Dyson and Featherstone 1996; Radaelli 2002.
[27] Radaelli 2002, pp. 225–6.   [28] Prodi 2001, p. 11.   [29] Radaelli 2002.
[30] *La Reppublica* May 5, 1992.   [31] See discussion in Schmidt 2006, p. 150.
[32] Prodi interview, in Moro 2011, p. 123.

The Introduction of the Single Currency

With such differing views—multiplied by the equally diverse perspectives of all the other euro members—it is small wonder that EU leaders could not come to agreement on how to govern deeper economic integration, let alone give up sovereignty over national fiscal matters. They moved forward with EMU nonetheless on the assumption that the "E" would be added when most needed, in the midst of crisis, because the EU had always managed to move forward in moments of crisis. But this time was different,[33] although there was a long lull before the storm.

Once the single currency came into being—as a banking currency in 1999, as money used by the public in 2002—the major fears over what would happen dissipated, since the euro proved itself to be a credible international currency. The transition from national monies to the euro was very smooth, with no panics and no major problems in any member states. The fact that the currency's value was initially very low, although of concern to some, was a boon to exports. Moreover, the economic boom, in particular in member states in the periphery, seemed to demonstrate that EU leaders were right after all to defy all the naysayers among economic experts and to disregard citizen opinion in some countries in order to forge ahead with monetary union even without economic union.

There was, however, a hiccup in the mid 2000s, when German Chancellor Schröder and French President Chirac demanded an exemption from the excessive deficit procedures, arguing that they should not cut public spending in a recession and that they needed to be given more time for recovery. Although many of the smaller member states, in particular the Netherlands, strongly objected on the grounds that they had themselves had to undergo painful budget cuts to stick to the rules, Germany and France prevailed. It is worth noting that as the jockeying for change began, in 2002, the EU Commission President himself, Romano Prodi, criticized the SGP rules as "stupid" in an interview in *Le Monde*, saying: "I know very well that the stability pact is stupid, like all rigid decisions. If we want to adjust them, one needs unanimity, and that does not work. It is not enough to have the information. That we have. We also need the power to make decisions."[34] This caused a firestorm of criticism from several member-state central banks and many members of the European Parliament (EP)—to which he responded a few days later, when speaking before the EP, by saying that he remained a staunch defender of the pact but that recognition of the positive aspects of the pact "should not blind us to the limitations of the institutional

---

[33] Parsons and Matthijs 2015.
[34] *Le Monde* Oct. 17, 2002 https://www.lemonde.fr/archives/article/2002/10/17/la-france-sera-en-minorite-si-elle-n-est-pas-le-levain-de-l-europe_294558_1819218.html?xtmc=prodi_stupide&xtcr=43

framework in which it is applied... Still less does it mean enforcing the Pact inflexibly and dogmatically, regardless of changing circumstances. That is what I called—and still call—stupid."[35]

Shortly thereafter, however, Prodi fell into line, as the Commission along with the ECB pushed hard to force Germany and France to follow the rules. But they were thwarted by the Council, which agreed in November 2003 to hold in abeyance the excessive deficit procedure against the two countries.[36] The rules of the Stability and Growth Pact were then revised in 2005 by strengthening surveillance and coordination and clarifying the excessive deficit procedure. As a result, the SGP moved from a quasi-automatic application of the rules to an emphasis on economic assessment.[37]

Other than this political wrangling over the rules, however, everything appeared to be going well. Little did anyone know that the conditions that would fuel the crisis had been gaining momentum. In the real economy, these included real estate bubbles building in the United States, United Kingdom, Ireland, Spain, and other countries. In the financial markets, they were the US subprime mortgages turned into mortgage-backed securities that were given A ratings by inattentive ratings agencies, and bought with alacrity not only by US banks but also by UK banks and even toward the end by German-based banks. As for monetary union, inflation targeting for all member states, rather than leading to the assumed convergence, had actually produced increasing divergence in all domains, making for the "one size fits none" rules.[38] Even during the early to mid 2000s, the divergences were clear, as ECB monetary policy fueled inflation in some countries (Ireland) while producing something close to deflation in others (Germany).

What is more, a little-noticed decision by the ECB had set the stage for the euro crisis. The ECB inadvertently compromised the safe asset status of government debt, in particular for the "weaker" member states, by linking eligibility for collateral to credit agency ratings. According to Athanasios Orphanides, in 2005 the ECB, concerned about the "moral hazard" potentially linked to the looser SGP rules pushed through by Germany and France, modified its collateral eligibility framework for government debt by explicitly linking it to private credit ratings. The decision effectively turned the ECB's collateral framework into a market-disciplining device for euro-area governments. During the crisis this left member states vulnerable to market (mis)judgments about their "fiscal fundamentals," an assessment the ECB itself should have been making. And ultimately, when market panic led to credit agencies' downgrading of their ratings, the weaker countries in the periphery were pushed into draconian formal (or informal) austerity programs because they were no longer able to access ECB collateral even as

---

[35] *BBC News*, Oct. 21, 2002 http://news.bbc.co.uk/2/hi/business/2345653.stm
[36] Mody 2018, pp. 149–151.   [37] Pisani-Ferry 2006, p. 839.   [38] Enderlein et al., 2012.

the stronger, better rated countries benefited (for no better reason) from the constant access to collateral along with lower interest rates.[39]

Initial Responses to the Eurozone Crisis: Doubling Down on the Rules

Two decades after the Maastricht Treaty, member states were still unable to agree on whether and how to deepen the economic side of monetary integration, in particular in the face of the sovereign debt crisis. In addition to the ongoing divides in ideas about the present and future of the "E" in EMU were the continuing differences in member-state preferences reflecting cognitive interest-based calculations about how much they might gain or lose and normative economic philosophies about the right way to respond under the circumstances. Moreover, the institutional impediments to action as a result of the unanimity rule were joined by legal constraints embedded in the treaties and laws. As a result, although there were institutional innovations, these came very slowly and incrementally. EU actors focused more on instilling discipline than on devising innovative responses capable of resolving the crisis once and for all.

Trials and Tribulations at the Inception of the Euro Crisis

In the run-up to the sovereign debt crisis, the old divisions remained while new ones emerged—most prominently the split between "creditor countries," mainly in Northern Europe, and "debtor countries" in the periphery. But there were also splits between the traditional leaders of the EU, between France and Germany, as French President Nicolas Sarkozy pressed for action while German Chancellor Angela Merkel resisted. This had already been seen in 2008, when Sarkozy, along with British Prime Minister Gordon Brown and US President Obama, led the push for fiscal stimulus in Europe while Merkel demurred, claiming that because Germans "save," a stimulus would do nothing (even though she relented shortly thereafter, and launched a spending program much more significant and successful than the French one).[40]

---

[39] Orphanides 2017.
[40] See, eg, Vail 2018. Germany's stimulus actually did a lot more with better results than France, which talked a good game but delivered much less. In addition to the new car-buying incentives of both countries, Germany engaged in a range of spending programs, including the highly successful "short-time work" that kept workers on the payroll in retraining programs, which encouraged firms to retain their skilled workers rather than laying them off by reducing their working time. The government compensated them up to as much as 67 percent of their net wages, while continuing to pay their social contributions and providing training and skill development when there was no work for them.

Institutional logics that required the unanimity rule for action, moreover, made it very difficult to do anything where even one member state disagreed. And because the main veto player, Germany, was also the most economically powerful member state, in line to pay the most in any bailout scheme, no action was taken as the storm clouds gathered. Chancellor Merkel could not be convinced that something needed to be done quickly, and she had strong support for her position not only from inside Germany—in particular from her Finance Minister Wolfgang Schäuble, along with legions of economists and the tabloid press—but also from allies outside, such as the Netherlands and Finland.

Resistance to action came from the unwillingness to create any kind of "transfer union" in which some member states would pay for the debts of others. This concern was particularly strong in Germany, which had already done this once before—for East Germany, in the greatest intra-country transfer of funds in modern history (it had done it willingly because this was for fellow Germans). It was not about to start again (in particular if it meant paying for Southern Italy). There were also constant discussions about the "moral hazard" of helping out Greece for fear that this would play havoc with the rule-following behavior of other member states if they felt they would always be bailed out.

The push for action instead came from concerns not just about what would happen to Greece and other member states that were under increasing market pressure, but about the future of the euro itself if nothing were done to stem market attacks. Differences in economic philosophies added to the divides, with ordoliberal ideas focused on stability pitted against more neo-Keynesian ones concerned with growth. While France, together with Southern European countries, pushed for neo-Keynesian, demand-led growth and for solutions like Eurobonds, Germany with its Northern European allies resisted on the basis of ordoliberal maxims about rules-based stability, and refused any mutualization of debt.[41] The main divisions can be summed up in terms of French and German leaders' very different political-economic visions of what to do and how to do it. As Mark Vail puts it, Sarkozy was imbued with France's longstanding statist liberalism, in which governments had long struggled with the fiscal constraints of the SGP, and used the state's macroeconomic levers to stimulate growth while supporting individual citizens' incomes. Merkel was instead sustained by Germany's corporate liberalism, in which the stability culture of the SGP fit better with governments' long-term commitment to preserving the system's fiscal balance while using their more selective, group-focused approach to economic management to promote export-led growth (in particular by subsidizing and sheltering skilled workers and firms in export-intensive sectors).[42]

---

[41] For an extended discussion, see Brunnermeier et al. 2016.   [42] Vail 2018.

Additionally, there were very real legal issues that constituted potential obstacles to action. Crisis response was uncharted territory with regard to the rules that applied. Some articles in the Treaty on the Foundation of the European Union (TFEU) seemed to explicitly prohibit the kinds of actions that the EU was contemplating. These include the "no-bailout clause" that forbids the EU and its members from assuming the financial commitments or liabilities of any member state; the stipulation that financial assistance to a member state can be granted only where its difficulties are caused by "natural disasters or exceptional occurrences beyond its control"; and the rule that the ECB is not allowed to purchase the debt instruments of its member states, including government bonds (and therefore could not act as a lender of last resort).

Given all of these constraints, it is no wonder that EU leaders dithered and dallied in response to the Greek crisis, precipitated in October 2009. This is when the new Greek government announced that its deficit was much higher than had been reported by the previous government, and the markets began to differentiate the interest rates on member-state debt on the basis of risk. But when the EU finally did act in May 2010, one needs to credit it with a lot of imagination in overcoming the obstacles to action—although it did not do enough to solve the crisis.

Initial Actions and Reactions

With regard to Greece, the EU skirted the no-bailout clause by making the bailout a loan at close to market prices. As for the loan guarantee mechanism for countries potentially at risk of market attack once Greece had been saved, the EU could be seen to have justified it by interpreting the contagion from the Greek crisis as involving an "unnatural" disaster beyond the control of the member states in question. But the EU did not attempt to set the mechanism up as a treaty, for fear of failing to achieve unanimity. Instead, it agreed to set up the largest part of the three-year loan package (€440 billion) as a "special purpose vehicle" outside the treaties, called the European Financial Stability Facility (EFSF), by way of multiple bilateral agreements, to which Eurozone members plus Sweden and Poland signed up. The further agreement in November 2010 to establish a permanent European Stability Mechanism (ESM) through a treaty amendment when the temporary EFSF ended in 2013 was a big gamble, given the difficulties stemming from the need for unanimity, but was done at German insistence. Finally, the ECB got around the prohibition against directly buying government debt by purchasing it on the secondary markets.[43]

---

[43] Schmidt 2010b.

The obstacles to EU action help to explain why this great leap forward in European integration was anything but a model of leadership: action came at the very last minute, after much hesitation and tremendous delay—largely because of German resistance—and offered only temporary relief. The crisis need not have happened had Germany not refused to deal with the question until almost too late, or had the ECB decided that it could act as a lender of last resort (LOLR) and buy member-state bonds in order to discourage market attacks, as had the US Federal Reserve Bank and the Bank of England since 2008. Had the rescue arrived in February, when the problem reached crisis proportions, or even in March rather than May, the markets might have been reassured and the EU may not even have had to come up with the collateral loan mechanism for the other Southern European countries. It is useful to note that the markets were actually very forgiving, all things considered, as they waited for EU leaders to take action in summit after summit—until they finally lost patience in May 2010, and priced interest rates on Greek bonds out of the market.[44] In short, although the Eurozone crisis is often blamed on the unfettered markets and the way in which greedy financiers, worried about recovering their investments, attacked Greece, the responsibility for the blow-up lies largely with Germany, which refused to agree to any kind of rescue plan as the clock ticked, and with the ECB's prior refusal to act as a LOLR.

The whole decision-making process was itself shambolic in the lead-up to the final agreement on the bailout, as many have chronicled.[45] Carlo Bastasin in particular meticulously details all of the many problems with regard to reaching agreement, including not only the bottom-up pressures from German citizens and the media but also the diverging viewpoints on what to do taken by the more orthodox ECB versus the newly dovish IMF; the role of US President Obama and other officials in the final negotiations; and the desperate shuttle diplomacy of the Greek Prime Minister Papandreou in efforts to get EU member-state leaders to act.[46] Ashoka Mody also has a lengthy discussion of just how complicated and inefficient the process was in terms of the exercise of leadership.[47] He points to, among other things, the mixed signals coming from German leaders themselves. For example, when Schäuble plumped for Grexit, insisting that countries that lived beyond their means needed to be punished aggressively, Merkel called it "idiotic" to punish countries in fiscal distress, but then used the possibility of Grexit to ratchet up pressure on Greece.[48] And then there were the *contretemps* related to persuading other member-state leaders to come on board, as well as the IMF, for which this was an unprecedented move.[49] Subsequent rounds of

---

[44] Jones 2010.
[45] See for example, Spiegel 2014; Bastasin 2015; Siani-Davies 2017; Mody 2018; Tooze 2018.
[46] Bastasin 2015, pp. 160–207.   [47] Mody 2018, pp. 233–67.   [48] Mody 2018, p. 245.
[49] Mody 2018, pp. 258–63.

negotiation ended up being more of the same, or worse. Not only was Merkel hesitant and slow to move, over and over again, but other EU leaders also threw in monkey wrenches along the way, generally over bottom-up political consider-ations involving coalition partners or electoral pressures.

This said, early resolution to the Greek meltdown might have only briefly put off the attack on the other weak economies, infamously called the PIIGS (acronym for Portugal, Ireland, Italy, Greece, and Spain) by all and sundry, or the equally politically incorrect (but accurate in terms of order of entry into crisis) GIPS, or GIPSI (!!) when Italy came under market pressure. Once the markets became concerned about sovereign insolvency, it was only a matter of time before the Eurozone's weaker member states with higher deficits and less competitive-ness became a target. Greece's deficit was at 13.6 percent of GDP in 2009[50] while Ireland's stood at 14.3 percent of GDP in 2009 and 12 percent by the end of 2010, not counting the bank debt that brought the deficit up to an estimated 32 percent of GDP. Spain's deficit was only slightly lower, at 11.2 percent in 2009. As for Greek debt, in 2009 it came to 115.1 percent,[51] while Italy's debt came in at 118 percent of GDP in 2010.[52]

Given these figures, and the markets' new concerns about sovereign debt default, it is clear that there was a great need for some kind of collateral loan guarantee mechanism or financial lending institution of last resort—such as a European Monetary Fund equivalent of the IMF or a European Debt Agency—to deal with the problem. No less a figure than German Minister of Finance Wolfgang Schäuble had called for one in March 2010, prior to the bailout.[53] But it would have actually been even better had a European Monetary Fund covering the entire EU been set up much sooner, arguably when the Central and Eastern European countries were in danger of default in 2008. Had the EU signaled to the markets then that it would take care of its own member states rather than send them to the IMF, it might have been able to avoid the whole sovereign debt prob-lem in the first place. Instead, the member states retained the "every man for him-self" principle, refusing to create a bailout for the Eastern European countries in response to the *cri de coeur* of the Hungarian prime minister against the creation of a new "economic iron curtain."[54] There were many good reasons for not doing so at the time, of course. These included the difficulty of quickly setting up such a mechanism, the lack of EU expertise compared to the decades of IMF experience, the concern that setting up a European equivalent to the IMF would undermine the latter, and the sentiment that it would be better to let the IMF be the scapegoat for the restrictive measures imposed on the EU member states in need. The refrain

---

[50] The real numbers were actually higher, having been revised upward to 15.4 percent of GDP once Commission officials were able to vet the Greek government's figures (Eurostat, November 15, 2010).
[51] This number was also revised upward by Eurostat (November 15, 2010) to 126 percent of GDP.
[52] See Schmidt 2010b.   [53] In an op-ed in the *Financial Times*, March 11, 2010.
[54] Schmidt 2009a.

that was most often repeated, however, was that a EU solution would create "moral hazard" if countries believed they would be bailed out for their bad debts and overspending. Instead, the EU created a "market hazard" with the development of an entire market betting against the EU rescue of any of its member states from sovereign debt default.[55]

The failure to act quickly, forcefully, and innovatively meant that country after country fell like dominoes to market runs on their sovereign debt, and therefore had to accept the harsh "conditionality" linked to entering a "program." European Council inaction on Greece, which allowed the crisis to simmer beginning in October 2009 and slowly come to a boil by May 2010, meant that first Greece had to accept a highly punitive bailout package that did not work (requiring a second bailout in 2012 and a third in 2015), then Ireland in November 2010, and Portugal in May 2011. And once these countries were in programs and out of danger, the markets turned their sights on Spain and Italy, which were countries "too big to fail" because "too big to bail" by the bailout fund in place. The pressures mounted to the level of existential crisis by July 2012, to which ECB President Draghi responded with his famous statement that he would "do whatever it takes" to save the euro. This stopped the markets' attacks dead in their tracks.

Institutional Innovations

The bailouts and accompanying loan bailout mechanisms set up in May 2010 were the *sine qua non* of the crisis response. But more was subsequently done in terms of deeper, positive integration—which, however, did not always appeal to the markets. The replacement of the temporary EFSF, established in 2010, with the permanent ESM as of 2013 was a case in point.[56] Although most member states supported simply making the EFSF permanent, Germany insisted on a treaty amendment for any permanent sovereign debt resolution mechanism, on the grounds that the German Constitutional Court would object to the constitutionality of continuing to operate using the temporary EFSF. By mid October 2010, Germany had enlisted France's support in exchange for giving up on its call for automatic sanctions on member states that had repeatedly exceeded the euro's SGP criteria and for agreeing to France's insistence that countries be dealt with "politically," on a case-by-case basis.

The biggest difference between the EFSF and the ESM was that the latter was not just a default resolution fund to which a country in trouble could turn for

---

[55] Schmidt 2010b.
[56] On the arguments for why such a sovereign debt crisis resolution mechanism was deemed necessary, whether with or without a treaty amendment, see Gianviti et al. 2010.

relief. It was equally one in which the bank creditors would also be expected to share the pain. This latter move was made because, as Chancellor Merkel argued, it was not fair that only taxpayers were asked to pay for the bad debts of the banks. But rather than calming the markets when the ESM was announced, the markets intensified their pressure on Ireland and on other Southern European countries. Interest rates on bonds skyrocketed as the specter of default for bondholders was raised explicitly for the first time, fueled by confusion as to whether current bondholders would also be held to account. No amount of subsequent reassurances by European leaders that "haircuts" for creditors would apply only to bonds emitted after 2013 could stop the run on Ireland, however. And by the end of November, Ireland very reluctantly turned to the EFSF, while Spain announced yet another round of painful budget cuts to fend off the markets and Portugal went for a highly restrictive 2011 austerity budget. The negotiation on the 2012 bailout for Cyprus was arguably even more problematic at the outset of the crisis. This is when the newly minted Eurogroup leader, Dutch Finance Minister Jeroen Dijsselboem, in his first days in the job, proposed a haircut for all bank account holders, which would have left the poorest pensioners destitute while having little impact on the Russian oligarchs' bank balances. This led to much brouhaha, and was quickly revised to apply only to bank accounts containing more than €100,000.

Another institutional innovation was banking union, agreed in 2012, which encompassed a Single Supervisory Mechanism (SSM) administered by the ECB and a Single Resolution Mechanism (SRM) to serve as a backstop for the banks. These instruments were established in response to pressure from the ECB, which was concerned that the EU needed to be able to regulate its biggest banks, and to ensure that in the event of another banking crisis the Eurozone would be able to come to the rescue.[57] But although the ECB was largely successful in crafting and gaining agreement on banking union, this too has had significant weaknesses. Most importantly, the Single Resolution Fund (SRF), intended to be the financial backstop for the Eurozone, remained without adequate funds. Similarly, the much discussed proposal for a European Deposit Insurance Scheme (EDIS), intended to guarantee individual deposit insurance up to €100,000 per deposit and needed to ensure banking stability, had yet to be agreed. Both the SRF and EDIS have been left in limbo because of German resistance, although there are signs that the Eurozone may be edging toward some solution.

Many other possible institutional innovations were also eschewed. No EU equivalent of the IMF was created, despite discussions early on, although the ESM is close to becoming an EMF (European Monetary Fund). There is no common debt issuance (often called Eurobonds) in EMU—and this remains the case

---

[57] De Rynck 2016.

despite subsequent proposals for different variants on this in the form of "safe assets" or most recently "green bonds." Also absent has been any sort of redistributive mechanism to balance inequalities and recompense losers, such as an unemployment compensation fund, a cyclical adjustment fund, or even a poverty alleviation fund. At the beginning of the crisis, EMU did not even have a central bank willing and able to act as a LOLR by buying sovereign debt at will, a key function of all national central banks, mandated to protect their "sovereign." That said, the ECB slowly backed into an LOLR function.

The ECB slowly moved toward an LOLR function by way of its increasingly big and bold bond-buying programs, in particular after July 2012. This began when Draghi announced the Open Monetary Transactions (OMT) policy, which promised to buy Spanish and Italian debt as necessary to stop market attacks on condition that these countries agree to enter a program of austerity and structural reforms. As it turns out, OMT was never put into effect because the markets calmed immediately on the belief that Draghi's statement that he would do "whatever it takes" meant that the ECB would indeed act as a lender of last resort, while Spain and Italy engaged in implicit conditionality to avoid a formal program. Following this, the ECB began an increasingly aggressive bond-buying program, culminating in 2015 with quantitative easing (QE)—something that the US Federal Reserve and the Bank of England had been doing since 2008.

The European Commission also gained greater powers with the "European Semester," a framework through which to coordinate member-state budgetary and economic policies, which gave the Commission increasing oversight and sanctioning powers.[58] It came to constitute the institutional architecture for the EU's approach to "governing by the rules and ruling by the numbers."

Reinforcing the Rules and Numbers

From the very start, in exchange for its actions, the ECB pressured the member states to engage in austerity and structural reform. Austerity soon became problematic in macroeconomic terms. Across-the-board cuts meant Eurozone recovery remained anemic at best, leading to Draghi's call to end austerity in 2013. Deflation followed as a serious risk—something the ECB itself acknowledged by 2014—leading to its promise that year to start quantitative easing in January 2015.

However, with or without the ECB, the member states had themselves decided early on to institute austerity and to demand structural reform of all countries, but in particular those in trouble. Already in June 2010, having gained agreement

---

[58] The European Semester was agreed in the Council meeting of September 7, 2010, and passed into legislation in 2011 via the Six-Pack, discussed below. See Hallerberg, Marzinotti, and Wolf 2012. For a brief overview and update of subsequent revisions, see Verdun and Zeitlin 2018.

that all member states would tighten their belts, Chancellor Angela Merkel announced cuts in the German budget of €80 billion by 2014—the biggest in postwar history—to set an example for the rest of Europe. This was despite the fact that Germany was already at the time a model for Europe with its comparatively low deficit of 3.3 percent, its debt of 73 percent, and its return to export-led growth. In doing so, moreover, it ignored the pleas of fellow member states, in particular France, to stimulate domestic spending in order to help lift growth across the Eurozone.[59] But France notably followed suit, instituting austerity budgets in 2011 and again in 2014.

This said, we might ask why all the member states went along with the austerity and structural reform program pushed by Germany, the Commission, and the ECB. For the "saints" of Northern Europe, the reasons were obvious: loss of trust in the "sinners" of the Eurozone periphery, perceived as having failed to follow the rules; belief that the markets expected austerity; a conviction that structural reform programs were the only answer for the sinners, as opposed to Eurobonds or any other risk-sharing mechanisms.[60] For the sinners, the answer was more nuanced. For Greece, this was all about TINA—there is no alternative—given market attacks. For Ireland, which had already imposed harsh austerity on itself following the financial crisis, entry into a conditionality program resulted from the direct threat by the ECB to cut off its access to liquidity. For Portugal, the markets' merciless attacks on its sovereign debt were the main reason. For Spain and Italy, which voluntarily chose a self-imposed informal program, it was largely about the fear of potential market attacks, and political coalitions willing to use the outside *vincolo esterno* (external constraint) to push internal reform.[61]

While austerity fell out of favor as a rallying cry by 2013, even if "fiscal consolidation" never disappeared as the European Semester's top headline goal until 2015, structural reform remained throughout. It was the elixir that was to cure all the ills of countries in trouble, in particular as the moniker for national reforms of labor and social policy. It remained a central part of Commission monitoring responsibilities in the European Semester, although the definition changed over time. At the same time that the fiscal rules went from a very strict definition to an increasingly loose one,[62] the definition of structural reforms moved slowly from a primary focus on market-making, economic reforms to more market-correcting, social reforms.[63]

Across the period of strong market pressure between 2010 and 2012, the main focus of legislation was on devising ever more stringent rules to instill discipline through ever more restrictive numerical targets for all the member states, along

---

[59] Schmidt 2010b.   [60] Matthijs and McNamara 2015.   [61] See, eg, Moschella 2017a.

[62] See discussion in Chapter 7 on the Commission.

[63] Copeland and Daly 2018; Zeitlin and Vanhercke 2018; see also discussion in Chapter 7 on the Commission.

with inescapable sanctions for the delinquents in exchange for the minimal "economic solidarity" embodied by the rescue mechanisms. A principal component of such legislation was the "European Semester," mentioned above, which served to reformulate as well as reinforce the various existing coordination processes of Eurozone governance, and was periodically revamped, most significantly in 2015. In addition to enforcing fiscal policies, to ensure sustainability of public finance, and preventing excessive macroeconomic imbalances, to guard against future problems, it was mandated to oversee structural reforms. These were intended to improve national economic competitiveness as well to promote growth and employment along with other social policy goals in line with the Europe 2020 Strategy.[64]

The Semester was formally established in 2011 as part of the "Six-Pack" legislation, which consisted of six measures intended to provide stronger fiscal and economic surveillance in Eurozone governance. The measures served to reinforce the pre-existing Excessive Deficit Procedure (EDP) of the Stability and Growth Pact (SGP)[65] while adding a new "Macroeconomic Imbalance Procedure" (MIP) for all twenty-eight member states.[66] Whereas the EDP is automatically triggered by the numerical rules, and follows a set process going from enhanced oversight through sanctions for countries that fail to comply, the MIP allows for greater discretion.[67] Both procedures are incorporated into the annual Semester cycle, which follows a set rhythm across the year, beginning with priorities set by the Commission in its Annual Growth Survey (AGS) (in November) and its Country Reports (in February), followed by National Reform Programs (NRPs) submitted by the member-states (in April), and then by Country-Specific Recommendations (CSRs) from the Commission on actions for member-states to take, based on the previous year's economic and social performance and the priorities set out in the AGS (in June).[68]

---

[64] For a brief review of the European Semester, see: Verdun and Zeitlin 2018; for a general overview of the European Semester, see: https://ec.europa.eu/info/business-economy-euro/economic-and-fiscal-policy-coordination/eu-economic-governance-monitoring-prevention-correction/european-semester/framework/eus-economic-governance-explained_en

[65] The Excessive Deficit Procedure first came into being as a protocol annexed to the Maastricht Treaty. It kicks in when member states breach the deficit or debt criteria, at which point the Commission subjects them to extra monitoring and sets a deadline to correct their deficit.

[66] For the details see: https://ec.europa.eu/info/publications/economy-finance/macroeconomic-imbalance-procedure-rationale-process-application-compendium_en

[67] The MIP operates by way of a scoreboard of indicators with indicative thresholds to enable the Commission to assess potential problems such as debt overhang or competitiveness decline, with an annual Alert Mechanism Report (AMR) to present findings from the scorecard and to indicate countries requiring further investigation via In-Depth-Reviews (IDRs). MIP decisions are based on four levels of procedures, including (since 2016) no imbalances, imbalances, excessive imbalances which require monitoring, and excessive imbalances which lead to the opening of an Excessive Imbalance Procedure (EIP). For more detail on the application of the procedure, see: Bokhorst 2019.

[68] For more detail on how these have been applied, see discussions in Chapter 7 on the Commission. For the specifics of the various aspects of the process, see: https://ec.europa.eu/info/

Beyond these measures, within the context of the European Semester, the Six-Pack mandated the Commission to engage in ongoing monitoring of whether member states' national budgetary plans were consistent with their Medium Term Objectives (MTOs), defined in terms of their aimed-for reduction in the structural deficit. The Six-Pack also enhanced surveillance by adding the examination of current account surpluses alongside current account deficits;[69] and it instituted a kind of reverse qualified majority voting (RQMV), in which a Commission decision under the excessive deficit and imbalance procedures could only be overturned by a qualified majority of the Council.[70]

The "Fiscal Compact" that followed was an intergovernmental agreement that mandated even stricter budgetary discipline, with member-state signatories expected to enshrine the rules in national law through "provisions of binding force and permanent character, preferably constitutional" (a balanced budget rule sometimes called the "Golden Rule"), to be monitored not only by EU institutions but also "at the national level by independent institutions."[71] The logic behind this was that whereas the Six-Pack, as secondary European law, could be revised through normal EU legislative procedures, a treaty law could not, ensuring an irreversible institutionalization of the balanced budget rule in EU and national law. In addition, the granting of assistance from the ESM was contingent on ratification of the Fiscal Compact and there was provision for the election of a euro-area president and an annual cycle of meetings of heads of state and government.[72]

The subsequent legislative "Two-Pack," which entered into force in May 2013, consisted of two measures that further specified the modalities of surveillance of national governments' budgets by the Commission, along with a timetable that

business-economy-euro/economic-and-fiscal-policy-coordination/eu-economic-governance-monitoring-prevention-correction/european-semester/european-semester-timeline_en

[69] But whereas excessive deficits are monitored beginning at 3 percent excess, excessive surpluses are only monitored beginning at 6 percent surpluses.

[70] This was pushed by the smaller Northern European countries like the Netherlands, intent on not allowing the big countries to avoid sanctions or, worse, change the rules, as France and Germany had done in 2004. The European Parliament introduced this as an amendment to the legislation in the co-decision process.

[71] This provided the rationale for setting up "Fiscal Councils" in all the member states.

[72] This was an intergovernmental agreement rather than a treaty, albeit called the "Treaty on Stability, Coordination, and Governance," which was to come into force once twelve euro-area member states adopted it (and did on Jan. 1, 2013, after Finland ratified it in December 2012). The fiscal part of it is called the "fiscal compact," and is binding only for euro-area member states, but will be binding for non-members once they adopt the euro, or earlier if they so choose. Other provisions include mandating that the Court of Justice of the European Union (CJEU) may impose financial sanctions (0.1 percent of GDP) if a country does not properly implement the new budget rules in national law and fails to comply with a CJEU ruling that requires it to do so. It runs alongside the Six-Pack, reinforcing certain aspects, such as RQMV, by applying it to all stages of the Excessive Deficit Procedure, even if not foreseen in the treaty. It was signed in December 2012 (after veto by the UK and opt-in by twenty-five member states—leaving out only the UK and the Czech Republic).

amended that of the European Semester.[73] Moreover, for countries experiencing or threatened with financial difficulties, the Commission was to engage in enhanced and ongoing surveillance. Countries falling foul of the rules and therefore put into an EDP would not only find themselves risking sanctions (of 0.2 percent of GDP per year, rising to 0.5 percent if statistical fraud were detected) but even a suspension of regional funds that cannot be blocked without a RMQV.[74] They would also be subject to Commission diktat on the extent of fiscal consolidation necessary and required to sign "economic partnership programs" which detail the fiscal and structural reforms (eg, on pension systems, taxation, or public healthcare) "that will correct Member-State deficits in a lasting way."[75] To get some sense of the extent of the oversight member-states, it is useful to note that in 2011, twenty-four member-states were subject to the EDP; and it was not until June 2019 that the last EDP dating from the crisis was abrogated (for Spain).[76]

Ideational Underpinnings of the Policy Responses

Underpinning all these agreements were a set of economic principles, often referred to as the "Brussels–Frankfurt consensus," which has three basic tenets for Eurozone economic policy: stable money, to be guaranteed by the ECB's role in fighting inflation and ensuring price stability; sound finances, to be assured by the member states, which were to eschew "excessive" deficits and debt; and efficient local labor markets, to be carried out by the member states, with each country responsible for making its own labor markets and welfare state "competitive" in whatever way it could.[77] This consensus combines an *ordo*-liberal philosophy focused on the need to impose austerity in order to ensure stable money and sound finance via rules-based governance with a *neo*-liberal philosophy focused

---

[73] The timetable specified at the time was that by October national governments would submit their annual budget proposals to the Commission (prior to their review by national parliaments), with the Commission having the right to demand a reworking of the budget.

[74] The EDP is triggered when euro members either have breached or are at risk of breaching the deficit threshold of 3 percent of GDP or have violated the debt rule with a government debt level above 60 percent of GDP, which is not diminishing at a satisfactory pace (ie, reduced by one twentieth annually on average over three years).

[75] See: https://ec.europa.eu/info/business-economy-euro/economic-and-fiscal-policy-coordination/ eu-economic-governance-monitoring-prevention-correction/european-semester/framework/ eus-economic-governance-explained_en For more detailed information, see: http://europa.eu/rapid/ press-release_MEMO-13-318_en.htm?locale=en and https://ec.europa.eu/info/business-economy- euro/economic-and-fiscal-policy-coordination/eu-economic-governance-monitoring-prevention- correction/european-semester_en

[76] https://ec.europa.eu/info/business-economy-euro/economic-and-fiscal-policy-coordination/ eu-economic-governance-monitoring-prevention-correction/stability-and-growth-pact/corrective- arm-excessive-deficit-procedure/excessive-deficit-procedures-overview_en

[77] Jones 2013b.

on "structural reform" of labor markets and welfare states as the answer to problems of growth.[78] Structural reform was generally understood as ensuring flexibility in labor markets and product markets, meaning in wages and prices. For the labor markets, this for the most part meant promoting labor mobility as well as dismantling the labor protections and laws that, it was assumed, would make it harder for business to respond "efficiently" in a downturn.[79]

In tandem with the general rules came assumptions about what was to be done with regard to the countries at greatest risk of default, subject to formal programs of conditionality or informal ones. This is where the EU essentially revivified the prescriptions of the "Washington consensus" that the IMF had itself abandoned— of short, sharp austerity adjustment combined with swingeing structural reforms—first seen in the 2008 IMF/EU programs for the CEECs.[80] Not taken into account, of course, was that the IMF programs were predicated on currency devaluation, with growth to pick up quickly through newly price-competitive exports buoyed by reduced wages and a devalued currency. But in the Eurozone, internal wage devaluation was the only alternative, given that members no longer had their own central banks able to buy government-issued debt *à volonté*.

The mindset can be illustrated by a conversation I had in spring 2013 with an eminent ordoliberal German economist who will remain nameless. The conversation went as follows:

VS: So you insist that the only way to reform is through increasing flexibility in labor markets and lowering wages to make Greece export competitive? So how much wage deflation would be enough: 30 percent?

EE (eminent economist): Yes.

VS: 40 percent?

EE: If necessary.

VS: But would such wage devaluation be politically sustainable if it immiserates its citizens to a very high degree?

EE: [No answer]

VS: But would this really help exports?

EE: Yes.

VS: So what would the Greeks export? Mercedes?

EE: No, of course not!

VS: Exactly. Quite obviously not! The Germans have the corner on this market. What about tomatoes?

---

[78] On Ordoliberalism, see Ptak 2009; Dullien and Guérot 2012; Blyth 2013; Schmidt and Thatcher 2013.
[79] For a full discussion of the issues involve, see Chapter 9 on the perversity of structural reform.
[80] Lutz and Kranke 2014.

EE: Yes, that's it.

VS: No, the Spaniards have the corner on that market. So what else? Olives? Perhaps, but the Greeks don't even have the olive oil refineries—those are in Italy and Spain.

The conversation continued onto other matters. But had my interlocutor been more empirically knowledgeable, he could have countered my last comment with the statement that Greek exports in areas such as shipping, tourism, and even pharmaceuticals had been doing reasonably well before, during, and after the crisis. My reply would have been that the export sector was too small to compensate for the losses imposed by austerity in the much larger domestic sector.[81] As for austerity, the point to be made is that it left the government unable to do much of anything for growth or investment in physical or human capital. Simply assuming that wage devaluation would solve the problems of the periphery fails to deal with the realities of contemporary export economies, in particular if the model to emulate is Germany, with its highly organized labor-management coordination that ensures that wage rises do not exceed productivity gains, and its high-skilled, well-paid, well-protected workers, which make for the country's manufacturing prowess. Such a "one-size-fits-all" model also fails to deal with the diversity of national political economies and the differences in growth models, let alone issues regarding state capacity.[82]

But regardless of their effects, these ideas focused on austerity and structural reform have proven highly resilient. They were enshrined in one treaty or agreement after another; adapted to changing circumstances since their beginnings with the Maastricht Treaty and the SGP; touted as effective and appropriate even when they failed to be implemented in the run-up to the crisis; and, once implemented, failed to work. But they nonetheless predominated over alternative ideas, most notably neo-Keynesian.[83] Germany, backed by many Northern European countries along with the ECB and the Commission, was the main proponent of these ideas, while the ideas themselves were institutionalized progressively, with their lock-in path-dependence through the stability-focused rules, making them difficult to alter.[84] Note, however, that the success of such ideas depended not so much on the power or single-mindedness of purpose of their proponents as on the absence of any alternative agreement on a framework for the exercise of discretion (as desired by the French), let alone any leap forward into full economic

---

[81] Thanks to Fritz Scharpf for the suggestion of this additional reply.

[82] See, eg, Scharpf 2010; Ban 2016; Hall 2018; Johnson and Regan 2018. For more detailed discussion, see the section on the problems of structural reforms in Chapter 9.

[83] Resilience can be explained following five lines of analysis: the generality, flexibility, and mutability of the ideas themselves; the gap between the rhetoric and a reality in which they are not implemented; their predominance in policy debates and political discourse against all alternatives; the power of interested actors who take up such ideas; and the force of the institutions in which they are embedded. See discussion in Schmidt and Thatcher 2013, ch. 1.

[84] Schimmelpfennig 2014.

government with fiscal union and political leadership.[85] Moreover, there were genuinely different points of view among the countries on the various policies, for which the resulting agreements were often a compromise. For example, while Southern European countries mostly found the structural deficit rule in the Fiscal Compact too restrictive and Northern European countries found it appropriate, some Central and Eastern European countries, such as the Baltic States, saw it, if anything, as perhaps too lax.[86]

We should also not forget that non-institutional actors, in particular experts with close links to EU institutional actors, were also highly active in the generation of ideas. In the heat of the Euro crisis, prominent think tanks greatly increased their production of expert reports, with innovative ideas about how to solve the crisis, such as on Eurobonds, a European Monetary Fund, a cyclical adjustment fund, and much more. They also produced assessments, often at the request and/or behest of EU institutions such as the Directorate General for Economic and Financial Affairs (DG ECFIN) in the Commission and the EP. Brussels-based think tanks such as Bruegel and CEPS in particular were at the center of vast but different networks of experts, drawing on a wide range of expertise, including from academic economists, central bankers, and researchers. As Ramona Coman shows in an illuminating visual map, while Bruegel carried on an international dialogue with senior experts from around the world with IMF and central banking experience, CEPS was more reliant on experts from the EU 28, and often brought in younger researchers.[87] Both served as sources of innovative ideas as well as legitimizing reports for EU institutional actors, even if in many cases their recommendations have yet to be implemented. In addition, more general debates among experts in international political economy over the value of neo-Keynesian ideas,[88] along with battles over revisionist, orthodox, or mixed economic ideas,[89] were also useful for EU actors as they sought to justify or deny departures from the foundational ideas of EMU.

Reinterpreting the Rules by Stealth in the Eurozone Crisis

While the ideas focused on austerity and structural reform remained resilient, there was increasing but unspoken recognition that the rules generated by such ideas were not working—and, as such, constituted a threat to output legitimacy. Increasing citizen dissatisfaction, as evidenced by the growing electoral losses of mainstream parties and the gains of populist challengers, also suggested problems of input legitimacy. As a result, informally, EU actors began incrementally changing their interpretations of the rules, seeking greater policy effectiveness so as to improve the Eurozone's still weak economic performance.

---

[85] Jones 2013b.   [86] Raudla et al. 2018.   [87] Coman 2019.
[88] Farrell and Quiggin 2017.   [89] Ban and Patenaude 2019, p. 7; Clift 2018.

The Commission became more and more flexible in its application of the rules, with derogations and exceptions becoming more and more frequent in the period beginning in late 2012 and early 2013, at the same time that social concerns gained traction. By 2015, the newly appointed Juncker Commission had even decided to institute rules governing flexibility to improve legitimacy, despite criticism from some Northern European member states. Having shifted its focus from fiscal consolidation to investment in the headline goal of the 2015 Annual Growth Survey (AGS), over the next few years the Commission continued to ease its application of the rules on the last of the countries in EDPs as well as on countries in MIPs, all in efforts to promote member state growth and employment along with investment. Moreover, it paid increasing attention to the social component of reform. The Commission added recommendations to its AGS and Country Specific Reports (CSRs) that pushed member states to ameliorate labor market conditions and social protection systems.[90] It also proclaimed the European Pillar of Social Rights in 2017, focused on delivering new and more effective rights for citizens with regard to equal opportunities and access to the labor market, fair working conditions, and social protection and inclusion.[91] And it put European Semester Officers in all member states in order to facilitate two-way communication between the national level and the Commission, in efforts to improve national ownership and inclusiveness in the deliberation process.[92] In 2019, moreover, the Commission went so far as to demand a fiscal stimulus in response to a mere slowdown of the European economy.[93] In the meantime, the Council engaged in more and more extensive political debates that had the effect of condoning Commission flexibility (despite condemnation in some quarters), even as it agreed to further institutional tools to fight the crisis. By 2012, the Council had agreed, at least in the discourse, to promote growth; by 2014, to accept flexibility; and in 2015, to provide for more Eurozone investment.[94] The ECB, as already noted, had engaged in increasingly aggressive bond-buying activities, with quantitative easing fully engaged beginning in 2015.[95]

In the process of reinterpreting the rules of Eurozone governance EU actors could be seen as having created a new "governance framework,"[96] by supplementing, if not supplanting, the formal rules with informal rules. This should not however be seen as the same as "informal governance," in which making exceptions to the rules is part of a process of negotiated agreement that actually reinforces the legitimacy of the formal governance processes (throughput), the impact of the

---

[90] See discussion in Chapter 7 on the Commission.

[91] See https://ec.europa.eu/commission/priorities/deeper-and-fairer-economic-and-monetary-union/european-pillar-social-rights_en

[92] Munta 2020.

[93] *Financial Times* Feb. 10, 2019 https://www.ft.com/content/eb58c17a-2bb4-11e9-a5ab-ff8ef2b976c7?fbclid=IwAR3aAGByXVSBx_DKu5oc4T-pe8wIUoFzYStal-qaRcDsvfrs3t4kRjhhepM

[94] See discussion in Chapter 5 on the Council.   [95] See discussion in Chapter 6 on the ECB.

[96] Alcidi et al. 2014.

rules (output), and their responsiveness to citizens (input). Informal governance in the case of Single Market regulations, for example, is when individual member states are occasionally given exemptions after Council-led investigation and agreement that the political fallout from domestic groups' objections could jeopardize consensual EU-level politics or national political stability.[97] In the Eurozone crisis, by contrast, governance in the period between 2010 and 2015 was not so much about making exceptions to the rules as about creating exceptional rules, while denying it.[98]

The problem for EU actors in the Eurozone crisis has been that the complexity of the decision-making processes, the formal rigidity of the rules, and the divisions among key players have ensured that admitting that they were actually reinterpreting the rules has been difficult if not impossible where they have feared legal challenges or worried that political deals may unravel. Both political and technical actors have in fact had very good reasons for not admitting publicly their reinterpretation of the rules by stealth. Added to the political splits among member states for or against austerity policies was the volatility of the markets as well as their inconsistency between 2010 and 2012, as they seemed to expect austerity and growth at the same time;[99] the uncertain reactions from different segments of the public within as well as between countries; and the threat of potential legal challenges (the referral of the ECB's Outright Monetary Transactions program to the German Constitutional Court being a case in point).

The problems with throughput legitimacy regarding the reinterpretation of the rules can also cast suspicion on output policy performance and leave political input responsiveness in question. Reinterpretation by stealth could make EU technical agents appear incompetent—or ideologically bullheaded—because they appear to be sticking to rules that do not work, thereby tainting public perceptions of the output policy performance. Moreover, by obfuscating on the reinterpretations, EU political agents tend to skew the politics, making them appear less responsive than they actually are. Worse, it leaves their actions open to critique by the political extremes—who claim to "tell the truth" while politicians lie, do not care, or care only about their own clientelist and/or class interests. But even without the populist take on this, the general public can get the wrong impression, given the disingenuous discourse of political and technical elites. Legitimacy, after all, is about perceptions of policy effects as much as it is about actual effects.

---

[97] See Kleine 2013.

[98] Another way of thinking about such reinterpretation comes from Italian constitutional theory, where the "costituzione materiale," or the constitution in practice, is accepted as malleable and legitimately reinterpreted through practice because the veto points and players make it impossible to revise the constitution. See Mortati 1940.

[99] See Olivier Blanchard on this: http://blog-imfdirect.imf.org/2011/12/21/2011-in-review-four-hard-truths/

Finally, in a system in which the focus on "governing by the rules and ruling by the numbers" created an increasingly rigid system of packs, pacts, and compacts, any exercise in political or administrative discretion demands rules for stretching or breaking the rules—or at the very least agreement on who has the authority to make or break those rules.[100]

This raises two questions: First, how does one legitimate such reinterpretations "by stealth," that is, by not admitting—or even denying—to the public what one is doing behind closed doors? Second, how does one go about legitimating the reinterpretation of the legally binding rules if there are no rules for bending or breaking those rules? Put another way, who judges the cognitive validity or normative appropriateness of the reinterpretations?

The answer to the first question—how to legitimate such reinterpretations to the public—remained elusive so long as EU institutional actors did not admit what they were doing, that is, reinterpreting the rules "by stealth." This was particularly problematic in the period from 2010 to 2015, during the Barroso Commission. Subsequently, the Juncker Commission began admitting to its flexibility, even setting out rules for flexibility, which improved perceptions of throughput legitimacy, especially since it also introduced greater social fairness content into the guidelines and recommendations for implementation of the rules. Moreover, as time has progressed, and as the reinterpretations have become increasingly contested, EU actors have more and more had to "give accounts" publicly of their actions—such as the ECB with regard to quantitative easing, and the Commission in terms of its derogations for member-states such as France, Italy, and Spain. This is one route to greater legitimacy, even if such public accounting has involved EU actors trying to hide the truth of what they are doing. Telling the truth—although more optimal in terms of accountability and transparency—remains problematic for output and input legitimacy, given member states' divergent interests and assessments of what needs or ought to be done.

The answer to the second question, how to go about legitimating rule reinterpretation, is embedded in EU institutional actors' own definitions of legitimacy as well as in the institutional settings in which they operate. Conceptualizations not just of efficacy but, even more importantly, of accountability need to be embedded in institutional understandings of what constitutes "democratic" norms and standards for evaluation, in particular in an "unsettled polity" like the EU, where principal-agent theories of compliance and control cannot account for the complexity of organizational relations.[101] To understand how EU institutional actors build legitimacy for their reinterpretations therefore requires looking at those

---

[100] Thanks to André Sapir for this comment, made in the wrap-up session of the Conference on "Europe in a Post Crisis World," Center for European Studies, Harvard University (Oct. 31–Nov. 1, 2013).

[101] Olsen 2013.

actors' own very different institutional configurations and frameworks for legitimation. And it entails recognizing that different sets of EU actors build their authority to change the rules on different bases following different pathways to legitimacy.

Conclusion

EU actors engaged in a dizzying amount of activity in response to the Eurozone crisis, at first delaying, then becoming more and more active in the initial period of crisis in legislating loan bailout funds and rules of behavior with restrictive numbers. Especially at the inception of the crisis, the governance processes that included intergovernmental decision-making by the Council in closed-door bargaining sessions, minimal action by the ECB, supranational rules elaboration and implementation by the Commission, and the relative absence of the EP in most decisions conspired to make the policies focused on "governing by the rules and ruling by the numbers" appear apolitical and technocratic. But they were indeed political—and highly conservative at that, as a result of demands that member states follow the ordoliberal stability rules of austerity and implement neoliberal structural reforms. These policies not only proved largely ineffective at solving the crisis, as evidenced by the weak Eurozone macroeconomic performance and poor socioeconomic outcomes, as we shall see in Chapter 9. They also deprived citizens of national-level political control over economic policy. This helps explain why, during the Eurozone crisis, citizens' attitudes toward both their national governments and/or the EU deteriorated dramatically in most countries, in lock step with their economies, to be discussed in Chapter 10. In response to these increasing problems of both output and input legitimacy, EU actors began reinterpreting the rules, which in turn raised additional problems of throughput legitimacy. In the next chapters, we look more closely at each EU actor in turn as it sought to legitimize its governance over time, and the Janus-faced ways in which the procedural legitimacy of such actions can be viewed.

5

The Council

"Dictatorship" or "Deliberative Body"?

In the Eurozone crisis, the demands on member-state leaders in the European Council for rapid responses requiring unprecedented kinds of actions, unanticipated in the treaties, ensured that intergovernmental decision-making would be the preferred mode of governance. But the institutional constraints imposed by the unanimity rule, combined with the differential economic weight of member states and the bottom-up political pressures on EU leaders, led to a supercharged intergovernmental mode of decision-making in which certain member-state leaders had an unparalleled hold on power. After a brief initial period of "duopoly" under the Franco-German partnership, Germany came to predominate, to govern by the "one size fits one" rules that privileged its own ideas and interests. Over time, however, in particular once the crisis slowed, Italy, supported by France, pushed for a reinterpretation of the rules—by adding first growth and then flexibility to the stability discourse—and finally for investment with the advent of the new Commission in 2015. So how should we characterize the Council in terms of procedural legitimacy?

Analysts are divided over whether the Council's approach to governance during the Eurozone crisis has constituted something of an illegitimate dictatorship, in which *diktats* from Germany have ruled the day, or has instead been more of a deliberative body, in which legitimacy was ensured through the search for consensus-based agreements. Those closer to the first interpretation cite Germany's power—economic and ideational—to dictate what to do and how, and point to its lack of accountability in any public forum. Those who prefer the second interpretation look more closely at the interactions between German and other Council leaders, to see deliberative and consensus-building processes that ensure a kind of mutual accountability among member states. Legitimacy has also come into question regarding Council efficacy, as the most powerful member state, Germany, delayed action until it was almost too late, and then continued to stymie attempts at crisis solutions. Even close to a decade later, Germany is the main impediment to agreement on the full range of measures necessary to put the Eurozone on a sound footing. As for transparency, inclusiveness, and openness, these have long been in short supply with regard to the Council, and the Eurozone crisis was no exception.

Europe's Crisis of Legitimacy: Governing by Rules and Ruling by Numbers in the Eurozone. Vivien A. Schmidt, Oxford University Press (2020). © Vivien A. Schmidt.
DOI: 10.1093/oso/9780198797050.001.0001

The chapter begins by discussing how to assess the Council's power and procedural legitimacy, in particular in terms of differences between traditional and new intergovernmentalists on how to establish legitimacy. The chapter next examines the many different facets of Germany's exercise of power in Eurozone crisis governance, to consider whether Germany's actions could indeed be seen as akin to a dictatorship with minimal accountability, and a particularly incompetent one at that because it served no one's interests well, including its own. The chapter then explores the alternative thesis: that the Council acted as a deliberative body with mutual accountability (even if in the shadow of Germany), especially over time. We end with a consideration of the Council's involvement in the loan bailouts for countries in trouble, both as a whole and via the Eurogroup of Finance Ministers. And in contrast to the open question about procedural legitimacy for "normal" countries during the Eurozone crisis, here we conclude that legitimacy was in short supply, with the Council and Eurogroup governance constituting either a harsh dictatorship or a kind of deliberative authoritarianism.

Council Power and Procedural Legitimacy

At the outset of the Eurozone crisis, the member-state leaders in the Council took charge as the only body with the authority to decide what to do and with the resources to commit to doing whatever was decided. Intergovernmental decision-making came to the fore, to the detriment of the co-decision process, as member states met to discuss what to do and how to do it. Member-state leaders argued that they, as the elected representatives of the citizens, could best represent their constituencies through the concentration of decision-making in the Council while also responding most rapidly to the crisis. German Chancellor Merkel, for example, explicitly commended this new "Union Method" in a speech at the College of Bruges in November 2010[1] while French President Sarkozy defined a more democratic Europe as "a Europe in which its political leaders decide" in a speech in Toulon in early December 2011.[2] Merkel followed up later that same month, in response to growing criticism of German leadership as inward-looking and self-serving, with a narrative suggesting that the "Europeanization" of domestic politics (*Europäischen Innenpolitik*) served to strengthen European democracy through the channels of electoral democracy and increased awareness of political developments beyond voters' own national setting.[3] This was essentially a legitimation of the greater impact of (German) bottom-up politics on Council politics at the top.

[1] Speech at the College of Europe in Bruges, Nov. 2, 2010.
[2] Speech in Toulon, Dec. 1, 2011.   [3] Sternberg et al. 2018, pp. 102–3.

At the point at which large sums of money were pledged by member states in the context of new initiatives that "bent the rules" on such things as the no-bailout clause, Council members believed that the new turbo-charged "executive intergovernmentalism," in which the member states played the central role in crisis management via Council meetings and Eurozone summits, was necessary.[4] They were, after all, the only ones capable of committing new financial resources to save the euro and/or other member states. But was it politically legitimate, as Merkel and Sarkozy seemed to assume? Did the actions taken by the EU member-state leaders in the Council pass the test of representation and responsiveness to the citizens in all member states? And if not, could the Council nonetheless be seen as procedurally legitimate, as a result of member-state leaders' mutual accountability in deliberative processes of decision-making? This question takes on added importance when remembering that conditionality accompanied the bailout for countries that fell foul of the rules. Here, we must further ask if Council governance was not about legitimacy at all, and rather more simply about power and interests, with the more powerful Northern European creditors imposing on the weaker debtor countries in the periphery?

Any answer to these questions is complicated by the split-level legitimacy of the EU. If we assume, together with traditional intergovernmental theorists, that member-state leaders are input legitimate as well as throughput accountable insofar as they represent their citizens' interests and can be held to account by their national parliaments, then there is little problem. This would mean that in the case of Germany, for example, so long as Chancellor Merkel's decision-making in the Council met with the approval of her national parliamentary forum and the forum of public opinion, her actions would be deemed procedurally legitimate, regardless of their impact on the Eurozone as a whole. And indeed, as Femke van Esch shows, Merkel scores high points at the national level on all "four vectors of legitimate leadership," including responsiveness to voters' preferences, skillfulness and efficiency in decision-making, upholding a common ideology or set of values, and ensuring social identification.[5] But as van Esch goes on to argue, this judgment does not hold when considered from the perspective of the EU level.[6] In the split-level EU, what may be seen as procedurally legitimate at the national level because it meets approval in the national accountability forum need not be seen as procedurally legitimate at the EU level by other member-state leaders or their national accountability forums.

Further problems arise in the case of countries in need of loan-bailout programs. As Fritz Scharpf has argued, intergovernmental decision-making can confer legitimacy only on decisions to which leaders agree for their own citizens,

---

[4] Fabbrini 2013; Wessels and Rozenberg 2013.
[5] Van Esch 2017, pp. 227–9.   [6] Van Esch 2017, pp. 229–31.

not those that they would impose on other member states' citizens.[7] But, he goes on to argue, even if it were legitimate for member states to agree to legally binding austerity measures for everyone, delegating to their agent (the Commission) the discretionary authority to implement such rules is not similarly legitimate, given the necessarily *ad hoc* nature of the specific application of those rules to any given country.[8] Greek, Irish, and Portuguese leaders had little weight in discussions of the terms of the bailouts, having been forced to acquiesce to Council decisions under pressure from the ECB and under threat from the markets, and were at a great disadvantage in negotiations with the Troika institutions (including the Commission representing the Eurogroup of Finance Ministers, the ECB, and the IMF). Moreover, their national parliaments were largely marginalized in the Troika negotiations, forced to rubber-stamp agreements under crisis conditions, and therefore unable to act in their role as accountability forums or representative arenas. And while their parliaments were effectively disenfranchised, the parliaments of creditor countries were in certain cases able to weigh in—most notably the German *Bundestag* in the third Greek bailout. The debtors also found that their potential bottom-up impact on Eurozone decision-making was reduced in other ways by the EU, whether by limiting referenda on bailout packages, delegating competencies to supranational organizations such as the Troika,[9] or further reducing national parliamentary authority.[10]

A traditional intergovernmentalist approach would thus consider what goes on in the Council as more like what happens in international treaty bodies, as a bargaining arena in which intergovernmental negotiation gives those leaders with the greatest bargaining power an advantage in closed-door negotiating sessions. There are certainly traditional intergovernmentalist scholars such as Frank Schimmelfennig who use a rational-choice institutionalist approach to show that crisis negotiation for program countries was the equivalent of a game of chicken in which the strong preference of all to avoid the breakdown of the euro area was combined with efforts to shift the costs to the weaker euro members most in trouble, whose leaders had no alternative but to accept the conditions in order to avoid catastrophic exit from the euro.[11] George Tsebelis further illustrates this in the case of the Greek bailout negotiations,[12] as does Yanis Varoufakis in his detailed account of his own experiences as Finance Minister during Greece's third bailout.[13]

But what about the more general negotiations focused on reinforcing the rules and innovating institutionally? Here, traditional intergovernmentalist scholars generally split between the many who emphasize the coercive power of Germany and its Northern European allies and the few who instead find accommodation and

---

[7] Scharpf 2013.   [8] Scharpf 2013, pp. 138–9.   [9] Schimmelfennig 2014, p. 323.
[10] Auel and Höing 2014.   [11] Schimmelfennig 2015a.   [12] Tsebelis 2016.
[13] Varoufakis 2017.

compromise. A recent rational-choice institutionalist study by Magnus Lundgren and colleagues, for example, argues, contrary to the conventional narrative, that Germany did not dictate the terms of Eurozone reforms even if it may have shaped the reform agenda, because it was constrained in negotiations by its extreme preferences and political commitments to the European project. Instead, the authors contend that member states "traded gains and concessions" and "exchanged wins and losses within larger reform packages," making for a procedural fairness able to allay concerns about legitimacy.[14]

This latter interpretation fits better with the more constructivist and discursive institutionalist approaches of new intergovernmentalist scholars, where the Council could be seen to have achieved a kind of mutual accountability by acting as a deliberative body in its collective decision-making. After all, each and every member state did seem to buy into the story of excessive public debt and failure to follow the rules, pledged their countries to austerity, and agreed repeatedly to reinforce the rules of the Stability and Growth Pact (SGP) in exchange for setting up the bailout mechanisms and/or receiving loan bailouts.[15] Moreover, as Luuk van Middelaar suggests, deploying the metaphor of an Elizabethan theater, the member-state leaders in the Council were mainly engaged in ongoing political improvisation, acting in response to the heat of the moment.[16] So perhaps one could insist that Eurozone governance in the Council does indeed make for procedural legitimacy based on deliberation (or bargaining)—unless of course many member states bought into austerity and agreed to Commission oversight only because they felt they had a gun to their heads.

Mutual accountability applies to Council governance only if decision-making meets certain deliberative standards, such that discursive processes of persuasion rather than coercive processes of imposition explain participants' changes in position, and that the deliberations worked according to such principles as fairness, inclusiveness, and openness for all concerned. Using these standards, Council decision-making would certainly not pass the bar in the case of the program countries. But it might for non-program countries, meaning all the other member states, for whom Eurozone crisis governance could be seen to meet the requirements of accountable deliberation—say, with regard to agreements on the various legislative packages and treaty agreements, on the adoption of Commission country report recommendations in the European Semester, as well as on the (re)interpretation of the rules over time.

Even with these normal, non-program countries, however, if we wish to stick to a deliberative framework then at the very least we have to recognize that in all the deliberations—or, better, contestations—going back to the beginning of the crisis, Germany held outsize power to pursue its own interests. That power was

---

[14] Lundgren et al. 2019.   [15] Fabbrini 2013; see also Schmidt 2015.
[16] Van Middelaar 2019.

coercive, resulting from Germany's political veto position as the strongest economy in Europe; it was institutional, as German opposition to doing anything delayed any decision on Greece until the markets threatened the very existence of the euro; and it was ideational, given German insistence on the reinforcement of the ordoliberal rules of the Stability and Growth Pact, and harsh austerity and structural reform for countries in trouble.[17] In short, if the Council has indeed been a deliberative body, it has been so in the shadow of German power.

Some might find the shadow of power as delegitimizing in deliberative terms. This is generally the case in Habermas-inspired studies of "deliberative democracy"[18] as well as of analyses of 'emergency politics',[19] which find German influence on member-states' collaborative exercise of power as having led to the abrogation of democratic processes of debate and consultation.[20] Others might not see deliberation in the shadow of Germany as delegitimizing if such power was wielded in the public interest. Here, international relations theory could lend a hand by addressing the question of whether Germany could fit the role of benevolent hegemon, exercising power in ways that serve not just its own interests but also those of all members for the common good of the whole. Hegemonic stability theory, as developed by Charles Kindleberger and updated by scholars for application to the EU, suggests that the stability of any political economic system can only be ensured if a single country acts as "first among equals," by playing a pre-eminent role in setting the rules, bearing a disproportionate burden of the costs, and mobilizing support for it.[21] In these theoretical terms, as Douglas Webber suggests, while the Franco-German partnership could be seen historically as the hegemonic "duopoly" in EU governance,[22] France's increasing marginalization has meant that Germany has now taken on that role on its own.[23] But Webber argues that in that role, Germany has been a "hobbled hegemon" compared to other regional hegemons such as the United States or China; that its federal structure is ill-adapted to decisive leadership in crises because it disperses rather than centralizes power; that its ordoliberal economic ideology in the Eurozone crisis led it to impose countercyclical economic policies that were not only counterproductive but also not in line with those of a hegemon expected to bear a disproportionate burden of the costs; and that in the role of EU "leader" it continued with its "leadership avoidance reflex."[24] This last characteristic ensured that Germany was equally a "reluctant hegemon."[25]

---

[17] Carstensen and Schmidt 2018a, 2018b.
[18] Puetter 2012, 2014—see discussion in Schmidt 2018a.
[19] White 2015; Kreuder-Sonnen 2019.   [20] White 2015; see discussion in Chapter 2.
[21] Kindleberger 1973; see discussion in Webber 2019.   [22] Webber 1999.
[23] Webber 2019.
[24] Webber 2019.   [25] Bulmer and Paterson 2013.

So did Germany ensure procedural legitimacy for the Council as a whole in its role as a hobbled or reluctant hegemon? The answer in terms of accountability depends in large part on our response to whether Germany's actions were in the interests of all, and thus output legitimate because it improved economic outcomes or input legitimate because it ensured political stability. The answer is negative on both counts. Output legitimacy was put at risk, as we shall see in Part III, as a result of the misframing and misdiagnosis of the crisis, the wrong remedies, and the lack of deep solutions that made for problems of economic performance. Input legitimacy was also in question, with the decline of mainstream parties and the rise of populist "politics *against* policy" a direct result of citizen discontent—economic, social, and political—with Eurozone crisis policies, politics, and outcomes.

Council Governance as Unaccountable "Dictatorship"

Germany's outsize power in the EU, in particular in the Eurozone, makes it count as a hegemon. But as we have just seen, it is a particularly "hobbled hegemon" because of its history, institutions, and ideas,[26] and a "reluctant hegemon" at that, given its unwillingness and inability to lead.[27] A reluctance to lead does not mean that Germany has not led indirectly, however, or that its coercive power has not been felt.

Coercive power, after all, involves not just the ability to impose but also—and more appropriately in the case of Germany—the ability to oppose, as in the delay on Greece, the foot-dragging on banking union, and resistance to most other proposals. But what then are the sources of German power? These include not only the material, institutional, and ideational sources mentioned above but also individual sources of power—linked to individual authority. A good explanation of Merkel's success in closed-door sessions of the Council can also be attributed to the fact that she came fully prepared, with total command of the dossiers, having consulted with the Bundestag, and therefore able to speak with great authority. This contrasts with her fellow leaders, many of whom reputedly came unprepared, not having read the files or unable to come up with alternative ideas.[28] Arguably similar qualities, plus simple force of personality, also explain German Finance Minister Schäuble's control of the Eurogroup, where anecdotal accounts suggest that in the more intense negotiations he talked and everyone else sat silently, listening.

---

[26] Webber 2019.   [27] Bulmer and Paterson 2013.
[28] Interview by author with a senior Commission official, Sep. 26, 2013.

Germany's Power to Impose "One Size Fits One" Rules

Germany's dominance has meant that German ideas and interests—economic, legal, and political—held outsize influence in Eurozone crisis governance.[29] Considerations of economic interest naturally fed into Merkel's initial calculations. She was troubled by German bank exposure to Greek debt, especially after having seen how expensive the bailout of HRE (Hypo Real Estate) had been in the 2008 financial crisis, although this was not communicated to the public at the time.[30] This fed into the economic calculations about Germany's financial self-interest in avoiding the costs of a "transfer union." It was much better for Germany to force program countries to pay back the German banks' risky loans without haircuts so that the German taxpayer did not have to save the country's own banks in the event of bankruptcy.

As for economic ideas, German ordoliberal orthodoxy was also in play. Hard on the heels of ECB President Trichet's urge to tighten monetary policy came German Minister of Finance Wolfgang Schäuble's call for a reversal of Keynesian policy in June 2010, with an extended opinion piece in the *Financial Times* that stressed the need for "expansionary fiscal consolidation," stating that Germany would not respond to the crisis by "piling up public debt."[31] A year later, he continued to insist that debt was the problem and austerity the answer in his assertion that "piling on more debt now will stunt rather than stimulate growth in the long run."[32] It is remarkable that even in November 2014, while a potentially new crisis was brewing—as deflation threatened the Eurozone and ECB President Draghi had already called for an end to austerity—Chancellor Merkel continued to insist on austerity and the German Finance Minister on a balanced budget.

German dominance was reinforced by legal issues, in particular with regard to the German Constitutional Court, which Merkel openly worried might block a Greek bailout on constitutional grounds. Court intervention was indeed a worry, given the history of Court decisions constraining German government participation in economic and monetary union (EMU) going all the way back to the 1993 judgment stating that should EMU fail to sustain price stability, German citizens could launch legal action against the country's participation in the single currency. The Stability and Growth Pact, which established member states' collective commitment to self-restraint, was negotiated in the shadow of that Court decision.[33] Moreover, the June 30, 2009 decision of the Court confirming the compatibility of the Lisbon Treaty with German fundamental law at the same time made clear than any further European integration or delegation of sovereignty could not be made in the context of the existing German constitutional framework.

---

[29] See Newman 2015.   [30] Bastasin 2015, pp. 15–22.
[31] *Financial Times*, June 24, 2010.
[32] *Financial Times*, Sep. 5, 2011.   [33] Jones 2010, p. 24.

It also affirmed that the government would have to consult the German Parliament for approval of any decisions with EU partners that would affect the living conditions of German citizens,[34] and that where policies are redistributive, thus affecting national fiscal decisions, national input-oriented decision-making is necessary since control via the European Parliament (EP) would not be sufficient given the nature of EU representation and governance.[35] Equally importantly, the Court listed among the powers that cannot be transferred "fundamental fiscal decisions on revenue and expenditure," which put a damper on hopes of using Eurobonds or other kinds of mutual risk sharing. The Court's rulings to ensure democratic oversight of the executive by its parliamentary accountability forum have additionally played havoc with European Council meetings, which have intermittently been broken up to allow the Chancellor to go to Berlin to consult the Bundestag. And finally, the Court has also inserted itself repeatedly into other EU matters, such as its hearings on the ECB's various non-standard programs to save the euro (including OMT), despite its lack of jurisdiction.

Such judicial activism may in and of itself be perfectly appropriate by the standards of national democracies. The point here is not that member states should do away with the national democratic processes they consider necessary to democratic legitimacy. But this can cause serious problems for the efficacy of European decision-making, in particular if these kinds of national judicial exigencies were to be multiplied across EU member states.[36] Moreover, as it is, this represents another instance of German dominance, since for the moment only the German Constitutional Court has interceded on a consistent basis, to impose its own concerns about democratic legitimacy.

All in all, however, Germany's overriding considerations were political.[37] Any agreement was not going to be easy for the governing coalition because of the change in coalition partner in September 2009 from the Social Democratic party (SPD) to the Free Democratic party (FDP), which was vehemently opposed to any bailout. But regional electoral politics was also a major consideration. Merkel delayed action on a bailout in the hopes that Greece would tighten its own belt sufficiently to calm the markets while allowing her party to win the North Rhine-Westphalia elections on May 9, 2010—a gross miscalculation given her party's resounding defeat.[38]

During the lead-up to the bailout, Merkel's political discourse was also problematic. It helped fuel the nationalistic media feeding frenzy that opposed any bailout because it would make "good" member states liable for the debts of "bad" ones and bolstered public resistance to any form of "transfer union" in which Northern Europeans would pay for debts accrued in the South.[39] Merkel made no

[34] Bastasin 2015, pp. 110–12.   [35] Nicoli 2017.   [36] Dehousse 2011b.
[37] Newman 2015.   [38] See Hennessey 2013.   [39] Schmidt 2014.

attempt to exercise leadership, for example by explaining why a bailout might be necessary or that this would in fact be a *loan* to be repaid rather than a transfer of German taxpayers' money. Nor was there mention of the interdependence of Eurozone economies, with German export-led growth depending on the low value of the Euro and benefiting from consumption-led growth in Southern European countries. Instead of leading, Merkel chose to follow public sentiment and the numerous opinion polls that had shown that about two thirds of German citizens opposed the idea of the federal government committing itself to financial help.[40]

What Merkel could have said to illustrate the deep and mutually beneficial economic interrelationships of Eurozone countries is illustrated in the following metaphor, which I proposed tongue in cheek at a conference at the Watson Institute of Brown University, subsequently picked up by National Public Radio in 2012. It went as follows: If we were to think of the Eurozone as a bar, with a never-ending happy hour, it may be true that the Irish, the Spaniards, and the Greeks were like drunkards on a binge. But who were the bartenders? The German and French banks! In the terminology of alcoholism, this is co-dependency. In the terminology of economics, it is interdependence. And legally, at least in the United States, bartenders can go to jail for irresponsibly selling liquor to their customers who end up in car crashes as a result.[41] Instead of this, the German and French banks were the major beneficiaries of the debt packages, not the citizens in the countries under the diktats of the Troika.

By not providing any legitimizing discourse related to a potential rescue, Merkel's anti-Greek, anti-action discourse made her about-face—with her new argument on May 10, 2010 that the bailout was needed "to save the euro"—all the more difficult to legitimize. When Merkel took to national television to explain her decision, she offered a very thin economic argument, maintaining that "the future of Europe depended on the bailout" and "it was essential to maintain the stability of the euro." The move was deeply unpopular. Critics like the conservative newspaper, the *Frankfurter Allgemeine Zeitung*, announced the next day that "all of the principles of monetary union have been sacrificed."[42] The negative

---

[40] Data from February 2010 by the German Institute for Statistics, available at http://de.statista. com/statistik/daten/studie/77453/umfrage/finanzielle-hilfen-der-bundesregierung-fuer-griechenland/

[41] These comments were picked up by National Public Radio, which eliminated the reference to the Irish at the beginning of the clip and then brought on an Irish bartender in Boston, who explained that he himself would be held liable if he sold too many drinks to a customer who then had an accident. My thanks go to the Irish bartender, and to NPR. NPR Marketplace in the Morning: http://www. marketplace.org/topics/world/economy-40/thinking-about-eurozone-bar. See also the panel "The European Project: Can Europe Survive the Euro?" at the conference "The Failure of the Euro? Causes and Consequences for Europe and Beyond" sponsored by the Watson Institute for International Studies and the Rhodes Center for International Economics, Brown University (April 17, 2012). http://brown.edu/web/livestream/archive/2012-euroconf.html

[42] *Frankfurter Allgemeine Zeitung* May 11, 2010, cited in Schmidt 2010b.

public reaction to the first Greek bailout also helps explain why two years later, in the discussion of the second Greek bailout of 2012, when Obama called to urge her to agree and as Sarkozy kept up the pressure, tears reportedly came into Merkel's eyes as she claimed: "you want me to commit political suicide!"[43]

In order to recover electorally as well as to appear more credible, Merkel's government therefore became the defender of the most rigid interpretation of the SGP, insisting on rapid deficit reduction and structural reforms along with macroeconomic conditionality. Her discourse, moreover, sought to reinforce the concept of the "stability culture," which the CDU had used since the mid 1990s to consolidate its own political position as it sought to legitimate the introduction of the euro in place of the Deutschmark, and would use again to undermine the Social Democrats while in opposition by claiming they had betrayed the stability culture by violating the SGP rules in the mid 2000s.[44] At the time of the Greek bailout, Merkel deployed it to reassure the German public that "I will take care that we make sure together with our partners that the whole of Europe commits herself to 'a new Stability Culture'" and that "Our Stability Culture has been tried and tested, and because of that I will not swerve one iota from it."[45]

German Power in the Franco-German Partnership

Germany's "power of one" has also undermined the "power of two" relationship of the Franco-German couple, which constituted the traditional balance in the Council as well as a kind of hegemonic duopoly, as noted earlier. In the past, although the big countries have always had the greatest influence in the bargaining process,[46] the differences in their starting positions tended to make the resulting compromise more acceptable to the other member states, who saw this as a "multilateralization" of a common goal.[47] In the Eurozone crisis, this was no longer the case. In the run-up to the sovereign debt crisis, while Sarkozy appeared as a "white knight" riding to the rescue of Greece (at least to the French and Southern Europeans), Merkel was seen as Europe's new "Iron Lady."[48] But the moment the crisis hit, Sarkozy reversed himself, taking on Merkel's positions— whether because he gambled that this was the only way to get the Germans to accept bailout of Greece and contagion funds; because of his fear of market speculation against France; or because of his calculation that this would assure him reelection by conservative voters.[49]

---

[43] Spiegel 2014.   [44] Howarth and Rommerskirchen 2013; see also Dyson 2002.
[45] Cited in Howarth and Rommerskirchen 2013, p. 762.
[46] Heipertz and Verdun 2010, p. 20.
[47] Webber 1999, p. 16; see also discussion in Fabbrini 2013.   [48] Crespy and Schmidt 2014.
[49] Schild 2013; Crespy and Schmidt 2014.

The result is that the relationship between Germany and France went from one of bilateral leadership to a bilateral *directoire* between 2009 and mid 2012,[50] but one increasingly dominated by Germany, with Merkel the major partner in the leadership duo.[51] While the press caricatured this Franco-German partnership as "Merkozy," public intellectuals went farther, characterizing it as "Merkiavellianism" because of the way in which German leaders managed to manipulate all other member-state leaders such that all they did was react to German initiatives.[52] Although largely led by Germany, which benefited from its economic and monetary power in contrast to France's lagging economy, the partnership worked mainly because of Germany's ability to reconcile French preferences with its own, which lasted only so long as Sarkozy remained President. While Germany got fiscal rigor and the debt brake (enshrined in the Fiscal Compact), France got an element of political discretion in the disciplinary measures.[53] Moreover, the two were for the most part able to make policy for the Eurozone as a whole.

German dominance of the Franco-German partnership can be seen not only in the content of the Eurozone policies, as the German preference for financial stability and economic "solidarity" through loan bailouts and harsh austerity and structural reform for countries in trouble replaced France's preference for neo-Keynesian fiscal stimulus and social solidarity. It can also be found in the ideas put forward about economic governance, as German ideas came to dominate France's concept of *"gouvernance économique"* with Commission-administered rules replacing the Eurogroup discretion that the French had long wanted.[54] The reversal can be seen in the content of the policies, with Germany's preference for reinforcement of the rules in legislative packs and treaty pacts winning out over France's push for some kind of proactive economic governance. And it is equally apparent in the discourse, as Germany's stability through balanced budgets became the *mot d'ordre* in place of France's push for solidarity and growth-enhancing policy.

The evolution in both leaders' views of what to do, with President Sarkozy largely acceding to Chancellor Merkel's ideas, is traceable through an analysis of leaders' pronouncements in their press conferences from 2010 to 2012 about the policy program and its underlying norms and values. During this time, Nicolas Sarkozy and Angela Merkel could be seen to have been playing an elaborate "discursive double game" between EU-level coordination and national-level communication, as Amandine Crespy and I found in an analysis of all thirty-five of their press conferences after European summits between 2010 and 2012 (see Figures 5.1 and 5.2).[55] In this double game, the two leaders continued to carry on different discourses with regard to their policy preferences, norms, and values, befitting

---

[50] Schild 2013.   [51] Fabbrini 2013.   [52] Beck 2013; Giddens 2014.
[53] Schoeller 2018.   [54] Howorth 2007.   [55] Crespy and Schmidt 2014.

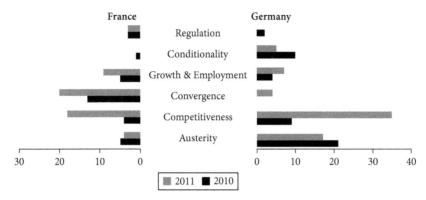

Figure 5.1. Policy preferences of French President Sarkozy vs. German Chancellor Merkel expressed in Press Conferences between 2010 and 2012
Source: Crespy and Schmit 2014

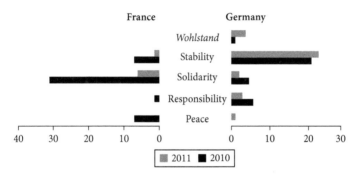

Figure 5.2. Norms and Values of French President Sarkozy vs. German Chancellor Merkel expressed in Press Conferences between 2010 and 2012
Source: Crespy and Schmit 2014

their differences in national context. That said, subtle changes can nevertheless be seen, mainly on the French side. Sarkozy gradually shifted away from an emphasis on the importance of "solidarity" for the bailouts, without, however, ever evoking the austerity frame in the national context. He instead focused on the idea of policy convergence within the Eurozone,[56] which was in tune with the French vision of a core Europe shaped by states' voluntarism, even as he increasingly talked of the importance of competitiveness. Merkel in contrast consistently talked of "stability," in keeping with the ordoliberal economic frame of EMU and longstanding German macroeconomic policy, while placing much greater emphasis on words such as competitiveness, austerity, conditionality, and responsibility, all of which Sarkozy was much more reticent to use.[57]

---

[56] *Le Monde* Dec. 13, 2011.   [57] Crespy and Schmidt 2014.

German domination of the Franco-German partnership brought with it that partnership's control of the European Council. This was managed mainly through prior Franco-German bilateral summits in which the two leaders thrashed out their differences and agreed on proposals for forthcoming meetings, pushing an austerity agenda. Because Council President Van Rompuy was generally assumed to follow their lead, he was seen as tainted by association, even though he did occasionally take an independent position.[58] Bilateral leadership itself was largely exercised by eliminating some options while reaching compromises on others that coalitional allies often, but not always, accepted.[59]

The most notable example of domination by the duo was in October 2010, when the two agreed, without consultation with any other member states or EU institutions, to a permanent bailout fund (the ESM) to replace the temporary fund (the EFSF) by 2013 with haircuts for bondholders.[60] This came much to the horror of the head of the ECB, Jean-Claude Trichet. Worried about the markets' response, he told Sarkozy: "You don't realize how serious the situation is," to which Sarkozy responded: "Maybe you're talking to bankers... We are responsible to citizens."[61] Sarkozy thus used political (input) legitimacy to justify a potential lack of procedural (throughput) legitimacy—understood in terms of accountability or inclusiveness in decision-making. At the time, many blamed the Merkozy ESM deal for the market panic that drove up the cost of servicing Irish debt, ultimately pushing it into a loan-bailout program.

Another example of Merkozy domination came in August 2011, when they sent a letter to European Council President Van Rompuy proposing that "payments from structural and cohesion funds be suspended in Euro area countries not complying with recommendations under the excessive deficit procedure."[62] The Commission took this up in its legislative proposal later that same month. And despite the objections of a majority of MEPs, regional funds were added to the potential sanctions.[63]

Yet another more subtle case of Merkozy imposition was when they succeeded in pushing Berlusconi to resign from his premiership. This came through a combination of behind-the-scenes pressure from Sarkozy and Merkel, worried about his unwillingness to do much to address the country's high debt, and the markets themselves, pricing up the cost of refinancing that debt. But the precipitating event was an exchange of smiles captured on camera by the press at a Summit meeting in October 2011, which signaled to the markets that the two leaders had lost all respect for Berlusconi. The markets then began increasing Italy's cost of borrowing toward unsustainable levels.

---

[58] Dinan 2014, pp. 126–7.   [59] Degner and Leuffen 2018.   [60] Tooze 2018, pp. 361–2.
[61] Wall Street Journal Dec. 27, 2010, cited in Tooze 2018, p. 362.
[62] Joint letter from Nicolas Sarkozy and Angela Merkel to Herman Van Rompuy, August 17, 2011, cited in Coman 2018, p. 547.
[63] Coman 2018, p. 547; see also discussion in Chapter 8 on the European Parliament.

Germany's exercise of power, in sum, ensured that its ideas about how to govern the Eurozone won out, that it dominated the Franco-German partnership and through Merkozy the entire process of Eurozone decision-making, that its internal judicial oversight mechanisms intruded on EU governance, and that its own economic and political interests were paramount. Such power-based governance raises serious questions for the Council's legitimacy, and lends credibility to the view that the Council acted as a dictatorship led by Germany. Germany's accountability has been in great doubt, given its lack of account-giving or being held to account by any public accountability forums other than its own national parliament. Add to this the fact that it was downright incompetent and inefficient in its delayed crisis response, high-handed in its Merkozy decision-making, and oppressive in its decision-making for program countries. From this perspective, we then need to ask to what extent "bad" throughput procedures thereby also skewed any political legitimacy the Council may have claimed as a representative body at the same time that it tainted the output legitimacy of the economic performance results even for Germany.

And then, what can we say about Germany's accountability as a hegemon, however reluctant? Ask German leaders and they might answer that "living by the rules" of the "Stability Culture" was in Europe's best interest. And certainly Germany's coalitional allies, in particular Finland and the Netherlands, would agree. But not Southern European countries. In the end, Germany's hegemonic governance is likely to lose out in the legitimacy contest, if only because rather than paying a larger share of the costs like a true hegemon, it made the weaker countries pay. Additionally, rather than ensuring all countries' best interests, the economic governance processes championed by Germany and its Northern European coalitional allies benefited them the most, to the detriment not just of Southern Europe but of the EU as a whole, when judged by the negative spillover effects on output and input legitimacy.

Council Governance as Mutually Accountable "Deliberative Body"

So was Germany really at the head of a Council dictatorship in the Eurozone crisis, benefiting from its power through (traditional intergovernmental) bargaining to delay any decisions until almost too late and then to impose its own ideas and interests with regard to Eurozone governing by rules and numbers? Or could we instead see what went on as more like (new intergovernmental) deliberative consensus-seeking in the shadow of Germany—and thus more throughput legitimate because it involved mutually accountable processes of deliberation, in which the ideational power of persuasion is more in play than the coercive power of simple *diktats*?

Deliberative Mutual Accountability in the Council

For Council decision-making to be considered mutually accountable deliberation rather than dictatorship, German leaders would have had to have gotten their way through ongoing discursive processes of persuasion rather than coercive imposition, and would have had at the same time to have been open to persuasion and accommodation in a process of consensus-seeking. The evidence for this can be found not only in the persuasive powers German leaders deployed at the beginning of the crisis when they got all member-state leaders to buy into the stability rules, but also in their own accommodation (however reluctant) to alternative views over time. Although German leaders kept insisting that the stability rules would not change, they nonetheless agreed to their reinterpretation to accommodate demands first for growth, then flexibility, and after that investment.

But for mutual accountability to operate deliberatively, an appropriate forum is also necessary. For the Eurozone crisis, although the Eurogroup of Finance Ministers already existed, there was no clearly constituted forum for member-state leaders of euro-area members to meet to deliberate on their own. Sarkozy created such a forum at the highest level in 2008 when he called an informal meeting of the euro-area heads of state and government, much to the displeasure of non-euro-area member states. There were no such objections in the first half of 2010, as the Eurozone crisis gained momentum, when European Council President Herman Van Rompuy began convening informal euro-area meetings at the fringes of regular European Council meetings. By October 2011, those meetings were formalized as the Euro Summit. As a result, there were now two mutual accountability forums: the Eurogroup of Finance Ministers, to deal with the day-to-day management of euro-area affairs, and the Euro Summit, to deal with the "big" issues involving financial assistance and the tightening of budgetary policy coordination.[64] Both forums, as Uwe Puetter explains, involved "processes of intensive intergovernmental policy deliberation" which, having developed initially at the lower level via the Eurogroup, then spread to the highest level with the need for the "constant generation of political consensus on particular policy measures among the heads [because] several of these decisions touched on the very existence of the euro area and, indeed, the fate of individual national governments."[65]

Such intensive intergovernmental policy deliberation can be seen in the Council approval process of the Commission's country-specific recommendations in the European Semester. In the Macroeconomic Imbalance Procedure (MIP), for example, once the Commission makes its recommendations (developed through an elaborate consultation process with national capitals, expert

---

[64] Puetter 2014, pp. 126–33.   [65] Puetter 2014, p. 132.

consultants, and internal Commission officials), a range of Council advisory committees such as the Economic Policy Committee or the Employment Committee discusses those recommendations and may propose amendments, after which ministers make their decisions in their Council formations. As a result, assessments come out of the collective agreements of member-state representatives, which also means that they are likely to put pressure on one another to comply with recommendations or legitimate why they have not.[66] There is some debate here as to whether the recommendations themselves tended to privilege economic policy decisions over social policy ones, given the asymmetrical influence of finance ministers in comparison with their counterparts in the Employment, Social Policy, Health and Consumer Affairs Council;[67] or not, in view of the growing preponderance of social policy recommendations in the Country Specific Reports (CSRs).[68] But whatever the interpretation, the deliberative processes in Council committees and meetings can be seen to serve as mutual accountability forums, with European Council and Eurogroup adoption of Commission recommendations a kind of stamp of approval.

For Germany's deliberative powers of persuasion, then, the Euro Summit and the European Council are where to assess Chancellor Merkel's persuasive abilities and deliberative accountability, just as the Eurogroup is the place to consider those of Finance Minister Schäuble. These persuasive powers were fully in evidence at the beginning of the crisis. Chancellor Merkel was intent on convincing all and sundry of the necessity and appropriateness of her own ideas about EMU governance, as not only the best but also the most legitimate way of solving the crisis. In the process, Merkel repeatedly invoked not only the ordoliberal mantra that following the rules was the way out of the crisis but also the neoliberal mantra that the rules themselves were needed to improve competitiveness.[69] To take just one example, in a press conference after a 2011 Council meeting, the word competitiveness appeared no fewer than three times in one of her sentences: "As a matter of fact, and this has been acknowledged everywhere, the competitiveness of the various Euro-countries is different, and we are helping ourselves to become the most competitive region in the world if we pay attention to the strengthening and the improvement of our overall competitiveness."[70] Schäuble not only backed up his Chancellor on these issues, he also generated his own arguments, including his early push to end fiscal stimulus, his insistence on the dangers of excessive state spending, his proposal for a European Monetary Fund (in an op-ed in 2010),[71] and his raising the possibility of Greek exit from the euro in the context of the third Greek bailout negotiations in 2015—at the same time that he expounded on the virtues of the *schwarze null*, the zero deficit, for Germany.

[66] Bokhorst 2019.   [67] Maricut and Puetter 2017.
[68] Zeitlin and Vanhercke 2014, 2018.   [69] See Crespy and Schmidt 2014.
[70] Council Meeting, February 4, 2011.   [71] *New York Times* March 9, 2010.

But even as German leaders were actively seeking to persuade other member-state leaders to accept their ideas, they were also willing to listen, and to compromise enough so as to forge consensus. We should not forget that German member-state leaders also changed their positions in response to pressures from fellow member states, from other EU institutional actors, and from internal German political actors, in particular the opposition Social Democrats, especially when they were part of grand coalition governments.[72] And naturally, Germany was not the only member state promoting its particular set of ideas, nor the only one appealing only to its own electoral constituencies in so doing.

Germany's main cheerleaders in Council meetings were the Finns and the Dutch. They were, if anything, even more convinced than the Germans of the need for austerity and structural reform in response to what they saw as the bad behavior of Southern Europeans. This came out ever so clearly not only at the height of the crisis—in the blind belief that austerity would bring growth—but also much later. One such example is Dutch Finance Minister Jeroen Dijsselboem, a lame duck after his party's defeat in national elections in 2017 but still in his position as head of the Eurogroup, who stated: "As a Social Democrat, I attribute exceptional importance to solidarity. [But] you also have obligations. You cannot spend all the money on drinks and women and then ask for help." Dijsselboem was greeted by a firestorm of criticism, but refused to apologize.[73]

In the various Greek bailouts, there were also Central and Eastern European leaders who saw Greece not so much as the profligate cousin as the richer one. In the second bailout, for example, the Slovakian government fell over internal divisions precipitated by the extreme right fourth member of the coalition government which rejected any bailout, while the Finnish government insisted on collateral from Greece for its participation, pushed by the extreme right Finns party.

In the end, even Sarkozy turned out to be perfectly willing to agree to a *quid pro quo* in which a rescue plan would be accompanied by an austerity program along with the "golden rule" for budgetary discipline (or debt brake) contained in the Fiscal Compact. This was not only more in line with the ideas of his own center right constituency; it also conveniently served to embarrass the opposition Socialists.[74] Sarkozy had himself begun advocating introducing the "golden rule" into the French Constitution in early 2010. Evidence of his persuasive power in this instance comes from that fact that in August 2011, a poll confirmed that one in two of the French approved the measure.[75] Subsequently, even President Hollande toed the line on sticking to the stability rules, in contradiction to his election campaign promises, insisting that France needed to regain economic

---

[72] Jacoby 2015.   [73] *Financial Times* March 21, 2017.
[74] Crespy and Schmidt 2014.   [75] *Le Point* August 25, 2011.

credibility before it could be credible enough to push for a change in rules.[76] In Hollande's case, however, he did not seek to convince the French public of the legitimacy of his acquiescence to the rules or his about-face on austerity, and paid the electoral price.

We should note in passing that a similar fate befell Emmanuel Macron, elected French President in 2017. He also bet that implementing domestic reforms to make France "more like Germany" would help to restore France's "credibility," and that this in turn would enable him to get the Germans to agree to his ambitious EU-level reform proposals. This strategy failed miserably both at the national level, where his popularity plummeted, and at the EU level, where Germany and its coalitional allies continued to stymie his ambitions.[77]

Germany's outsize persuasive power, in short, also lies in the political coalitions constructed with it and around it, to push forward its agenda in deliberations in which it has managed to persuade other member states that its own position is the correct one. But if we left it just to the discourse, then we could not be certain that the deliberations consisted of mutual accountability forums, or were even deliberation at all in the shadow of German power.

The Council's Interactive Processes of Deliberative Accountability

The proof that deliberative persuasion rather than dictatorial imposition occurs comes where discursive interactions can be shown to involve not just listening but also accommodating the other side or accepting a failure to persuade. On both counts—accommodation and failed persuasion—Council deliberation can be confirmed, in particular once the crisis slowed after 2012. This is when the European Council's discourse gradually shifted from an exclusive focus on maintaining stability and strict adherence to the rules to one that by 2012 admitted that "growth" was important and, by 2014, that even "flexibility" was acceptable, with the need for "investment" following shortly thereafter, with the appointment of the new Commission in 2015. It is also when Council President Herman van Rompuy launched his 2013 initiative on the Social Dimension of EMU, accompanied by a declaration of EU Social and Employment Ministers demanding a rebalancing of the European Semester. This in turn contributed to an enhanced role for the Commission directorates involved in social and employment policy relative to their economic policy counterparts.[78] At the same time, German attempts to persuade other member states of the value of adding even more stringent conditions to the rules failed.

---

[76] Glencross 2018.   [77] See Crespy 2018.
[78] Zeitlin and Vanhercke 2014, 2018. See also discussion in Chapter 7 on the Commission.

An example of failure in "German" persuasion efforts was a proposal introduced in the "Four Presidents" report of December 2012[79] and reinforced by a joint letter from French and German leaders in May 2013 calling for "contracts" signed between member states and the Commission (with buy-in from national parliaments), pledging even more binding adherence to the rules as well as structural reform where deemed necessary. By December 2013, however, the European Council had rebuffed Merkel's continued push for such contracts on the grounds that the incentives were paltry and the approach counterproductive, even though the discussion revived briefly in spring 2014. Equally significant is the fact that banking union, pushed by the ECB and the Commission, was agreed by the Council in 2012 in the face of German resistance (in particular from the Bundesbank).[80]

Evidence for deliberative accountability as a result of taking into account divergent views came most notably in 2012 and thereafter. Growth entered the discourse toward the end of 2011. As the EU economy continued to deteriorate while national politics became increasingly volatile—as populist parties grew, incumbent governments were defeated, and weak countries fell like dominoes under market attack—the political dynamics among member-state leaders in the Council began changing. Growing contestation of the ordoliberal orthodoxy and the stability rules led to Council deliberations that produced changes in the discourse and the application of the rules.

In Italy, the replacement of Italian Prime Minister Silvio Berlusconi with the "technical" Prime Minister Mario Monti in November 2011 was significant not just for Italy—by making it almost immediately more credible with the markets— but also for the EU, because he was the first member-state leader to challenge ordoliberal orthodoxy by arguing for growth. At the EU level, Monti promised to implement austerity and structural reform in Italy, but in exchange he pushed EU leaders to promote growth. In Italy, he engaged in a much more positive communicative discourse about the EU, claiming, for instance: "You will never hear me ask for a sacrifice because Europe asks for it, just as you will never hear me blame Europe for things that we should do and that are unpopular."[81] But Monti was equally persuasive, at least initially, in speaking to the markets, to the people, and to EU leaders all at the same time. In his end-of-year 2011 press conference he spoke to the Germans, by describing himself as the "most German of Italian economists"; to the markets, by claiming that Italy was now moving with the winds behind it "to the north-west, towards Brussels and far from Greece"; and to fellow EU leaders, as he insisted that "the turbulence is absolutely not over" and that more had to be done.[82] That discourse worked with the markets,

---

[79] Van Rompuy et al. 2012.   [80] Spiegel 2014; de Rynck 2016; Dehousse 2016.
[81] *New York Times* Dec. 5, 2011.   [82] *Financial Times* Dec. 29, 2011.

bringing the spread back down to sustainable levels. But his policies proved very unpopular in Italy.

In France, the Socialist presidential candidate, François Hollande, took up Monti's rallying cry in his campaign in early 2012. Once elected President, Hollande pushed further for growth in meetings of the European Council, while Monti continued his pressure—even as both instituted austerity programs at home. The result was a lot more talk of growth—in contrast to the stability discourse—although little was actually done by the Council to change the rules. Nonetheless, political communication had changed. Most notably, the staunch supporter of stability herself, Chancellor Merkel, now talked of the importance of growth *and* stability—by 2013 even using it in her re-election campaign (in which austerity had disappeared completely, although "staying competitive" remained the mantra).[83] Importantly, this discursive support for growth was a message taken to heart by the Commission in its oversight function, and was most evident in its granting exceptions to the rules and recalibrating the numbers—much to the very vocal irritation of Northern European finance ministers in the Eurogroup. Equally important for the Commission was Herman van Rompuy's 2013 initiative on the Social Dimension of EMU (requested by the European Council of December 2012). It helped spur EU Social and Employment Ministers to demand the rebalancing of European Semester governance to include more social content, with an enhanced role for their directorates-general, which occurred from 2013 on.[84]

In 2014 a new discourse appeared, focused on flexibility in the application of the rules, accompanied by an intensification of the discussion of growth. This time, the new Italian Prime Minister, Matteo Renzi—emboldened by the impressive 40 percent score of his newly created *Partito Democratico* (PD) in the European Parliamentary elections—came to Brussels with demands for greater flexibility in the application of the rules, which were echoed by Hollande. Renzi pushed for greater flexibility from the EU while reiterating the need for growth and criticizing the stability rules as he argued: "we certainly have to call into question the Maastricht treaty because the [3 percent deficit] is based on a model in which Europe's economy was growing, and now it isn't any more." At the same time, his European commissioner Antonio Tajani declared that he would press to allow Italy to breach EU budget commitments as had Germany in 2003 (which was like waving a red flag in front of a bull, given the German narrative that this was the source of the problem in the first place).[85] This verbal contestation of the rules came in tandem with pledges to follow the rules. Even as Renzi criticized the "stupidity pact" (echoing Romani Prodi's famous line in the late 1990s) in his communicative discourse to the public, he promised to undertake major

---

[83] *New York Times* Sept. 14, 2013.   [84] Zeitlin and Vanhercke 2014, 2018.
[85] *Financial Times* February 18, 2014.

structural reforms of Italian labor markets, its tax system, and more.[86] But in exchange he expected that Italy be able to invest.

The upshot of the confrontation was that Renzi and Hollande won modest concessions that marginally violated the rules on austerity. But Merkel also won by ensuring that they too had to make modest concessions toward greater austerity. As a result, again with much hesitation and political contestation, Merkel added flexibility to the discourse, on condition that it remained "within the stability rules." As Merkel explained in summer 2014 (in a speech to the Bundestag), there was no need to change the rules since the Stability and Growth Pact already contained all the necessary flexibility.[87] But this lent even further support to the Commission's reinterpretations of the rules, for which it had come under even more fire from Northern European finance ministers in the Eurogroup for overstepping its authority.[88]

During this same time period, behind the scenes, Renzi had also pushed for investment to be a major priority for the new Commission—something he is said to have made conditional on his support for the new Commission President, Jean-Claude Juncker.[89] And in fact, with the new Commission in 2015, investment did indeed become a major new part of Council discourse *and* policy.

Thus, by 2015, the Council's "one size fits one" governance had been softening even as contestation continued, with Southern Europe and France pressing for greater flexibility and Northern European leaders pushing for continued discipline. Indeed, the Euro Summit no longer met as frequently once the initial turmoil between 2010 and 2012, and then the 2015 third Greek bailout, had passed. Skirmishes continued, but were no longer a major source of tension except occasionally, as when the Italian populist coalition government consisting of the League and Five-Star parties proposed a deficit-busting budget in fall 2018. But even here, this was not a question for the Euro Summit but rather a matter of discussion in the Eurogroup, of action by the Commission. After a short wrangle, however, with the Commission giving a little and the Italian government a little, the problem went away, with only the Germans complaining, yet again, that the rules were not being respected. A similar scenario played out in summer 2019, when the Commission threatened to open an Excessive Deficit Procedure (EDP) against the Italian government but then delayed judgment until the fall of 2019— at which point a new coalition government of the PD and the Five Star successfully negotiated on the issue.

By the time Emmanuel Macron became French President in 2017, the discourse had shifted to the question of how to complete the Eurozone's architecture,

---

[86] Picot and Tassinari 2017.   [87] *Reuters* June 18, 2014.   [88] Schmidt 2016a.
[89] Interview with author, high-level Italian member of the European Parliament, September 30, 2015.

with the missing elements of the banking union, a Finance Minister with a budget for investment, and more. But Germany hesitated, with Merkel feeling more constrained by internal politics, including the rise of the Alternative for Germany (AfD) and challenges from the Christian Social Union (CSU) on migration policy. Italy had not helped matters, with the populist coalition government in 2018 having proposed a potentially rules-busting budget. The upshot was that little further progress was made in the Council with regard to resolving the continuing vulnerabilities of the Eurozone.

Council Governance as Harsh Dictatorship or Deliberative Authoritarianism in Program Countries?

The Council's action with regard to program countries was different. Although one may be torn between seeing the Council as a dictatorship or a deliberative body for regular (non-program) countries, in particular after 2012, Council actions with regard to program countries were highly problematic across time, especially when it comes to the role of the Eurogroup of Finance Ministers. As already discussed, accountability was flawed at best, given Council members imposing their "remedies" in the form of harsh austerity and structural reform on program countries in exchange for bailouts. The question would be whether to label such Council governance harsh dictatorship, because of the coercive power exercised over vulnerable member states, or authoritarian deliberation, given that member-state leaders did deliberate about their policy impositions in the Euro Summit as well as in the Eurogroup. Transparency was equally in question, with secrecy sometimes used not so much to better manage the crisis as to exploit the crisis situation to gain concessions otherwise impossible if made public. Inclusiveness and openness were also missing from negotiations that went from the top down, with minimal consultation of national parliaments and none with those groups most negatively affected by the policies, such as workers, pensioners, the poor, and the ailing.

To assess the procedural legitimacy of Council governance of program countries, we need to distinguish between Council governance in the formulation and negotiation of the policies—which takes place at the EU level in the general context of Council meetings, whether in the European Council, the Euro Summit, or the Eurogroup of Finance Ministers—and the implementation of those policies. At the implementation stage, most significant is the role the Eurogroup played in directing the actions of the Troika (later called "Institutions" to soften the image and account for the fact that the ESM was also included). But how the program countries responded is also significant, in particular with regard to whether they were perceived as having taken "ownership" of the national process.

National "Ownership" and Accountability

With regard to procedural legitimacy of the conditionality programs for the countries needing bailouts, "ownership" was a key concept. Ownership could be understood as a measure of the accountability a national government felt with regard to the procedural legitimacy of its "giving accounts" to the Troika. And where governments "took ownership" of their program, the governance processes could be seen as instances of deliberative authoritarianism. This was largely the case for Ireland, Portugal, and Cyprus, even though there were varying degrees of buy-in from key national institutional players such as the parliament and constitutional court, as well as the citizens. Each of these countries was subject to a program that lasted three years (Ireland's from December 2010 to December 2013, Portugal's from May 2011 to June 2014, and Cyprus' from May 2013 to March 2016). In Greece, in contrast, none of its successive governments took ownership, with national players generally experiencing the governance processes as harsh dictatorship. The country was subject to three programs lasting eight years (the first bailout starting in May 2010, the second in 2012, and the third running from August 2015 to August 2018, with continued enhanced surveillance thereafter).

Ireland, for one, took full ownership of its program. Not only did the government commit itself to harsh austerity and structural reform but also the citizens largely acquiesced, with no substantial opposition from potential veto players. The Irish blamed themselves for the crisis because "we all partied," and therefore accepted the "bitter medicine" without significant protest.[90] An editorial in the *Irish Times* said it all when, after asking whether Ireland's long fight for independence was for naught because it had surrendered to the Troika, it stated that "the true ignominy of our current situation is not that our sovereignty has been taken away from us, it is that we ourselves have squandered it" and that responsibility lay with "the incompetence of the governments we ourselves elected."[91]

In Portugal and Cyprus, in contrast, governments took ownership of the reform program but met with stiff opposition not only from citizens but also institutional veto players, including the courts and national parliaments. These governments nevertheless managed to overcome opposition to program implementation by way of coercive strategies that included using pressures coming from the Troika (eg, withholding the next tranche of credit) and fears of the costs of non-agreement.[92] In Portugal, for example, the government of Prime Minister Pedro Passos Coelho, elected in June 2011 with a substantial parliamentary majority and a strong consensus that the costs of non-agreement would be very

---

[90] See, eg, Kiersey 2018.
[91] *Irish Times*, November 18, 2010, cited in Tooze 2018, p. 362.
[92] Lütz et al. 2019.

high, was able to act swiftly and decisively on a bailout that it saw not "as a hostile act but as an unfortunate necessity."[93] Government success had much to do with its ability to legitimate its policy imposition with a depoliticizing narrative that insisted that there was no alternative,[94] and to contrast the problems of Greece with its own performance. It cast itself as "the good pupil" of austerity, which had learned its lesson and implemented the necessary policies with little fuss or delay.[95] Popular mobilization against austerity was very high in the first two years, but largely ignored and/or suppressed.[96] By 2012 and 2013, however, the government was encountering greater difficulty in fulfilling the terms of the Memorandum of Understanding (MOU) because the constitutional court struck down a number of measures for which it had increasing difficulty finding substitute legislation. But by then the pressures from the markets had eased off, and the country soon thereafter exited its loan-bailout program.[97]

In the case of Greece, governments' repeated failure to take ownership of the successive loan-bailout programs was a result not only of their lack of commitment but also of major opposition by the parliament, the court, and the citizens. All saw Greece as the victim of harsh dictatorship on the part of the EU, given a loan-bailout program that was bound to fail—as the IMF itself conceded in 2013—because it provided no debt relief and a loan at too high interest rates, with almost all the money from the loans going to debt repayment, not to people in need. *And* austerity went on and on! Evidence of the lack of government ownership—and the Troika's concomitant loss of trust in the country—can even be seen in the evolution of the oversight process. In comparing the programs, André Sapir and colleagues found that only in the Greek case did the program become more stringent over time. By 2014, it had many more pages setting out its two programs than any of the other countries under conditionality (1800 versus around 1000 for Portugal, more than 900 for Ireland, and 400 for Cyprus). And it was the only program country that was subject to a greater specificity in the detail of its required reforms over time.[98] To be fair, however, that specificity was not just focused on draconian cuts at any cost, as is often assumed. For example, the second bailout package did call for the Greek government to ensure that the burden of consolidation did not fall on the most vulnerable, while the third bailout package included recommendations for a guaranteed minimum income and universal access to health care, delinked from employment status. The fact that such recommendations were not fully implemented suggests that national governments also share the blame, since they often took the route of political expediency to the detriment of social justice.[99]

---

[93] Lütz et al. 2019.   [94] Standring 2018.
[95] Magone 2014, p. 353; see also Standring 2018.   [96] Accornero and Pinto, 2015.
[97] Lütz et al. 2019.   [98] Sapir et al. 2014.
[99] Siani-Davies 2017; Perez and Matsaganis 2017; Featherstone 2011; see also discussion in Chapter 9 on austerity and structural reform policies in the periphery.

Anecdotal accounts of why the programs turned out so differently among countries under conditionality suggest that the problems were due not only to variations in national responses but also to the people involved "on the ground" on the side of the Troika. By all accounts, the personalities engaged in the national-level implementation were seen as more rigidly "orthodox" in their economic prescriptions for Greece than in the other member states. This counts not just for the representatives of the Commission—who in any case had to follow the orders of the Eurogroup—but also for the representatives of the ECB and the IMF.[100] The communicative discourse of senior EU (and IMF) officials prior to and during the Greek crisis from 2008 up to the arrival in power of the Syriza government in January 2015, as detailed by Dimitris Papadimitriou and colleagues in a discursive institutionalist study of their pronouncements, shows that distrust also colored EU leaders' views of Greece. The narrative frames went from "suspicious cooperation" between May 2010 and October 2011 to "blame" from November 2011 through June 2012 and then "reluctant redemption" from June 2012 to January 2015.[101] And of course, once the Syriza government came in, the distrust only deepened.

In the third Greek bailout in 2015, a range of additional factors came into play. Most significant, first of all, was the fact that an extreme left populist government had been elected promising to stop austerity and to negotiate a better deal. Equally significant was that it had no certain political allies among mainstream Council leaders, although it had counted on the center left for support. Also making for difficulties were the personalities involved, and in particular the new Greek Finance Minister Yanis Varoufakis, who came into conflict with German Finance Minister Wolfgang Schäuble, as a matter of (arrogant) style as well as radical (for the Germans) policy proposals. Additionally complicating matters was the fact that the European Stability Mechanism was now involved in the negotiations, which had by now replaced the EFSF and the Troika as the main institutional lender.

In this new institutional context, negotiations went from a purely intergovernmental, *ad hoc* process in which Eurozone leaders agreed on bailouts to one in which national legislatures could be directly involved in the approval of rescue packages by the ESM. As Manuella Moschella explains, negotiations were radicalized (to the detriment of Greece) in large measure because the German Bundestag now had to vote both *ex ante* (on starting negotiations) and *ex post* (on the outcome of negotiations). Conservative German legislators who were loath to provide Greece with another bailout had the power to block not just the end

---

[100] There is a big difference between the research branch, quick to admit error, and the operations branch, which was as implacable as the Eurogroup and the ESM, although its demands differed somewhat from theirs. See discussion in Chapter 6 on the ECB/IMF comparisons.

[101] Papadimitriou et al. 2019.

agreement but even the start of negotiations, and used that power to force Chancellor Merkel to take a much harder line than she might have. As a result, unlike in 2012, when Merkel opposed her Finance Minister's push for Grexit, she now backed his proposed five-year time-out from the Eurozone for Greece (as an "organized Grexit") in front of the Bundestag.[102] That hardened stance made for discontent among the creditor member states in the negotiations, including France, which wanted to keep Greece in the Eurozone, and Finland, which had initially backed Germany.[103] The end product, according to the *Financial Times*, was "the most intrusive economic supervision programme ever mounted in the EU."[104]

But beyond the problems of accountability were those of input legitimacy. As Manuela Moschella argues, national parliaments' involvement in the ESM has done the reverse of what might be expected when EU affairs are brought to the domestic level so as to legitimize them, because "it is not EU policy that is 'domesticated' but (some) domestic politics are elevated to EU-level policy."[105] The result was that the domestic legislature of one member state (Germany) largely dictated the bailout terms for another member state (Greece) whose legislature had no real say in the process.

Council Secrecy as Crisis Management or Crisis Exploitation?

Transparency was also at issue with the loan-bailout programs, and necessarily so given the formal secrecy of all Council meetings, including those of the Eurogroup. But here, we need to go back to Kreuder-Sonnen's very useful distinction between crisis management, where the secrecy of deliberations is deemed vital to manage the public's perception of threat while avoiding further deterioration of the situation, and crisis exploitation.[106] Secrecy as part of crisis management was very much in play in the behind-the-scenes negotiations prior to the first Greek bailout as well as in the creation of the "group that doesn't exist," set up to consider how to deal with the dangers of contagion and made up of senior French and German officials along with representatives of the Commission, the ECB, and the office of the Eurogroup President.[107] It was seen as necessary for impression management, to keep the markets from panicking, and so to protect the countries most at risk by avoiding any further deterioration of the situation as a result of unfiltered or poorly timed information.[108] As such, it can largely be

---

[102] Moschella 2017b, pp. 254–6.   [103] Moschella 2017b, pp. 256–7.

[104] *Financial Times* July 13, 2015, cited in Moschella 2017b, p. 253.

[105] Moschella 2017b, p. 242.

[106] Kreuder-Sonnen 2018b, Kreuder-Sonnen 2019b; see also discussion in Chapter 2.

[107] *Wall Street Journal*, September 24, 2010—cited in Kreuder-Sonnen 2018b, p. 968.

[108] Kreuder-Sonnen 2018b, pp. 968–9; see also Kreuder-Sonnen 2019b.

deemed procedurally legitimate, with the lack of transparency balanced out by the beneficial results as output legitimacy.

Another instance of secrecy as crisis management for purposes of ensuring positive outcomes is the case of the European Stability Mechanism (ESM). As we have already seen, it acts as a quasi-monetary fund and began operation in 2013 as the permanent follow-up mechanism to the EFSF, the mandate of which is to provide financial assistance to European sovereigns and financial systems in distress. It makes its decisions for lending to countries in need of bailout in complete secrecy, on the grounds that transparency would hurt the very countries it sought to help. The trade-off here is between throughput transparency and output performance, since making clear the ESM's assessment of the country's needs could give investors incentives to make money from taking positions against the debtor countries that the ESM is trying to assist.[109] That secrecy is also meant to ensure that the ESM, as a new financial assistance fund, maintains credibility in the markets, which in turn hinges on the continued support of the states whose bond market reputation backs the ESM, that is, those with the highest market credibility (eg, Germany and the Netherlands). This means that accompanying the secrecy promoting good crisis management is a narrow kind of accountability to the creditor states, and to its board of governors, the Eurogroup of Finance Ministers, whose voting privileges are proportional to their debt exposure as members of the ESM. But this latter kind of legitimation for secrecy also brings with it dangers of crisis exploitation, in particular because of the strong position of creditor nations in the Eurogroup.[110]

Crisis exploitation is when authority holders use a crisis to present their policies as necessary while eschewing the normal standards of evidentiary reasoning, often in order to impose policies that would not be politically possible otherwise. This was in play in the case of the Eurogroup of Finance Ministers, as the effective decision-making body of the ESM, which operates as an informal body outside the EU legal framework and therefore with legally unregulated executive discretion. And with no judicial review by the Court of Justice of the European Union (CJEU), it is obligated to give accounts to no one. In consequence, it can delegate authority to the Troika to impose strict fiscal conditionality and to demand and monitor far-reaching reforms.[111]

In practice, the Eurogroup via the ESM has generally instructed the Troika to present its demands on a take-it-or-leave-it basis, where taking it meant accepting *diktats* that subjected national executives to its legislative tutelage, while relegating national parliaments to the role of rubber stamps.[112] Under the cover of secrecy, moreover, the Eurogroup informally instructed the Troika to implement their

[109] Ban and Seabrooke 2017; Ban and Schmidt 2017.
[110] Ban and Seabrooke 2017; Ban and Schmidt 2017.
[111] Kreuder-Sonnen 2018a, p. 457.   [112] Kuo 2014, p. 85.

demands without taking any of the responsibility—indeed, making it appear through their public communications that the technocrats were the ones calling the shots, making expertise-related decisions for which there were no alternatives (TINA).[113]

As such, procedural legitimacy was in question in the many loan bailouts as a result of the lack of transparency as well as accountability—not to mention the lack of policy effectiveness (output). Even if one were to defend the Troika or 'Institutions' in the bailouts in output terms, by pointing to the social content of its recommendations—for example, its call in the second Greek bailout package to ensure that the burden of consolidation did not fall on the most vulnerable, or its mandate in the third Greek bailout to establish a guaranteed minimum income and universal access to health[114]—throughput legitimacy with regard to the negotiation process remained in question. In the case of Greece, as Martin Sandbu of the *Financial Times* put it, such Troika policies constituted the "tyranny of technocracy" which served to "infantilize the Greek body politic" with its mandatory cuts in public services and reform measures in the labor market and sheltered services sectors.[115]

Greek Bailouts as Harsh Dictatorship or Deliberative Authoritarianism?

Finally, in particular in the case of Greece, our main question remains whether the negotiations met the requirements of procedural accountability. And here, the only real question is whether the negotiations represented harsh dictatorship or deliberative authoritarianism.

Deliberative authoritarianism could be applied to many aspects of the negotiations surrounding Greek governments' referenda-related decisions, because Greek leaders were in constant dialogue with other member-state leaders, and acquiesced to their demands. For example, when Greek social democratic Prime Minister Papandreou retracted his call for a referendum on the bailout package, he felt forced to do so in response to an "outpouring of anger" from other EU political leaders.[116] As French President Sarkozy recounted in a BBC interview, he told Papandreou that

> if you want to hold a referendum, hold one, but on whether you the Greeks want to stay in or leave the EU...But you can't hold a referendum on whether the measures agreed in the program are good or not. That would mean that 9 million Greeks could decide against 450 million Europeans. That's not acceptable.[117]

---

[113] Kreuder-Sonnen 2019b.   [114] Thanks to Jonathan Zeitlin for this point.
[115] Sandbu 2015, p. 130.   [116] Spiegel 2014; see also Moschella 2017b, p. 250.
[117] BBC 2019.

Sarkozy's remarks highlight a fundamental dilemma for the EU as a result of its split-level legitimacy. In re-enfranchising the Greek public, Papandreou would singlehandedly have been disenfranchising the greater public of Eurozone countries for whom the fate of the euro itself was likely to depend on the outcome of the Greek referendum.[118]

A similar dilemma faced the extreme left Prime Minister Tsipras in the 2015 bailout, when he held a referendum on the third bailout package that required continued harsh austerity, and got the resounding "no" vote for which he himself had campaigned. But that very night, Tsipras realized that he had no alternative other than to accept the package or risk default, and capitulated. Council President Donald Tusk recounts that he told Tsipras prior to the referendum that he should "be aware that other prime ministers, they can organize their own referenda on one question: Would you like to pay the Greek bill? Imagine the result...You will find yourself with your referendum in deep shit."[119] What is more, right after the referendum vote, as Yanis Varoufakis, the short-lived Finance Minister in the first Syriza government, tells it, Tsipras, flush with victory, spoke by phone with President Hollande, who told him: "You won, but Greece has lost. And the risk now is that those who never wanted Greece to stay in the Eurozone will decide at the next EU Summit to push Greece out. Do you want to stay in the Euro?" Tsipras' response was yes, and later that evening he announced that he would go back to the negotiating table. This was the moment that Varoufakis resigned as Finance Minister on the grounds that "we were elected to challenge a program that failed and put our people in debtor's prison and destroyed the prospects of a whole generation."[120]

While for Tsipras we could argue that the negotiations may have constituted deliberative authoritarianism, for Varoufakis there is no doubt that the negotiation processes in all the bailouts constituted a harsh dictatorship, and an inefficient and unaccountable one at that. He described the process beginning with the 2010 negotiations as "fiscal waterboarding" because of the way in which Greek governments were starved of liquidity each time up to the very last minute, while being banned from defaulting on creditors, so that

> Instead of confessions, they were forced to sign further loan agreements...Exactly like waterboarding, the liquidity provided was calculated to be just enough to keep the subject going without defaulting formally, but never more than that. And so the torture continued with the government kept completely under the troika's control.[121]

Varoufakis' dramatic account of what went on in Council negotiations suggests that Germany ganged up on Greece while the other member states were cowed

---

[118] Dehousse 2011a.   [119] BBC 2019.
[120] BBC 2019.   [121] Varoufakis 2016, pp. 160–1.

into submission, and time after time imposed requirements without listening to Greek leaders' concerns and without taking account of the consequences of their demands on Greek citizens, as suicide rates went up along with the general immiseration of the population.[122]

A whole raft of scholars and even EU Commission officials support Varoufakis' view of the negotiations. Christian Joerges has no doubt that "this exercise of authority is neither based upon democratic process, nor upon an exchange of reasons among equals; this is an authoritarian type of rule characterised by the kind of decision-making which Carl Schmitt foresaw and asked for in a state of emergency."[123] In addition, Pierre Moscovici, Commissioner of the Directorate General for Economic and Financial Affairs (DG ECFIN), minced no words in September 2015 in criticizing the third Greek crisis Eurogroup negotiations on legitimacy grounds, stating that "its decisions do not have a face to them...(and) a decision without a face is a decision for which no one is accountable." He added that the Eurogroup "organises the debate among national interests rather than fostering the emergence of a common interest in the euro area. This is not effective and it most certainly is not democratic."[124]

Not all commentators have been so critical with regard to the EU Council or the Eurogroup, of course. On the eve of the Greek referendum vote, EU Council President Donald Tusk claimed in an interview: "For sure, it's not a black and white story...Maybe the biggest mistake, but I'm not talking only about Greece, was this blame game, the political game between creditors and Greece. Nobody here is an angel."[125] In that "game," moreover, the Greek government made a serious miscalculation when it thought it held the trump card: fear of the contagion effects of "Grexit."

The "Greek tragedy" that unfolded over the course of the spring and summer of 2015 resulted from the Syriza government's misjudgment of the "game" that was being played, in particular between Greek Finance Minister Yannis Varoufakis and German Finance Minister Schäuble, who turned out to be the "master gambler."[126] Varoufakis, himself an economist with a specialization in game theory, thought that he held the trump card, believing that the member states' greatest fear would be the destabilization resulting from a Greek exit from the Eurozone. But neither he nor the Greek Prime Minister Alexis Tsipras had bargained on Schäuble's calling their bluff. Schäuble had his ministry leak an informal paper to *Die Welt am Sonntag* arguing for a temporary "Grexit" just after the Greek referendum and in the middle of a EU finance ministers' meeting in Brussels. Even before this, however, Greek leaders had not expected center left and Southern European member-state leaders' refusal to concede much to the Greek push for an end to austerity beginning in February 2015.[127]

---

[122] Varoufakis 2017.   [123] Joerges 2014, p. 34, cited in Kreuder-Sonnen 2018a.
[124] Moscovici 2015.   [125] *Politico* July 3, 2015.   [126] Sauerbrey 2015.
[127] Featherstone 2016.

That expectation was arguably politically naïve, since the Greek government was not simply asking EU member states to take on board another member state's democratic vote to end its adjustment program. It was asking Eurozone finance ministers to suspend the EU rules on austerity and structural reform, agreed by all, which those very ministers had been applying in their own countries. It was not just the Irish and the Portuguese, who had recently exited adjustment programs, who refused to let Greece off the hook. It was even the Italians and the French, who had been clamoring for increased flexibility in the application of the rules, but who were equally engaged in pushing reforms in their own countries. To give Greece a break would be to open up debate in their own countries on past and present conditionality programs. Moreover, supporting a hard left government's demands was not only politically risky from the point of view of center left leaders, and politically out of the question for center right leaders; it could also have fueled electoral support for the populist extremes. Such parties would use any Greek exception to argue for an end to EU-related programs in their own country—in particular for Spain, where Podemos had become a serious threat to the Conservative government of Prime Minister Rajoy. Better to envision Grexit! This was at least the case in the view of German Finance Minister Schäuble, since Grexit no longer carried the economic contagion risk it had back in 2010. As he insisted, in response to Greek Prime Minister Tsipras' claim that he had a democratic mandate to demand change in Europe: "I have also been elected."[128] All of this, as Kevin Featherstone suggests, illustrates the tension between the national exercise of democratic choice and supranational agreements, which "appear imperious and unaccountable."[129]

Conclusion

Council governance in the Eurozone crisis leaves us with the question whether it constituted a largely unaccountable dictatorship under the leadership of Germany or a mutually accountable deliberative body in the shadow of Germany. The answer may be either, depending in some measure on whether one opts for a traditional intergovernmentalist view that centers on the coercive power of member states in Council bargaining or a new intergovernmentalist approach that considers the persuasive power of member states in Council deliberations. The two options are not incompatible. The response to the question "Was one country dominant?" is certainly yes. The response to the alternative question, "Was there a genuine discussion?" is also yes. As for the Council's governance with regard to program countries, here the options are two sides of the same coin, suggesting a

---

[128] *Financial Times* June 15, 2015.   [129] Featherstone 2016, p. 9.

lack of procedural legitimacy, whether as harsh dictatorship or deliberative authoritarianism.

The spillover effects of Council governance on the two other kinds of legitimacy are telling: In terms of output legitimacy, as we will see in Chapter 9, the Council's excessive intergovernmentalism, whether seen as unaccountable dictatorship or mutually accountable deliberation, served to mandate the "one size fits one" policies that produced the Eurozone's comparatively poor macroeconomic performance and deleterious socioeconomic results. With regard to input legitimacy, although the program countries suffered the greatest loss of democratic responsiveness via Troika diktats, non-program countries were also affected, with citizens' displeasure evidenced in the decline of mainstream parties and the rise of populist challengers, as we will see in Chapter 10. But it is also the case that the consequences in terms of input politics on individual member-state democracies has been highly differentiated: while Germany was largely able to ring-fence its own national democracy from the impact of the Eurozone crisis, Greece, under its various bailout agreements, offers the most extreme example of the hollowing out of national democracy.[130]

The only procedurally legitimate way forward for the Council is to give up on the excessive intergovernmentalism of the "one size fits one" rules through which it governed at the height of the crisis, when the Council was characterized mainly by unaccountable dictatorship. Moreover, although legitimacy subsequently improved, as the Council increasingly resembled more of a mutually accountable deliberative body, intergovernmental decision-making remains highly problematic. Procedurally legitimate governance is more likely to be assured where the Council acts in continued consultation with the ECB and/or the Commission and in co-decision with the EP and the Commission. Beyond this, the Council itself is likely to appear not only more throughput accountable but almost more input legitimate were it to become more transparent by engaging in more public debates, however politicized. In other words, the Council needs to become not just a more truly "deliberative body" but also a more communicative one, while overcoming the last vestiges of the seeming "dictatorship" of Germany's "power of one."

---

[130] See, eg, Matthijs 2016, 2017b.

6

The European Central Bank

Hero or Ogre?

At the inception of the Eurozone crisis, the European Central Bank (ECB) took the minimal action necessary to stabilize the euro, leaving it to member-state leaders in the Council to come up with solutions. ECB President Jean-Claude Trichet had a restrictive reading of the bank's mandate. He articulated a legitimizing discourse focused on maintaining the central bank's "credibility," meaning keeping its distance from political leaders, while insisting that it would never become a "lender of last resort" (LOLR). But as the crisis deepened in the absence of effective Council action and in the face of escalating market attacks, the ECB shifted its approach, most dramatically in July 2012 when Trichet's successor, ECB President Mario Draghi, promised to "do whatever it takes" to save the euro. But even before this, the discourse had shifted from a focus on "credibility" to "stability" in order to legitimate increasingly "non-standard" or unconventional monetary policies that moved the bank ever nearer to LOLR status. At the same time, the ECB President coordinated closely with influential political leaders to ensure acceptance of the policies while communicating more effectively to the markets and the public. In this process, the ECB incrementally went from a very narrow understanding of the "one size fits none" rules of its Charter to an increasingly expansive interpretation "by stealth," that is, by proclaiming that it was faithfully following the rules even as it radically reinterpreted them. In other words, the ECB hid its reinterpretation of the rules "in plain view," through a discourse that claimed that everything it did was in keeping with its Charter.

The ECB's discourse and actions, in particular since 2012, made it appear to be the legitimate "hero" of the crisis to all and sundry, in particular in comparison to a fractious Council, a sidelined Commission, and an absent European Parliament (EP). But the *quid pro quo* expected by the ECB, that in exchange for its more expansive monetary policies the member states would agree to austerity and structural reform, instead suggests that the ECB played the role of the unaccountable "ogre" of the crisis. The ECB's push for rapid fiscal consolidation during the fast-burning phase of the crisis, its use of monetary tools and other forms of coercive pressure to push countries in trouble into loan-bailout programs, and its role in the Troika as the champion of socioeconomic cuts that hit program countries particularly hard, together served as a counter to the narrative of heroism.

Europe's Crisis of Legitimacy: Governing by Rules and Ruling by Numbers in the Eurozone. Vivien A. Schmidt, Oxford University Press (2020). © Vivien A. Schmidt.
DOI: 10.1093/oso/9780198797050.001.0001

So how can we assess the legitimacy of the ECB's governance? At the inception of the crisis, we could characterize the ECB's decision-making as one focused mainly on procedural (throughput) legitimacy, with an assumption that a restrictive reading of its mandate and a harsh approach to countries in trouble would ensure its effectiveness and, thereby, Eurozone performance (output legitimacy). But as output performance was increasingly at risk, the ECB, helped by a change in leadership, began to reinterpret its mandate more and more broadly. It sought to legitimate such actions not only through greater communication to the public, often via its reports to the EP, its political accountability forum, but also through informal coordination with member-state leaders, as well as, equally importantly, with the expert networks that served as its technical accountability forums. As such, the ECB could be seen generally as having moved slowly over time from ogre toward hero, with increasing procedural legitimacy.

The chapter begins with a consideration of the nature of ECB power and throughput legitimacy. It considers the relative power of the ECB compared to other central banks, and then explores how the ECB legitimated its reinterpretations of the rules via expert accountability forums and innovative leadership. The chapter next examines the different facets of the ECB's incremental shifts in its rules interpretation, which led to its being hailed as the hero of the Eurozone crisis as it moved from a discourse of credibility to stability, and from never lender of last resort to almost one. The chapter subsequently explores the alternative view, that the ECB was actually an ogre all along, using its power to impose its own austerity and structural reform agenda on all Eurozone members as well as to push the most vulnerable member into conditionality programs, with detrimental results in particular for countries under conditionality. Here, we consider the ECB's orthodoxy in contrast to IMF revisionism, its mantra of austerity and structural reform, and its role in the Troika. The chapter ends with a consideration of what it may take for the ECB to continue to be a hero into the future.

ECB Power and Procedural Legitimacy

As a non-majoritarian institution noted for its institutional independence, the ECB has generally seen itself and has been seen as legitimated by the effectiveness of its monetary policies, as judged by the macroeconomic performance of the Eurozone. But that performance is inextricably linked to the quality of the ECB's governance processes. Regulatory governance of non-majoritarian institutions like the ECB has been characterized as a "fourth branch of government" in which authority is to be exercised by consent, with expert consensus ensuring procedural legitimacy.[1] In other words, while the ECB is empowered to govern autonomously,

---

[1] Majone 1993.

that autonomy goes hand in hand with its accountability to expert forums. The other criteria of throughput legitimacy are less present, with transparency going only as far as central bankers deem necessary to guide the markets, while inclusiveness and openness are not of great relevance here. But efficacy is paramount, with leadership mattering a great deal not only in terms of the efficiency and timing of ECB actions but also with regard to the persuasiveness of its public communication, both to signal to the markets and to ensure public acceptance of its monetary policy.

ECB Independence and Its Accountability to EU Majoritarian Actors

Although all central banks in advanced industrialized countries have over the years become increasingly insulated from politics, the ECB is the example of this par excellence, given that it is by charter the most independent of central banks. This also limits its accountability. On a recent cumulative chart using a range of indexes to measure central banks' comparative accountability and independence, Fraccaroli and co-authors score the ECB above 0.8 points on a 0.9-point scale for independence, in contrast to the much lower independence of the Fed, at close to 0.4 points, and the Bank of England, at slightly over 0.5 points. As for accountability, they score the ECB at a low of around 6.5 points on a 12-point scale, in contrast to the Fed's much higher rating of over 8 points and the BoE's over 11 points.[2]

The problem for the ECB's legitimacy is that the kind of legitimizing logic generally applied to national central banks—that is, that they operate in the "shadow of politics"—does not work nearly as well for it as it does for other major central banks with a purely national mandate. Top officials in national central banks are for the most part not only appointed by the legislature in combination with the executive but also have an obligation to report regularly on their actions to parliamentary oversight or monitoring committees, to respond to questions, and to explain their actions. They can also be subject to formal sanctions. In legislative hearings, moreover, they generally seek to establish their "political accountability," meaning their accountability to political forums, by building trust, ensuring credibility, and persuading legislators of the necessity and appropriateness of their policies. According to Sir Paul Tucker, Deputy Governor of the Bank of England, "Monitoring is, therefore, about more than collecting the evidence for formal sanctions. It is about generating legitimacy through discursive accountability."[3]

---

[2] Fraccaroli et al. 2018, p. 58.
[3] Conversation with author, February 25, 2015 and follow-up correspondence with this quote from a manuscript then in progress, but now published (Tucker 2018). Tucker noted that his use of the term

The ECB acts much less in the shadow of politics than the Bank of England or any other national central bank. This is not only because of the complexity of its appointment process and its far removal from "politics" but also because the most the ECB has to do formally with regard to accountability is for the ECB President to explain ECB actions and respond to questions in its four yearly mandated meetings with the EP's Committee on Economic and Monetary Affairs. This interactive engagement certainly provides an opportunity to build "discursive accountability," but the ECB President need not heed EP advice. Be this as it may, ECB President Draghi has used the EP as an important tool not only to enhance the ECB's political legitimacy through the public communications reported in the media, but also to ensure procedural legitimacy. This helps explain his introductory remarks at one of his meetings with the EP Committee on Economic and Monetary Affairs, in which he declared: "The ECB's accountability to you, the European Parliament, is a central counterpart to the ECB's independence. And transparency is a precondition for your holding us to account."[4]

The Council has even less ability to influence the ECB than the EP. The Council does not in any way constitute a political accountability forum for the ECB, since the ECB is by charter not required to take direction from member-state leaders. Indeed, to be "credible," the ECB initially at least sought to avoid direct contact with member-state leaders in the Council. But during the Eurozone crisis, the ECB over time increased its informal contacts with member-state leaders, in particular the most powerful, in order to win them over so as to avoid taking actions that might meet with too much politically delegitimizing opposition. As such, not only has the ECB become more politically strategic in communicating "to the markets and to the people," but it has also become much more politically interactive "at the top" in its coordination with other EU institutional actors.[5] Such coordination has been in direct contrast to ECB policy at its founding, when the first President, Wim Duisenberg, and the second, Jean-Claude Trichet, avoided interaction with the member-state leaders in the Council for fear of even the appearance of allowing political considerations to influence ECB decisions.

Since Draghi's presidency, however, the ECB has opened up dialogue with the more powerful governments to gain tacit agreement for politically sensitive departures from orthodox ordoliberal monetary policy before taking action. This happened most notably just prior to President Draghi's announcement that he would do "whatever it takes" to save the euro and set up the Outright Monetary Transactions (OMT) program.[6] But not all approved of the actions. The ECB came under attack, most notably by the Bundesbank (BB). These attacks came

---

"discursive accountability" was to avoid using Jane Mansbridge's "deliberative accountability," which is tied to deliberative democracy, which does not describe this interaction.

[4] Draghi 2015b.   [5] Schmidt 2014, 2016a.   [6] Spiegel 2014.

initially from the inside, by the BB representatives on the board of governors, and then from outside, when the BB found itself isolated and outvoted internally. Meanwhile, the ECB has steadily and deliberately engaged in public communication of its actions,[7] taking every opportunity not only to speak to the markets, in order to calm them, but also to the people, in order to legitimize its actions.[8] Thus, while President Draghi has long used his quarterly interrogations by the EP as a vehicle for getting his message across to the people via media reporting, he—along with other high-level ECB officials—has also taken every opportunity to speak in public venues.

Public perceptions naturally also matter. These may be shaped not only directly, by citizens' own experiences of the euro, but also indirectly, by the ECB's communicative discourse and/or by the range of groups engaged with the ECB in building, implementing, or assessing the euro's effectiveness. These include the policy networks that coordinate with the ECB, the competing functional interests such as labor unions and employers' associations that respond to ECB signals, and the independent experts whose opinions may influence the policy's credibility.[9] Ultimately, public perceptions of the ECB's procedural legitimacy may depend not only on how well these groups coordinate to ensure the proper functioning of the euro but also on how positively they communicate about the ECB, whether in terms of its effectiveness or its efficacy, to the media.[10] And, needless to say, how the markets perceive ECB performance and then act in response is also central to its legitimacy (output and throughput).

ECB Accountability in Expert Forums

Procedural legitimacy also entails determining that the ECB meets the technical requirements regarding efficacy, meaning its competence and efficiency in making monetary policy and guiding the markets. This largely depends upon whether the ECB meets standards established on the outside by experts in the forums of central banking expertise, as well as on the inside by its own various boards. As such, efficacy assessment is at the same time an exercise in accountability, that is, about how the ECB is held to account by and gives account of its monetary governance to relevant expert forums.

Any such account-giving is necessarily an interactive discursive process involving generating ideas and building consensus for such ideas. This was no easy task during the Eurozone's unexpected and unprecedented crisis, as the ECB sought to develop and legitimate its new approaches to monetary policy, and in particular as it slowly reinterpreted its mandate. Because the ECB's pre-crisis "paradigm" on

---

[7] Asmussen 2012.   [8] Schmidt 2014.
[9] See Scharpf 1999, and discussion in Jones 2009, pp. 1091–1.   [10] Jones 2009, p. 1097.

what to do in the event of a crisis did not cover all the contingencies, the ECB had to engage in a continual process of *"bricolage"*[11] in the context of emergency crisis management via monetary policies that were unimagined and arguably unimaginable prior to the crisis. These were the *ad hoc* responses of ECB agents puzzling their way through a fast-burning crisis rather than the result of "willful actors" seizing the moment.[12] Any reinterpretation of the rules was not easy because of the very different ideas held initially by different members of the ECB board, with more pragmatic central bankers willing to take an increasingly expansive interpretation of the rules and more orthodox ones insisting on following the rules as heretofore strictly defined.

The interactions inside the ECB mainly entailed the exercise of persuasive ideational powers. Member-state representatives to the ECB governing board were engaged behind closed doors in internal coordination processes of discussion, deliberation, and contestation. Initially, the more orthodox bankers, mainly from Northern Europe, formed a blocking coalition around Germany, and could not be persuaded to do anything much beyond minimal tinkering around the edges. But this changed over time, as more and more Northern European countries rallied around the ECB President in a process of what could be seen as "deliberative (new) intergovernmental" decision-making.[13] This left the Bundesbank (BB) increasingly on its own in espousing the most orthodox positions.

There are other ways to explain the interactions, of course. Traditional intergovernmentalists might see the changes in ECB actions solely as calculated responses, in hard-bargaining negotiations, to failing performance and increasing political pressure, without considerations of legitimacy. The problem is that even if such rationalist analysis were essentially correct, we still need to explain how the ECB was able to develop the new ideas that enabled it to persuade previously opposed central bankers—with notionally fixed opposing preferences and divided interests—to shift their support to a more flexible reading of the rules, and thereby to isolate the Bundesbank. Traditional supranationalists might have another reading of the events, related to the rules-based path dependencies, with other kinds of problems. Here the unanswered question would be how it was even possible to generate new policy ideas within the context of the "stability paradigm" that had been slowly built up over the previous decades. National central banks, Ministry of Finance officials, and experts, including the economists in academia and in research departments of banks, had all developed and elaborated the paradigm in replacement of the Keynesian one.[14]

In terms of discursive interactions, the inside story has yet to be told. But it is likely that the ECB managed to generate this shift in coalitional support through its own conscious process of opening up to a larger expert epistemic community

[11] Carstensen 2011.   [12] Braun 2013.
[13] Puetter 2014; Bickerton et al. 2015.   [14] Heipertz and Verdun 2010, ch. 5.

consisting of banking experts, think tanks, and central bankers with different ideas, as it had done before. The ECB had already in the past followed an expert-based process to persuade banking actors to change the rules, when its coordination with a transnational epistemic network managed to alter the collateral strategy of the banks.[15] And there is no question that as the crisis proceeded ECB officials were in constant contact with the other major central banks and expert networks, as well as the financial policy community.

The opening up to deliberation among experts served not only to help generate new ideas about how to cope with the crisis but also to promote greater procedural legitimacy for any ECB reinterpretation of the rules. After all, in the case of monetary policy, throughput legitimacy—understood as the efficacy of applying the rules—is generally assessed by the community of peers, meaning other central bankers and monetary experts, and is enhanced by the accountability that comes from wide-ranging and ongoing consultation and deliberation. Over time, the deliberations in expert forums helped reshape central bankers' views of what to do, and even their analysis of the crisis itself. It is thus likely that the ECB executive managed to generate a shift in coalitional support through a process of opening up to a larger expert epistemic community with less orthodox ideas, in efforts slowly to generate a shift in coalitional support within the bank which was ultimately to leave the veto-playing Bundesbank isolated.

Importance of Individuals' Ideas and Leadership

Ideational entrepreneurship is an added factor in the explanation of the ECB's changing ideas and discourse over time. The switch in ECB presidents was of great significance, and needs to be added to the deliberative coordination of internal consensus among ECB bankers and the ECB's changing communicative discourse to the public. Trichet was the consummate civil servant whereas Draghi was much more innovative, having had a more diverse professional background.[16] Trichet's response to the crisis was much more hesitant—very little, rather late— by comparison with the much more flexible and innovative Draghi.

Trichet's single-minded focus on "credibility," which dictated his policy of maintaining autonomy through non-interaction with member-state leaders, could be explained first of all by his long civil service career in monetary affairs as head of the French Treasury and then the Bank of France. This was a period in which, because France had less "credibility" with the markets compared to Germany, it got the worst of the currency fluctuations despite its stronger currency and better economic fundamentals.[17] Trichet's focus can be understood,

---

[15] Gabor and Ban 2016.   [16] Basham and Roland 2014.
[17] Howarth and Loedel 2003, p. 120.

secondly, as a function of his long career in ECB institution building, even before gaining the ECB presidency. He was seen as the "perfect civil servant" in his promotion of Mitterrand's conception of *"la construction européenne"* and in his unquestioning acceptance of the changes in central banking. After all, it was he who oversaw the move to French central bank independence from monetary authorities, and then its loss of autonomy to the ECB. And of course, in the process he also accepted the non-negotiability of the (German-dictated) stability rules.[18] We should add to this the political nature of his appointment as ECB head—through Chirac's insistence on a "pre-agreement" that the first head of the ECB withdraw for "health reasons" halfway through his term. This was likely to have made him even keener to demonstrate his "credibility" with regard to resisting even the hint of political influence.

No such politics was involved with Draghi's appointment, which meant he had less to prove in terms of his own political autonomy. But he had arguably more to prove with regard to his suitability for the job, given that he was Italian, at a time when Berlusconi was that country's Prime Minister. His career history, however, prepared him well for the job of renovating the ECB, given that he had had to face an uphill battle in rebuilding Italy's credibility when he took over as governor of the Bank of Italy upon the resignation amid scandal of his predecessor, who had sought to insulate the domestic financial sector from the effects of euro-related integration. Moreover, in addition to having had a career involved in promoting institutional change, in contrast with Trichet's institution building, Draghi had a more mixed career trajectory. Not only had he spent less than half of the time that Trichet had spent in the ECB (while he was on the ECB board as governor of the Bank of Italy), but he had academic training in economics rather than professional training in public administration, had been an economics professor and an Executive Director of the World Bank, and had worked in private finance, as well as having been Director-General of the Italian Treasury before becoming Governor of the Bank of Italy.[19] All of this helps explain why Draghi was more innovative and flexible.

The styles of management of the two heads of the ECB were also very different. Trichet tended to gain consensus within the board, before going to the board of governors to get agreement (which they generally approved). But this meant that compromises were already made prior to the board decision. Draghi instead tended to decide what he thought was best, and went with his recommendations directly to the board of governors, without consulting the inner board and thus without making compromises. This meant that he brought more innovative or out of the ordinary decisions directly to the board—necessary in particular in

[18] Dyson and Featherstone 1999; see also discussion in Basham and Roland 2014.
[19] Basham and Roland 2014, pp. 11–13.

times of crisis—without watering down the recommendation ahead of time. And he generally then was able to persuade the board of his proposals.[20]

Additionally, Draghi was a bridge-builder. In the progressive reinterpretation of the rules to "save the euro," not only did Draghi gain the trust and respect of fellow bankers; he also, as noted above, managed to develop sufficient rapport with Council leaders—and in particular Chancellor Merkel—so as to gain their trust and support as well. As such, Draghi could be seen as a highly successful "policy entrepreneur"[21] who was able not only to develop a new set of actionable ideas acceptable to the broader central banking epistemic community, but also to legitimate this to the satisfaction of political as well as technical actors in potential veto positions. The ECB itself, in fact, has been very successful as a policy entrepreneur overall, as in the case of banking union.[22]

Finally, charisma was equally a factor in helping establish Draghi's leadership authority. Charisma is Max Weber's second way of establishing the legitimacy of any governing authority (the first is based on tradition, the third is on legal-rational grounds), and can be seen as another element helping to lend support to the legitimacy of the ECB's expanding governing activities. In the case of Draghi, we could say that he increased his authority by way of the charismatic qualities of his rhetoric during the Euro crisis that "spoke to the people" in ways that reassured them, and that made the ECB appear the "hero" of the crisis.[23] ECB President Mario Draghi was notably hailed as "super Mario" at the height of the Euro crisis. That said, even the previous ECB President, Jean-Claude Trichet, was endowed with similar such qualities of leadership.

The ECB as "Hero"

The ECB may have been slow to respond to the crisis, but in the end it did rescue the euro when all other actors—notably member-state leaders in the Council— failed to act in any of the many ways that could have stemmed market attacks. And in the absence of any positive action taken by these other actors, the ECB was ultimately hailed as the hero of the crisis—after Mario Draghi had finally stopped market attacks with his famous pledge to "do whatever it takes." The actual process that led to the ECB's being the hero was slow and incremental, requiring changes in ideas about how to manage the crisis and discourses of legitimation intended to demonstrate that all the new policies were already in the ECB's mandate.

---

[20] Conversation with high-level Commission official, Boston, Nov. 1, 2017.
[21] Kingdon 1984.   [22] de Rynck 2016; see also Dehousse 2016.
[23] Tortola and Pansardi 2018.

As a "hero," the ECB deployed its persuasive ideational power in three ways: first, by legitimating its changing monetary governance through communication to the public, seeking to win in the "court of public opinion"; second, through its coordination with member-state leaders, in order to gain tacit approval; and third, by opening up its coordinative discourse to a larger network of experts in order to gain support for its ideas, which in turn enabled it to convince EU institutional actors—its own board members as well as political leaders—that its new initiatives would be effective and were appropriate.

From a "Credibility" Discourse to a "Stability" Discourse

Initially, the ECB sought to manage perceptions with a communicative discourse focused on the quality of its governance processes, by emphasizing the importance of maintaining its "credibility" through strict adherence to its (throughput) rules of inflation fighting while resisting any political (input) pressures from member-state leaders. This was the main mantra of the ECB presidents in the first ten years of the euro, first Wim Duisenberg and then Jean-Claude Trichet. This credibility discourse continued as the financial crisis turned into one of the real economy and then a sovereign debt crisis, even as ECB President Trichet engaged in what he called "non-standard" monetary policies to shore up the currency once the 2008 crisis hit. A part of that non-standard policy went a lot farther than publicly acknowledged. As Carlo Bastasin explains, the ECB, concerned about the parlous state of banks in many member states following upon the financial crisis, created a secret "grand bargain" in March and April 2009 in which it provided extra liquidity to the banks on condition that they buy member-state debt. This was effectively an indirect way for the ECB to buy government debt, and as such forbidden in the Treaties. But all the member states agreed, not only because this came before the sovereign debt crisis of the euro, when national debt was considered the safest of all investments, but also because it seemed the only way to shore up the failing banks in many countries, given the lack of Council action. Even the German Bundesbank, the "purest defender of banking autonomy from politics," did not protest, and understandably so given that German banks benefited greatly. The bankrupt Hypo Real Estate bank, for example, benefited from 80 billion euros in loans from the ECB over the course of 2008–9.[24]

All the while, however, Trichet insisted that the ECB was not and could not ever be an LOLR like the Fed or the Bank of England by buying member-state debt, given the no-bailout clause in the Treaties. This came out most clearly for the first time in May 2009 when, in conjunction with the ECB's program of "credit

---

[24] Bastasin 2015, pp. 96–9.

easing" (cutting rates and buying "covered bonds") in response to the credit crunch in the real economy, Trichet announced that this was not the ECB's equivalent to the UK and US quantitative easing schemes.[25] And yet, in 2010 Trichet did buy member-state debt, claiming that this was always allowed so long as it was bought on the secondary markets, and he justified this by quickly "sanitizing" the debt—that is, reselling within a relatively short period.

Even Mario Draghi, when appointed head of the ECB in late 2011, initially continued with the discourse of "credibility" while denying that the ECB could be an LOLR, thereby seeming to signal his continuation of the Trichet approach. In his first press conference, Draghi insisted that "continuity, credibility and consistency are of the essence in the way we carry out our jobs." And when asked whether he would do whatever was necessary to keep the Eurozone in one piece, including act as an LOLR, he responded: "No, I do not think that this is really within the remit of the ECB. The remit of the ECB is maintaining price stability over the medium term."[26]

Soon thereafter, however—in spring 2012, as Draghi began to engage in increasingly bold, unconventional monetary policies in response to the unfolding crisis—his legitimizing discourse changed from one focused on "credibility" to one focused on "stability" (see Figure 6.1). In a randomized sampling of Draghi's speeches and press conferences from his appointment in late 2011 through 2013, although "credibility" appears in the first months of his mandate (winter 2011/ spring 2012), it largely drops out of his vocabulary subsequently (with the exception of a small increase in spring 2013). In contrast, "stability" remains the most prevalent term between 2011 and 2013. It is rivaled only by the word "competitiveness," which shoots up in spring 2012 and again in fall 2013. Meanwhile, "inflation" was a low-level yet steady presence, as was "structural reform," at an even lower level. "Save the euro" appears only once, and minimally, in winter 2012/13, since Merkel's use of the phrase in 2010 had panicked the markets— something of which the ECB was well aware. ECB Executive Board member Jörg Asmussen used that event explicitly in a speech to illustrate the problems of communicating to the people with the markets listening.[27]

The switch from a discourse emphasizing credibility to one focused on stability was not uncontroversial. The stability discourse was intended to help legitimate bond buying while overcoming the resistance of those who retained a narrow reading of the "no-bailout clause." Already with Trichet, the modest "non-standard" bond-buying policies had led to internal fights within the ECB, and even the resignation in protest of the two German members of the ECB governing board, Axel Weber in April 2011 and Jürgen Stark in September 2011.[28] This led to the appointment of the more moderate Jörg Asmussen to the governing board, which

---

[25] Trichet 2009.   [26] Draghi 2011.   [27] Asmussen 2012; see discussion in Schmidt 2014.
[28] Matthijus 2016.

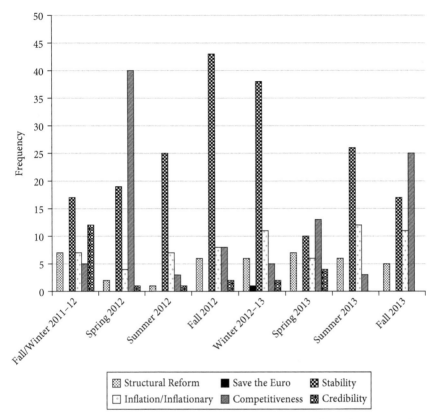

Figure 6.1. Word Use Frequency by ECB President Mario Draghi (Fall 2011 to Fall 2013)

Source: Speeches and Press Conferences, randomized choice, 3-4 per season. See ECB website http://www.ecb.europa.eu/press/key/date/2013/html/index.en.html

facilitated further discretionary policies by the ECB. But only once Draghi was appointed did the ECB move toward a more expansive view of its mandate. Even so, stability was not accepted as on a par with credibility until the euro itself was clearly in danger.

The word "stability" was itself central to the legitimation of the slow and subtle shift in central bank policy. In using the word, the ECB sought to conjure up the "stability paradigm" underlying European Monetary Union (EMU),[29] and thereby to reassure all and sundry that the ECB remained committed to its basic philosophy and mandate, as outlined in the Charter. At the same time, however, it signaled a move away from the "credibility" associated with a narrow interpretation of the ECB's remit. As ECB officials themselves explained in an article in the

---

[29] Heipertz and Verdun 2010, p. 93.

Journal for Common Market Studies, in a crisis the central bank "must stand ready to back up the market while increasing its communication to explain that its primary objective has not changed in crisis mode,"[30] as they insisted that the "exceptional measures are temporary in nature—to ensure price stability in the medium term."[31]

In other words, the ECB legitimated stretching or even breaking one set of rules (not buying sovereign debt) in the short term in the name of the cardinal rule—stability in the medium term. One could think of this as a question of Kantian conflict between categorical imperatives. The issue is which rule comes first: the rule that forbids ECB debt purchases as a way of ensuring price stability, or the more basic one that gives the ECB responsibility for the euro? Clearly, if the euro explodes, price stability cannot be sustained. Thus, rescuing the euro overrides the ban on debt purchases.

The switch to a stability discourse also opened up space for ECB President Draghi to engage in informal interactions with EU leaders in the Council. Unlike Trichet, who seemed most concerned about maintaining his autonomy vis-à-vis member-state leaders for purposes of "credibility," Draghi sought to coordinate with Council leaders. This included engaging in a "charm offensive" (as some described it) or, more accurately, in a concerted yearlong effort to persuade Chancellor Merkel in particular that "non-standard" bond-buying programs and banking union were essential. All the while, the bank was working to fashion policy packages acceptable (to Germany) and workable (for EMU)— against opposition from the Bundesbank.[32] Draghi succeeded in getting around Bundesbank opposition largely via Merkel and after bypassing the objections of the German representative on the ECB board. This opened the way to increasingly unconventional monetary policies, including low-interest loans to the banks via "long-term refinancing operations" (or LTROs) in late 2011 and early 2012. Both of these could be seen as a form of quantitative easing that largely bailed out the banks while doing little for the countries that had now accumulated much larger debt loads.

From "*Never*" Lender of Last Resort to "*Almost*"

Importantly, however, even as the ECB quickly switched its discourse from credibility to stability beginning in 2011 and undertook a range of bond-buying programs, it took much longer for the discourse and practices to shift with regard to measures that would bring the ECB closer to acting as an LOLR, or something akin to one.[33] Any such shift was arguably more difficult given the lack of explicit

---

[30] Drudi et al. 2012, p. 890.   [31] Drudi et al. 2012, p. 894.   [32] Spiegel 2014.
[33] For an excellent overview of the ECB as an LOLR, see Ban 2020.

mandate in the ECB Charter, plus the clear prohibition in the Treaties against buying member-state debt as a result of the no-bailout clause. Moreover, German reluctance, once the rule against buying member-state debt had been breached or, rather, "reinterpreted" to allow for "non-standard" buying policies, made it difficult for the ECB to do much more.

As a result, despite the switch to a stability discourse, the ECB continued to deny publicly that it could act as an LOLR despite slowly and incrementally layering on an increasingly unconventional bond-buying policy that brought it closer and closer to one.[34] When Draghi was asked early in his term whether the bond buying was Europe's version of "quantitative easing," his response was: "Each jurisdiction has not only its own rules, but also its own vocabulary. [The bond-buying programs] are certainly unprecedented. But the reliance on the banking channel falls squarely in our mandate, which is geared towards price stability in the medium term…We call them non-standard measures."[35] Such measures, however, did little to change the course of the crisis itself between 2010 and 2012, since the discourse of denial about acting as an LOLR kept the markets worried, and primed for panic and attack, while the actual policies created their own knock-on effects for member states, the banks, and the ECB itself.[36]

The ECB's denials with regard to its being a LOLR were clearly intended to reassure member states and central bank members, most notably Germany and other Northern Europeans, that even as the ECB engaged in increasingly "non-standard" monetary policies (Trichet's term as of 2010), it was sticking to a restrictive reading of the Charter.[37] But the denials had unintended consequences. Trichet's nay-saying helps explain why, as the Greek crisis unfolded, the markets became increasingly nervous about the possibility that the ECB would not act as a classic LOLR by standing behind the sovereign debt of its member states, in particular as the member states in the Council failed to reach agreement on what to do about the Greek crisis.[38] The markets remained unimpressed following the Greek bailout and the "shock and awe" of the contagion fund, soon stepping up their attacks on the member states most at risk of default: Ireland and Portugal, forced into loan bailouts, and then Spain and Italy. It was only in July 2012, as the markets had begun massive attacks against Spanish and Italian sovereign debt, that Draghi pledged to go what seemed the last mile, stating that "the ECB is ready to do whatever it takes to preserve the euro" and adding, after pausing for effect, "and believe me, it will be enough." The markets took this as a pledge

---

[34] Buiter and Rahbari 2012.   [35] *Financial Times* Dec. 19, 2011.
[36] Blyth 2013; Mody 2018, Ch. 8.
[37] Note that ECB executive board member, Jörg Asmussen, in a speech at the European Conference 2013 organised by UBS in London (12 November 2013), reiterated the point that ECB policy was not "unorthodox," it was simply "non-standard." https://www.ecb.europa.eu/press/key/date/2013/html/sp131112.en.html
[38] Blyth 2013.

to act as lender of last resort, although the ECB never stated that it was an LOLR. In actual fact, Draghi's full sentence, not often reported in the media, began with: "Within our mandate."[39] This qualification was to ensure against potential legal challenges, in particular given the German Constitutional Court's previous decisions.

By this time, only the Bundesbank and its head Jens Weidmann, plus a large number of German economists, were against the ECB's reinterpretation of the rules on the grounds that they violated the Charter and risked long-term inflation. As Erich Keller, rector at the Deutsche Bundesbank University of Applied Sciences, said at the time to explain his virulent opposition: "We have a mantra, only one goal—price stability...This stability orientation is in the genes of the Bundesbank...We are bringing in those genes."[40] The question of the ECB's right to institute OMT was even taken up by the German Constitutional Court in a case brought by the German economists and supported by the BB. It pitted Weidmann, who vehemently opposed ECB intervention on the grounds that its remit was to control inflation and that only the politicians had the legitimacy as well as the obligation to deal with the rest,[41] against the ECB's Executive Board member Jörg Asmussen. Asmussen justified the increasingly non-standard monetary policy measures as a response to unusual circumstances, insisting: "We are in a situation of one size fits none [and] that is why we have extended these non-standard instruments."[42] Draghi also sought to reassure the Germans in a press conference on a major German television station, ZDF, in saying that "the risk to German taxpayers is considerably lower today than it was a year ago" even as he promised to remain true to the spirit of the stability rules: "I can guarantee that we won't simply inflate our way out of debt."[43]

Significantly, the German Constitutional Court's decision, which sided with the Bundesbank's analysis of the illegality of the ECB's never-instituted OMT program, nonetheless referred the case to the Court of Justice of the European Union (CJEU). And the CJEU ultimately decided that the ECB was in its right.

The ECB's pledge in fall 2014 to engage in quantitative easing (QE) to stave off deflation, begun in early 2015, was yet another step toward becoming an LOLR without admitting it—and it too was questioned by German central bankers and economists. In this case, however, after initial criticisms, even the Bundesbank head Weidman seemed to come around to accepting the ECB's proposed move to QE when he stated in an interview that in light of a strong currency and in view of deflation risks, the ECB could in fact buy Eurozone member bonds or top-rated private sector assets, and the door was therefore open to quantitative easing (QE).[44] Draghi himself confirmed support for QE in mid July 2014, when he said

[39] Draghi 2012.   [40] *New York Times* Dec. 15 2012.   [41] *Financial Times* June 12, 2013.
[42] *Financial Times* June 12, 2013.   [43] *Financial Times* June 11, 2013.
[44] *Euroactiv* March 26, 2014.

to the European Parliament that "the Governing Council is unanimous also in using unconventional measures to address the risk of a too prolonged period of too low inflation," and added: "QE falls squarely in our mandate."[45]

Once the program of quantitative easing through bond buying had begun, however, Weidman and other German members of the ECB expressed doubts and dissatisfaction—citing worries about inflation and the impact on creditors, whose savings would lose value. In response, on December 4, 2015, Draghi again reiterated his commitment to QE, insisting: "Like central banks everywhere, we have those that dissent. But the bottom line is that Q.E. is here to stay."[46] And in order to leave no room for doubt, he said that the ECB had "the power to act and the determination to act and the commitment to act," adding: "There cannot be any limit to how far we are willing to deploy our instruments, within our mandate, and to achieve our mandate."[47]

For countries vulnerable to high interest rates on their bonds, quantitative easing was a real boon, since it enabled them to refinance public debt at very low rates. It was no boon to pensioners in Germany, of course, who saw little return on their savings. But it also saved the Eurozone from the threat of deflation, and was a spur to economic recovery, at least for a while.

The ECB, in sum, did "whatever it takes to save the euro" as it reinterpreted its mandate to engage in increasingly expansionary monetary policy, even though this took a very long time as compared to other central banks that had aggressively begun QE already in 2008. And as such, the ECB was seen as the hero, with Draghi himself hailed as "super Mario" in the press.

The ECB as "Ogre"

Throughout the Eurozone crisis, even as the ECB reinterpreted its own rules to come increasingly closer to an LOLR—and in so doing became the "hero" rescuing the euro—it continued to press for austerity up to 2013 and structural reform thereafter, with particularly harsh austerity recommendations for program countries as part of the Troika. These actions made it the "ogre" of the Eurozone crisis, in a counternarrative focused on the fact that the ECB, having been the only actor with the financial capacity and legal authority to make decisive interventions, was largely able to set the agenda for the other institutional actors.[48] And that agenda was a politicized one, in which the ECB worked hand in hand with the more powerful countries to favor the "creditors" to the detriment of the "debtors,"[49] which the ECB pushed into conditionality programs.

---

[45] *Euractiv* July 15, 2014.   [46] *New York Times* Dec. 5, 2015.
[47] *Financial Times* Dec 4, 2015.   [48] Braun 2013, pp. 6–8.
[49] See discussion in Tortola 2019.

As an "ogre," the ECB's power—institutional and ideational—was in evidence as it made clear to all Eurozone members that its heroic actions came with strings attached, linked to austerity and structural reform. With regard to the program countries, moreover, one could easily argue that the ECB's demands reflected coercive power, pure and simple. The program countries had no alternative other than to accept conditionality, given that exit from the euro was not a viable option. And here, the ECB's power was operative in two ways: first, by having been able to coerce member states into a program by cutting off their access to liquidity; second, by institutionally enforcing harsh austerity and structural reform through its role in the Troika.

ECB (Lack of) Efficacy

Concerning the ECB's procedural legitimacy in the Eurozone crisis, questions can be raised in the first instance about the ECB's efficacy, since it came relatively late to the promise to "do whatever it takes." The ECB's stability-based ordoliberal reading of its Charter, along with its initial focus on procedural "credibility" instead of performance results (believing these would necessarily follow), meant that the ECB initially did much less than it could and should have done (at least compared to the Fed's effective performance for the United States or the Bank of England's for the United Kingdom).[50] Had the ECB engaged in aggressive quantitative easing in 2009 and thereafter, like the other central banks, the run on Eurozone sovereign debt would never have happened.[51] Instead, the ECB took five years after the inception of the Euro crisis to begin the kind of quantitative easing that the US and UK central banks had engaged in since 2008—and only because deflation threatened.[52]

The ECB could have legitimized such action by interpreting its mandate more broadly from the beginning. As Mark Blyth has noted, instead of focusing on the initial part of Article 127 of the Treaty on the Functioning of the European Union (TFEU), which stated that the ECB's primary objective "shall be to maintain price stability," the ECB could have paid attention to subsequent phrases stating that "without prejudice to the objective of price stability, the ESCB shall support the general economic policies in the Union with a view to contributing to the achievement of the objectives of the Union as laid down in Article 3 of the Treaty on European Union". Article 3 says that

The Union shall...work for the sustainable development of Europe based on balanced economic growth and price stability...aiming at full employment and

---

[50] Blyth 2013; Legrain 2014; Tooze 2018, Ch. 18; Mody 2018, Ch. 8.
[51] Lonergan 2019.   [52] See. e.g., Mody 2018, Ch. 8.

social progress, and a high level of protection…It shall promote economic, social and territorial cohesion, and solidarity among Member States.[53]

The ECB also made mistakes in monetary policy, in particular under Trichet's watch. Not only did it fail to see signs of trouble throughout the first years of the euro, but it also misread market signals after the boom had turned into a bust. The very day before the Greek crisis went almost out of control—on the morning of May 6, 2010, as Greece had voted in what Adam Tooze calls "the most draconian austerity program ever proposed to a modern democracy"—Trichet still refused to even discuss buying Greek bonds. Only by evening, in response to the dramatic plunge of the euro and panic in the markets, did he change his mind, and the next day pledge to buy bonds (albeit on the secondary markets and not as an LOLR).[54] Other examples of mistakes and hesitations include the fact that a year later, in 2011, the ECB twice raised interest rates, despite market panic and spiking Italian bond yields along with a deteriorating European economy.[55]

So why did the ECB not act with efficacy, and why this particular agenda, in which it resisted doing much that brought it closer to an LOLR even as it pushed for rapid deficit reduction through fiscal consolidation? For an answer, we need first to look more deeply into the ECB's attempts to ensure its own procedural legitimacy, by considering its economic ideas about macroeconomic and fiscal policy and the expert networks that serve as the ECB's technical forums of accountability.

ECB Orthodoxy versus IMF Revisionism

The best way to illustrate the ECB's Janus-faced image as hero on monetary policy and ogre on fiscal policy is to contrast its fiscal policy recommendations with those of the IMF in terms of both ideas and expert networks. As Cornel Ban has shown, while both the IMF and ECB defended core neoliberal theory favoring consolidation of public finances through cutting public expenditures in order to inspire the confidence of sovereign bond markets, the ECB was much more orthodox in its views of when, how, and how much to consolidate. Whereas the IMF viewed fiscal consolidation as unlikely to have expansionary effects on output, and recommended gradual introduction of fiscal consolidation (backloading), the ECB saw fiscal consolidation as expansionary, and recommended frontloading it immediately in all countries. While the IMF recommended that fiscal consolidation proceed through a combination of spending cuts and revenue increases, including through taxes, the ECB preferred only spending cuts and no

---

[53] See discussion in Blyth 2013, ch. 3.   [54] Tooze 2018, p. 340.
[55] Legrain 2014, pp. 222–3.

tax increases. Although both targeted public jobs programs, social transfers, public sector wages, employment, housing, and agricultural subsidies for spending cuts, the IMF exempted public investment, whereas for the ECB nothing was exempt.[56] In terms of ideas, then, as Ben Clift argues, the IMF put down a number of intellectual markers when it directly critiqued the "expansionary fiscal contraction" thesis while putting a high value on expansionary fiscal policy and public investment in periods of recession.[57]

These differences in ideas about how to manage the macroeconomy, between the IMF's revisionism and the ECB's orthodoxy in fiscal policy, can be related to a number of factors. Leadership of course plays a major role. The shift in IMF policy toward a more revisionist approach dates to the appointment of Dominique Strauss-Kahn as head and Olivier Blanchard as Chief Economist, just as the change in the ECB's monetary policy to do "whatever it takes" dates to Draghi. The institutional context also matters, whether as constraints or opportunities. The IMF is more autonomous as an institution than the ECB because it is the delegated agent of such a large number of nation states, with representatives from each of the member states on its governing board, who have very different views of monetary and fiscal policy. But for policies even to be envisioned, let alone to be perceived as both workable and legitimate (in technical output terms), they must also have a strong connection to the networks of experts informing and legitimating technical actors' policies in the coordinative discourse of policy construction.

The IMF's ideas are largely in tune with the revisionist wave of macroeconomic thinking beginning in the 2000s that generated a kinder and gentler (new) Washington Consensus very different from the more orthodox Brussels–Frankfurt Consensus at the core of the ECB position.[58] Cornel Ban provides a fascinating visual map of the ecology of these institutions between 2008 and 2014 through a combination of content, network, and regression analysis of the professional career trajectories of the staffs and their citations in papers and other documents to show that they tapped into very different networks for ideational support and legitimation.[59] As Ban argues, the IMF's revisionism has much to do with the research done by the less orthodox economists from its own Research Department, by parts of the Fed, by several European central banks, and by faculty from some elite US academic institutions. Instead, the ECB's orthodoxy can be explained by how much it drew on the research of its own more orthodox internal researchers, other parts of the Fed, and different external allies, including a think tank (CEPR), the orthodox resistance within the IMF (ie, the Fiscal Affairs Department), the Bank of International Settlements, and an assortment of central banks and prestigious US academic departments.[60]

---

[56] See discussion in Ban 2016.   [57] Clift 2018, Chapter 5.   [58] Ban 2016; Clift 2018.
[59] Ban and Padenaude 2019.   [60] Ban 2016.

The ECB's beliefs, much as those of the Commission, reflect the economic theory of "expansionary austerity" advocated by influential economists such as Alberto Alesina of Harvard and Roberto Perotti at Bocconi University, who maintained that the frontloading of cuts would have a beneficial effect in jump-starting stalling economies.[61] This view was echoed by Trichet in an interview with the *Wall Street Journal*, when he stated that "fiscal retrenchment in countries that need it is part of growth enhancement, because sustainable public finances makes a difference in terms of improving confidence of households, enterprises, investors and savers, which is decisive to foster growth and job creation."[62] We could add the views of Reinhart and Rogoff (2009) in *This Time Is Different*, suggesting a 90 percent limit for sustainable levels of debt (that later proved not to be sustained by the evidence)—also cited approvingly by the Commission Vice-President and Commissioner of DG ECFIN, Olli Rehn.[63] These differences help explain why the economists in the research division of the IMF issued reports critiquing the pace and the content of the Eurozone's move to austerity, as well as the IMF's own role in the Greek crisis, in great contrast to the ECB, which was a major proponent of Eurozone austerity and a supporter of the harsh measures for Greece.

This said, it is important to differentiate the IMF's revisionist research branch from its operations branch, which was every bit as orthodox as the ECB. But this was a different kind of orthodoxy. In the third Greek bailout in particular, while the IMF pushed for significant debt restructuring (along with further painful cuts to the welfare system, strongly resisted by the Syriza government), the ECB wanted its money back (having Greek bonds on its balance sheets), as did the German Finance Minister (in the Eurogroup), who would not countenance any loss for German taxpayers. The ESM was in a more ambiguous position. Having just refinanced Greek debt at very low rates for a long period (thirty years), it was happy to "extend and pretend" (that the debts would be repaid), in contrast to the IMF, which worried that Greece would never regain market confidence with such a high GDP-to-debt ratio.

The ECB's Mantra of Austerity and Structural Reform

Equally important for judging the ECB's governance was its *quid pro quo* pressure on the member states for austerity policies and "structural reform." This has been problematic not only in terms of the economics but also in terms of the politics. How legitimate is a non-majoritarian institution like the ECB, after all, when it

---

[61] Helgadottir 2016; Clift 2018, pp. 128–132.   [62] *Wall Street Journal*, Jan. 23, 2011.
[63] Cassidy 2013.

pushes democratically elected governments to impose policies that, in many cases, go against what they and their constituents want?

The ECB had been focused on austerity and structural reform even before the Greek crisis put it on the agenda, when it became Merkel's *quid pro quo* for the loan bailouts. Already in January 2009, the ECB's Governing Council (led by Trichet) issued a broadside against the 2008 fiscal stimulus on the grounds that "if not reversed in due time, this will negatively affect in particular the younger and the future generations;" in September, it asked for "a swift return to sound and sustainable public finances," to be paid for by spending cuts since "the focus of the structural measures should lie on the expenditure side, as in most euro area countries tax and social contribution rates are already high."[64] But the Greek bailout negotiation provided the ECB with the opportunity to force the issue, as it demanded that its own bond buying be accompanied by a massive bailout fund (the EFSF) along with member states' pledges of austerity.

Draghi continued the message of austerity and structural reform. In his first press conference, in addition to insisting that the ECB would not act as an LOLR, as mentioned above, he went on to say:

> the real answer [rather than the ECB being an LOLR] is actually to count on the countries' capacity to reform themselves with the right economic policies…first, put your public finance in order and, second, undertake structural reforms. In doing so, competitiveness is enhanced, thereby fostering growth and job creation.[65]

Moreover, when Draghi finally did pledge to "do whatever it takes"—which the markets mistook as the ECB acting as an LOLR—there was a major difference between the ECB's proposed actions and those of a true LOLR. The ECB made clear in September 2012 that it would use the OMT for the potentially unlimited purchase of Eurozone bonds to stop market attacks on Spanish and Italian bonds only if the Italian and Spanish governments asked for such purchases and in exchange agreed to a conditionality program. By insisting on conditionality, the ECB appeared to be trying to legitimate a break with one set of rules (ie, the prohibition against buying member-state debt) by reinforcing the others (in particular the imperative of conditionality).

Such conditionality made the program more akin to an IMF-style lending program, focused on dealing with insolvency, than to an LOLR program, focused on illiquidity.[66] Even German leaders largely accepted this shift in policy,[67] with the exception of the more orthodox Bundesbank, which supported the court case in the German Constitutional Court that opposed the ECB's right to institute OMT.

---

[64] ECB, cited in Ban 2016.   [65] Draghi 2011.
[66] Mody 2015.   [67] Newman 2015.

But while the German Bundesbank pushed for orthodoxy against the seeming laxness of the ECB, one should not assume that the ECB had therefore gone soft. It may have moved to unconventional monetary policy to "save the euro," but it pushed austerity and structural reform all the more. Illustrative are the remarks of ECB Executive Board member Yves Mersch at a conference in Athens in which, after having hailed the historic success of Greece in achieving a primary surplus and in reforming the pension system so as to make it "comparable to others," while calling the high unemployment rates a "tragedy," he insisted that "fiscal sustainability—and hence intergenerational justice—is not yet assured" because the country had not reached its surplus targets; therefore, he said, "fiscal consolidation has to continue."[68] His comments of course beg the question of intergenerational justice, given the high levels of youth unemployment. Most significantly, however, there was no suggestion that the ECB could do more within its own purview, or ease the program.

The ECB's Role in the Troika

Possibly the most compelling case for depicting the ECB as the ogre comes from the ways in which it dealt with program countries, both by forcing them into programs and then in pushing harsh austerity and structural reform.[69] These actions were very much a political exercise of coercive power over the countries in trouble. This was exemplified by the ECB threat to withhold emergency support for Irish banks unless the government agreed to enter a harsh conditionality program.[70]

In what has since been regarded as a major overstretch in terms of its mandate and, indeed, an attack on member states' democratic (input) legitimacy, in August 2011 ECB President Jean-Claude Trichet sent secret letters to Italian Prime Minister Silvio Berlusconi and Spanish Prime Minister José Luis Rodriguez Zapatero (which the latter denied receiving at the time, but published in his memoirs in 2013) demanding austerity and structural reform. In the case of Spain, Trichet ordered Zapatero to decentralize the labor markets, break the monopolies of certain professions, and institute cutbacks "whatever the circumstances."[71] The revelation of the contents of the letter in late fall 2013 unleashed a debate in Spain about how much the President of the ECB had overstepped his bounds, whether by violating his own mandate to focus solely on Eurozone monetary policy, by interfering with the

---

[68] "Intergenerational Justice in Times of Sovereign Debt Crises." Speech by Yves Mersch, Member of the Executive Board of the ECB, at the Minsky Conference in Greece organised by the Levy Economics Institute Athens, 8 November 2013. http://www.ecb.europa.eu/press/key/date/2013/html/sp131108.en.html#

[69] See discussions in Eichengreen 2013; Tooze 2018.

[70] See discussion in Tooze 2018, pp. 362–3.   [71] Zapatero 2013.

democratic control of elected governments, or in taking over the role of the Commission to make radical recommendations which even the Commission would not have made.[72] It is useful to note that even earlier, in May 2010, the ECB held the Spanish banks hostage to ensure that Zapatero would agree to Council leaders' demands that the country adopt significant debt reduction measures plus labor market deregulation.

A similar controversy hit Ireland in November 2014 when it came to light that Trichet had written Irish PM Brian Lenihan a letter that essentially pushed the country into a harsh bailout package (to the tune of 84.5 billion euros, with an annual cost of 8 billion euros). Trichet threatened to withhold emergency support (Emergency Liquidity Assistance) for the country's failing banks unless Ireland applied for an international rescue, at the same time as protecting senior bond-holders from losses to preserve confidence in the European banking system.[73] While this certainly was a breach of input legitimacy, as the unelected ECB head sought to dictate policy to elected leaders, it was also a problem for throughput legitimacy. Not only was the action unaccountable—and not accounted for in any political accountability forum—but its secrecy was a gross violation of transparency, as another instance of crisis exploitation.

Notably, while many blame Merkozy in the Council for causing the market panic that forced Ireland into a program by announcing the establishment of the ESM that would impose haircuts on banks beginning in 2013, Adam Tooze argues that Trichet "had the whip hand." In addition to Trichet's secret letter, the ECB in short order insisted that Ireland enter a program, threatened to withdraw support if it did not, leaked to the media that Ireland was about to apply for a loan, and demanded further fiscal consolidation and structural reform while recapitalizing its banks.[74] The governor of the Bank of Ireland at the time, Patrick Honohan, later criticized such policies, noting that an alternative monetary-fiscal mix with less fiscal contraction and more expansionary monetary policy "would have allowed even the more stressed governments to achieve lower inequality (and a more rapid growth recovery) without risking loss of market access."[75]

As for Greece, the ECB was particularly harsh with regard to the austerity and structural reform program, working hand in glove with the Eurogroup of Finance Ministers. Not only did Trichet adamantly oppose any Greek debt restructuring in May 2010 but the ECB had also bought Greek bonds, thus giving it a vested interest in opposing any such restructuring.[76] Yanis Varoufakis had very strong words for the ECB, in particular under Trichet. He described the various ways in which loan bailouts were structured as an elaborate "Ponzi scheme" in which

---

[72] *El Pais* Dec. 1, 2013.   [73] *New York Times* Nov. 7, 2014.   [74] Tooze 2018, p. 362.
[75] Honohan 2019, p. 15. He was on the ECB board from September 2009 to November 2015. This came as a side-comment in a 2019 paper on future central banking policies.
[76] Legrain 2014, p. 222.

program countries were further and further loaded with debt as banks made out like bandits. He also criticized the ways in which the various ECB schemes for saving the banks, including through LTROs, the OMT, and even QE, were unable to do what it really took to save the euro. This is because of the constraints imposed by the interpretation of the no-bailout clause. The EFSF loans were set at market interest rates not just for the program countries but also for the lending countries, making those at greater market risk pay higher interest; and the ECB was forced to buy bonds from all Eurozone members at the ratio of their notional bond-holdings in the Eurozone (eg, for Germany at approximately 27 percent), rather than only from the member states in need, such as Greece, Italy, or Spain.[77] Interestingly, while Varoufakis was clearly disdainful of Trichet, whom he called "arguably the world's worst central banker," he was kinder about Draghi, whom he saw as "frightfully smart."[78]

Conclusion

ECB governance in the Eurozone crisis leaves us with the question whether it represented a hero acting to save the euro or an ogre imposing harsh austerity and structural reform on member states in trouble. Both arguments are valid. The ECB did achieve its key objective, to save the euro, even though it used ogre-like methods to coerce the program countries. If we add a time dimension, we might be tempted to pile much of the blame for the ogre-like qualities on Trichet, whose responses failed to stem a crisis that never needed to have happened, by refusing to allow the ECB to act as an LOLR. This jeopardized output legitimacy, as did his push for the Council to implement policies focused on austerity and structural reform, and to join with the IMF and the Commission as part of the Troika to impose harsh conditionality on program countries. Moreover, Trichet was on thin ice indeed with regard to input legitimacy when he sent secret letters to Prime Ministers threatening withdrawal of Central Bank support if they did not follow ECB demands.

But we cannot let Draghi entirely off the hook, even though the measures he took quickly made him the hero of the crisis, as he hid his reinterpretations of the ECB's mandate "in plain view." In so doing, he continued to lend validity to the earlier interpretations by insisting that his unconventional policies were temporary, to deal with the problems of the moment. In consequence, he missed an opportunity to communicate clearly to the public that the new instruments were not only necessary but legitimate for then and into the future.

---

[77] Varoufakis 2016, pp. 161–4, 169–71.   [78] Varoufakis 2016, p. 169.

But Draghi's was an act of understandable omission, given German opposition to the ECB's reinterpretation of the rules. The ECB's act of commission, in contrast, and the one that made it more of an ogre, was its continued demands for austerity in the program countries as part of the Troika long after the worst of the crisis was over. Thus, while the ECB appears to have managed incrementally to legitimate reinterpreting the rules (throughput) so as to move slowly toward better economic performance (output), the question of its legitimacy remains.

For ECB governance to become more fully legitimate, two things are required: First, the ECB needs to concentrate on continuing to do "whatever it takes" in monetary policy as quasi-lender of last resort and as bank supervisor. This means that, as Benjamin Braun and Leah Downey put it, the ECB needs to move definitively beyond the ideas of the "holy trinity" of monetary policymaking developed over the previous thirty years, focused on inflation targeting, with price stability the goal, banking independence the institutional arrangement, and short-term interest rates the instrument.[79] Second, it needs to focus on continuing to be the "hero" in monetary policy, and give up the last of its "ogre"-like pressures on member states.

But to be a hero from now on, even more will be required of the ECB. This is not simply because much still needs to be done to bring the Eurozone back up to a "stable" rate of inflation (at 2 percent) if not beyond. Equally if not more important are the other threats to monetary "stability," most importantly the challenges related to inequality and climate change.

A discussion among central bankers has already begun on the pros and cons of greater central bank activism with regard to both sets of challenges. On inequality, beyond studying the effects of QE,[80] some even propose using "helicopter money," first brought up in 2014,[81] in the form of cash grants to every person in the economy, made by national governments to avoid legitimacy problems were unelected central banking actors to decide on their own.[82] On climate change, former central bankers such as Honohan have argued for rethinking bond-buying neutrality (since it is not neutral with regard to buying bonds with a large carbon footprint),[83] while outgoing ECB Executive Board Benoît Coeuré has favored supporting the transition to a low carbon economy: "first, by helping to define the rules of the game and, second, by acting accordingly, without prejudice to price stability."[84] As to be expected, BB President Weidman's rejoinder was that he

---

[79] Braun and Downey 2020.

[80] At the moment, the effects are uncertain: while long-term bond-buying may favor richer people who hold such bonds in contrast to low-income households, easing as such may favor employment stability for low-income households and thus have an equalizing effect on income inequality. See Honohan 2019, pp. 9–10.

[81] Lonergan and Blyth 2014.   [82] Honohan 2019, p. 13, 19.

[83] Honohan 2019, pp. 17–18.

[84] Speech by Mr Benoît Coeuré, at a conference on 'Scaling up Green Finance: The Role of Central Banks', organised by the Network for Greening the Financial System, the Deutsche Bundesbank and the Council on Economic Policies, Berlin, 8 November 2018, p. 5.

would view "very critically" any such attempt to redirect ECB monetary policy to address climate change on the grounds that these kinds of initiatives remained the responsibility of politicians.[85] But this flew in the face of the commitment by the new head of the ECB, Christine Lagarde, to make climate change a "mission-critical" priority for the central bank.[86]

In conclusion, the problem for a more "political" ECB is that it needs to guard its own independence to ensure the procedural legitimacy of its monetary policy while coordinating with more input legitimate EU institutions—EU member-state leaders in the Council as well as the members of the EP—in ways that effectively address both inequality and climate change while continuing to govern the euro. This is no easy task, given an increasingly politically divided Council and a weakened EP. As a result, the ECB also needs to make sure to communicate directly to the public in order to legitimate charting an innovative pathway to the future.

---

[85] Speech by Jens Weidman at the German Bundesbank, Oct. 29, 2019 https://www.bundesbank.de/en/press/speeches/climate-change-and-central-banks-812618
[86] *Financial Times* Nov. 27, 2019 https://www.ft.com/content/61ef385a-1129-11ea-a225-db2f231cfeae

7

The EU Commission

"Ayatollahs of Austerity" or "Ministers of Moderation"?

The Commission has a difficult role to play. It is at one and the same time an independent executive, responsible for the initiation of legislation and acting as "Guardian of the Treaties"; a subordinate bureaucracy, charged to "execute" the decisions of the Council, the political authority to which it is directly account-able as its delegated agent; and a legislative co-decision maker in tandem with the Council and the EP, to which it has also become increasingly accountable. The Eurozone crisis has intensified the contradictions in its role. While the Council's increased intergovernmental decision-making during the crisis initially appeared to have turned the Commission into something of a secretariat when it came to the preparation of Eurozone legislation,[1] the Commission nevertheless was able to play a powerful role in Eurozone governance. Not only did the Commission provide many of the ideas for Eurozone governance that were then approved via Council-led intergovernmental agreements or legislated with the EP via the co-decision method. The resulting intergovernmental pacts and legislative packs also served to enhance the Commission's own discretionary powers of oversight and enforcement in the context of the European Semester.

Public perceptions of the EU Commission's approach to governance can be encapsulated by two very different stories that have crystallized over the course of the crisis. The first depicts EU Commission officials as the unaccountable and secretive "Ayatollahs of Austerity" who zealously pushed rules focused on fiscal consolidation and structural reforms targeting economic competitiveness. In contrast, the second story paints EU Commission officials as "Ministers of Moderation" whose legitimacy stems from their efforts to reconcile demands for strict enforcement of the rules with needs for greater flexibility and social ori-entation. Neither storyline entirely fits the complex reality, which has in any case changed over time. The Commission's initial responses to the crisis better reflect the "Ayatollahs of Austerity" framing, especially from 2010 to 2012, as Commission officials appeared to rigidly implement the restrictive stability rules and structural reforms that they had a major role in designing. "Ministers of

---

[1] Fabbrini 2013; Schmidt 2015a.

Europe's Crisis of Legitimacy: Governing by Rules and Ruling by Numbers in the Eurozone. Vivien A. Schmidt, Oxford University Press (2020). © Vivien A. Schmidt.
DOI: 10.1093/oso/9780198797050.001.0001

Moderation" increasingly came to define the Commission's subsequent years, as its officials slowly reinterpreted the rules with greater moderation and more social content, albeit "by stealth," hiding it with their Ayatollah-sounding discourses under the Commission led by President José Manuel Barroso. As of 2015, however, the new self-described "political" Commission led by Jean-Claude Juncker admitted to its reinterpretations, even going so far as to specify rules for its reinterpretations so as to promote greater accountability along with transparency. It also further 'socialized' the European Semester, culminating with its proclamation of the European Pillar of Social Rights in 2017, as it sought to balance the push for fiscal consolidation and economic competitiveness with recommendations focused on improving labor market conditions and welfare state protections. The main exception to the view of the Commission as a moderating force is with regard to the program countries under Troika rule, where the Commission's push for austerity came under direct orders of the Eurogroup Finance Ministers, and thus was not always acting for itself but rather as the voice of the Council.

The Commission's procedural legitimacy has been highly contested, whatever the perspective on its Eurozone governance. From outside the EU institutions, scholars and analysts have condemned the Commission for its Ayatollah-like rigidity in implementing the rules, in particular with regard to program countries. From the inside, the Council saw the Commission as lacking in accountability, but has been divided between Northern European member-state leaders, who accused it of bending the rules too much, and Southern European leaders, who said it did not bend them enough. And of course, transparency was in jeopardy as a result of the Commission's reinterpretation of the rules "by stealth." As such, the Commission has found itself between a rock and a hard place in the Eurozone crisis, sandwiched between the leaders of countries seeking greater flexibility—namely non-program as well as program countries under Troika surveillance—and member-state leaders in the Council insisting on applying the rules strictly—the Germans most prominently but also the Finns and Dutch, who kept close tabs on the Commission, and held it to task in Eurogroup meetings on the European Semester.

This chapter starts with a discussion of the Commission's power and procedural legitimacy. It considers the relative power of the Commission in relationship to the Council and the political dynamics of interaction between the two bodies. The chapter next examines the ways in which the Commission can be seen as acting as "ayatollahs of austerity"—as the harsh enforcer of the European Semester, in particular during the fast-burning phase of the crisis between 2010 and 2012—and then goes on to explore its shift to moderating ministers with their increasingly flexible interpretation of the rules and efforts to socialize the Semester. The chapter ends with a consideration of the problematic impact of Commission oversight in the European Semester on national sovereignty and democracy, and the way in which this may have been alleviated over time.

Commission Power and Procedural Legitimacy

As befits a bureaucracy, the EU Commission depends for its legitimacy primarily on the quality of its throughput legitimacy, that is, the efficacy, transparency, inclusiveness, and openness of its performance of the duties assigned it by the input-legitimate bodies to which it is accountable—the Council and, increasingly over time, the EP. With the onset of the Eurozone crisis, however, the "master" to whom the Commission saw itself accountable was narrowed to the Council as a result of the massive increase in intergovernmental decision-making and the sidelining of the EP.[2] In this context, the Commission appeared to have lost much of its powers of initiative to the increasingly active European Council.[3] But Council legislation focused on reinforcing the Eurozone's "governing by rules and numbers"—itself mostly proposed by the Commission itself—further strengthened the Commission's powers as enforcer in the European Semester. The Commission's own legislative proposals in fact vastly increased its powers of oversight as it built in the discretionary authority that enabled it to reinterpret the rules[4]—if only "by stealth." Although the Council took charge with regard to the big decisions over what to do, the Commission exercised ever-increasing control, much of which resulted from its enhanced institutional competences and innovative ideas.[5] In the European Semester in particular, the Commission vastly increased its supranational powers, with discretionary authority to enforce the various oversight functions of the macroeconomic imbalance and excessive deficit procedures. With such new powers, the Commission's legitimacy also became linked to the output performance of the policies it administered. As for input legitimacy, its (throughput) processes of oversight over national governments' budgets undermined the member states' parliamentary prerogatives over budgetary matters and, thereby, national political legitimacy.

But there were nonetheless significant limits to what the Commission could do. In the absence of real remedies to the crisis, such as a fiscal union or Eurobonds, and in light of a Council narrative focused on the sinners who overspent, the Commission was stuck with searching for solutions, in the inimitable words of Deborah Mabbett and Waltraud Schelkle, "like the drunk who looks for his lost keys under the lamp post" because "that is where the light is."[6] Recognizing this reality, in particular as output performance deteriorated, the Commission increasingly made exceptions and flexible adjustments for non-program countries while slowly redefining the rules and orders of priority in its Annual Growth Surveys and paying growing attention to social policy. But it tried to avoid acknowledging its rules reinterpretations publicly, not only because it lacked the

---

[2] Fabbrini 2013.   [3] Bickerton et al. 2015.   [4] Dehousse 2016.
[5] See discussion in Chapter 3, on "politicization at the top."
[6] Mabbett and Schelkle 2014.

independent authority of the ECB but also because it felt constant pressures from the member states in the Council either to make exceptions to the rules or to deny them. As a result, between 2010 and late 2014 the Commission maintained a harsh discourse focused on the necessity of austerity and structural reform so as to circumvent the political pressures and objections from pro-austerity Council members. Beginning in 2015, however, the new more "political" Commission changed the order of priorities of the Annual Growth Survey toward investment for growth, proclaimed its flexibility, and socialized the European Semester.

The Politicization of Commission Governance

Unlike the ECB, which has the autonomy to reinterpret its own rules and therefore communicated that its reinterpretations remained true to its cardinal rules, the Commission had none of the ECB's independence and none of its legitimating discourse. At the same time that the Commission's enhanced oversight responsibilities in the European Semester have given it a tremendous amount of "political" discretion to make decisions, such decisions are subject to member states' ability to amend most of them. The member states in the Council, moreover, have increasingly subjected the Commission to political scrutiny for discretionary decisions that they have interpreted as political rather than purely technical. Commission governance, in other words, has become highly politicized in the context of the Eurozone crisis. Such politicization comes not only as a result of the changes in Commission leadership but also in consequence of the increasingly politicized dynamics of interaction between the Commission and the Council as well as within them.

Politics has of course always been present to some extent in Commission dealings with member states in the Council. But it has only been since the mid 2000s that such politics has been acknowledged. José Manuel Barroso was appointed President of the Commission because his political "color" reflected that of the majority in the newly elected 2004 EP. This was later made official by the Lisbon Treaty, which mandated the European Council to take the EP elections into account when nominating a candidate, on the grounds that political orientation in appointment is acceptable even though party politics within the Commission must be avoided.[7] That said, what "politics" means for the Commission has changed over time both within the presidency of Barroso (2004–14) and between it and that of Jean-Claude Juncker (Nov. 2014–2019).

If the Barroso Commission at the onset of the crisis was often seen as a secretariat to the Council, and aligned with Northern European leaders, by the end of

---

[7] Schmidt 2006, p. 162.

Barroso's term it was regarded as anything but. Initially, the Commission, imbued with the ideas of the Brussels–Frankfurt Consensus, not only enforced harsh austerity, but its communicative discourse repeatedly emphasized its strict adherence to the stability rules, framing the crisis as stemming from fiscal profligacy and demanding that member states put their houses in order.[8] But by 2013 the Commission's practices had changed. It became increasingly flexible in its macroeconomic judgments, despite the fact that the discourse remained the same, as it reinterpreted the rules by stealth in order to improve performance.[9] And it introduced more social content into its structural reform recommendations. Much of the change in the Barroso Commission's practices was incremental and can be chalked up to experience, that is, to the time it took for the Commission to "learn" how to navigate during the fast-burning crisis as well as to recognize that the harsh initial measures did not work, producing a double-dip recession in which performance plummeted while citizen dissatisfaction increased, to the detriment of both input and output legitimacy.[10] Internal pressures to be more inclusive in consultations on drafting recommendations, in particular with regard to social policy, also played an important role in changing practices.[11] In contrast, the decision not to admit the changes was clearly political—the result of the fact that the Commission had to deal with a Council divided between Northern Europeans putting on the pressure for continued discipline, come what may, and the Southern Europeans pushing for greater flexibility to promote growth.

But however "political" the Barroso Commission may have appeared to members of the Council, the changeover from the Barroso to the Juncker Commission constituted a difference in kind and not just in degree. This followed not only from differences in policy agenda but also from changes in the discourses of legitimation about that agenda. Institutionally, Barroso's appointment in 2004 was the decision of a Council that took into account the political orientation of the majority. Juncker's, instead, was the choice of a Council that found itself unable to circumvent the EP's clever campaign to have the *Spitzenkandidat* named as Commission President—despite great reluctance in particular in the cases of British PM David Cameron and German Chancellor Merkel.[12] The new Commission President was therefore more directly tied to the (input-legitimate) EP than the previous one, who owed his job more to the Council, even if vetted by the EP. As a result, the Commission gained a fuller sense of its dual accountability, to the EP as well as the Council, which also served to reinforce Commission autonomy by enabling it to play one actor off against the other. Increasingly over the course of the crisis, however, this meant enlisting EP support against the Council.

---

[8] Warren et al. 2017.   [9] Schmidt 2016a.   [10] Schmidt 2016a.
[11] Copeland and Daly 2018.   [12] Dinan 2015.

The ideas also changed. Barroso was politically a neoliberal who maintained the fiction of an apolitical Commission. Juncker was a Christian Democrat (with a strong social conscience) who had already announced in the electoral campaign of 2014 that his would be a "political" Commission. By this he did not mean that the Commission would engage in partisan politics but rather that it would be politically sensitive to citizens' (input) concerns and preferences. In this, Juncker was clearly attempting to respond to growing citizen discontent, evident in the rise of Euroskeptic parties and the decline in public trust in the EU. The differences in the "political" orientation of the Presidents came out clearly in their discourses of policy legitimation. A qualitative content analysis of the State of the Union Addresses of Barroso and Juncker reveals that whereas Barroso's legitimizing speeches focused on the "rationality" of EU decisions mainly in terms of economic outputs, Juncker's were more politically charged, referencing input-related concerns of democracy and popular sovereignty.[13]

All of this helps explain why, as the EPP candidate to the Commission Presidency, Juncker positioned himself as a political leader rather than a technocratic one as he detailed his "Political Guidelines for the next European Commission." Moreover, intent on making sure that the Commission was no longer seen as "the bad guy,"[14] he committed himself to socializing the European Semester while introducing greater flexibility, albeit with more clearly specified "rules" for flexibility within the existing SGP rules, announced in January 2015.[15] The new guidelines codified three clauses: first, the "investment clause," in which member states' contributions to EU-linked investment projects were not to be included in deficit and debt calculations (with more specific conditions for countries subject to the Excessive Debt Procedure);[16] second, a "structural reform clause," which excluded the costs of such reforms from deficit calculation if they were "major," "fully implemented," and foreseen to "have long-term positive budgetary effects, including by raising potential sustainable growth"; and third, the "cyclical conditions clause," which stipulates that the fiscal effort should be "modulated" with respect to economic cycles and possible economic downturns.[17] With these new guidelines, the Commission directly acknowledged the flexibility that had increasingly been in play in previous years but denied in the discourse, at the same time as giving itself even more leeway for rules reinterpretation.

The publication of these guidelines drew immediate support from the EP, which had long been pushing for greater flexibility in the interests of input and

---

[13] Pansardi and Battegazzorre 2018.   [14] Zeitlin and Vanhercke 2018, p. 168.
[15] Commission 2015.
[16] Eligible investments are national expenditures on projects co-funded by the EU under the Structural and Cohesion Policy, Trans-European Networks and the Connecting Europe Facility, as well as national co-financing of projects financed by the European Fund for Strategic Investments.
[17] Commission 2015; see discussion in Crespy and Schmidt 2017.

output legitimacy, and direct opposition from the ECB and Germany. Within the Council, the polarization on the issue of flexibility only intensified. But this did not faze the Commission, where officials from 2015 on readily acknowledged their more "political" role. One official in the Secretariat General's office quoted Commissioner Katainen as saying that "we're allowed to be more political" and went on to note that it helps to have so many former Prime Ministers as Commissioners because they have a different authority in the member states.[18] Juncker himself, in legitimation of this exercise of increasing political discretion, declared in his first State of the Union speech to the EP: "You cannot run a single currency on the basis of rules and statistics alone. It needs constant political assessment, as the basis of new economic, fiscal and social policy choices."[19]

Finally, Juncker also sought to exercise "political" leadership, through innovative suggestions for the future of the EU, as in the Five Presidents' report[20]— although it had little success. However, Juncker's organizational reforms, such as making Vice-Presidents project term leaders and strengthening the role of the Secretariat General, reinforced his powers in relation to other actors, including with an increasingly assertive European Council and a more autonomous European Parliament.[21]

The Commission's Inter-Institutional Political Dynamics

A major problem for the Commission over time has been the growing politicization of its interactions with members of the Council. Increased political tension between the Council and the Commission has arisen from the ambiguity involved in who is assumed to be responsible and/or accountable for the policies. The Council set the rules but shunned political debate on the priorities, even as individual member-state leaders would complain about the Commission's "political" decision-making—meaning any exercise of technical discretion of which they disapproved. The Commission generally carried out the policies, using its own discretion even while relying on informal understandings of the member states' will, often gained through informal contacts with individual member states.[22] Over the course of the Eurozone crisis, so long as the Commission maintained a highly restrictive definition of austerity and structural reform, it had the approval of the more powerful "core" Northern European creditor countries, but naturally not that of the countries found in violation of the rules. Later, however, as it became more flexible in its application of the rules to ensure better results, France

---

[18] Cited in Schön-Quinlivan and Scipioni 2017.
[19] Juncker, State of the Union speech to the EP, September 9, 2015 http://europa.eu/rapid/press-release_SPEECH-15-5614_en.htm
[20] Juncker et al. 2015.   [21] Bürgin 2018.   [22] Crum 2015.

and Southern European creditors were less critical whereas powerful Northern European leaders complained bitterly.

The Commission has naturally had to be sensitive to the Council's authority not only because of how the Council might react as a body to its decisions but also due to how individual member states may respond. This can often push in opposing directions. One instance of such pressure was French President Hollande's angry outburst against the Commission's 2013 European Semester recommendations on structural reforms of the French pension system on the grounds that "the Commission has no right to dictate what we have to do."[23] As one high-level EU official noted, the Commission pulled back, having learned its lesson, explaining: "Countries want to remain masters of their reform agenda, and don't want in any way to be subordinated to a Commission whose legitimacy in these matters is fragile at best."[24] And yet, in 2014, the Commission criticism of France's 2015 draft budget drew angry reactions again. The French Finance Minister Michel Sapin invoked French sovereignty, and declared that the country would not modify its budget given its social and economic difficulties. But two weeks later he provided some "*précisions*" and new measures to reduce the deficit by 3.6 billion euros more.[25] The incident became highly politicized "at the bottom," with the extreme right National Front targeting the "complacent attitude of the French government in the face of budgetary injunctions from the European Commission" and claiming that "We should not act like a penitent and contrite student in response to a Commission blinded by austerity-based dogmas."[26]

While the Commission has to pay attention to French and Southern European leaders pushing for growth and flexibility, it also has to deal with Northern Europeans demanding strict adherence to the rules. The Northern Europeans saw Commission action as unacceptable politicization because instead of remaining rules-based, it "moved [macroeconomic policy decision-making] into the sphere of collectively binding decision-making."[27] Northern European countries' increasing opposition to flexibility came to a head in 2014, with Germany and Finland making a frontal attack on the Commission in an eight-page memo in which they claimed that the Commission used "a somewhat arbitrary approach" in granting budgetary flexibility, and went so far as to suggest that "a separate pair of eyes" was needed to ensure that the rules were properly applied.[28] German Finance Minister Schäuble went on record repeatedly in calling for an independent agency to take over the European Semester budgetary oversight from the Commission, so unhappy had he become with what he saw as the Commission's "politicized" flexibility. And in 2016, the President of the Bundesbank himself stated:

[23] *Le Figaro* May 29, 2013.   [24] Cited in Quatremer 2016.
[25] *Le Monde* Oct. 27, 2014; *Le Point* Oct. 27, 2014, cited in Schön-Quinlivan and Scipioni 2017.
[26] *Le Point* Oct, 27, 2014, cited in Schön-Quinlivan and Scipioni 2017.
[27] Zürn 2016, p. 167.   [28] *Financial Times* Feb. 28, 2014.

"I do not believe that a Commission which interprets its mandate as politically as the current one is best suited to ensure budget surveillance in Europe."[29]

Matters were not helped that same year when Commission President Juncker quipped, when asked about making exceptions to the rules for France, that the reason was "because it is France."[30] This, naturally, led to a firestorm of accusations by Northern European finance ministers in the Eurogroup and conservative politicians in the Council that the Commission President was playing politics, with political discretion exercised in the context of budgetary oversight for Southern European countries as well as France.[31] Since then, moreover, Northern European leaders have continued to condemn the Commission's "political" turn. The most recent incident came in February 2019 when the Dutch Minister of Foreign Affairs, Stef Blok, in a wide-ranging opinion piece in the *Financial Times*, made a point of insisting that "[a] Commission that prides itself on being political undermines its own objectivity" while complaining with regard to the compromise decision on the Italian budget with the populist coalition government that "it appears the rules of the stability and growth pact were bent for the sake of political expediency...In Europe, a deal must be a deal."[32]

Council members' criticism of the Commission was not limited to its actions regarding France or Southern European countries, however. The Germans engaged in equally politically charged debates with the Commission, in this case on the issue of fiscal space.[33] It had a harsh response in 2016 to the Commission push for all countries (without even naming Germany) to engage in fiscal expansion, insisting that "the Commission has no right to decide on its fiscal space."[34] The previous year, moreover, Germany had managed to quash the European Commission recommendation in its draft Country-Specific Report (CSR) that Germany reduce its fiscal surplus in order to "further increase public investment in infrastructure, education and research, including by using the available fiscal space." Over Commission objections, the final recommendation approved by the Council did not include any references to the fiscal space.[35] But despite what were highly politically charged debates, the Commission continued to press Germany on its fiscal surplus, by doing more to raise wages for workers as well as to increase investment so as to provide a fiscal stimulus not just for Germany but for the Eurozone as a whole.

More generally, any country that finds itself in the sights of the Commission is likely to protest, which it often does also on grounds of political (input)

---

[29] Reuters, Nov. 25, 2016.
[30] Reuters, May 31, 2016 http://uk.reuters.com/article/uk-eu-deficit-france/eu-gives-budget-leeway-to-france-because-it-is-france-juncker-idUKKCN0YM1N0
[31] Der Spiegel online, June 17, 2016 http://www.spiegel.de/international/europe/eu-commission-president-juncker-under-fire-a-1098232.html
[32] *Financial Times* Feb. 4, 2019 https://www.ft.com/content/0f306466-286a-11e9-9222-7024d72222bc
[33] Buti and Turrini 2017.   [34] *Irish Times*, Nov. 18, 2016.   [35] Coman 2019b.

legitimacy. It is therefore not surprising that when Belgium was pressed to further cut its budget for 2013 or face sanctions, Belgian Minister (and EU democracy scholar) Paul Magnette responded "Who is Olli Rehn?" in reference to the Finnish Commissioner for Economic and Monetary Affairs. That the Hungarian PM echoed the statement shows that the spectrum of concern goes from the left through to the (authoritarian) right. But equally significant, despite the protests, is that national governments generally complied with Commission requests, if only after a period of wrangling over the details.

In short, the Commission has had to navigate very narrow "political straits" in its European Semester governance. On one side it has had member states under surveillance, seeking fiscal space for economic growth in order to respond to citizens' demands while reducing their deficits and paying off their debts. On the other, it has had member states pushing for stricter and more punitive application of the rules, in response to their own citizens' worries about having to pay the debts of others. This suggests, as Bauer and Becker contend, that the Commission engaged in "highly political activity to deliver opinions and recommendations— be it in terms of financial stability support or policy surveillance."[36]

Moreover, ideational lines of battle were not just drawn between Northern and Southern European member states in the Council, but also within the Commission as well as between the Commission and the Council, and took place in a number of different contexts in diverse venues. The European Semester is deliberated and negotiated with different actors at different stages of the process, including discussions within the Commission on the elaboration of the Annual Growth Surveys and Country Reports, bilateral meetings between the Commission and the member states on the Country Reports and Country Specific Recommenations (CSRs), and further discussions within the Council and the Commission. For the CSRs, themselves, there is a complex process characterized by cooperation and bargaining, as the CSRs are reviewed and refined.[37] And finally, deliberation and bargaining also takes place in the Council, when the Commission invites the Council to "comply or explain" any attempt to deviate from its initial proposal (which since 2012 requires a written explanation from

---

[36] Bauer and Becker 2014, p. 226.

[37] First the implementation of the previous year's CSRs is reviewed in the Council Advisory Committees, including the Economic Policy Committee (EPC), the Employment Committee (EMCO) and Social Protection Committee (SPC), which produce a multilateral view of each country's actions and performance. Then the new CSRs proposed by the Commission are reviewed in these committees, and amendments are proposed by member states. Where the Commission does not accept the proposed amendments, then these can be passed by a Reinforced (not Reversed) Qualified Majority Vote, following the rules introduced by the Treaties of Nice and Lisbon (not the Six-Pack), which changed in 2017. Where the CSRs fall into areas of overlap between the different committees, the final text is settled in a jumbo meeting between the EPC-EMCO-SPC, or in a meeting of the Economic and Finance Committee (EFC) attended by the Chair of the SPC. When the text of a CSR is amended by the committees, they write the Comply-or-Explain text on behalf of the Council. Thanks to Jonathan Zeitlin for these details. See for further information Zeitlin and Vanhercke 2014, 2018.

the Council for any modification) and a vote involving reverse qualified majority voting (RQMV) to reverse a Commission recommendation.[38]

Finally, as one high-level Commission official said to me, in response to my comments about the seeming rigidity of the Commission's application of the rules in the 2011–15 period: "But Vivien, after all, rules are rules!"[39] For Commission officials, the exercise of discretion was constrained by the legal and practical limits imposed by the legislative and treaty-based rules, like them or not. Moreover, there were also internal divisions within the Commission, not just between it and the Council. Many officials were prepared to defend strict interpretations of the fiscal rules and to focus structural reforms on economic competitiveness, while others pushed for greater flexibility and more attention to the social concerns of the Europe 2020 goals. This was as true for lower and mid-level officials as for those at the highest level. As Ramona Coman shows, the Commission at the level of the "College" (made up of the Commissioners) was itself divided on the question of flexibility and sanctions even in 2015 and later, with newer members of the College of Commissioners appointed under Juncker in favor of increased flexibility in the interests of output performance, and those who served under Barroso's Commission supporting the strict application of the rules to preserve their credibility in the defense of procedural legitimacy.[40]

Commission as Ayatollahs of Austerity

Paul Krugman once called the Commission "the Rehn of terror," in a play on the name of DG ECFIN Commissioner Olli Rehn, for its promotion of austerity policies.[41] I prefer to call the Commission "Ayatollahs of Austerity."[42] The question is whether this is an accurate depiction of the Commission. Certainly, in an initial period, between 2010 and 2012, the Commission seemed to be unreasonably rigid and inflexible, as cheerleaders for the harshest austerity and the most restrictive of definitions of structural reform. The Commission, after all, is the EU actor that proposed the European Semester as an oversight mechanism in the first place, and that initiated the Six-Pack and Two-Pack legislation that specified the sanction-triggering numbers. And the Commission was also the actor that, following up on the recommendation of Merkel and Sarkozy in August 2011, sought to ensure the automaticity of the sanctions by proposing a regulation to allow it to suspend all EU funding, including structural and investment funds, to any

---

[38] Coman 2019b.   [39] Interview with author, June 8, 2015.   [40] Coman 2018, p. 11.
[41] *New York Times* February 22, 2013 https://krugman.blogs.nytimes.com/2013/02/22/paul-de-grauwe-and-the-rehn-of-terror/
[42] And I did actually call DG ECFIN "Ayatollahs of Austerity" at the first conference of my part-time fellowship in Sept 2014. By the end, however, I came to see it as more Ministers of Moderation, as I announced in the last of the fellowship conferences.

member state that "fails to take effective action in the context of the economic governance process."[43] Subsequently, moreover, even once the Commission began to reinterpret the rules by stealth, its failure to admit its growing flexibility meant that Commission officials continued to be seen as akin to ayatollahs, at least from the outside. Only starting in 2015 did the image of the Commission begin to soften.

Governing by Rules

Most notable in the Commission's governance of the sovereign debt crisis begin-ning in 2010 was the reversal of its approach from the period immediately before, during the financial crisis and the crisis in the real economy. In the mid 2000s, as the rules of the Stability and Growth Pact (SGP) were eased, there was some ques-tion as to whether the SGP itself could survive. Its death knell seemed to have been sounded with the onset of the crisis in 2008, when the Commission champi-oned deficit spending through the European Economic Recovery Plan (EERP), in line with the Council's preferred move toward Keynesian demand policies in response to the crisis.[44] But by setting up the EERP as an exceptional response to a major fast-burning crisis even as it continued to apply the SGP rules, the Commission found a way of bringing the rules into harmony with the crisis-fighting response. Thus, while continuing to open up EDPs suggested principled com-mitment to "sound finances," creating the EERP sanctified non-compliance by "stretching the boundaries of exceptionality."[45] This approach to Eurozone gov-ernance also ensured that the Commission had little problem dropping the exceptional EERP when the Council switched to austerity policy and a focus on structural reform in May 2010 while the ECB pressed for stronger fiscal control mechanisms.

As already noted in Chapter 4, the Commission itself proposed the European Semester in May and June 2010 as its new precision instrument for "governing by the rules and ruling by the numbers." The European Semester provided the Commission with the framework through which to coordinate member-state budgetary and economic policies and monitor their budgets on an ongoing basis. The various legislative pacts and intergovernmental compacts that the Commission drafted—at Council request and German and ECB instigation—served to rein-force the rules, specify the numbers, and increase the sanctions on member states found in violation. The Commission's institutional power came not only from its Semester-based responsibility to monitor member-state compliance and even propose sanctions but also from the fact that the Council's hands were tied

---

[43] COM(2012)0496, cited in Coman 2018; see also discussion in Coman 2018.
[44] Larch et al. 2010.   [45] Pelc 2009, 335.

through the RQMV that made it difficult for the member-state leaders to counter Commission recommendations. But even as the rules and numbers of the European Semester tied the hands of the member states, they also tied those of the Commission, by limiting its room for manoeuver as a result of the increasingly precise definition of rules and numerical targets. However, rather than weakening the Commission, it actually strengthened its hand.

Although increasingly precise, the rules themselves still left the Commission greater margins for flexibility than it admitted publicly. The Six-Pack regulations increased Commission discretion in evaluating a member state's fiscal position and adjustment effort, since the Commission was to take into account the "range of relevant factors" when judging non-compliance—including mitigating or aggravating ones—along with "exceptional circumstances."[46] All of this, as Scharpf has argued, ensured the Commission a kind of built-in discretion without any built-in accountability, in particular with regard to the Macroeconomic Imbalance Procedure (MIP), which the Commission was essentially free to decide when to launch (or not).[47] The Commission's flexibility comes from the fact that although Article 4 of the Regulation (European Union 2011) lists the items to be included in the MIP scoreboard, it makes the Commission responsible not only for setting up the MIP scoreboard but also for gathering further evidence, contextualizing it with regard to the Eurozone and EU area, and even changing the criteria. This, as Manuella Moschella notes, "gives the EU Commission both flexibility and a high degree of discretion in interpreting the data."[48]

But whatever the increasing flexibility of the Commission over time in its interpretation of the rules, the actual calculations matter, giving way to a "politics of numbers" that is extremely important for any assessment—and that raises questions about the "accounting" end of the exercise of discretion.[49]

Ruling by Numbers

Numbers matter, and how they are calculated matters a great deal to the countries in danger of falling under fiscal surveillance procedures or needing a bailout. The determination of the numbers is not solely in the Commission's hands, though, because the country statistics upon which the Commission bases its decisions are the domain of the statisticians of Eurostat. Eurostat statisticians decide whether to classify bailouts of loss-making public enterprises as capital transfers on grounds of poor recovery prospects, or as financial transactions, which do not

---

[46] Reg 1177/2011, Article 1(2)(a)—see discussion in Mabbett and Schelkle 2014, pp. 12–13.
[47] See Scharpf 2012a.   [48] Moschella 2014, p. 1276.
[49] On the issues involved in the politics of numbers, see, eg, Mügge and Stellinga 2014.

show up in a country's deficit.[50] Although the norms are applied to all member states without prejudice, in unstable macroeconomic situations calculations of country deficit and debt based on such norms tend to disadvantage countries that the markets consider less viable.[51]

As a result, although Ireland, the Netherlands, and Germany all had bank bailouts, only Ireland's were classified as capital transfers, thereby increasing its debt by 20.2 percent of GDP in 2010, despite the fact that the actual recovery for Germany turned out to be no better. But because Germany's bailouts were classified as a financial transaction, they had no effect on its balance sheet.[52] Thus, statisticians' accounting procedures and classifications, with no political bias intended, can nevertheless make it much harder for already weak countries to recover and makes it more likely that they will fall foul of the rules. It may even make it appear that countries are hiding debt figures, whereas it is only the case that in worsening economic environments, statisticians reclassified their public enterprises as capital transfers because of the magnitude of their losses—as with both Greece and Portugal.[53]

The game of numbers had the greatest impact on the program countries that, in exchange for a bailout, were subject to conditionality via the Troika. On the basis of the numbers, they have been forced to legislate harsh pro-cyclical austerity measures, with enforced cuts pushed by the Troika for Greece, Ireland, and Portugal. But the game of numbers was also problematic for the other member states of the Eurozone which were not in programs.[54] In the first years of the crisis, demands for rapid deficit and debt reductions for countries which breached the deficits and debt numbers, accompanied by recommendations for structural reforms that included slashing welfare-state budgets and deregulating labor markets, led virtually all European governments to adopt major austerity plans which translated into massive cuts and "efficiency measures" in welfare and public services.[55]

In all such cases, in non-program and program countries alike, Commission governance came in for criticism not only on grounds of output legitimacy, given the deteriorating macroeconomic and socioeconomic picture—to be discussed in Chapter 9—but also on grounds of procedural legitimacy. One such criticism had to do with the initial centralization of the evaluation process in the Directorate General for Economic and Financial Affairs (DG ECFIN), reinforced by Commission President Barroso's decision to grant autonomy of decision to the Vice-President and Commissioner for Economic and Monetary Affairs, Olli Rehn. This dispensed Rehn from discussion, let alone decision, by other Commissioners in

---

[50] Mabbett and Schelkle 2014, pp. 12–13.
[51] See discussion in Mabbett and Schelkle 2014, pp. 15–17.
[52] Mabbett and Schelkle 2014, p. 18.   [53] Mabbett and Schelkle 2014, pp. 18–19.
[54] See discussion in Chapter 9 on the socioeconomic impact of austerity.
[55] See Crespy 2016, ch. 6.

regular meetings of the Commission. The result was a process in which DG ECFIN was perceived even in other parts of the Commission—perhaps with a bit of exaggeration—to work out the numbers on its own, largely in secret, to make its decisions, and only then to inform the rest of the Commission.[56] While this may have improved the efficacy of the application of the rules, DG ECFIN's secrecy was problematic in terms of transparency. Lack of inclusiveness in the evaluation process was also an issue, in particular at first, since it shut out other Directorates General that could have provided more nuanced information to moderate judgments about the numbers as well as the effects of any cuts (although as we will see presently, this changed over time).

Another critique comes with regard to the Commission's role in the Troika, where it was largely responsible—arguably along with the ECB—for pushing hard on austerity. Already in 2008, with the loan bailout programs for the CEECs, the Commission had insisted on the strictest conditionality, against the wishes of the IMF, making this the European "rescue of the Washington consensus."[57] The strict conditionality imposed on Eurozone members as of 2010 was also due to Commission insistence, in particular with regard to the harsh terms imposed on Greece that set the ground rules for all future bailouts. The IMF itself later not only conceded that the policy on Greece was a major mistake, because it assumed that severe austerity would lead in short order to growth;[58] it also condemned the Commission's emphasis on the throughput rules to the detriment of output performance, because "the Commission, with the focus of its reforms more on compliance with EU norms than on growth impact, was not able to contribute much to identifying growth enhancing structural reforms."[59] This critique was echoed in a June 2014 report by the French Commissariat on Strategy, which also noted that in the European Semester, the efficacy of the approach "merits discussion" in view of the formalism and heaviness of the procedures, the possible inefficacy of sanctions, and the poor integration of the social and employment dimensions—considered only in terms of costs and not with regard to their possible productive effects.[60]

For program countries, moreover, the demanded reductions in the substantive level of protection resulted in across-the-board cuts in wages, pensions, health care, social assistance, and education, and produced increased penury, misery, and violations of human rights, at the same time as negatively affecting growth. It should be noted that blame also lies with member state governments, whose politicians went for across-the-board cuts rather than targeted reforms that might have hurt their own particular constituencies more. Different members of the Troika also occasionally pointed to the need for, say, increased spending on social assistance for the poor and training for the unemployed in Latvia, and for

---

[56] Interview with a senior Commission official, September 2013.   [57] Lütz and Kranke 2014.
[58] See discussion in Chapter 9.   [59] IMF 2013, p. 13.   [60] Nicolaï and Valla 2014, p. 16.

unemployment insurance in Italy.[61] But whatever the attribution of responsibility between Troika and member-states, the resulting programs can be seen as violations of the understandings at the basis of the European Union itself, in which social policy was left to the member states in order to ensure that it would remain input-legitimate to the citizens, even as the EU provided output legitimacy via better performance through freer markets.[62] It is significant that, in a textual analysis of the massive number of documents related to the programs of the countries under conditionality between 2010 and 2014, André Sapir and colleagues found that the main concern that appeared over and over again involved fiscal matters, while poverty was never mentioned once for any of the program countries except for Greece—and that only later on, when it became so acute an issue that it could not be avoided.[63]

Only in 2013, and for non-program countries, did the Commission tacitly acknowledge the failure of fiscal consolidation policies by agreeing to ease the policy on rapid deficit reduction (in light of the ECB call for an end to austerity). This came with a significant change in the way in which deficits were calculated, now in terms of a "primary" surplus (deficit minus interest payments). The change enabled the Commission to allow countries posting a primary surplus to delay rapid deficit reduction in order to propel growth, as seen with France and Italy, which were given two-year delays in 2013 to meet their targets.

But Commission spokespeople nonetheless stuck to a discourse that claimed that it was prior success, not failure, which allowed for a more flexible policy. Commission Vice-President and head of DG ECFIN Olli Rehn, for example, in particularly obtuse language, claimed that things were getting slightly better only because the crisis response offered "a policy mix where building a stability culture and pursuing structural reforms supportive of growth and jobs go hand in hand."[64] In response to the Northern Europeans in particular, moreover, the Commission insisted that the increasing complexity of the rules constituted a "methodological refinement," and was "no change in policy, only a change in circumstances" since "we now have more room for manoeuver" because cutting deficits was no longer such an urgent priority.[65] In cases where derogations were granted, moreover, Rehn made sure they came with extra demands for economic reforms.

In addition, continued belief that structural reform produced growth also meant that the Commission recommended but did not require member states to take into account the Commission's own Europe 2020 agenda that sought to create the conditions for growth by promoting employment, improving education, and reducing poverty and social exclusion. The "one size fits all" rules entailed not only assuming that all countries needed rapid deficit and debt reduction in the

---

[61] Zeitlin and Vanhercke 2018, p. 13; see also Crespy 2016.   [62] See Chalmers et al. 2014.
[63] Sapir et al. 2014, p. 17.   [64] Rehn 2013.   [65] *New York Times* May 17, 2013.

first two years. It also meant that structural reforms targeting labor market deregulation and welfare-state retrenchment were seen as the main answer to countries' problems with growth, thus ignoring the fact that the countries' very slow rate of increase in economic activity, which ensured little demand for new workers, was the real culprit.[66] As a result, while social retrenchment was pushed forcefully for countries with little "fiscal space," meaning those with or at risk of an excessive deficit, debt, or macroeconomic imbalance, social investment was optional, and therefore unlikely to be implemented by those very countries, given their lack of fiscal room for manoeuver.[67]

Moreover, even though Commission recommendations in the CSRs did indeed pay increasing attention to social concerns during the period from 2011 to 2015, the content of those recommendations tended to be more focused on improving economic competitiveness than social justice. In an analysis of all of the relevant Country Specific Recommendations during this period, Paul Copeland and Mary Daly found that only a small fraction of social policy recommendations (7 percent) tended to target "market-correcting," meaning redistributive measures such as ensuring adequate income and social protection. The bulk of recommendations were instead concerned with "market making" (41 percent) alone or mixed the two (52 percent). The market-making recommendations focused on such measures as deregulating employment, cutting back on benefits and services, downgrading income redistribution, and reframing social policy to emphasize activation and human capital development. Those involving a mix of recommendations generally focused on enhancing labor market participation or reorganizing service provision.[68] With the exception of the Commissioner for Employment and Social Policy Laszlo Andor, the Barroso Commission systematically downgraded market-correction in the European Semester during this period.[69] But obstacles to promoting more market-correction also came from member states resisting Commission 'competence-creep' (mainly Northern Europe) or worried that such areas could eventually be linked to macroeconomic governance (Southern Europe).[70]

The Commission also kept a rather inflexible approach to the remaining rules. Thus, Rehn continued to allow only those countries that posted a primary surplus to increase their deficits in order to propel growth. This is why France and Italy were allowed delays but Spain was not, until the Commission agreed to change the calculation of the "structural deficit" as proposed by the Spanish government (on the grounds that it underestimated the impact of unemployment) so that it

---

[66] Crespy and Schmidt 2017.
[67] Crespy and Schmidt 2017; Crespy and Vanheuverzwijn 2017; see also discussion in Chapter 9 on the perversity of structural reforms.
[68] Copeland and Daly 2018, pp. 1005-6.
[69] Copeland and Daly 2018, p. 1006; Crespy and Menz 2015.
[70] Copeland and Daly 2018, p. 1013.

would also have a primary surplus. But although the Commission's "Output Gap Working Group" agreed to make an ad hoc methodology change for Spain because the normal calculation appeared so improbable, it refused to generalize this calculation out of "concern in some capitals" (read Germany) about the implications of using better estimates—which might ease up the pressures on program countries.[71] Subsequently, moreover, Rehn appeared to remain uncompromising—at least in his discourse—when Italian Prime Minister Renzi pushed for greater flexibility, declaring that "piling new debt on top of this old debt does not seem to improve the economic competitiveness of Italy."[72]

The inconsistency in this "game of numbers" thus also raises questions about (throughput) fairness and consistency in the application of the rules, even as it helped ensure better (output) performance. Transparency was naturally also at issue, given the discourse that constantly denied the Commission's increasingly flexible practices as it focused on member states maintaining policies of austerity (up until 2013) and structural reform throughout.

To illustrate, we take the discourse of the main public spokesperson for the Commission with regard to the European Semester between 2011 and 2014, Commissioner for Economic and Monetary Affairs Olli Rehn. Rehn's communicative discourse was all about fiscal consolidation and structural reform in order to bring down excessive deficits and address macroeconomic imbalances. Especially in the first few years, his speeches invariably referred to the need for consolidation along with structural reform. In terms of word use frequency between fall 2011 and fall 2013 (using the same set of words as in the graph for ECB President Draghi), we find similarities between Rehn's discourse and that of ECB President Draghi, despite the differences in their responsibilities (see Figure 7.1). This was most apparent in the absence of considerations of "inflation," "lender of last resort," or even "save the euro" in Rehn's public pronouncements. But although Rehn, like Draghi, repeatedly referred to the importance of stability, Rehn's discourse emphasized the "stability culture" and/or the need for financial stability through deficit and debt reduction in the member states, not price stability.[73] Additionally, Rehn's focus on competitiveness was even more pronounced than Draghi's, especially by late 2012 into 2013. Competitiveness served as a justification for the push for market-making structural reforms, which also appeared steadily at an increasingly high level. Finally, interestingly enough, while Draghi largely dropped credibility as a reference point, Rehn continued to use it, but to different ends. The word was used to recommend that the

---

[71] *Wall Street Journal* Sept. 24, 2013.   [72] *Financial Times* Feb. 18, 2014.
[73] See, eg, Rehn's speech at European American Press Club, Paris, October 1, 2013; Debate in the European Parliament, Strasbourg, June 13, 2012; Speech at the European Economic and Social Committee public hearing/Brussels, February 19, 2013.

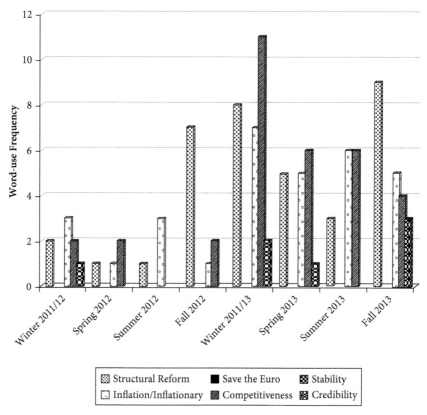

Figure 7.1. Word use frequency by Olli Rehn, EU Vice President in charge of Economic and Monetary Affairs and the Euro (Fall 2011 to Fall 2013)
* Note that the blank space left for 'Save the Euro' indicates that no mention was made of this term.
Source: Speeches and Remarks, randomized choice, 3-4 per season

member states regain credibility by consolidating their finances,[74] or that Europe regain "credibility on our road towards a stability union of both responsibility and solidarity."[75]

But hidden behind this discourse focused on stability, credibility, and competitiveness were practices that were becoming incrementally more flexible in the application of the rules and calculation of the numbers, and more socially focused.

[74] See, eg, Rehn's speech on the adoption by the Italian government of extraordinary fiscal and economic measures on Dec. 4, 2011; at the Conference on the European Semester/Warsaw on March 8, 2013; at the European American Press Club, Paris, Oct. 1, 2013; and at the Press Conference in Strasbourg, Feb. 14, 2012.
[75] Speech at the EPC Policy Breakfast in Brussels, Jan. 11, 2013.

Commission as Ministers of Moderation

While the Commission's communicative discourse remained largely uncompromising from 2010 through 2014, and outside analysts saw the Commission as tone deaf to the socioeconomic impact of numbers-targeting rules, the actual internal coordinative bureaucratic discourse—as contained in the official reports, including the Annual Growth Surveys (AGSs) and the Country-Specific Recommendations—became incrementally more inclusive of such concerns. This resulted not only from Commission responsiveness to Council admonitions as output performance deteriorated but also from an internal opening by DG ECFIN to other Directorates-General as well as to the member states in the context of the sectoral advisory committees on employment and social policy. The changes were even more dramatic from 2015 on, as the new Commission revamped the European Semester, switching the type and order of the recommendations, with investment now first and fiscal "responsibility" last, at the same time that it sought to ensure enhanced "ownership" of the Semester by national actors and civil society.[76] But even so, only those countries with "fiscal space" (read, those not under procedures for deficit or debt) were encouraged to promote growth through investment—leaving out those most in need of growth-enhancing measures.

Moderating the Rules and Numbers in the Barroso Commission

In the Annual Growth Surveys, subtle changes came in between 2011 and 2015. But the order of priorities remained the same. Austerity, or "fiscal consolidation," came first in the list of general recommendations, with structural reforms second and growth-enhancing and social measures, which slowly crept in across these years, a distant third. The harshest recommendations for austerity and structural reform came in the 2011 and 2012 exercises, since by 2013 the ECB had begun to call for an end to austerity, and that same year the Commission began softening its approach to structural reform while giving derogations on deficit procedures. But until then it meant that member states under European Semester surveillance for excessive deficits, debt, or macroeconomic imbalances were all pushed to deregulate labor markets and/or cut welfare and pension benefits, often to the detriment of socioeconomic concerns as well as of growth.

The initial experiences did indeed confirm critics' worst fears of a "one size fits all" approach in the European Semester that subordinated social cohesion goals to fiscal consolidation, budgetary austerity, and welfare retrenchment. This was clear in the first AGS (Annual Growth Survey) and Country-Specific

---

[76] Crespy and Vanheuverzwijn 2017; Vanheuverzwijn and Crespy 2018; on ownership see also Chapter 5 on the Council, regarding program countries.

Recommendations.[77] In the 2011 Semester exercise, the AGS' first priority was "to set budgetary policies on a sound footing through rigorous fiscal consolidation." The second priority, concerned with structural reform, was to engage in "rapid reduction in unemployment through labour market reforms" focused on wage devaluation for countries with high deficits and debt through implementing "concrete corrective measures" (these could include strict and sustained wage moderation, including the revision of indexation clauses in bargaining systems). Only the third proposed "growth enhancing measures," while there was no mention of social concerns such as the increase in poverty.[78]

Subsequent exercises of the European Semester were less narrowly targeted, however, at least on paper. Moreover, even in the assessment of the results of the 2011 European Semester and guidance on 2011–12 written in June 2011, the Commission was already highlighting problems with the (output) results, regarding "reaching the targets in the areas of employment, research and development, energy efficiency, tertiary education and poverty." But the focus on austerity remained, with the first substantive section, involving recommendations on the "pre-requisites for growth," beginning with: "(The) Commission considers that it is essential to stick to agreed deadlines for the correction of excessive deficits and to consolidate swiftly, moving towards the medium-term budgetary objectives specified by the Council." That said, the Commission did signal awareness of problems with questions about the inclusiveness and openness of the exercise, as well as input legitimacy, when it noted that "to build the legitimacy and effectiveness of the new EU economic governance, the Member States should decide on the best ways to involve their national parliaments, as well subnational authorities and other stakeholders, in the development and follow-up of their programs."[79]

The 2012 AGS (Annual Growth Survey) of November 2011 recommended a more socially balanced set of priorities, including "tackling unemployment and the social consequences of the crisis" together with "pursuing differentiated growth-friendly fiscal consolidation," which were reaffirmed in the 2013 and 2014 AGSs. Moreover, Country-Specific Recommendations sent to member states addressed issues of poverty reduction and social inclusion (seven in 2012, eleven in 2013, twelve in 2014) as well as issues of education, training, and active labor market policies, pensions, and health policy. This concern with socioeconomic issues was the result of a more and more collaborative process over time within the Commission itself, through more bottom-up involvement of desk officers and support from horizontal policy units across a wide range of DGs. This made for a drafting process that became increasingly deliberative and "evidence-based," in particular because it was enhanced by greater openness to

---

[77] Pochet 2010; see also discussion in Zeitlin and Vanhercke 2014, pp. 12–14.
[78] 2011 Annual Growth Survey (AGS, COM 2011, p. 9).   [79] COM(2011) 400 final, June 7.

amendment by employment and social policy actors in the specialized sectoral committees of the member states.[80] That openness increased even further after the revised procedural framework was adopted following highly charged conflicts in the Council about the second European Semester.[81] As a result, the initial conflicts with other DGs, in particular with the Directorate General for Employment, Social Affairs and Inclusion (DG EMPL) in the first years, slowly eased, in particular as the Secretary General's office increasingly orchestrated the process. As such, we can conclude that the procedural legitimacy of Semester exercises increased over time between 2011 and 2015 through the greater deliberative mutual accountability and inclusiveness of internal processes, even if doubts remain as to the output legitimacy of the market-making ideas contained in social policy recommendations, as discussed earlier.

Importantly, although the stated objectives and recommendations did become more 'social' on paper, and the Comission more accountable and all-inclusive in the Semester process, the actual impact of their recommendations in practice remained in question. The problem with the continued pressures for fiscal consolidation was that member states had little room in their budgets for growth-enhancing or socially responsive measures, and many were in any event not necessarily inclined to spend in these areas. Moreover, the CSRs themselves provided limited guidance on how best to address the social and employment problems. The focus on cost, evaluated through macroeconomic measures and the push for money-saving cuts above all largely trumped socioeconomic considerations.[82]

The fact that the first priority in the Annual Growth Surveys from 2011 to 2015 remained fiscal consolidation also helps explain why member states cut first, and then naturally found there was nothing left for growth-friendly policy based on the Commission's Agenda 2020, let alone for poverty alleviation and employment promotion. Notably, the countries themselves were most worried about market pressures, and therefore would have naturally focused on fiscal consolidation—in particular given that this was the headline goal in the CSRs—despite increasing moderation in the subsequent two categories. In 2012, for example, the member-states had on average done much what was required of them under the EU's fiscal rules.[83]

Increasing Moderation of the Rules and Numbers in the Juncker Commission

Only with the inception of the new Juncker Commission in November 2014 did the moderating practices seem to come into greater alignment with a discourse

---

[80] Zeitlin and Vanhercke 2014, pp. 21, 28; see also Zeitlin and Vanhercke 2018.
[81] Zeitlin and Vanhercke 2014, pp. 25–6.
[82] Crespy and Schmidt 2017.   [83] Buti 2017.

that was itself changing its message. New Commission initiatives ensured that it shifted the focus of its discourse away from fiscal consolidation toward investment at the same time that it began presenting structural reform as a *quid quo pro* for greater flexibility through slower deficit reduction. Structural reform itself was redefined, with the new catchphrase, "upward convergence," signaling that structural reforms were not to be equated with social regression but rather that such reforms (mainly focused on education and training and the redesign of social protection) could generate incentives and increase the level of employment. As part of this, the Commission also pledged to do more to alleviate the social costs of the crisis, and to promote growth through a new investment fund—the European Fund for Strategic Investment (EFSI).[84] Finally, the Juncker Commission together with the Council began to stress the concept of a "positive fiscal stance," that is, one that would be neither restrictive (read: austerity) nor fully "expansionary" (read: Keynesian-type spending)—in which the Eurozone was to achieve an overall balance and convergence in competitiveness and welfare by tackling what it considered a "telling paradox: those who have fiscal space do not want to use it [read: Germany]."[85]

Most importantly, the 2015 Annual Growth Survey for the first time put fiscal consolidation—renamed "fiscal responsibility" (defined as "growth-friendly fiscal consolidation")—in third place, following investment for growth in first place and structural reform in second place—the latter with a much wider set of recommendations instead of the narrow focus on labor market flexibility of the AGS of 2011. In the introductory section, the first item described was a "coordinated boost to investment" followed by a "renewed commitment to structural reforms." Only the third item mentioned "pursuing fiscal responsibility," in which member states "still need to secure long term control over deficit and debt" while those "with more fiscal space should take measures to encourage domestic demand," with a particular emphasis on "investment" while "addressing tax fraud and tax evasion."[86] The labor market recommendations were more labor-friendly, less focused on destroying labor market protections, and more open to working out reforms with the social partners.[87]

[84] Crespy and Schmidt 2017.
[85] Commission 2016, p. 3; see discussion in Crespy and Schmidt 2017.
[86] AGS COM (2014) 902 final, Nov. 28.
[87] The statement reads: "Employment protection rules and institutions should provide a suitable environment to stimulate recruitment, while offering modern levels of protection to both those who are already in employment and those looking for a job. Member States must do more to remove obstacles to job creation, with the involvement of social partners [but] still need to complete the correction of pre-crisis trends, with wages outpacing productivity gains. The role of social partners is crucial. Collective agreements should allow a certain degree of flexibility for differentiated wage increases across sectors and within sectors, according to specific productivity developments." AGS COM (2014) 902 final, Nov. 28, pp. 11–12.

By 2015, most member states had exited the Excessive Deficit Procedures (EDPs), and the Commission therefore largely shifted its attention to the MIPs. There is a big difference between the MIPs, which allow significant flexibility in the assessment, and the EDPs. Whereas in the former, a range of calculations make up the decision on whether or not to initiate a procedure, in the latter merely hitting a certain number would trigger the procedure. Moreover, whereas the EDPs can be seen as procedurally hierarchical, given that a country found in violation is put under great pressure to comply, the MIPs, as David Bokhorst explains, can be interpreted as more procedurally deliberative, since it is seen as something of a "health check" in which Commission recommendations serve to signal problems. Additionally, because the MIPs do not force action, and the sanction procedure is not very credible, they operate much more in terms of the "force of argument," in particular because over time they have become virtually co-terminus with the normal CSR Semester.[88] It is significant that whereas EDPs were the main focus of the Barroso Commission, which appeared most Ayatollah-like and hierarchical in its dealings with member states, MIPs were the focus of the Juncker Commission, which was much more deliberative in its interactions with the member states.

The Juncker Commission was also much more concerned about socioeconomic issues than its predecessor, and was intent on paying greater attention to social fairness. This is why it changed the European Semester to introduce more social and employment indicators to the existing list focused on economic and financial indicators, and in 2016 announced "Structural Reforms 2.0," in which it promised a better mix of policy actions.[89] DG ECFIN at the time also saw its central role in the European Semester reduced, with the coordinating role of the Secretariat General reinforced to its detriment, along with a major reorganization that saw a number of staff transferred to other DGs, including DG EMPL. Moreover, the Commission sought to improve coordination with national capitals by creating a multilevel structure for permanent bilateral discussion in which it also created European Semester officer positions in each Commission Permanent Representation across the EU, thereby establishing new decentralized channels for national stakeholders to interact with the European Commission.[90] Such nationally based officers were expected to improve the European Semester's procedural legitimacy by providing new channels of communication and information as well as deliberation with a more inclusive group of national actors, including labor and civil society, in the interests of enhancing national ownership of structural reforms.[91]

---

[88] Bokhorst 2019.

[89] See speech by Commissioner Pierre Moscovici, "Structural Reforms 2.0, for a stronger and more inclusive recovery" (Brussels, 9 June, 2016): https://ec.europa.eu/commission/presscorner/detail/en/SPEECH_16_2124

[90] Schön-Quinlivan and Scipioni 2017; Crespy and Schmidt 2017; Bokhorst 2019.

[91] Munta 2020.

The major shift in the headline goals of the Annual Growth Surveys suggests that Commission officials had indeed moderated their approach to rules-based governance, in particular with regard to austerity policies related to rapid deficit reduction. This shift in approach was also mirrored in decisions related to countries in danger of breaching the rules.

In 2015, the new Commission agreed to delay the application of the deficit rules to France and Italy for another two years. In the case of France, Economics Minister (and future President) Emmanuel Macron had unilaterally declared that the country would not meet the 3 percent deficit target before 2017. The Commission was split over whether to grant France an extension, with the Northern European ministers in charge of economics-related portfolios—including the Latvian and Finnish Vice-Presidents (both of whom had been part of the Barroso Commission)—pushing to sanction France, while Economic Affairs Commissioner Moscovici resisted, and Juncker arbitrated in his favor. The angry reaction of former Commission President Rehn is evidence enough of the shift in Commission approach. Rehn condemned the decision on throughput as well as output legitimacy grounds, insisting that it

> is eroding the credibility of eurozone [rules] that the Commission did not have the guts and sense to say 'no effective action' to France, even though it is obvious to any even slightly informed observer...[that] this is watering down the [crisis-era] reform of economic governance, and erodes economic stability and sustained growth.[92]

In 2016, the Commission even recommended suspending fines for member states in violation of the rules (Spain and Portugal), to which the finance ministers of the Economic and Financial Affairs Council (ECOFIN) agreed. This again came after much internal dispute within the Commission as well as with (and within) the Council. While Northern European Commissioners pushed on grounds of procedural legitimacy to impose at least symbolic sanctions so as to "apply the rules," including the Latvian, Finnish, and German Commissioners, others argued for clemency on grounds of political legitimacy.[93] French Commissioner Moscovici, for one, argued that punitive actions could spark off anti-EU feelings because "we're at a time in Europe when people are having their doubts about Europe and we have to be careful about how the rules and the implementation of these rules are perceived." Moreover, in response to critics who saw the move as undermining the credibility of EU rules, he responded that the rules gave room to cancel the fines, while highlighting that many more countries respected the rules today than when the rules were introduced.[94]

---

[92] *Financial Times* March 8, 2015.   [93] See discussion in Coman 2018, pp. 551–2.
[94] *EU Observer* Aug. 10, 2016.

By 2019, the Commission was continuing to monitor a number of countries in the MIP, with ten member states signaled as experiencing imbalances (Bulgaria, Croatia, France, Germany, Ireland, Portugal, the Netherlands, Romania, Spain, and Sweden), and three member states excessive imbalances (Cyprus, Greece, and Italy).[95] In the case of Italy, which was in trouble for its planned extra spending at a time when its debt remained too high and its deficit had started climbing, things came to a head in summer 2019. But after some grandstanding by the populist coalition government as well as the Commission, the agreement was to kick the can down the road, to October 2019, when a new Commission was to be seated. And by then, a new and more accommodating Italian coalition government turned out to be in charge. It is worth noting in this regard that in its 2019 report, the European Fiscal Board (EFB), charged with advising the Commission on matters of economic governance, found that the Juncker Commission had made use of every possible loophole within the flexibilized SGP to avoid imposing penalties under the EDP, in particular on Italy. And this led to growing demand for reform of the EU fiscal framework, and to Juncker's commissioning a report from the EFB on the topic.[96]

All in all, the 2019 CSRs were mainly focused on socioeconomic concerns. The overall report was primarily focused on market-correcting social policy. It cited such things as "improving the quality of public spending" to "enhance the ability of public finances to support growth and social cohesion," including "favoring education, employment and investment"; "help[ing] support inclusive growth" through tax and benefit systems; addressing problems in labor markets by reducing gender inequalities in employment and pay and ensuring access to quality education and training "in a life-long learning perspective"; and dealing with poverty, including in-work poverty. Moreover, social dialogue was again singled out as a key factor for the successful design and implementation of policies, because "the involvement of social partners and other stakeholders improves ownership of policies and leads to better and more sustainable policy outcomes."[97] In the 2019–20 recommendations, moreover, attention to regional and territorial disparities appeared for the first time, in an effort "to better identify specific investment needs and promote accelerated economic and social convergence" with the help of "the EU's investment resources, including the Juncker Plan and structural funds investments."[98]

In sum, although the Commission began ministering greater moderation in rules-based governance under President Barroso once the crisis slowed, beginning in 2013, aspects of its ayatollah-likeness remained. Not only did the Commission continue to lack transparency and accountability, as the discourse of

---

[95] Commission 2019, p. 5.   [96] Thanks to Jonathan Zeitlin for this point.
[97] Commission 2019, pp. 6–9.   [98] Commission 2019, p. 9.

strict enforcement of the rules hid the reality of increasing flexibility, but its shift to social policy concerns retained a bias toward economic competitiveness (or market-making) over social fairness (or market-correcting). With President Juncker, the Commission was not only more transparent and accountable, as it set rules for its flexibility, but it was also more inclusive via Semester consultations and more focused on social fairness concerns in Semester recommendations. As of today, the European Semester, and in particular the MIP, continues to promote a range of goals, including social fairness and economic competitiveness, sound public finances and quality administration.[99]

Commission Governance versus National Sovereignty and Democracy?

A final problem for the Commission, even if seen as "Ministers of Moderation," is that its very role seems to challenge in essential ways longstanding conceptions of national sovereignty and democracy, in particular with regard to the role of national parliaments. The Commission's remit to enforce the various oversight functions of the macroeconomic imbalance and excessive deficit procedures in the European Semester, which include the power to vet national budgets even before governments submit them to national parliaments for approval, not only challenges national governments' sovereignty, by diminishing their autonomy with regard to budget development, but also undermines one of the main pillars of national parliaments' representative power—control over national budgets. Because the European Semester process is one in which national governments coordinate with the Commission often prior to national parliaments' discussion of the national budget, many of the major decisions are taken beforehand, and the parliaments may therefore be relegated to the role of rubber-stamp institutions.

That said, increasingly over time national parliaments have been able to debate EU economic policies, both prior and subsequent to European Council meetings, while the relevant parliamentary committees have been debating the programs.[100] Even so, as Ben Crum finds, while parliaments may have expanded their scrutiny of national budgets in the European Semester, this occurs only at the lower ranges of accountability mechanisms, including information, consultation, and debate, but not in relation to the substance of the budget, which they leave to the EU-level process.[101] In this process, national parliaments are themselves partially to blame for their lack of impact, since while their powers have expanded, there is considerable cross-country variation in the extent to which they use those

---

[99] Bokhorst 2019.   [100] Chalmers 2016, p. 293; Jančić 2016; Crum 2018.
[101] Crum 2018.

powers to hold their national executives to account, and where and when debates take place.[102]

As for the governments themselves, within the limits of the agreed-upon rules, the Commission has the discretionary power to demand reforms, so long as the Council agrees, regardless of whether the government in question or its parliament is agreed. Such supranational intervention in the management of national economies flies in the face of national input legitimacy. The fact that the Commission can also sanction governments that do not mend their ways only adds insult to injury.

The problems are compounded for program countries that agreed to memoranda with the European Stability Mechanism (ESM), where there is no provision for parliamentary involvement. In many cases where governments have to secure parliamentary assent for conditionality programs, it comes primarily because parliaments see no alternative, and the budget as a fait accompli.[103] The consequences of such memoranda include negative effects on activities historically associated with sovereign power, meaning those activities that enable "bare life," in Agamben's words, including the different programs allowing people to be housed, fed, and cared for in terms of health care or pensions.[104]

So if the operation of the European Semester and the ESM appear to undermine democracy and even sovereignty taken from a national-level perspective, why does it continue? With regard to the European Semester, one answer is that national parliaments have simply accommodated themselves to the new realities, without contesting their input legitimacy.

Another answer is that constitutional courts have deemed these acceptable within the context of the "community of risks" in EMU and the mutual commitment to manage such risks established by the Six-Pack and the Fiscal Compact.[105] For example, in the case of the "Golden Rule" of balanced budgets, as Damian Chalmers shows, all member states' constitutional courts accepted the principles while national parliaments embedded it in national law, even though the specifics of court judgments and national legislation differed. The German Constitutional Court found the golden rule unproblematic on the grounds that it did not overly constrain budgetary policy, in particular because the national legislature had already constitutionalized the golden rule in the Basic Law. The French Constitutional Court also found the golden rule unproblematic, but not the French legislature, which incorporated it as an organic law rather than a constitutional amendment. And while Portugal saw much parliamentary debate on the issue, there was minimal constitutional response or debate in Estonia, Finland,

---

[102] Such variation includes differences in whether the debate takes place at the parliamentary level; whether the European Affairs or finance committees are involved; and whether involvement comes before submission ofcountry-specific recommendation or after. See Hallerberg et al. 2018.

[103] Crum and Curtin 2015; Chalmers 2016, pp. 290–1.

[104] Agamben 1998, p. 142, cited in Chalmers 2016, p. 281.   [105] Chalmers 2016.

Luxembourg, or the Netherlands.[106] Moreover, although the legality of the ESM was challenged in the case of *Pringle*, the CJEU ruled that it was constitutionally acceptable since it was established by national executives collectively, that its power was virtually limitless, and that since the ESM was outside the treaties, it was not subject to legal controls. Significantly, no constitutional courts challenged this on grounds of violation of national sovereignty—including the Greek Council of State, because the Greek government had autonomously accepted the memorandum.[107] In short, the courts have sanctioned national legislatures' ceding of control over budgetary processes to the Commission and, by extension, to the Council.

There are two final reasons why the European Semester may have come to be accepted. First, as we have already seen, the Semester has become more deliberative over time—with greater mutual accountability for all and sundry and with greater involvement of national parliaments and civil society actors—and therefore more readily acceptable because more procedurally inclusive. Second, beyond the first couple of years of the fast-burning phase of the crisis, the Semester has had little "bite," meaning that the member states did not implement a majority of the recommendations.

Although the discourse of the Commission has been positive all along about the record of member-state implementation, the actual numbers suggest a different picture. The Commission's report on the 2019 European Semester country reports touted the fact that between 2011 and 2018, "More than two thirds of the country-specific recommendations issued until 2018 have been implemented with at least '*some progress*'" (9 percent full implementation, 17 percent substantial progress, and 44 percent some progress). But the Commission's own report finds declining compliance, such that during the first two years of annual assessments (2011 and 2012) implementation was highest (at 90 percent in 2011 and about 72 percent in 2012), with decreasing numbers thereafter, to slightly above 40 percent in 2018.[108] While for the Commission this signaled success, and there is evidence to suggest that even some progress can be meaningful in difficult-to-reform areas like labor markets in difficult-to-reform countries like Italy,[109] analyses by the think tank Bruegel in 2015 and again in 2019 concluded that this record was actually very weak.[110] The Bruegel report of 2015 found the European Semester "rather ineffective" and questioned whether the European Semester was worth the effort, but ultimately answered in the affirmative mainly because "some form of dialogue is needed."[111] A Bruegel report in 2019 painted a similar picture of declining compliance, with an even sharper drop in 2018. It

---

[106] Chalmers 2016, pp. 278–80.   [107] Chalmers 2016, pp. 282–3.
[108] Commission 2019, pp. 3–4.
[109] Brokhorst 2019.   [110] Darvas and Alvaro 2015, 2016; Efstathiou and Wolff 2019a.
[111] Darvas and Alvaro 2015.

concluded that "the overall picture is thus one of deteriorating implementation of reform recommendations during a period during which market pressure was subsiding and the economy was improving in general," including "in the context of tighter surveillance."[112] In other words, absent the pressures of the first two years for rapid deficit reduction for the most vulnerable countries, implementation was anemic at best for almost all countries. But the solution is not, according to report authors Kostantinos Efstathiou and Guntram Wolff, to therefore reinforce the legal obligations and tighten the monitoring (as called for by Northern Europeans), because compliance is mainly affected by macroeconomic fundamentals and market pressures. Rather, the answer is to limit the recommendations to issues "with significant macroeconomic spillovers on the EU as a whole" (such as the German current account surplus or the Italian debt crisis), while "leaving other goals at the national level, in the spirit of subsidiarity."[113]

So does this mean that the European Semester is an empty vessel or a pointless exercise? Not necessarily. This amazing architecture of economic coordination plays an important role in creating a "health" assessment exercise in which member states, experts, and officials in the Commission and the Council, and to a lesser extent the EP, all engage together in a deliberative mutual accountability forum about the state of the EU and national economies. Such coordination can be seen as somewhat akin in approach to the abandoned Open Method of Coordination of the early 2000s, which was entirely voluntary, with benchmarking and naming and shaming the only sanctions. The European Semester has more formal "teeth," but as we have seen, no one really believes any longer that it will ever really bite, since that would be economically and politically counterproductive. Nevertheless, Commission recommendations have exerted influence on member state reform agendas not just by creating pressure on national officials but by empowering them to use those recommendations as coercive justification and/or discursive legitimation for reforms.[114]

The problem with the European Semester remains the fact that although it has become increasingly horizontal and deliberative, from the outside it may still be perceived as hierarchical and dictatorial (in particular by populist Euroskeptics), as well as a point of contention between member states in either mode. The problems for it are therefore not only that it is has not been particularly procedurally efficacious in what it set out to do (given the lack of compliance) or transparent in the processes (given the discourse of denial in the Barroso years). It is also that it has been seen either as oppressive by Southern European countries or as biased in their favor by Northern European countries, and as such has had negative spillover effects on political legitimacy. Nonetheless, the process has become an integral part of Eurozone governance, and is here to stay.

---

[112] Efstathiou and Wolff 2019a.   [113] Efstathiou and Wolff 2019b.
[114] Bokhorst 2019.

Conclusion

Much like the ECB, the Commission has managed incrementally to legitimate its reinterpretations of the rules, in particular once it stopped doing so by stealth. Moreover, after an initial phase of support for rules-based orthodoxy, the Commission has played a leading role in arguing that risk sharing and risk reduction should go together, rather than the former being delayed until sufficient progress is made with the latter. In so doing, the Commission did indeed move toward increasing moderation of the policy content of the European Semester. But politicization of policymaking has continued to be an issue, with the Commission caught between the Council's rival coalitions, and in constant danger of contestation. In response to the question of whether such politicization is a good or a bad thing, as discussed in Chapter 3, we could argue that the Commission's public defense of its increasingly flexible governance, just as much as its verbal jousts with different member states, can be seen as legitimizing in throughput terms, as a form of rendering accounts in the forum of public opinion, which also ensures greater transparency. Politicization is a worry only if the Commission appears unfair or biased in its judgments, oppressive in its decisions, or partisan. Over time, the Commission has moved away from its Ayatollah-like character as the enforcer of austerity and more toward being a Minister of Moderation, as it has come to recognize that legitimacy depends upon squaring the circle between throughput, output, and input legitimacy.

Our main question is about the European Semester itself. If indeed it has been less and less efficacious in ensuring compliance but the processes are nonetheless seen as intrusive with regard to national democracy, what should be done? Jettisoning it is not an option, constitutionalized as it is in EU treaties and national laws, and by now embedded in national and EU practices of macroeconomic governance. Moreover, it remains the only instrument by which to take stock of the EU economy, as well as to appear to keep member states in line with EU economic goals. Its problems are that the method of recommendation still appears at least from the outside as hierarchical and top-down. The diminishing returns with regard to member states' records of implementation suggest that this approach is not working, and that for the member states to take national ownership, they need to have *real* ownership.

In other words, the European Semester would do better to become and to be seen as horizontal and bottom-up rather than vertical and top-down. For this, the best way forward would be to keep the architecture of coordination but make the governance process more of a decentralized exercise in thinking about how to make the national economy prosper. At the EU level, the Commission should conceive of itself less as community "enforcer" for Council decisions and more as "enabler" or "advisor" to national governments, with even more flexible interpretations of the rules and with 'structural reforms' focused on whatever measures would help to make member states' very different national political economies work better.

At the national level, a decentralized Semester would mean that the national fiscal councils, rather than serving as technical bodies focused on ensuring fiscal discipline, should be in the business of assessing how to ensure the country's fiscal well-being along with economic growth. Moreover, the national productivity councils should be more like industrial policy councils, to propose ways to foster sustainable growth through investment in industries of the future and in human capital via education, training, and so forth. But rather than being made up mainly of experts, they should be made up of the social partners—labor unions and businesses—as well as civil society, to ensure not only greater throughput accountability but also political input legitimacy. Much like the French "Plan" of the 1950s, this could bring the *forces vives* of the society, providing businesses with information as well as state investment where appropriate. But in addition, it would be a place for improving trust and common vision between labor unions and businesses as well as civil society.

At the EU level, moreover, beyond the European Semester, the Commission also needs to be a generator of innovative ideas for the medium and long-term, as a *"vivier d'idées"* to meet the challenges of the 21st century. This would entail, for example, developing industrial policies targeting investment in the growth industries of the future, in particular in areas needed to address the threat of climate change. Although already done on a small scale, such as in EU support for the development of electric car batteries, with exemption from state aid rules,[115] any such industrial policy demands greater ambition and a much larger store of funds—perhaps via the ECB, as mentioned in the conclusion to the previous chapter, in tandem with the European Investment Bank (EIB) and/or a beefed up Juncker Fund. But the Commission also should develop a range of ways to combat inequality, including through various kinds of adjustment and solidarity funds (e.g., unemployment compensation, migration integration, and poverty alleviation funds), harmonization of corporate tax regimes which today allow major corporations to avoid tax on profits in the member-states in which they earn them, or setting basic minimum EU standards for social assistance and income support.

Finally, serving two masters through its double accountability to the EP and to the Council may actually enable the Commission to be a more independent and resourceful institutional leader. Leadership, in other words, is the watchword, even if this means "leading from behind" by providing the ideas for input-legitimate actors to take up at the EU and national levels.

---

[115] *Financial Times* Dec. 2, 2019 https://www.ft.com/content/140e560e-0ba0-11ea-bb52-34c8d9dc6d84?shareType=nongift

8

The European Parliament

From Talking Shop to Equal Partner?

This is the shortest chapter in Part II, which is appropriate to the comparatively marginal role the European Parliament played in Eurozone crisis governance, particularly at first. If during the Eurozone crisis the Council grappled with its "one size fits one" governance and the European Central Bank (ECB) had to contend with the "one size fits none" rules of the structure of the euro, while the Commission sought to moderate over time the "one size fits all" ruling by numbers, then the European Parliament could be seen as having initially served as little more than a "talking shop" with almost "no size at all." Over time, however, this too changed, as the EP pushed to become more of an "equal partner," even if it still has a long way to go.

The EP's lack of "size" resulted first and foremost from its lack of legal and institutional weight in Eurozone governance. Unlike its increasing powers in everyday policymaking as part of the co-decision method with the Council and the Commission, the EP has never had much power with regard to Eurozone governance. Moreover, unlike all the other EU institutional actors, which increased their governance powers in the crisis, the EP was left on the sidelines. The Council took back the initiative from the Commission, the ECB took action, and the Commission exercised oversight through the European Semester. The most the EP could do was to take on the role of a public accountability forum, through its use of voice whenever it had the opportunity, whether in response to EU actors' testimony in committee and plenary hearings and "dialogues" or in critical reports. But it did little of this at first, acting instead as a cheerleader for harsh austerity and structural reform with regard to the Council dictatorship, the ECB ogre, and the Commission ayatollahs. Over time, however, the EP increasingly held the other EU actors to account for their actions, questioning their legitimacy in terms of output performance and procedural quality, as they sought to act as the input-legitimate representative for citizens' concerns and the public interest more generally. Moreover, as the Council became more of a deliberative body, the ECB a hero, and the Commission ministers of moderation, the EP recognized and served to legitimate their reinterpretations of the rules.

This chapter begins with a consideration of the EP's limited power and its growing procedural legitimacy, as it has struggled to make itself heard as an accountability forum. The chapter next examines the ways in which the EP was

Europe's Crisis of Legitimacy: Governing by Rules and Ruling by Numbers in the Eurozone. Vivien A. Schmidt, Oxford University Press (2020). © Vivien A. Schmidt.
DOI: 10.1093/oso/9780198797050.001.0001

little more than a talking shop at the inception of the Eurozone crisis, and then explores the ways in which it managed to increase its informal institutional powers and to exercise voice in ways that brought it closer to, but still far from, an equal partner in Eurozone governance.

EP Power and Procedural Legitimacy

The EP's power and procedural legitimacy comes first and foremost from the fact that it is in theory the most input legitimate of EU institutions, because directly elected by the citizens. The EP's input-legitimate status also ensures its procedural legitimacy as a participant in EU governance and/or as a public accountability forum. The Council granted the EP increasing governance powers over time as a result of its clear recognition that the more EU integration deepened, the more the EU had a problem with political legitimacy. The Council empowered the European Parliament first by granting it representative authority through its election in 1979 and then incrementally over time by adding to its governance competences, in particular as the co-decision process increasingly became the primary *modus operandi* of the EU while the EP gained more and more oversight over EU administrative procedures and appointments.[1] Beginning in the 1990s, this was explicitly related to attempts to respond to the EU's perceived democratic deficit.[2] Co-decision was introduced in 1992 with the Treaty of Maastricht, which put the EP on an equal footing with the Council of Ministers and then was expanded in every subsequent treaty, to culminate with the Lisbon Treaty of 2009 that made co-decision the "ordinary legislative procedure" of the EU.

But although in theory the EP is the most input legitimate of EU institutional actors because it is directly elected by citizens, it is less so in practice, given that citizens have long had little interest in EP elections or understanding of the EP's role. In the Eurozone crisis, moreover, the EP's minimal role in decision-making meant that it could not act in a representative function. Over time, however, it increasingly sought to hold EU actors to account for their actions, thereby reinforcing its own role as a public accountability forum. But it did this differently depending upon the actor. Because it had no formal role as such as an accountability forum with regard to the Council, it took on that role informally, through critiques of its lack of efficacy, accountability, and transparency. In contrast, with the ECB and the Council, the EP did what was in its (limited) power to hold them to account. With regard to the ECB, as we have already seen in Chapter 6, it acts as the sole accountability forum for the ECB through its quarterly appearances in the EP, but has little power to hold it to account. As for the Commission, the EP

---

[1] Rittberger 2005; Hix and Hoyland 2013; Fasone 2014; Dinan 2014; Héritier et al. 2016.
[2] Costa and Magnette 2003; Rittberger 2005.

has increasingly served as its primary political accountability forum, in particular since the *Spitzenkandidat* process and Commission President Juncker's insistence on the political nature of his mandate.

The problem for the EP, with regard to input as much as procedural legitimacy, is that it has remained largely invisible to or irrelevant for the majority of EU citizens. EP elections have long been characterized as having a "second-order" status in which national political concerns have dominated political debate and national electorates have tended to use the elections to punish or reward incumbent national governments.[3] Much of the literature on the media content of public debates during EP elections shows that they have been mainly domestic, despite weak trends toward greater emphasis on EU issues in more recent EP elections.[4] That said, party manifestos for EP elections have been focused on EU matters, while domestic party manifestos, even when not dealing much with the EU, tend to take similar positions to the EP manifestos.[5] Party positions in EP election manifestos, moreover, have become increasingly politicized over time, with Euroskeptic parties mainly focused on constitutive questions (ie, what the EU is and how it affects national sovereignty and identity) and Euro-friendly parties more concerned with policy issues.[6]

But however intense the debates and whatever the content of the manifestos, citizens' interest has been minimal. This has been evidenced by, if nothing else, the increasingly high rates of abstention over time in voting in EP elections, with the exception of the 2019 election. Turnout in EP elections declined from 70 percent in 1984 to 59 percent in 1994, 49 percent in 1999, 45 percent in 2004, 43 percent in 2009, and 42.54 percent in 2014. Although the jump in participation in 2019, to 50.95 percent, was hailed as a turnaround in participation, it came on the back of a major rise in Euroskepticism and fears of populist challenger parties gaining upwards of a third of the vote—in the end, they got approximately one quarter of the vote, up from a fifth in 2014.

Although the EP's representation *of* the people, which is the first definition of input legitimacy discussed in Chapter 2, may therefore be found wanting, this is not the case for the EP's representation *by* the people—to do what it thinks right *for* the people to promote the common good—in the second sense of legitimacy considered in Chapter 2. The EP has long seen its role as governing in the public interest, with partisan politics less important than reaching agreement on issues with broad public appeal, as "a way of defending effectively the general interest or the sum of particular interests," as Olivier Costa has put it.[7] As such, what counts is less how much the EP is representative of the electorate in all its diversity and more the nature of the ideas that MEPs defend, and how effectively they defend

---

[3] Franklin, and van der Eijk 2007; Mair 2006; Hix 2008.
[4] Boomgaarden and de Vreese 2016.   [5] Braun and Schmitt 2018.
[6] Braun et al. 2016.   [7] Costa 2009.

them. This helps shed light on why the EP, with its traditional grand coalitions of center right and center left, has shied away from ideological divides to govern in the public interest. Such governance was arguably also the only kind viable for an EP squeezed between a Council concerned mostly with serving national interests and a Commission engaged in mediating among organized interests.[8] Successes in the EP's defense of the public interest include interventions in very different spheres: for example, its engineering of a compromise in the controversy over the Bolkestein directive on posted workers in response to the high level of public mobilization and protest against the "Polish plumber,"[9] or its push for a reduction in the costs of mobile roaming charges. In fact, it is the EP's ability to deal with "civil society" as represented by social movements from outside the established channels as much as from insider interest groups that makes for another source of its legitimacy—throughput as well as input. The EP alone has been able to give voice to extra-parliamentary opposition in the absence of traditional left/right opposition in the EP.[10]

That said, whatever the EP has gained in input legitimacy over the years, its biggest problem has been that it remains far removed from the citizens and even national parliaments. Attempts to improve the linkages between the EU and national levels include the creation of an EU Ombudsman in 1992 by the Maastricht Treaty and the European Citizen's Initiative (ECI), introduced by the Lisbon Treaty of 2009, that gives citizens the right to be heard via petition with a million signatures from seven or more states. While the Ombudsman has been reasonably successful in creating a sense that the EU is listening to individual citizens' concerns, in particular with its focus on improving EU institutions' transparency and accountability,[11] the ECI has so far done little to increase citizen access.

As for national parliaments, as discussed in the final section of Chapter 7 on the Commission, most have relatively little ability to hold their own governments to account on budgetary matters in the context of the European Semester. Nor do they have much say over Eurozone governance, with the exception of the ability of some to vote on (and thus affect) new bailout financing via the European Stability Mechanism (ESM), in particular the power of the German Bundestag in the third Greek bailout as discussed in Chapter 5 on the Council. That said, national parliaments have gained more general powers that could be deployed in the future with regard to Eurozone governance, among other areas. The most notable innovations came with the Lisbon Treaty of 2009, which allowed time for prior national scrutiny of EU legislation by national parliaments (eight weeks) to ensure that subsidiarity was respected, with the possibility that legislation would be reconsidered if a certain number of national parliaments provide a "yellow

---

[8] Schmidt 2006, pp. 161–2.   [9] Crespy 2012.
[10] Crespy and Parks 2017.
[11] See, for example, the Ombudsman's report on the Council's lack of legislative accountability due to its lack of transparency https://www.ombudsman.europa.eu/en/press-release/en/95029

card." But it has yet to be used to reverse ongoing legislation, even as discussions continue about adding a "red card" that would give national parliaments the power to stop EU legislation, or even a "green card" to propose new legislation.

Moreover, as already noted in Chapter 2 on conceptualizing legitimacy, a majority of national parliaments also have difficulty holding their national executives to account in intergovernmental decision-making in the Council. While some Northern European legislatures have managed to establish mechanisms for parliamentary consultation by their executives, most legislatures have not, in particular in Southern and Central and Eastern European countries.[12] This results not only from the lack of competences of most national legislatures with regard to intergovernmental decision-making but also from the fact that they have little direct knowledge of what actually was said, and generally depend upon their national government's word for what it said and did in the Council. Ironically, as Katrin Auel has found, individual parliaments are more likely to be better informed by their national governments where they are involved in informal negotiations outside of public scrutiny, which therefore arguably ensures accountability to the detriment of transparency.[13]

More promising has been the process set up by the Lisbon Treaty for interparliamentary cooperation between national parliaments and the EP. The first yearly "Article 13" meeting was held in Vilnius in October 2013 and the second in Brussels in January 2014, under the title "European Parliamentary Week," which included the interparliamentary event on the European Semester.[14] So far, however, the focus of such meetings has been mainly on procedural issues. As a result, the yearly one-day consultations between the EP and national parliaments have been little better than a finger in the dike, even if they are an important beginning nonetheless.[15]

The main channel for direct citizen representation, then, remains via the EP. That channel has been reinforced over the years in most areas of legislation. Eurozone governance has been an exception to this from the very beginning. And rather than getting better at the time of the Eurozone crisis, it got worse.

EP as Talking Shop with No Size at All

For the EP, the Eurozone crisis constituted a major reversal in its slow and steady gains in power and influence through the co-decision method, at least at first. At the height of the crisis the EP was largely marginalized, as most decisions were

---

[12] Auel 2007; Crum 2017; Kreilinger 2019.
[13] Auel 2007; see also discussion in Papadopoulos 2010.
[14] EP 2016 *Relations between the European Parliament and National Parliaments under the Lisbon Treaty Annual Report 2014–2015* (June 22, 2016) http://www.europarl.europa.eu/relnatparl/en/publications/annual-reports.html
[15] Ballesteros et al. 2014; Fromage 2018.

taken by the Council and/or through international treaties with the International Monetary Fund (IMF), from which the EP was excluded by international law. From the very beginning, in fact, all the way back to the Maastricht Treaty, the EP had little formal legislative role in Eurozone policy formulation, which has mainly been the domain of the Council. Therefore, when the crisis hit the EP was unable to influence the new architecture of Eurozone governance, including all the loan bailouts and guarantees, or agreements on governance by the "Troika" of the IMF, EU Commission, and ECB. The only exceptions were the legislative packages of the Six-Pack and Two-Pack, along with the European Semester, which the Commission insisted needed approval via the regular legislative (meaning co-decision) procedures. But even with these, Council leadership predominated with regard to the framing of crisis causes and remedies.

Surprisingly, perhaps, the EP voted for the European Semester and the Commission's discretionary authority without even demanding an oversight function. In the Six-Pack and Two-Pack, for example, it voted to give the Commission exclusive power to apply the rules, denying itself the ability to oversee the Commission's decision even as it limited Commission discretion by specifying numerical targets for intervention. Here, the heightened sense of crisis, together with the "no alternative" discourse, was such that most MEPs voted in favor of austerity and fiscal tightening—and indeed pushed for more stringent measures than were on the table.[16] Happy to gain some power as a result of the Commission bringing it into Eurozone decision-making via the various legislative pacts, it allowed itself to be stampeded into reinforcing the rules. This was not only because of the Conservative majority in the EP, led by the EPP. It was also because even social democrats bought into the narrative of debt and bad behavior, in particular those in Northern Europe. The result is that the EP did not simply go along with Council demands for stricter rules on fiscal discipline; it made them even more restrictive by demanding reverse qualified majority voting (RQMV) in cases of Council opposition to Commission recommendations.[17]

This said, the Six-Pack and the Two-Pack legislation did marginally increase the EP's powers in Eurozone governance. The EP gained the possibility for its President to be "invited to be heard" in the Euro Summit and the obligation of the President of the Euro Summit to present a report to the EP after each Euro Summit meeting; the ability to enter into "Economic Dialogues" on the application of economic governance rules with EU institutions and member states; and a mandate to discuss such issues with national parliaments in the framework of the European Parliamentary Week and the Interparliamentary conference on Stability, Economic Coordination and Governance.[18]

[16] Barbier 2012.   [17] Warren 2018.   [18] Fromage 2018.

These ensure that the EP has the right to be informed, to discuss, and to give advice. But they are procedural rather than legislative functions. Without a legislative role, the EP cannot be the deliberative forum in which Eurozone policies are debated and contested, or even changed through the co-decision procedure. And without more formal control over the European Semester, it also can do little to provide greater oversight over the Commission.[19] As a result, the EP has no formal role as an accountability forum not only with regard to the Council, as already discussed, but also with the Commission with regard to the European Semester, even if its dialogues may help increase transparency and a kind of informal accountability.

The EP has had even less of a role to play in negotiations on bailouts, with no input into Troika decisions. In the case of the third Greek bailout in spring/summer 2015, for example, Commissioner Pierre Moscovici, head of DG ECFIN, noted that the EP was "the great absentee" in the discussion, and then asked: "to whom should it have turned? To the Commission in its capacity as negotiator? To the president of the Eurogroup, who is not answerable to it? To the IMF, which is even less answerable to it? Or to the European Stability Mechanism, which is a purely intergovernmental organization?" He then added: "how much weight did the European Parliament carry in the [third] Greek crisis by comparison with the German *Bundestag* or the Finnish *Eduskunta*?"[20]

Resizing the EP as Potential Equal Partner

As the crisis slowed, however, the EP was able to formally strengthen its powers to be informed, consulted, and to hold hearings and issue parliamentary commission reports.[21] Notably, the EP has been particularly active in deploying ideational power to persuade other EU institutional actors as to the input legitimacy of increasing its competencies, mainly with reference to its own electoral status as the only directly elected EU body.[22] In some instances requiring the creation of new regulation related to new Eurozone crisis instruments, the EP was involved in co-decision processes as an active partner, in particular in discussions of banking union and financial regulation. And in these cases, such as where trilogues are involved, the EP can exert pressure by drawing the Council into the political arena, since it can "go public" as a means of influencing the course of trilogue negotiations—and thereby assert its identity as a normal legislator on a par with the Council.[23]

---

[19] Crum and Curtin 2015; Crum 2018.   [20] Moscovici 2015, p. 2.
[21] Fasone 2014; Crum and Curtin 2015; Crum 2018.   [22] Hix and Høyland 2013.
[23] Roederer-Rynning and Greenwood 2015.

In Eurozone governance, despite the fact that this is a policy area in which the EP has been singularly devoid of competence, especially initially, it nevertheless had a role to play. That role came about in part as a result of the Lisbon Treaty, which gave the EP some powers of oversight and strengthened its ability to hold the executive accountable. Such accountability established the EP's right to be informed or occasionally consulted by the Commission on matters of multilateral economic surveillance, and ensured the EP's ability to invite the Commission, national ministers, and the Presidents of the Council, the Eurogroup, and the European Council to an Economic Dialogue or Exchange of Views.[24] Moreover, the ways in which the EP engaged in co-decision on the "Six-Pack" and the "Two-Pack," and then in banking union and the Single Supervisory Mechanism (SSM), were cases where it intermediated between supranational actors' legislative proposals and lobbies' pressures.

Illustrative of the EP's (minimal) powers was its opposition to the Commission proposal (following the Merkozy letter) to include the structural funds in macroeconomic conditionality, which was to empower the Commission to suspend funds if a state has failed to correct its excessive deficit, submit a corrective action plan for macroeconomic imbalances, and/or implement an adjustment plan. The EP was almost unanimously opposed from the moment the proposal was published in September 2011. MEPs argued that it was inappropriate to sanction regions for their government's failure to comply with Eurozone governance requirements, and all EP committees voted against including the provision in Regulation 1303/2013. Nonetheless, in the co-decision process, which included a record number of trilogues, the President of the EP and the Council and Commission engineered a compromise. As a result, the final regulation included an only slightly modified measure, with the words "macroeconomic conditionality" replaced with "measures linking effectiveness of European Structural and Investment Funds to sound economic management."[25] That MEPs were unable to stop the measure demonstrates the EP's continued fundamental weakness. But that they were able to change the language at all suggests that by 2013 the EP was already able to have a marginally greater impact on Eurozone governance than it had had in the past.

The EP has additionally managed to exercise increasing influence over policy in informal ways. Even in areas where the EP has very little formal power, it has come in earlier and earlier in the negotiations in attempts to influence the Commission on policy, with the credible threat that if it is not informed of the process, it can veto the initiative or slow the process. The EP has also increased its institutional influence by using blocking or delaying tactics to exercise leverage over other EU actors, as well as by going public with any concerns.[26] Such tactics

---

[24] Fasone 2014, p. 183f; Héritier et al. 2016, p. 80.
[25] Coman 2018, pp. 548–50.   [26] Héritier et al. 2016; Meissner and Schoeller 2019.

have equally led to increases in formal powers. In the case of banking union, for example, the EP was able to extract institutional concessions from the Commission and the member states. These involved strengthening the EP's scrutiny powers vis-à-vis the supervisory board as well as obtaining the right to formally approve (and dismiss) the chair and vice-chair of the Single Supervisory Mechanism (SSM).[27] In the case of the SSM giving the ECB surveillance of banks, more specifically, the EP blocked the decision-making process with both the Commission and the ECB until the ECB conceded rights of information to the EP. What is more, in the case of banking union, the EP managed to invent its own right to hold hearings for appointments to head new boards, mainly because the Commission and the ECB felt they could not say no to this. Although the new "rule" is totally informal, decision-makers now would not consider going for a candidate the EP finds unacceptable.[28]

While the EP's actions may in some cases seem like a grab for more institutional power, in particular from the viewpoint of intergovernmental or supranational actors, it could equally be explained in terms of the EP's commitment to the idea that intergovernmental initiatives should be converted wherever possible into the more "constitutional" approach represented by the co-decisions of the Community Method. This is why the EP was in many instances willing to trade its preferences with regard to substantive policy for the institutionalization of a more co-decisional process. This helps explain the EP's (often failed) amendments to the Six-Pack and the Two-Pack as well as its (failed) efforts to influence the Fiscal Compact.[29]

Moreover, despite its minimal formal institutional power, the EP has nevertheless been able to establish some political accountability for action by the three "executives": the Presidents of the European Council, the Commission, and the European Central Bank. As a result of the Six-Pack, for instance, the President of the European Council is mandated to come before a committee of the European Parliament (normally ECON—the economic affairs committee) to inform it and engage in an "economic dialogue."[30] Council President Herman Van Rompuy's economic dialogues with the EP, for instance, encompassed fifteen debates in plenary sessions and three with ECON. These involved much imparting of information, some debate, but hardly anything in terms of judgment, since the EP held no formal powers in terms of approval or denouncement.[31]

In the case of the Commission, the EP does have some formal powers as a result of various rules and regulations related to economic and budgetary matters.[32] In the 2009–14 legislature, this entailed for the most part asking the Vice-President of the Commission, Olli Rehn, to attend plenary sessions, in which he gave speeches imparting extensive information on the European Semester among

---

[27] Rittberger 2014, p. 1180.   [28] Héritier et al. 2016.
[29] Héritier et al. 2016, p. 69.   [30] Fasone 2014, pp. 175–6.
[31] Bovens and Curtin 2016, pp. 195–7.   [32] For the specifics, see Fasone 2014.

other matters, but responded little in the ensuing debates or to direct questions.[33] Moreover, plenaries were held for the Annual Growth Surveys for 2016 and 2017 prior to their adoption, with Commission recommendations the object of an exchange of views with the Commission and the Eurogroup.[34]

Finally, the EP has more formal powers with regard to the ECB, which is mandated to present an annual report on its activities to the EP as well as to appear before the ECON committee at least four times a year. In the cases of both ECB Presidents Trichet and Draghi, this generally involved very informative and intensive dialogues, along with some critical debates, to which attention was paid.[35]

More generally, we also need to take note of the EP's growing exercise of voice, with increasingly noisy demands for accountability from both supranational and intergovernmental actors. The EP enhanced its exercise of oversight over other EU actors not only through the increasing numbers of hearings and expert testimony but also in its committee reports—all of which focused on enhancing both EU institutional accountability and transparency. Increasingly over the course of the Eurozone crisis, the EP explicitly criticized Council and Commission actions. For example, the EP stepped up its criticism of the Troika in terms of its governance processes and its policies' output effects on the bailout countries. In two non-binding reports, the EP condemned the "lack of appropriate scrutiny and democratic accountability as a whole," along with the negative social consequences due to a lack of a "proper impact assessment" on citizens with regard to such matters as cuts in healthcare, increased unemployment, youth migration, and rising poverty. Additionally, it blamed finance ministers and the Eurogroup for "failing to give clear and consistent political pointers to the Commission and for failing to shoulder their share of responsibility in their capacity as final decision-taker."[36]

Equally important has been the EP's self-empowerment through the "*Spitzenkandidat*" in the 2014 EP elections, as the EP effectively anointed the leader of the winning political party Commission President.[37] This could be conceived as having increased the EP's own powers at the expense of European Council autonomy, but also in favor of Commission autonomy through its now double accountability to the EP and the Council. The fact that the Juncker Commission called itself "political" although not "politicized" in response to Council accusations that it did not apply the rules suggests that the Commission was fully aware of the value of its connection to the EP, as a way of reinforcing its autonomy from the Council along with its overall appearance of accountability.

Finally, even where the EP is completely left out of the decision-making process, it can still play a role, having increasingly become the "go-to" body for other EU actors concerned about their legitimacy. There is evidence to suggest that the

---

[33] Bovens and Curtin 2016, pp. 200–2.   [34] Fromage 2018, p. 287.
[35] Bovens and Curtin 2016, pp. 205–10.   [36] *Euractiv*, March 14, 2014.   [37] Dinan 2015.

EP's formal and informal powers in legislation, comitology, Commission investiture, budget, economic governance, and international agreements have increased at least in part because of member-state and Commission concern for democratic legitimacy.[38] Notably, Moscovici, after lamenting the EP's lack of involvement in the Greek negotiations, said that he intended to expand the EP's role in Eurozone governance in order to enhance the legitimacy of Commission decisions in the European Semester.[39] In the case of the ECB, moreover, as we have already seen, although the ECB President does not have to follow the EP's advice in his mandated four yearly appearances, he gains in procedural legitimacy by speaking to the EP—plus he can use this venue as part of his communicative strategy with the public more generally.

But be careful what you wish for. The increasing politicization of the EP has its downside. With approximately a quarter of the EP controlled by the extremes, the thinning mainstream has to form the equivalent of an even grander "grand coalition" than was necessary in the past to ensure the required supermajorities for the passage of important legislation. Up until now, extremist groups have had little power in the EP, since they had no control over major committees, and used the EP more for their own electoral purposes than to try to exert influence. But the difficulties involved in forming coalitions with three or more parties—center right, center left, liberals, and Greens—let alone in reaching compromises on more contested legislation could mean that the EP will have less, rather than more, influence than it had in the past. Efficacy in the co-decision process is in play, as is EP accountability in cases where MEPs of extremist parties might chair key committees.

This relatively new polarizing politicization via the presence of extremist challenger parties in the EP is not the only way in which political cleavages have affected the EP. Over the course of the Eurozone crisis (among other crises), MEPs have divided along a number of different cleavage lines, leading to what Maurizio Ferrera has called the EU's "clash syndrome."[40] The clashes are based on four lines of conflict, including the market-making versus market-correcting priorities of EMU; national social sovereignty and discretion versus EU law and conditionality; supporters versus opponents of fiscal stability or cross-national transfers (creditor versus debtor conflicts); and high wage and high welfare (Western European) member states versus low wage and low welfare (Central and Eastern European) member states.[41] These divisions have been very much in evidence in the context of many EP debates, including over implementing the European Pillar of Social Rights, and have increased the difficulties of coming to common conclusions about how to strengthen the EU's social and employment policies.[42]

---

[38] Héritier et al. 2016.   [39] Moscovici 2015, p. 3.   [40] Ferrera 2017.
[41] Ferrera 2017; see discussion in Vesan and Corti 2019.   [42] Vesan and Corti 2019.

Conclusion

All in all, the EP will still not be able to have much sway over Eurozone govern-ance unless the decision-making process were to move from highly intergovern-mental toward a co-decision format. For this to happen, however, the formal legislative set-up would need to change. For one, treaty-based rules would have to become ordinary legislation, meaning they would have to be open to amendment through political debates and compromise. Excessive intergovernmentalism through the focus on treaty-based or multilateral agreements and the supercharged supra-nationalism exemplified by the European Semester, however understandable as an initial response to the crisis, now needs at the very least to be counterbalanced by the enhanced involvement of the EP as well as national parliaments. Legitimacy is at stake not only in input terms, by giving citizens the sense that their votes matter, but also in throughput terms, by ensuring that Eurozone governance is more accountable through being subject to parliamentary scrutiny and to demo-cratic deliberation sufficient to legitimate any compromises.

In short, the EP needs to get more "size" in Eurozone governance, to become more of an equal partner, beyond the talking shop to which it had originally been relegated by its lack of formal role in Eurozone governance. But it needs to do this also by bringing national parliaments and citizens into the delibera-tion process. Overall, Eurozone governance needs to become like most other areas of EU legislation, which means it should mainly use co-decision for legisla-tion, in which the EP is a major player alongside the Council and the Commission. This would entail "resizing" the EP by bringing it into all Eurozone decision-making while reducing the intergovernmental dominance of the Council in Eurozone governance.

Ultimately, however, procedural legitimacy—whether of the EP, the Commission, the ECB, or the Council—cannot stand on its own. However efficient, account-able, transparent, inclusive, and open the processes, if these EU institutional actors do not produce good results or if they are perceived as not responding to citizen concerns, they fail the ultimate tests of legitimacy. This is why in Part III we turn to output and input legitimacy, to evaluate Eurozone performance and citizens' political responses.

PART III

OUTPUT AND INPUT LEGITIMACY IN THE EUROZONE CRISIS

9

Policy Effectiveness and Performance in the Eurozone Crisis

Eurozone governance during the crisis was not only problematic with regard to throughput legitimacy. Output legitimacy was also put at risk because of the ineffectiveness of the policies devised in the initial response to the crisis, which failed to promote the economic performance of the Eurozone as a whole. As the EU slowly initiated policies focused on governing by rules and ruling by numbers, along with a few institutional innovations such as loan bailout funds and banking union, the Eurozone stagnated. Although some member states continued to prosper, in particular in Northern Europe, many others fell back into recession and unemployment rates climbed, along with poverty and inequality. The distributive impact of crisis policies was felt very differently across the core and periphery of the Eurozone,[1] with comparatively little impact on the core countries compared to the long and painful recessions of periphery countries.[2] The worst problems came in the first two years of the crisis, from 2010 through 2012, as austerity took its toll, although it was not until 2015 that a page was turned for the Eurozone, with the ECB's move to quantitative easing and the Commission's shift toward more a social, market-correcting focus for the European Semester.

The lack of policy effectiveness comes down to four main elements. First, EU leaders framed the crisis as caused by too much public debt, whereas the real cause, acknowledged by all prior to May 2010, came from private debt, from banks over-extending (in the financial sector) and over-lending to individuals (especially in real estate). Second, EU leaders diagnosed the crisis incorrectly, by claiming that the problem of public debt stemmed from bad behavior, even though—with the exception of Greece—the countries in trouble, such as Ireland and Spain, had the best fiscal behavior prior to the crisis. The structure of the euro was in fact to blame, pushing increasing divergence in member-state economies in place of the expected convergence. Third, EU leaders chose the wrong remedies: pro-cyclical policies centered on austerity and "structural reform" instead of countercyclical policies focused on growth and investment. The austerity policies insisting on rapid deficit reduction only intensified recessionary pressures, while the "one size fits all" structural reforms, pushing wage devaluation, labor market

[1] Copelovitch et al. 2016; Matthijs 2017a; Schmidt 2015b.
[2] Braun and Hübner 2018; Parker and Tsarouhas 2018.

Europe's Crisis of Legitimacy: Governing by Rules and Ruling by Numbers in the Eurozone. Vivien A. Schmidt, Oxford University Press (2020). © Vivien A. Schmidt.
DOI: 10.1093/oso/9780198797050.001.0001

deregulation, and cutting the welfare state, did little to promote productivity or reduce unemployment. And fourth, EU leaders provided solutions that were inadequate to the task at hand, leaving the European Central Bank (ECB) to do what it could legitimize doing.

The ineffectiveness of the policies initially devised in response to the Euro crisis was directly responsible for the poor performance of the Eurozone in the first five years of the crisis. Assessed on most economic measures, such as growth, investment, and social well-being, the poor economic outcomes are clear, and even more so when comparing Eurozone performance in general to the US "dollarzone." The Eurozone fared worse in terms of growth because of the high costs of austerity that cut deficits too quickly and the perversity of structural reforms that weakened labor without doing much to strengthen national economic institutions, material resources, or human capital. Lack of investment was also a major problem. And all of this in turn had a deleterious impact on the socioeconomics, evaluated on measures such as unemployment, poverty, and inequality. Even though some countries, in particular in Northern Europe, did particularly well through the crisis, the average figures suggest that their better performance could not make up for the poor performance of countries in the periphery. Moreover, for program countries, the success stories have had much less to do with their implementation of austerity and structural reform-based prescriptions than with nationally specific economic pathways to growth. In contrast, the failures, most notably in the case of Greece, were due to the excessive costs of austerity and the perversity of structural reforms in a context of nationally specific problems.

In this chapter, we begin with the Eurozone policies' (lack of) effectiveness, including their (mis)framing, (mis)diagnosis, (wrong) remedies, and (inadequate) solutions, using statistical data with charts and graphs for evidence. We then consider Eurozone performance in terms of austerity and structural reforms, by providing a cross-national picture of the socioeconomic impact of crisis responses. Finally, we discuss the performance of the main countries in conditionality programs, with a consideration of Southern European countries followed by a contrast with Ireland. The main focus of this chapter is on the period between 2010 and 2015 (although not to the exclusion of subsequent developments), since this is when the Eurozone's governing by rules and ruling by numbers was most pronounced, before the shift from the Barroso Commission to the Juncker Commission also signaled a change in priorities, and the last of the bailout programs was negotiated (Greece's third bailout).

Misframing of the Crisis

The first of the Eurozone's problems with regard to output legitimacy stems from the (mis)framing of the crisis as one of public debt, which was generalized from the case of Greece. Seemingly forgotten were the real reasons for the crisis in all other countries: private debt that resulted from the massive overstretch of the banks, the increasing indebtedness of households, and the mispricing of sovereign risk by the markets.[3] It was as if EU actors had caught a major case of collective amnesia in 2009 and 2010,[4] as they painted the crisis as caused by public profligacy rather than private debt, in what Mark Blyth has called "the greatest 'bait and switch' in history."[5] The narrative that stuck, in particular in Germany, was about the profligacy of the "lazy Greeks" versus "Germans who save"[6]— ignoring the fact that the Greeks work longer hours with shorter vacation periods for less pay than their German counterparts.[7] And this was then generalized to all the countries in trouble. This misframing of the crisis as one of public debt in the periphery helped fuel resistance to any form of "transfer union," in which Northern Europeans would pay for debts accrued in the South, and helped close off proposed remedies such as Eurobonds or a European Monetary Fund.[8]

The reality was of course very different, since although Greece had indeed been profligate in terms of its public spending, the private sector was the main culprit in all the other countries, whether in terms of over-leveraged banks or households. This included some of those hardest hit by the crisis, such as Spain and Ireland, the governments of which had been scrupulous before the crisis in maintaining low public deficits and reducing their sovereign debt (see Figure 9.1). Public sector finances were largely steady or even reducing in the cases of Ireland

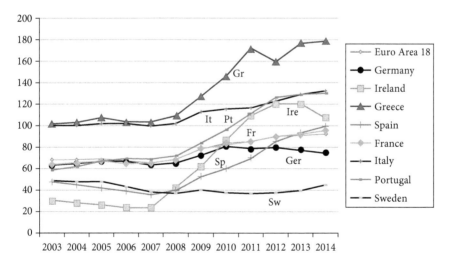

Figure 9.1. Public sector finances, 2003–2014
Source: Eurostat 2016

---

[3] De Grauwe and Ji 2012; Blyth 2013.   [4] See Barbier 2012.   [5] Blyth 2013.
[6] Newman 2015.   [7] Jones 2010, pp. 29–30.   [8] Schmidt 2015b.

and Spain as well as Sweden, while in countries like Italy and Greece, where the debt level was high (at around 100 percent of GDP), it was not increasing. Commission officials had themselves already drawn attention to the problems of private debt and the current account imbalance arising from asset price bubbles and private credit expansion in a 2006 report.[9] And Chancellor Merkel, among others, had, only just before the sovereign debt crisis exploded, been blaming the banks and, thus, private profligacy for the debt problem.

The level of public debt changed only once the financial crisis hit, and the Euro area as a whole moved up from approximately 68 percent to 92 percent debt as a percentage of GDP. The increase in debt was due to the fiscal stimulus programs instituted in all EU countries, while the massive increase in some countries' debt followed from the banks' rescue with taxpayers' money. Ireland's debt skyrocketed from 24 percent of GDP in 2007 to 109 percent of GDP in 2011—at which point it went into a Troika-led loan bailout program—and then moved up to 120 percent of debt to GDP by 2013—when it was feeling the full effects of the austerity program that, in shrinking the economy through cuts in public spending, also increased the ratio of debt to GDP. In comparison, Italy did not experience nearly as significant a jump in its debt-to-GDP ratio, having gone from 100 percent of GDP in 2007 to 116 percent in 2011. But while Italy's debt continued upward, to 135 percent in 2014, Ireland was able to reduce its debt-to-GDP ratio to 108 percent by 2014. This is because Ireland benefited from a reduction of its debt in 2013 and began to grow again, whereas Italy's economy continued to slow, and its debt-to-GDP ratio crept upward. The latter's increasing debt ratio was also a result of the country's "implicit" conditionality.[10] Italy and Spain had had to engage in self-imposed austerity to keep the markets from pricing up their debt. In so doing, they sought to avoid the explicit conditionality of an austerity program through the Open Monetary Transactions (OMT) initiative offered to them by the ECB in 2012 (but never taken up). By 2018, while Ireland's debt was down to 64 percent of GDP, Italy's remained at 135 percent.

In short, the problem was never one of public profligacy (with the exception of the Greek case). Significantly, EU institutional actors themselves later went back to the original story of the crisis being caused by private debt. First, in 2013 the ECB, in a speech by its Vice-President, acknowledged that the narrative was incorrect;[11] then in 2015, the President of the European Commission, in an analytical note written in "close cooperation" with the Presidents of the European Council, the Eurozone Finance Ministers, and the President of the ECB, set the record straight—the crisis had begun with private debt, which then turned into the sovereign debt crisis as a result of government need to bail out banks and stimulate their economies.[12]

---

[9] CEC 2006.   [10] Sacchi 2015; Pavolini et al. 2015; Perez and Matsaganis 2017.
[11] Constânci 2013.   [12] Juncker 2015.

Misdiagnosis of the Crisis

The second problem with regard to the Eurozone crisis was the (mis)diagnosis of the problem as behavioral rather than structural. The narrative that framed the problem as public debt diagnosed it in terms of member states' failure to follow the rules of the Stability and Growth Pact (SGP).[13] This goes back to the early days of the SGP, when a disciplinarian view of sanctioning public deficits gave way, in the face of rebellion by France and Germany in the mid 2000s, to a more regulatory view focused on the long-term sustainability of public finances, to be ensured through emphasis on common national budgetary standards and procedures. But when Greece appeared to have lied about its debt, the disciplinarian theme returned—since it appeared that regulation had failed because a member state had flouted the rules, just as the French and Germans had done in 2005.[14]

The problem with the behavioral narrative, however, is that it does not fit the facts. Throughout the 2000s, member states in the periphery such as Spain and Ireland were models of rule-following on deficits and debt (as seen in Figure 9.1 above), in contrast to core countries such as Germany and France, which broke the rules on deficits in the mid 2000s. But there were good reasons for this—in particular, avoiding cutting spending in a recession and, in the case of Germany, creating the space to institute unpopular, painful reforms of pensions and unemployment insurance (Hartz IV). But Merkel paid no attention to such nuances. Instead, she portrayed Germany's own breaking of the rules as a cardinal sin, and fed it straight into her behavioral narrative about the need to tighten the rules.

The rules-breaking narrative was reinforced by a focus on competitiveness. The German view was that the country had regained competitiveness as a result of the major structural reforms of the Hartz IV program in the mid 2000s. In contrast, it saw the countries in the periphery as having lost competitiveness through egregious wage inflation—and the failure to engage in similar kinds of reforms. The chart on real wage compensation lent credence to their view, since in the graph using 2000 as the baseline, other countries, in particular in the periphery, charted inflationary spirals of wage increases compared to Germany (see Figure 9.2).

In the chart, we can see that German wages fall significantly below the line, making them much more competitive in comparison to Southern Europe's sharp increases in wages. Greek and Irish wages in particular moved up more than 20 points above the baseline at their peak in 2009, putting them at a serious competitive disadvantage with Germany, which had fallen below the baseline by 2–3 points. From the German government perspective, then, the conclusions were clear: the wage increases in countries in the periphery were irresponsible and unsustainable. These countries, it was argued, needed to do what Germany had

[13] Jabko 2015.   [14] Schelkle 2009.

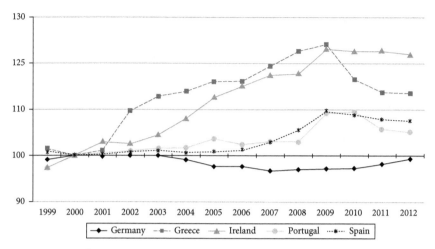

Figure 9.2. Real compensation per Employee, 1999–2012
Source: Ameco Database; Scharpf 2013

done in the mid 2000s to regain competitiveness, through structural reforms focused in particular on wage reduction. What this also meant, of course, is that German workers had been seeing their real wages decrease while those of Southern Europeans boomed.

What was missing from the German perspective is the full story of how Germany had achieved its wage competitiveness. One part of the story is that Germany's corporatist bargaining between labor and management had kept wages way below gains in productivity in the high value-added manufacturing sector. This enabled German industrial goods to be much more cost competitive inside the Eurozone as well as outside, ensuring that German companies would have an edge over European rivals. And it also helped it to corner the Chinese market in a number of high-end areas, such as automobiles—in particular when the exchange rate was favorable. We should add here that German export price competitiveness also depended upon membership in the euro, for which Southern Europe played a vital role in reducing the external value of the common currency.[15]

Another part of the story, more hidden from view, is that the Hartz IV reforms opened the door to a major increase in temporary and part-time jobs at very low pay—the so-called "mini-jobs" that came without benefits or job security—which led to the dualization of the work force and a massive rise in inequality.[16] Putting the two parts of the story together, the wage restraint on manufacturing workers' salaries that kept wage increases well below productivity gains, together with the proliferation of low-wage service jobs, enables us to understand why German citizens may have felt a sense of outrage at Southern Europeans' seeming profligacy,

[15] Streeck and Elsässer 2017.   [16] Palier and Thelen 2010; Hassel 2011.

given what appeared to be unsustainable wages on top of excessive deficits and debts, ultimately at Germany's expense.

Yet another missing piece of the story is that the inflationary spiral of wages in the periphery was mainly in the construction industry (linked to the real estate booms in Ireland and Spain in particular). This was pushed in good part by the excessive investment of German banks[17]—motivated to export savings because the returns on investment were much higher in the periphery than in Germany itself, where workers' lack of wage increases pushed them to save rather than to borrow.

But regardless of the real story, the behavioral tale stuck, spun not only by Germany but also by its Northern European allies, the Commission, and the ECB. As a result, the Eurozone failed to come to terms with its most serious problem, which was structural rather than behavioral. The ECB's "one size fits none," inflation-targeting monetary policy produced growing divergence rather than the expected convergence between countries.[18] This was apparent not only in the increasing wage differentials but also with regard to current account balances. As Figure 9.3 shows, Germany's current account surpluses continued to rise, and since 2016 have remained steady at a very high level. This contrasts with most other Euro area countries, which mostly declined and/or went into current account deficits until 2015 or so. The exceptions were other Northern European countries such as the Netherlands, which however posted surpluses at a much lower value. For Germany in particular, critics have suggested that its huge surpluses contributed to the problems of the periphery. In an incisive op-ed in 2013, Martin Wolf noted: "a large country [read: Germany] with a huge structural current account surplus does not just export products. It also exports bankruptcy and unemployment, particularly if the counterpart capital flow consists of short-term debt."[19] By pushing up the value of the euro as an international currency, Germany's surpluses made the periphery's exports less price-competitive, while Germany's low domestic demand and low wage growth, based on a wage-bargaining system that delivers wage restraint even when the labor market is tight and corporate profits high, pushed wages and prices in the periphery even lower, enhancing their deflationary spiral.[20]

German policymakers kept to their narrative, however, with the prescription for countries under market threat to engage in wage devaluation and labor market deregulation, along with rapid deficit reduction through policies of austerity. And this in fact was then done.

So if the Germans were right, and the behavioral failure to follow the rules was indeed the problem, the main question would be why, once all member states

---

[17] French banks were equally involved here.
[18] Enderlein et al. 2012; De Grauwe 2013; De Grauwe and Ji 2012.   [19] Wolf 2013.
[20] See, eg, Tilford and Springford 2013; Matthijs and Blyth 2011.

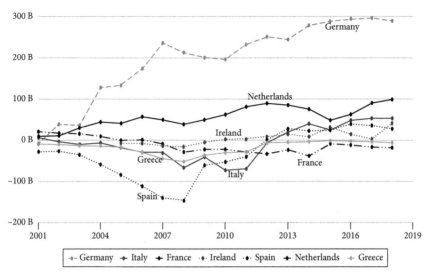

Figure 9.3. Current Account Balance with Rest of World, 2001–2019 (Balance of Payments, current US dollars)
Source: Worldbank 2020

began to follow the rules, the Eurozone did not emerge from the crisis more quickly, and why deficit countries did not return to surplus once wages had been so radically suppressed. One answer is naturally that the rules were themselves counterproductive, leading to weak economic performance—which will be further developed below. Another answer, as many critics pointed out from the very beginning, is that insisting that the model to emulate is Germany, through export-led, surplus-producing growth, violates Keynes' "fallacy of composition" (ie, what works for one country will not necessarily work for all). Such policies fail to deal appropriately with the interdependence of EU economies, in which surplus countries beget deficit countries. In this context, austerity policies simply make the problem worse. Insisting that all countries tighten their belts at the same time to become more "competitive" ignores the interdependence of surplus and deficit countries and the moving average problem at the heart of such efforts.[21]

But none of this figured in EU analysis at the time. And notably, even when EU officials began to acknowledge the problem of surplus and deficit countries, they underplayed their importance by penalizing deficits above 3 percent but only problematizing surpluses above 6 percent—without penalty. It is useful to note that everyone was aware of the issue, because French leaders had been continually harping on the need to do something about the increasing current account balances once the financial crisis hit between 2008 and 2010. French Finance Minister

---

[21] See, eg, Skidelsky 2013; Matthijs and Blyth 2011; Wolf 2013.

Christine Lagarde in particular repeatedly focused on the joint responsibility of deficit countries and surplus countries, and the need for the latter to consume more, raise wages, and reduce savings, much to the reported irritation of Merkel in March 2010.[22] Merkel insisted over and over again that she was not about to undermine the very element that contributed to German competitiveness—its "competitive" wages—or to reduce its surplus, which she insisted was merely the manifestation of the success of its export-oriented industries. Only in May 2010 did the French stop talking about the problem, in exchange for the Germans finally agreeing to allow the EU to take action on the now existential crisis of the euro.

It was a number of years before the issue came back on the table. In 2014, the Bundesbank, backed by the ECB, pushed German employers and trade unions to increase wages in response to the threat of deflation in the Eurozone, endorsing a new minimum wage to begin in 2015. At the same time, however, Finance Minister Schäuble stuck to his *"schwarze Null"* (in the black, zero deficit) budget as a matter of pride, even as the German infrastructure continued to crumble from lack of capital expenditure and investment. Having been the first Finance Minister since 1969 to balance the budget in 2014, he was not about to give that up then or in subsequent years, with popular support domestically and in the face of criticism from everywhere else.[23] The problem with the "stability" rules was not just that federal spending did not keep up with an expanding economy, despite years of budgetary surpluses, or that the lack of spending constituted a drag on the Eurozone economy as a whole. It was also because in Germany's federalized system—with the Länder responsible for university education, and local governments for local infrastructure—the rules limited new investment for the poorer (and therefore already more indebted) regions and localities, thereby increasing inequalities among sub-federal units while stunting growth potential.[24]

Wrong Chosen Remedies

The third problem comes from the chosen remedies in the first years of the crisis, centered on pro-cyclical policies of "sound" money, budgetary austerity, and "structural reform," instead of countercyclical policies that could have generated growth through macroeconomic stimulus, industrial investment, and socioeconomic support.[25] This suggests a critique of the economic ideas at the basis of the "Brussels–Frankfurt consensus."[26] According to Martin Heipertz and Amy

[22] *Der Spiegel*, March 17, 2010 http://www.spiegel.de/international/europe/tension-in-the-euro-zone-france-germany-bicker-over-export-surplus-a-684185.html

[23] Deustche Welle, July 2016 http://www.dw.com/en/sch%C3%A4uble-clings-to-black-zero-fetish-in-german-budget/a-19382452

[24] Roth and Wolf 2018.   [25] Scharpf 2012b, 2013, 2014; De Grauwe 2013.

[26] De Grauwe 2006; Jones 2013a.

Verdun, the "stability paradigm" at the basis of this consensus sees price stability (low rates of inflation) as a precondition for growth rather than as a trade-off; an independent central bank as key to setting interest rates independently of political processes (and opportunistic politicians); and conforming wage policy (ie, no excessive wage bargains) and fiscal policy (no excessive levels of public deficit and debt) as further requirements.[27] To critics, this philosophical mindset ensured that EU actors focused on the wrong factors, in particular for member states under surveillance or in programs. Eurozone problems have had much more to do with the "sudden stop" of market finance than with indebtedness (as noted above, before the crisis Ireland and Spain in particular had very low deficit and debt) or lack of "competitiveness" (all exported at decent rates, while wages were "excessive" mainly in relation to Germany's hypercompetitive wage restraint). Importantly, as Erik Jones has convincingly argued, that sudden stop can itself be seen as related more to the uncertainty generated by EU leaders' pronouncements or (in)action with regard to deeper European economic integration than to the health of those member states' economies.[28]

Monetary Policy

The differential effectiveness of the chosen remedies can be seen in the comparative economic outcomes in the Eurozone economy versus those of the United States. Even if there are some who would argue that the United States is a special case, with the markets much more willing to accept more expansionary policy despite high deficits and debt, it is useful to see that differences in the economic policies of these two close-to-equivalent regions in economic terms yielded significant differences in economic outcomes.

Despite the fact that the United States suffered a massive blow to its economy as a result of the financial crisis and was in recession from December 2007 to June 2009, with a longer road to recovery, it steadily improved, and without a double-dip recession. The Euro area was in recession technically from January 2008 to April 2009, and then fell back into a longer recession from the third quarter of 2011 through the third quarter of 2013. Moreover, although the United States fell much farther and faster following the financial crisis in terms of its output gap (potential GDP versus actual GDP), it reduced that gap much more quickly than the Euro area between 2013 and 2016 (see Figure 9.4). Only in 2017 and thereafter did the Euro area reduce it gap between potential and actual GDP more rapidly than the US.

The explanation for these differences in economic recovery trajectories between the two largest regional economies in the world has much to do with the policies.

---

[27] Heipertz and Verdun 2010.   [28] Jones 2010, 2015b.

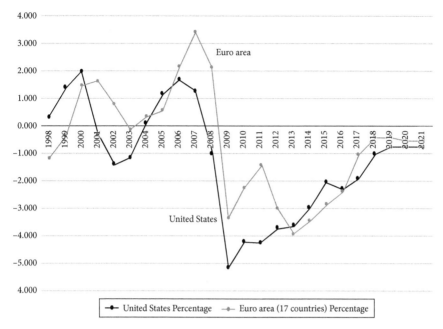

Figure 9.4. Output Gaps: Euro Area vs. the United States, 1998–2021 (Deviations of actual GDP from potential GDP as % of potential GDP)
Source: OECD 2019

The Eurozone demanded austerity for all, with rapid deficit reduction from all countries breaching the rules, austerity and structural reform for countries in trouble in the first years of the crisis. In contrast, the United States continued fiscal stimulus much longer, with the federal government bailout of the big banks—paid by all taxpayers—ensuring against high debt and the threat of insolvency for the federal states. In other words, whereas in the Eurozone the taxpayers of the debtor countries bore the brunt of the crisis and paid the costs, in the dollarzone all taxpayers shared the costs and gained the benefits. What is more, less affluent taxpayers were also protected by individual deposit insurance, the FDIC, which guaranteed accounts up to $100,000.

In the United States, moreover, the Federal Reserve Bank acted immediately and decisively at the inception of the financial crisis with quantitative easing (extensive buying of government debt), to deter any market attacks while supporting the US sovereign. The ECB did not. Had the European Central Bank acted as a lender of last resort (LOLR) from the very beginning, the sovereign debt crisis would most likely have been stopped almost before it started. The lessons from the United States in terms of the actions of the Federal Reserve Bank are clear, but so are those from the Bank of England. One of the most important functions of central banks is to act as lenders of last resort, to protect the sovereign. Even if one believes the United States to be exceptional—as the home of the world's reserve currency—the United Kingdom was not. Its deficit and debt from the financial crisis was much greater than that of the main Eurozone countries, yet it never came under sustained attack. But unlike the Fed and the BoE, as we have already seen, the ECB only very slowly and incrementally increased its bond-buying programs between 2010 and 2012, with the great leap forward through the promised (but never taken up) OMT for Spain and Italy, and the even bigger leap into quantitative easing (QE) in 2015.[29] But while the massive injection of liquidity by the ECB did have positive effects, helping to close the output gap, it was insufficient to ensure robust growth for the Eurozone economies. This is because quantitative easing came late, and was not enough on its own to stimulate the economy (given interest rates close to zero). Moreover, the liquidity created by the central bank could not in any event easily filter into the real economy as a result of the "liquidity trap," which results from hoarding by financial institutions.[30]

The ECB's various schemes to provide money to the banks to ensure liquidity, such as the VLTROs (very long term refinancing operations) of 2011, worked well with regard to creating market confidence and, thereby, calming the crisis.[31] But its success was limited with regard to promoting bank lending to firms so as to boost growth and investment, in particular in the countries in the periphery that were in trouble. Often the banks were overburdened with bad debt, as in Spain—until it agreed to a partial program in 2012 to restructure and recapitalize its banks—and in Italy—which continued to limp along, with some banks (most notably Monte dei Paschi) finally being restructured only beginning in 2017. The ECB's liquidity in many cases enabled banks to renew their loans to unproductive "zombie firms" that often had a disproportionate share of capital stock and employment, particularly in places such as Italy, Spain, Portugal, and Belgium.[32]

Alternatively, the domestic banks often took the money from the ECB but hoarded it (the liquidity trap), and/or loaded up on government debt rather than lending to business. In some euro-area members, this ended up reinforcing the already problematic interdependence of banks and governments, often termed the "diabolic loop" between domestic bank solvency and the fiscal standing of the sovereign, which banking union and the yet-to-be-agreed individual deposit insurance was supposed to break.[33] As economic historians Markus Brunnermeier, Harold James, and Jean-Pierre Landau explain, the diabolic loop comes in two forms. First, if banks cut back on lending, leading to less credit for the economy, then growth slumps, lowering tax revenues while raising government expenditures (eg, on unemployment insurance). This in turn threatens overall government sustainability, which therefore lowers government bond prices while driving up interest rates on new bond issues. Second, weaker banks only further threaten

---

[29] See Chapter 5 on policy ideas for the details on OMT and quantitative easing.
[30] De Grauwe 2016.   [31] Brunnermeier et al. 2016, pp. 350–2.
[32] McGowan et al. 2017.   [33] See, eg, Schoenmaker and Gros 2012.

government sustainability, thereby again lowering government bond prices and further hurting banks. Prime examples of this at the height of the crisis were Ireland and Spain.[34]

Disagreements among euro-area members on how to solve the diabolic loop help explain why banking union has remained incomplete. According to Brunnermeier, James, and Landau, the stalemate comes down to the incompatible ideas of the French and the Germans, supported by their different coalitional allies. For the French, "bail-ins" through bank bailouts by taxpayers are necessary to stabilize the economy and the sovereign. In contrast, for the Germans, "bailouts" through "haircuts" for creditors, along with higher equity requirements for banks, are required. This sheds light on why in 2015, when the Bundesbank and other Northern European banks pushed to limit banks' holdings of domestic government debt in order to break the loop by limiting exposure, French and Southern European central bankers strongly resisted. They insisted that at the height of a crisis only domestic banks would buy and/or hold on to their government's debt, and that this ensures that governments will not default on their debt. The problem here is that this close bank–government interrelationship can make also for a "straitjacket" in which it becomes nearly impossible for governments to restructure banking debt.[35] A prime example of this has been Italy, where successive governments did little to tackle the country's banking crisis because to do so would have involved haircuts to small Italian savers, meaning ordinary Italians rather than big foreign creditors.

Investment

In addition to these drawbacks regarding the relationship between the ECB and the banks, or the banks and businesses, is the problem of investment. In countries suffering from high deficits and debts, the rules make it nearly impossible for governments to stimulate the economy in the usual ways, through investment in infrastructure or in growth-enhancing areas such as research and development, education and training, or renewable energy. But even in countries with low deficits and comparatively low debt, investment has been long in coming. As economist Paul de Grauwe has noted, the "debt brake" or golden rule that demands that investment by Eurozone countries be funded by current tax revenues rather than bond issues puts serious limits on growth. It prevents public investment from taking off, to sustain recovery or to develop a "green" economy. Moreover, despite the fact that some countries in the Eurozone periphery may have "limited capacity" to increase their public debt under the current rules, de Grauwe suggests that

---

[34] Brunnermeier et al. 2016, pp. 182–3.   [35] Brunnermeier et al. 2016, pp. 184–5.

countries such as Germany, France, Belgium, and the Netherlands could do so almost for free, by borrowing at very long maturities at extremely low cost (given interest rates at 1 percent or lower).[36]

This is the same point stressed by the International Monetary Fund (IMF) in its *World Economic Outlook* of 2014, where it concluded that "debt-financed projects could have large output effects without increasing the debt-to-GDP ratio, if clearly identified infrastructure needs are met through efficient investment."[37] It is worth noting that the OECD in its 2016 *Economic Outlook* devoted a whole chapter to the need for more investment, including two highlighted, set-aside boxes to the EU. One such box used Germany as the example to demonstrate that debt-financed public investment would have no long-term effect on debt to GDP ratio.[38] The other suggested two ways to revise the SGP to promote investment: the first by using even more discretion and flexibility in the interpretation of the rules; the second by excluding net public investment spending from assessment of compliance with the fiscal rules, as is already done in the case of countries contributing to the European Fund for Strategic Investment (EFSI).[39]

On investment, as in other areas, the differences between the US and the EU are striking. These demonstrate the importance of the fiscal stimulus in the United States, and how it also spurred private investment, in contrast to the belt-tightening austerity across Europe. But it was only in 2015 that EU officials acknowledged how serious the problem was. This was when Juncker announced the EFSI, while ECB President Draghi, in a 2015 speech in Sintra to the ECB Forum on Central Banking, referred to the "crisis in investment."[40] The OECD *Economic Outlook* in 2016 found that investment in the euro area in particular lagged far behind that in the United States (see Figure 9.5). Whereas investment in the United States had returned to its 2007 level by 2014, and had risen above it by close to 4 points by 2016, the euro area continued to struggle at way below the 2007 baseline level—at its best around 12 points below the baseline in 2016, which put it 16 points behind the United States. Notably, only Germany overtook the United States, albeit only marginally, despite being the powerhouse of Europe. And while France came in 11 points below Germany, it still came in significantly ahead of the euro area as a whole. Italy and Spain, in contrast, show the effects of austerity programs and the problems of their banks, with both countries coming in with their best scores since the crisis in 2016, at a disastrous 30 points below the 2007 baseline. By 2018, after three years of emphasis on investment, although the euro area was doing better, it continued to lag behind the US in terms of public investment (at 84 points versus 90 points, where the baseline was 100 in 2007) as well as in private investment (95 versus 105).[41]

---

[36] De Grauwe 2016.   [37] IMF 2014.   [38] OECD 2016, pp. 75–6.
[39] OECD 2016, pp. 89–90.   [40] Draghi 2015a.
[41] OECD 2018, *OECD Economic Outlook: Statistics and Projections* (database).

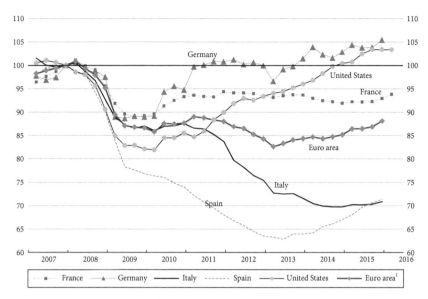

Figure 9.5. Investment: United States compared to Euro area and select countries
[1] Euro area member countries that are also members of the OECD (15 countries).
Source: OECD (2016), *OECD Economic Outlook: Statistics and Projections* (database)

Economic Divergence

The differential investment figures between Germany and Southern European countries such as Italy and Spain are only one illustration of the growing divergences between Northern and Southern Europe. The differentials in potential and actual output among euro-area members are equally dramatic, and serve to demonstrate how problematic the chosen remedies for the debtor states turned out to be, in particular for Greece (see Figure 9.6). Germany recovered quickly from its large output gap related to the financial crisis, and sailed through the Eurozone crisis. In 2011, it came close to par on its potential versus actual GDP, and by 2015 and after it was outperforming its potential. In contrast, Southern Europe's output gaps only increased in the main crisis period. Spain and Greece in particular went into freefall at the beginning of the financial crisis and continued to plummet during the heat of the Eurozone crisis, between 2010 and 2012. While Spain dipped to a negative output gap of minus 10 percent before it began to recover, Greece dropped even more precipitously, with a negative output gap of almost minus 15 percent, and with only anemic moves upward thereafter.

For Greece in particular, the bailout packages administered by the Troika provided anything but remedies to its problems. The initial loan bailout at above 5 percent interest was very high—too high, in fact, for any chances of repayment, in particular given the failure to erase any of Greece's debt, which then

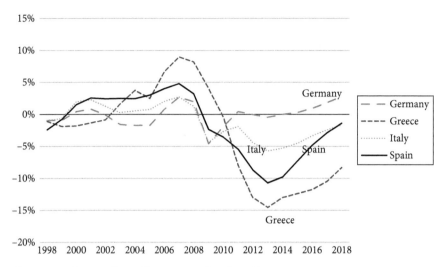

Figure 9.6. Output Gaps: Germany vs. Southern Europe, 1999–2018
Source: OECD 2017

skyrocketed as a percentage of GDP as the country's economy shrank in response to the mandated austerity policies. The IMF itself issued a report in 2013 in which it admitted that it had made major mistakes in the bailout of Greece. Its assumption that severe austerity would lead in short order to growth was very far off the mark, in particular in light of the failure to restructure Greek debt. Part of the report summary reads, damningly: "Market confidence was not restored, the banking system lost 30 per cent of its deposits, and the economy encountered a much-deeper-than-expected recession with exceptionally high unemployment."[42] Without an immediate haircut to major bondholders, the program was unsustainable from the very beginning.

But for EU leaders this was more about saving the euro than saving Greece, which they felt had put the euro in jeopardy, and which had lied from the very beginning about its numbers (including not just its deficit in 2009 but also its readiness for membership in the early 2000s). Most importantly, at the time of the bailout in May 2010, EU leaders were mostly concerned about market panic spilling over to the rest of the Eurozone were bondholders not to be paid in full. Another piece of the story was that this was also about saving the German and French banks, which were heavily invested in Greece and other debtor countries in the periphery.[43] No initial haircut for major bondholders meant that such heavily exposed banks were able to sell off their loans.[44]

After a few years, the shareholders most at risk from a loss were not the German or French banks but German and French taxpayers, because of the

---

[42] IMF 2013, p. 1.   [43] Blyth 2013; Thompson 2015.   [44] Minenna 2018.

transfer of ownership of debt to the ECB and the European Stability Mechanism (ESM) (backed by the member states), which had become the largest holders of Greek debt. In this regard, it is important to note that far from losing money on the bailout—as the German discourse suggested at the time of the crisis, when it insisted that it would be the first to pay for the debts of the periphery—Germany made money on the deal. German financial authorities earned €1.34 billion from Greek bonds in the two-year period 2015–17,[45] even as Greece went through repeated cuts in public sector expenditure, in particular regarding salaries and pensions, and as it continued to suffer from record unemployment.

Lack of Adequate Solutions

The final problem results from the EU's lack of adequate solutions. The contrast with the US may again prove useful: In the US, all the necessary institutions and policy capabilities were already in place to make it possible to produce real solutions to the financial crisis. The government had the authority and the capacity to rescue the banks; it had the money for the fiscal stimulus as a result of a big federal budget; and the Fed could buy government debt and even print the money, if necessary. In contrast, as Waltraud Schelkle has shown, the EU suffered from a lack of adequate solutions that left an incomplete risk pool and insurance mechanism put in place more by default than design to respond to the pressures of global financial markets and the challenges of global competition.[46] What was needed was a response that could at the very least approximate US responses in a minimal way, through some form of debt sharing, redistributive mechanisms, or fiscal union. Although many policy solutions to the crisis were proposed—for example, some form of Eurobonds or mutualization of debt,[47] a "European Monetary Fund" to rescue countries in trouble, a joint tax system with EU institutions' own resources, plus macroeconomic stabilizers such as an unemployment fund or a "cyclical adjustment fund"[48]—Eurozone governments did the minimum, through loan bailout mechanisms and close oversight of compliance with the reinforcement of the SGP through restrictive rules and stringent numbers.

That said, Eurozone governments went much farther than was initially intended, in particular by Germany and its Northern European allies. Honoring the no-bailout clause of the Maastricht Treaty was not really a viable option in May 2010. The contagion effect would have been much too difficult to contain, given the lack of sufficient EU-level resources and the likelihood of market attacks

[45] *Reuters*, July 12, 2013. For more information see: https://www.dailysabah.com/economy/2017/07/13/germany-earned-134-billion-euros-in-greek-crisis
[46] Schelkle 2015, 2017.   [47] Eg, Delpla and Von Weizsäcker 2011; Claessens et al. 2012.
[48] Dullien 2014; Enderlein et al. 2012; Enderlein et al. 2013.

on countries "too big to bail" with banks "too big to fail" (Spain and Italy) once the other dominoes fell (Greece, Ireland, Portugal). As Martin Sandbu of the *Financial Times* argued, had the EU allowed the member states to become insolvent, with bail-ins of the owners and creditors of private banks and a radical restructuring of sovereign debt, the crisis might have been resolved without the imposition of tight fiscal constraints.[49] That said, had this been agreed, it would not only have caused major losses to national holders of their countries' debt and that of international investors, but would also have entailed major losses for German and French banks with exposure to Greek debt—something neither Merkel nor Sarkozy were willing to countenance.

This brings us back to the structure of the euro and its original incomplete architecture. As discussed earlier, in exchange for the go-ahead on unification, Kohl accepted monetary union, which was pushed by Mitterrand, who wanted to end German dominance of the European Monetary System for economic reasons, and not just political ones. Italy also saw monetary union not simply as a political issue, to ensure national pride, but also as an economic one, by constituting the "*vincolo esterno*" that would force the country to undertake the necessary economic reforms. Every other member state had equally compelling economic and political reasons for moving forward. As Schelkle has argued, there are good rationalist logics for member states to cooperate in a mutually beneficial "risk-sharing" insurance union, based on diversity and inequality, where the members could better ensure their economic prosperity together than they could apart.[50] The only problem with such a union is that those shared risks have not been randomly distributed but rather, as Fritz Scharpf has contended, have fallen disproportionately on Southern European deficit countries, given Eurozone rules.[51] So the question remains: can EMU survive given its high level of diversity, where the risks have turned out not to be shared equally?

For many top economists, in particular those in the United States such as Barry Eichengreen and Martin Feldstein, EMU was doomed from the start. They roundly criticized the decision to go ahead with it as a faulty political decision that was unworkable precisely because of the diversity of euro member economies. Their critique was that the Eurozone could not work because it was not an Optimum Currency Area (OCA).[52] They argued that the Eurozone as a whole lacked sufficiently integrated markets for labor or goods, that many of its member states were insufficiently flexible to manage any negative shocks, and that it also lacked a budgetary union that would have cushioned such shocks.[53] The Eurozone was in fact as distant from an OCA as could possibly be imagined. This was illustrated in an illuminating chart produced by JP Morgan in 2012. The chart

---

[49] Sandbu 2015.   [50] Schelkle 2017.   [51] Scharpf 2014, 2015.
[52] Eg, Eichengreen 1991, 2012; Feldstein 1997.   [53] Eg, De Grauwe 2013.

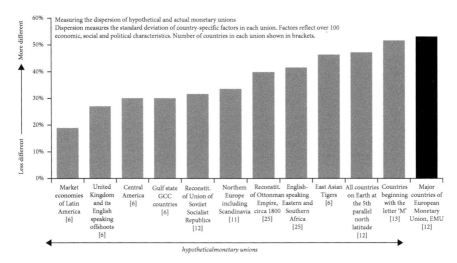

Figure 9.7. Measures of Dispersion in the Structure of EMU

Source: World Economic Forum Global Competitiveness Report, J.P. Morgan Asset Management--
J.P. Morgan, "Eye on the Market," May 2, 2012

shows the degree of dispersion of hypothetical and actual monetary unions, with EMU more dispersed than even the most random agglomeration of countries, for example, those on the 5th parallel north latitude of the world or those countries beginning with the letter "M" (see Figure 9.7). Note that the US is missing from the list of potential OCAs. This is because it could be seen as having as much dispersion in terms of its economic, social, and political characteristics as the EU, if we were to contrast, say, Louisiana, Missouri, and Alabama with California, Wisconsin, and Massachusetts.[54]

More generally, as Kathleen McNamara has argued, the OCA literature fails to explain the woes of EMU because it does not consider the history of monetary unions. These succeed only when they are embedded in a set of political and social institutions capable of providing a solid foundation for a monetary union. This means that a monetary union requires not only a "true" LOLR, fiscal redistribution and sovereign debt pooling (fiscal union), along with financial market regulation, resolution mechanisms, and deposit guarantees (banking union), but also legitimate and democratic institutions of governance (political union).[55] It remains questionable whether any such economic solutions, alone or together, are enough without a full-fledged "political union" to serve to democratically legitimize decisions taken.[56]

---

[54] Schelkle 2017.   [55] McNamara 2015b; see also Jabko 2015; Jones 2015a; Schmidt 2015a.
[56] McNamara 2015b.

Excessive Costs of Austerity

The evidence for the lack of effectiveness of Eurozone policies comes not only from the macroeconomic performance indicators, including the low overall growth of the Eurozone, the output gaps between the EU and the US, and the program countries' initial increase in deficits and debt-to-GDP ratios. It also emerges from any consideration of the socioeconomic indicators, whether in terms of wages, jobs, and unemployment or measures of inequality and poverty, in particular for Southern Europe. Although the performance results are generally better for Northern Europe, output legitimacy demands general improvement for all—not that some are much better off while others much worse. Notably, even those touted as success stories among program countries, such as Ireland, have achieved this at the initial cost of major emigration of their populations in search of jobs and increases in poverty and social exclusion.

Wages, Jobs, and Employment

One of the most dramatic illustrations of the effects of austerity has been on real wage compensation. Although the story at the time of the Eurozone crisis was that the other economies in the South had overinflated wages, and this made them uncompetitive (using the year 2000 as the baseline, as in Figure 9.2), the story looks very different when seen from a more recent vantage point (using the year 2010 as the baseline), after the austerity "cure." In Figure 9.8, the graph shows that real wage compensation declined rapidly following the sovereign debt crisis as recession set in and public employees' salaries were slashed, initially by an average of 30 percent in program countries, with private sector salaries

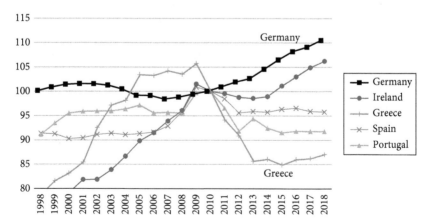

Figure 9.8. Real Compensation per Employee 1998–2018
Source: Ameco 2017

following suit. The tale of Greece is especially dramatic, since from 2013 on salaries fell back down to the level of 2001, just before it had entered the euro, and way below even the other member states that had been in trouble at the height of the crisis. As for Germany, wages largely remained in line with inflation, but still well below productivity growth.

Equally at issue is how much recovery from the crisis occurred in terms of jobs lost and jobs regained. The comparative numbers on employment of 20–64 year olds in the EU as a whole provides a very telling picture of the differential effects of the crisis on member states (see Figure 9.9). By 2016, most member states subject to conditionality did not recover to their pre-crisis level (of 2008), although there is a marked difference between Central and Eastern European countries, which largely raised their overall employment rates to a reasonably high level, and Southern Europe, which lost in employment at an already lower level. Greece is the worst case, having dropped to a catastrophic level of employment, at around 56 percent. In contrast, Northern Europe clearly more than recovered.

The figures on employment are only part of the picture with regard to the recovery. The quality of the jobs being added to the Eurozone economy is another. Because such jobs were generally low paid and in the services sector, they made for a recovery in which many continued to be left behind.[57] There was little growth in traditional blue-collar industrial jobs, with the increase in employment in manufacturing coming mainly in the higher-paid professional and technical engineering jobs. The recovery itself was fueled in part by extended working lives

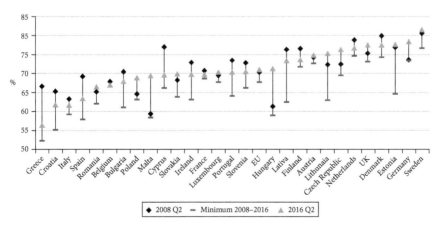

Figure 9.9. Employment rates of 20-64 years olds by member-state, 2008 Q2–2016 Q2
Source: EU-LFS (Eurostat 2017)

[57] World Economic Forum *Global Competitiveness Report* 2016–2017.

and later retirement—the share of workers aged 55+ was 18.6 percent of the workforce in 2017, up by 4.6 percentage points from 2008.[58]

The other side of the employment story is unemployment. It reached record highs at the peak of the crisis, with 12.1 percent for the Euro area as a whole in 2013, but topped 23.6 percent in Greece, Portugal, and Spain taken together. In contrast, Continental European countries, including Austria, Germany, and Luxembourg, together went no higher than 5.5 percent unemployment that same year (see Figure 9.10). That said, there were big differences even among so-called normal countries. While the French jobless rates hit a new record of 12.2 percent in April 2012, Germany was at a low of 5.4 percent.[59] In 2014, the Catholic charity Caritas Europe reported that the seven countries hardest hit by economic crisis (Cyprus, Greece, Ireland, Italy, Portugal, Romania, and Spain) had experienced a massive rise in unemployment, with 50 million jobs lost, and an increase of job seekers to 80 million. Recovery came slowly but steadily, however, once austerity policies eased beginning in 2013, and unemployment in the euro area continued to fall thereafter. That said, the unemployment statistics remained highly differentiated: while the Euro area had fallen to 8.5 percent by 2018 and Continental European countries to 4.6 percent, Southern European countries remained at a very high 14.9 percent (see Figure 9.10).

It is useful to note that the unemployment figures would be even higher were it not for outward migration. In Ireland in particular, unemployment figures were lower because of the large number of young adults who left the country in search of employment elsewhere in Europe, in Australia and the Americas. According to Caritas, the Irish unemployment rate would have been around 20 percent by 2013 had this emigration not occurred.[60] Although all of the countries in trouble experienced increased emigration after the crisis, Irish citizens left in much greater numbers per capita—largely explainable by their English-language skills, training, and networks abroad.[61]

A related problem is the emigration of high-skilled workers, often trained at great cost, who leave to find jobs with better pay and working conditions. In Greece, for example, the brain drain of engineers and doctors has been estimated at an outflow of around 17,000 a year between 2008 and 2018,[62] for what amounts to the outflow of approximately 427,000 (Bank of Greece estimate) highly educated Greeks from 2008 through 2016.[63] For doctors alone, the outflow increased steadily between 2010 and 2016 to a total of 9,300, even as the healthcare system was facing shortages of specialized medical staff.[64]

---

[58] Eurofound 2017.   [59] Eurostat 2013.
[60] Caritas 2015.   [61] Glynn 2015.
[62] Oxford Analytica, August 2, 2018 https://dailybrief.oxan.com/Analysis/GA236556/Greece-will-struggle-to-reverse-brain-drain
[63] Endeavor, July 19, 2016 http://endeavor.org.gr/en/latestnews/2137/
[64] *Ekathimerimi*, Nov. 11, 2016. Note that the number is based on licenses issued by the Athens Medical Association for medical doctors to practice abroad. See: http://www.ekathimerini.com/213843/article/ekathimerini/community/greek-doctors-continue-to-emigrate-in-large-numbers

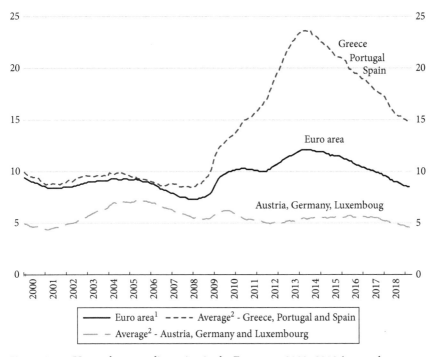

Figure 9.10. Unemployment dispersion in the Euro area, 2000–2018 (unemployment rates in percentages)

[1] Euro area 19 countries.
[2] Unweighted average.

Source: Eurostat (2018), "Employment and unemployment (LFS)", *Eurostat Database*; OECD Economic Surveys—Euro Area 2018

Youth unemployment was the biggest problem, though, and remained stubbornly high everywhere. To illustrate, despite the return to growth in the euro area as a whole, in 2019 youth unemployment was still at 16.9 percent. In southern Europe, the numbers were 32.17 percent in Italy (but down from 43.1 percent in March 2015), 34.4 percent in Spain (down from 50.1 percent in March 2015), and 39.9 percent in Greece (down from 50.1 percent in January 2015).[65] In this context, of greatest concern has been the rate of youths who are not only not employed but are also not in education or training programs, the so-called NEETs (not in employment, education, or training). Again, the north/south differences have beeen staggering. But that is not to say that there are not problems across the EU. For some countries most affected by the Eurozone crisis the level remained catastrophically high, including in Greece, which hit a high of 30.8 percent at its worst in 2013 but was only down to 25.6 percent in 2016, and Italy, which hit a high of 26.2 percent in 2013 and was only down to 26 percent in 2016, marginally above Greece (see Figure 9.11).

[65] Eurostat 2015, OECD 2020.

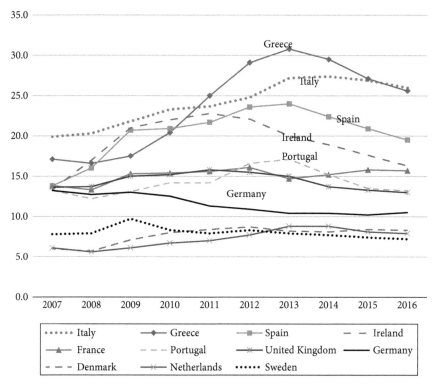

Figure 9.11. NEETs (youth not in employment, education or training) in percentage rates from 2007 to 2016

Source: Eurostat 2017

Inequality and Poverty

The impact of the Eurozone crisis on youth unemployment, general unemployment, job quality, and real wage compensation together contributed to growing inequalities across Europe—within member states, not just between them. Although inequality has been on the rise for a very long time, austerity policies have contributed greatly to its increase. But this is an area where the differentials also have a lot to do with longer-term trends of national political economies, and not just the effects of the euro crisis.

Germany is of special interest, given that its high economic performance did not translate into greater prosperity for the ordinary German. Not only did workers' real wages stagnate through much of the 2000s but ordinary Germans may actually be proportionately poorer next to comparable Southern Europeans. An ECB survey in 2013 put the net wealth of median households in Germany last, compared to all of Southern Europe as well as Continental and Nordic Europe. The survey itself unleashed media polemic reinforcing the discourse that asked why "we Germans" should pay for a richer, profligate South. But as economists Paul de Grauwe and Yuemei Ji pointed out at the time, while the median German household may be poor, Germany is wealthy, with wealth highly concentrated in the upper part of household income distribution or held by the corporate sector and the government.[66] A 2018 analysis by the German Institute for Economic Research suggests that levels of inequality may be even worse than those found in the ECB 2013 study, because it had failed to take account of the superrich, with the top 1 percent of German households owning a third of the country's wealth and the wealthiest 5 percent in Germany holding 51.1 percent of the country's entire wealth. The contrast with Spain and France is striking, since the richest 10 percent of households own less than half of their country's wealth, whereas in Germany they own close to two thirds of the nation's wealth.[67] The fact that family ownership of major corporations may hold much of this wealth—with profits reinvested in businesses so as to spur growth and ensure employment stability—does little to mitigate the political inequalities of access and influence that follow from the economic inequality. Nor did it do much for German workers, whose real wages stagnated through much of the 2000s as the inequalities grew.

Inequality has in fact increased everywhere as a result of general trends linked to national governments' liberalizing responses to the competitive pressures of globalization. One part of the explanation comes from the fact that progressive taxation (ie, the income tax) has given way to an emphasis on regressive taxes (eg, VAT and fees), and that "mobile capital," meaning multinational companies, has benefited from increasingly favorable low domestic tax regimes, along with tax avoidance schemes through offshore tax havens, creative accounting, and special tax deals for the biggest companies (such as those revealed in Luxleaks and the Panama Papers). Another piece of the puzzle is the rise of financial capitalism, which has sped up capital accumulation for the top players at the same time as it has provided increasing returns to the holders of capital—those Thomas Piketty has called the 1 percent.[68] Yet another part of the explanation comes from the dualization of the workforce through deregulatory labor market reforms that have split the labor force increasingly between the "insiders," with decent salaries, social benefits, and job protections, and the "outsiders" in temporary and part-time jobs with lower salaries, low benefits, and no job protection.[69] Such dualization was instituted in Germany through the Hartz IV reforms, but it has been a more generalized phenomenon, which has been particularly pronounced for

---

[66] de Grauwe and Ji 2012.

[67] Bach et al. 2018 http://www.diw.de/sixcms/detail.php?id=diw_01.c.575700.de, reviewed in *Der Spiegel* Jan. 26, 2018: http://www.spiegel.de/international/business/inquality-and-wealth-distribution-in-germany-a-1190050.html

[68] Piketty 2014.   [69] Hassel 2011; Palier and Thelen 2010.

countries under conditionality programs, and is in part responsible for rising inequalities across Europe.[70]

But even though inequality is rising, there is no necessary linkage between it and growing poverty and social exclusion. France, for example—with significant inequality compared to Sweden (in GINI coefficient), and high wealth differentials—nonetheless has comparatively low levels of poverty. That said, the financial crisis in 2008 and the euro crisis in 2010 reversed the previous downward trend in poverty and social exclusion everywhere, which rose to new levels during the peak years of the crisis, in particular for countries in explicit conditionality programs (ie, Greece) or implicit ones (ie, Italy) (see Figure 9.12).

In 2013, a Council of Europe report concluded that austerity programs in response to the crisis had undermined human rights in key areas, largely as a result of public social spending cuts, and especially in countries under loan bailout programs (where the Troika demanded that public spending in program countries not exceed 6 percent of GDP). The report particularly condemned increasing homelessness in Southern Europe, Ireland, and the United Kingdom, as well as failures to provide adequate safeguards to ensure access to the minimum essential levels of food (as governments limited food subsidies), and even of water in the case of Ireland (resulting from Troika insistence on new fees for domestic water).[71] For 2014, moreover, a Caritas Europe report detailed the

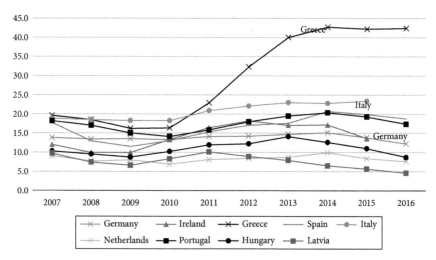

Figure 9.12. At-risk-of-poverty rate anchored at a fixed moment in time (2005) by age and sex from 2007 to 2016
Source: Eurostat 2017

[70] Emmeneger et al. 2012.   [71] Council of Europe 2013.

extent of the humanitarian problem resulting from responses to the Eurozone crisis, finding that more than one third of the population in five EU Member States was at risk of poverty or social exclusion[72] and that one in three children, or more, lived in poverty in fourteen of the twenty-eight EU countries.[73] Additionally, a 2015 European Parliament (EP) report on seven countries (Belgium, Cyprus, Greece, Italy, Portugal, and Spain) detailed the austerity-related slashes in spending on education, the transfer of health costs from state to citizen, the reversal in gains in citizen health, the critical shrinking of pension benefits, and the rise in unemployment.[74] Most damning in the EP report was the finding that spending cuts, rather than being specifically targeted at wasteful uses of public resources, tended to "impose horizontal and indiscriminate cuts across the policy areas they targeted, to meet financial savings that were determined in advance."[75]

We could add that austerity policies in program countries also negatively affected those areas highlighted in the Europe 2020 targets as expected to promote growth in the medium and long term, such as education. Between 2008 and 2012, following the financial and Eurozone crises, while poverty and social exclusion went up, government spending on education was cut significantly—by 17 percent in Greece, 13 percent in Portugal, 10 percent in Ireland, 8 percent in Spain and 6 percent in Italy.[76] By 2015, spending on education had fallen even more dramatically for these countries, and there was little change in the numbers thereafter. Between 2009 and 2017, Greece had experienced a drop of 23 percent in spending; Cyprus 17 percent; Portugal 16 percent; Spain 11 percent; and Italy 10 percent.[77]

If output legitimacy is to be judged on the basis of the effectiveness of policies, as measured by the impact on citizens' lives, that is, in terms of socioeconomic performance, then it is no exaggeration to say the EU failed miserably in its response to the Eurozone crisis. The indicators—from the quantity and quality of decent jobs through to poverty and inequality—show deterioration for all euro members, although they are naturally worse for the countries in the periphery that underwent major conditionality programs. Such deterioration can be attributed not only to the costs of austerity but also to the perversity of the structural reforms demanded via the European Semester and the conditionality programs.

---

[72] The numbers were: Bulgaria 48 percent; Romania 40.4 percent; Greece 35.7 percent; Latvia 35.1 percent; and Hungary 33.5 percent.

[73] Caritas 2015.   [74] Caritas 2015.

[75] Study for the EP: "The Impact of the Crisis on Fundamental Rights across Member States of the EU: Comparative Analysis." Study prepared for the Committee on Civil Liberties, Justice and Home Affairs of the EP, PE 510.021 2015. See: http://statewatch.org/news/2015/mar/ep-study-cris-fr.pdf

[76] Lindner 2014.   [77] *Euractiv* Sept. 8, 2017.

Perversity of EU-Led Structural Reforms

The meaning of structural reform tends to be left vague and undefined, as an "empty signifier" which can be infused with any number of meanings.[78] Technically it can connote any reforms that involve neither macroeconomic policy (focused on debts and deficits) nor fiscal policy (focused on public tax and spending). Mostly, structural reform under the influence of neoliberalism in the first years of the crisis has been taken to mean wage devaluation along with the deregulation of the labor markets, for example, by limiting collective bargaining, decentralizing wage setting, and reducing the costs of firing workers.[79] The assumption behind increasing "labor market flexibility" was that lowering of workers' wages and job protections would improve deficit countries' wage and price competitiveness. The other main element was "rationalizing" welfare, meaning cutting spending and reducing the generosity of pensions. Specific reforms additionally targeted such things as improving tax collection, liberalizing closed professions, ameliorating state administration, and deregulating product markets. But for EU policymakers, in particular during the first years of the crisis, the magic bullet was labor market reform, under the assumption that this would encourage export-oriented growth. This "one size fits all" approach was blind to differences in varieties of national political economies and their growth models, and failed to deal with the complexities of labor markets as well as their embedding within very different national systems of capitalist production, supported by different national welfare systems.[80]

The Problems with the Structural Reform Policies

The structural reform policies have raised as many problems as the austerity policies with regard to Eurozone performance. The emphasis on labor market reform was based on the belief that labor market "rigidities" had contributed to countries' lack of competitiveness and failure to recover quickly after the crisis—it took no notice of the structural issues with the euro or the sudden stop in market finance. Equally importantly, the neoliberal assumption that all national political economies required the same remedies imposed special burdens on countries that differed from the ideal.

That ideal, focused on export-oriented, manufacturing-based growth, requires institutions able to repress wages and hold down domestic demand. This fits perfectly the coordinated market economies (CMEs) of Northern Europe, with their

---

[78] Laclau and Mouffe 1985; see also Crespy and Vanheuverzwijn 2017.
[79] Myant et al., 2016; Crespy 2016; Crespy and Schmidt 2017; Crespy and Vanheuverzwijn 2017.
[80] See, eg, Scharpf and Schmidt 2000; Schmidt 2002; Emegnegger et al. 2012; Beramendi et al. 2015.

organized (corporatist) wage bargaining between business and labor.[81] It does not fit as well the liberal market economies (LMEs) of Anglophone Europe[82] or the state-influenced market economies (SMEs) of France and Southern Europe.[83] These are countries that have traditionally benefited from demand-led growth based on allowing wages and credit to expand[84]—even if countries such as France and Italy also have sectors with strong export-oriented growth. These are also countries that tend to have less organized labor markets, either because they are already highly flexible (as in the United Kingdom since the 1980s and Ireland post 2008) or because the state plays an organizing role instead, whether through state-led "social pacts" (as in Spain until 2010 and Ireland between 1986 and 2008)[85] or state intervention in labor-management bargaining and wage-setting (as in France).[86]

The structural reform remedies that demand major belt-tightening with cuts to the welfare state along with deregulation of the labor markets tend to penalize countries that have traditionally been more demand-led, with domestic consumption a driver of growth.[87] Where such countries do not have a large export sector, as Lucio Baccaro and Jonas Pontusson argue, they will be unable to offset the worst effects of austerity and wage devaluation on domestic demand, and thereby will be at pains to generate growth.[88] In other words, the so-called "growth friendly fiscal contractions" purported to spur growth while reducing deficits and debt, as propounded by Alberto Alesina and colleagues,[89] would do the opposite in the very countries most in need.

Moreover, Eurozone deficit and debt requirements that served to limit state investment and macroeconomic stabilization capabilities also led to an even greater reduction in the state's role. This has been particularly problematic for countries where the state has traditionally served as an engine for growth (via planning or investment) and/or as an organizer of labor-management relations, whether in SMEs such as France and Italy or in an LME like Ireland.[90] In Ireland, most notably, while the crisis-generated pressures led the state to abandon its longstanding state-led labor-management coordination in favor of radical decentralization, it stepped up its "enterprising" role with regard to business.[91] In contrast, Southern European SMEs abandoned both the state-led "social pacts" that

---

[81] Hall and Soskice 2001; Thelen 2004.   [82] Hall and Soskice 2001.
[83] For state-influenced market economies see Schmidt 2002, 2009b; Vasileva-Dienes and Schmidt 2018.
[84] Eg, Hancké 2013; Iversen et al., 2016; Johnston 2016; Baccaro and Pontusson 2016; Iversen and Soskice 2018.
[85] Teague and Donaghy 2004; Molina and Rhodes 2007.
[86] Howell 2009; Schmidt 2009b; Vasileva-Dienes and Schmidt 2018.
[87] Johnston and Regan 2018.
[88] Baccaro and Pontusson 2016; see also Iversen and Soskice 2018.   [89] Alesina et al. 2012.
[90] Schmidt 2009b; Vasileva-Dienes and Schmidt 2018.
[91] Regan 2012; Regan and Brazys 2018; Brazys and Regan 2017; and see discussion to follow.

had contributed to their success in the 1990s and early 2000s (especially Spain) and their state-led investment strategies.[92] Even France, which was not as seriously affected by the crisis, ended up engaging in more talk than action when it came to its traditional state-led investment role, whether under President Sarkozy or Hollande.[93]

For the program countries under "conditionality" in particular, the Troika specified wrenching labor market reforms focused on reducing wages, easing rules on hiring and firing, and loosening worker protections. These, together with mandated cuts in social welfare and public health, interfered with individual and collective economic and social rights enshrined in the Charter of Fundamental Rights, at the same time as abrogating any number of domestic law provisions regarding rights to labor protection, social security, and health. In the case of Greece, the Troika forced the repeal of all collective bargaining agreements and demanded a change in the whole collective bargaining system.[94] The Troika also pushed Portugal to radically deregulate labor markets. For countries under "implicit conditionality"—Spain and Italy—which reformed under the threat that if they did not do it of their own free will, market pressure would force them into a program, the cuts to welfare and reforms of labor markets were also severe (albeit more for Spain than Italy), even though these were the decisions of governments rather than the explicit demands of the Troika.[95]

This single-minded focus on labor market reform neglected other possible remedies, such as investment in infrastructure, education and training, renewable energy, and the technologies of the future, while ruling out any neo-Keynesian stimulus linked to investment, that would have kept money in workers' pockets, thereby ensuring a demand-led recovery. But equally importantly, policymakers failed to consider the contradictions between goals, for example, that export-led growth in high value-added manufacturing generally needs more regulated and coordinated labor markets, not less—as evident from the Northern European experience. Moreover, wage reduction alone will not solve the problem where export industries cannot compete; where there is insufficient investment to maintain existing firms, let alone create new ones; and where bank lending remains very low and risk averse. The belated shift to an emphasis on structural reform—after austerity had already taken its toll—was meant to address the problems of "competitiveness." But there was too much of a focus on increasing the flexibility of the labor markets—meaning crushing the unions and lowering wages—instead of on the myriad other ways of restarting growth.[96]

---

[92] Molina and Rhodes 2007; Perez and Matsaganis 2017; Parker and Tsarouhas 2018.
[93] Clift 2012; Vail 2018.
[94] Fischer-Lescano 2014, pp. 48–52; see also discussion in Kreuder Sonnen 2018.
[95] De la Porte and Heins 2015; Sacchi 2015, 2018.
[96] Crespy 2016; Crespy and Schmidt 2017.

To be clear, the problem with Eurozone crisis governance has not been the focus on structural reform per se: it has been its neoliberal bias, in particular in the years between 2010 and 2015.[97] Most member states would do well to reform their social systems and labor markets by promoting greater equity in pension systems and more progressive taxation or by putting an end to the dualization of the workforce that protects insiders to the detriment of outsiders and by improving education and training for lifetime learning. Combating corruption and getting everyone to pay taxes, in particular the very rich and the biggest corporations, are equally important structural reforms. And, indeed, the Commission, in its Country-Specific Reports (CSRs) under the macroeconomic imbalance procedure, has included these kinds of structural reforms in its recommendations— albeit to limited effect, as discussed in Chapter 7.

What has made the push for neoliberal structural reform particularly perverse is the fact that the very reforms believed to produce convergence have only increased the divergence among member states. We should not forget that the success of export-oriented Northern economies is in large part due to the more highly organized and protected labor markets of their high value-added manufacturing industries, where highly skilled workers with good wages benefit from constant on-the-job retraining and a range of work protections. Pushing for more flexible labor markets as such, without considering the overall industrial landscape of the country (eg, which industries have growth potential), let alone ensuring retraining and up-skilling of workers, leaves those member states under structural reform "diktats" not only at a disadvantage with regard to competition with Northern Europe but also vulnerable to competition from developing countries with lower wages and potentially more highly skilled workers. As Servaas Storm and C. W. M. Naastepad have argued, the kinds of labor market deregulation that are pushed for program countries would, ironically, reduce the very forms of labor market coordination that make for the strength of export-competitive Northern Europeans, thereby locking the Southern European economies into low- and medium-technology activities in direct competition with China.[98]

Taken to its logical conclusion, some scholars have suggested that the EU structural reform obsession risks blowing up the Eurozone as a whole. Fritz Scharpf has argued that any such policies in the context of a Eurozone that works well for the export-led, surplus-producing model of growth and competitiveness of member states in Northern Europe cannot work for member states in the periphery, mainly in Southern Europe.[99] These countries have traditionally flourished via a domestic-spending, deficit-producing model of growth that requires periodic currency devaluation to right the balance and therefore demands control

---

[97] Schmidt and Thatcher 2013; Crespy 2016; Crespy and Schmidt 2017. See discussion in Chapter 7 on "Ayatollahs of Austerity."
[98] Storm and Naastepad 2015.   [99] Scharpf 2012a, 2014; see also Hall 2012.

of its own currency. Without the ability to devalue because of the euro or to run deficits because of the stability rules, Southern European member states have no alternative but to enter into a never-ending downward spiral of wage repression accompanied in the end by the suppression of social and political democracy—or to leave the euro.[100]

The alternative to exit from the Eurozone is, of course, changing the rules that govern it. But that is a different issue.

Austerity and Structural Reforms in the Eurozone Periphery

Although Eurozone members in formal programs imposed by the Troika (Greece, Ireland, Portugal, and Cyprus) or in informal self-imposed programs (Spain and Italy) engaged in rapid deficit and debt reduction along with structural reform of labor markets and welfare states, the economic impact of such policies was highly differentiated, mainly as a function of how the recommendations were "translated" into the national context.[101] The differences were related not only to the policies instituted but also to the political context in which they were implemented.

Structural reforms in which countries slashed wages and radically decentralized their countries' labor markets played a major role in the differential socioeconomic outcomes. In Greece, radical decentralization combined with a major cut in the minimum wage served to create a negative feedback loop between massive job destruction and economic depression—which also contributed to the major rise in poverty and inequality.[102] In Spain and Portugal, the radical decentralization of the labor markets, legitimated on the grounds that it would reduce labor market segmentation between insiders and outsiders, did nothing of the sort. While segmentation remained, job precariousness increased because firm-level agreements (which could now supersede more centralized collective bargaining) made for more and more jobs outsourced to less regulated contractors. The end result was major wage devaluation—as was intended—but also major increases in inequality, mainly for Spain, due to its greater job destruction.[103] The only countries to escape these destructive impacts on jobs were Italy, where labor market deregulation came later and was less radical, and Ireland, where the quick economic rebound based on export-led growth enabled the country to escape the worst.

National politics played an important role in the policies adopted, along with the relationship of the government to the Troika and other EU institutional actors. Greece was largely powerless in the face of the Troika, and got little

---

[100] Scharpf 2013, 2014.   [101] Ban 2016.
[102] Perez and Matsaganis 2017, pp. 9–10.   [103] Perez and Matsaganis 2017, pp. 9–10.

sympathy from other EU institutional actors, given its large deficits and debt plus its role in triggering the crisis in the first place. But internal political conflicts also undermined Greek governments' ability to moderate Troika demands, as did patronage-driven efforts to protect key constituencies from the full impact of reforms focused on public employment.[104] This was as true for mainstream parties in power between 2010 and 2015 as it was thereafter for the Syriza government. This said, the Syriza government's focus on "socialist" structural reform did ameliorate the socioeconomic results by the time Greece successfully exited the third bailout program in 2018, in particular for the very poor.[105] The emphasis on social issues and distributional effects ensured that instead of further wage cuts, the Syriza program focused on providing a universal basic income along with transfers to low-income families and the unemployed, while increasing tax rates to achieve the required high primary surpluses of 3.5 percent. The contrasts in the official statistics between the 2015–18 program and that of 2011–14 are revealing: an increase of seven percentage points in the hourly wage versus a drop of 14.3 percent previously; a reduction of 6 percentage points in poor or socially excluded people versus an increase of 28 percent; a drop of 24 percentage points of persons with severe material deprivation versus an increase of 83 percent; and a decrease of 7.2 percentage points in unemployment versus an increase of 13.8 per cent in the previous program.[106]

In Portugal, public employment was not as politically charged an issue for the government, which benefited from cross-party agreement on the measures to be taken. At the same time, historical legacies of the democratic transition, in which protests played a positive role, also ensured that the government was more responsive to popular concerns, and moderated its policies through a progressive approach to tax and spending.[107] Equally importantly, with the 2015 arrival in power of a left-of-center government coalition, policies changed, with the government undertaking a dual strategy. At the same time as staying within the austerity guidelines—indeed, lowering its deficit to historic levels—it sought to boost growth through investment in industries such as tourism and to encourage demand through more redistributive policies, including raising the minimum wage, lifting a freeze on pensions, and canceling future civil service pay cuts—all of which also made it very popular. Much of the success in terms of increasing growth and employment was attributed to the economic strategy of Socialist Minister of Finance Mario Centeno, who, when asked what advice he had for Greece building on his own experience, suggested that the answer was to "regain

[104] Siani-Davies 2017; Perez and Matsaganis 2017; Featherstone 2011.   [105] Kaloniatis 2019.
[106] Hellenic Statistical Authority, Eurostat, Greek Independent Authority for Public Revenue—cited in Kaloniatis 2019.
[107] Perez and Matsaganis 2017.

ownership, to take control of the whole process and to find alternatives for what is on the table."[108]

In Spain, in contrast, the institutional capacity to impose unpopular reforms, combined with a historical legacy in which protest was not seen as legitimate enough to warrant response, enabled minority governments to impose a deeper austerity than expected.[109] Such excessive austerity reflects longstanding ideas founded in ordoliberalism along with the more recent embrace of neoliberal ones by left as much as right-leaning political elites.[110] Only with the unexpected arrival in power of the center-left Sanchez minority government on the back of a center-right corruption scandal in 2018 did the policies change, with Sanchez following the Portuguese playbook of rejecting austerity without defying Europe. He announced a "shock plan" for youth unemployment, labor market reforms to reduce the number of contracts, investment in education, and more.[111] Public satisfaction with his track record can be gauged by the fact that he won the May 2019 elections, albeit without a clear majority.

Italy avoided much of the pain felt by its Southern European counterparts not only because it came into the sights of the markets later but also because of its bicameral political institutions and fragmented politics. To begin with, Berlusconi resisted doing anything until forced; he then backslid, for which he was ultimately pushed out. Policies such as short-time work contracts similar to those in Germany helped limit job shedding in the first couple of years, while the Monti government's attempt to radically reduce job protections was largely neutralized in Parliament.[112] It was only with Renzi's "Jobs Act" of 2015 that significant labor market flexibility was instituted, which deregulated the use of fixed-term contracts and apprenticeships while reducing dismissal protection for open-ended contracts.[113] Such flexibility was moderated, however, by more "security" via the expansion of unemployment insurance and training programs and by efforts of both the Monti and Renzi governments to increase workers' "social rights," leading to a welfare state that was more comprehensive than it had been before the crisis.[114]

The economic crisis also hit Ireland very hard. The collapse of major banks, followed by government rescue, in 2008 left the country in the deepest recession of any advanced economy (according to the IMF). By 2012, however, Ireland had returned to healthy growth, led by its export sector, although unemployment and poverty remained serious problems, as did massive emigration (as noted above).

---

[108] Centeno (2018) "Portugal's economic recovery: from sick man to poster boy" Center for European Studies, Harvard University (April 18) video at https://ces.fas.harvard.edu/recordings/portugals-economic-recovery-from-sick-man-to-poster-boy

[109] Perez and Matsaganis 2017.   [110] Ban 2016; Perez and Matsaganis 2017.

[111] La República, Nov. 13, 2018 https://www.larepublica.co/globoeconomia/pedro-sanchez-anuncia-un-plan-economico-con-una-inminente-reforma-laboral-2792872

[112] Perez and Rhodes 2015; Perez and Matsaganis 2017.   [113] Picot and Tassinari 2017.

[114] Sacchi 2018.

This helps explain why Ireland was the first program country touted by the Commission as a success, and as the model to emulate. But that success had little to do with the "structural reforms" that successive Irish governments had imposed with alacrity, and was not imitable.

Ireland's ability to pull out of recession and exit its program had mostly to do with its unique growth model. This rests on the Irish state's ability to bring in foreign direct investment (FDI) in the computer and information services sector, attracted by its unique position as the only native English-speaking country in the Eurozone; its low corporate tax regime—the lowest in the EU at 12 percent, without counting the special deals for multinational giants like Apple or Microsoft (which may have paid less than 2 percent tax); and the ability to hire high-skilled workers from the rest of the EU in a country that is a member of EMU as well as the Single Market.[115] Additionally, Ireland benefited from a deal on its massive debt in 2013, in which the ECB approved its exchange of the short-term promissory notes of the Anglo Irish bank (the failure of which in 2008 precipitated Ireland's crisis) for long-term government bonds. This served to slice billions off the country's borrowing needs and cut its budget deficit.[116]

Is the Irish growth model transferable? Clearly not, given its unique characteristics. But is it even sustainable? The problem, as Aidan Regan and Samuel Brazys convincingly argue, is that because the economic recovery has mainly been felt by those in the Foreign Direct Investment (FDI) sector, and Irish fiscal policies have not redistributed gains from that recovery to the broader population, the country may be vulnerable to a political backlash from those who feel "left behind."[117] Moreover, one part of the growth model itself may be unsustainable, given that the EU is not likely to put up much longer with Ireland's "beggar-thy-neighbor" tax regime, in which taxes on corporate profits from across Europe are paid at massively reduced rates.[118]

Conclusion

The EU's Eurozone problems of output legitimacy result from failures of framing and diagnosis as well as poorly chosen remedies without lasting solutions. The lack of effectiveness of austerity policies in the first years of the crisis was evidenced by the anemic macroeconomic performance of the Eurozone as a whole, in particular when compared to that of the US, and the disastrous socioeconomic performance of Southern Europe, especially when contrasted with Northern

---

[115] Regan and Brazys 2018s.
[116] While the promissory notes had an average maturity of between seven and eight years, the bonds had an average maturity of more than thirty-four years (making the first principal repayment in 2038 and the last in 2053). *Reuters*, February 7, 2013.
[117] Regan and Brazys 2018.   [118] Regan and Brazys 2018.

Europe. Policy prescriptions with regard to structural reforms that assumed that what worked for Northern Europe would work for Southern Europe failed to recognize the differences in national varieties of capitalism and growth models.

"Real" structural reform requires equitable growth which can only be ensured where the state plays a strong role in public investment strategies focused on childhood and tertiary education along with training for workers in growth industries, such as high tech services.[119] Although the shift in Commission recommendations in the European Semester after 2015 supported such a move toward more equitable growth, the rules limiting deficit spending have continued to undermine advancement in this area. In addition, Eurozone members need industrial policy and planning, with investment in renewables and industries of the future, as well as to spend more on education and retraining and on those "left behind." All of this necessarily demands not "one size fits all" structural reform kits, where member-state "ownership" is defined as compliance with top-down prescriptions, but rather more bottom-up control and planning by the member states themselves, as discussed in the conclusion to Chapter 7 on the Commission.

But beyond this, the Eurozone needs real investment in all members' economies, North and South, with at least some of the proposed remedies finally implemented. Most importantly, the Eurozone requires some form of mutual risk-sharing that could stabilize the euro once and for all while ensuring that all euro members benefit from the euro as a savings reserve. In addition, debt reduction for countries still at risk is a must, along with greater solidarity across countries on things like unemployment insurance as well as individual deposit insurance and a substantial financial backstop for failing banks. But it is equally necessary for the Eurozone to develop a vision of how to build economic capacity and sustainability in an increasingly unstable world economy under threat of climate change, trade wars, and political disruption.

Finally, Eurozone policies jeopardized many of the EU's overarching output-related goals, both material and symbolic, including economic prosperity and social solidarity. And because of this, input legitimacy also increasingly came into question, as part of the feedback loop in which citizens' political judgments feed into their political demands and concerns as expressed in their voting preferences and political activities. This is the focus of the next chapter.

---

[119] See, eg, Wren 2013; Beramendi et al. 2015.

10

National "Politics *against* Policy" in the Eurozone Crisis

In democratic polities, when economic prosperity plummets and policies go awry, we generally assume that citizens will elect new leaders with mandates for political change in the expectation that both the policies and the economics will improve. Not so in the European Union (EU), where citizen dissatisfaction in the midst of the Eurozone crisis did little to change the policies forged at the EU level. The result has been the increasing national-level politicization of EU policies, as mainstream national party politics struggles to respond to the challenges generated both by EU-level technocracy and national-level populism.

During the Eurozone crisis, as output legitimacy was put to the test by ineffective policies and poor economic performance, input legitimacy also deteriorated. Citizens' trust in national and EU political institutions declined dramatically while their support for Euroskeptic political parties grew exponentially against a background of increasing feelings of insecurity, both economic and social. The sources of discontent that served to mobilize were not just socioeconomic, however, resulting from rising unemployment and industrial decline. They were also sociocultural, related to people's worries about loss of social status and identity-related fears of migrants. The socioeconomic and sociocultural actually fed into one another, in particular because of the regionally differentiated patterns within as well as among countries.

The traditional electoral landscape has changed as a result, with the frequent turnover of incumbent mainstream governments, the rise of new (or reinvigorated) challenger parties on the extremes of the left and right, and even the takeover of government by populist parties, occasionally in unlikely left–right extremist coalitions. As Euroskeptic anti-system parties with radical agendas jumped in numbers and adherents, mainstream parties in the center lost electoral support to the populists, with some centrist parties collapsing entirely, in particular on the social democratic left.

In all of this, the EU for the first time became a major issue of debate in national as well as European Parliament (EP) elections. Before the Eurozone crisis, EU policy issues simply did not have great salience for national electorates, which tended to be more focused on national tax-and-spend issues. The exceptions were the Euroskeptic parties on the margins, for which the EU and/or the euro were

Europe's Crisis of Legitimacy: Governing by Rules and Ruling by Numbers in the Eurozone. Vivien A. Schmidt,
Oxford University Press (2020). © Vivien A. Schmidt.
DOI: 10.1093/oso/9780198797050.001.0001

frequently central campaign issues.[1] But this changed with the crisis, as electorates in debtor countries suffered with austerity policies seen as imposed by Brussels while creditor states saw "their" tax money going for bailouts to the debtors. This fueled the success of populist leaders who blamed national elites and the EU for the sorry state of affairs, and then later added to their support by capitalizing on the migrant crisis.

But although the populists' playbook may be similar on the surface, via leaders' anti-establishment discourse and approach to the media, the differences in ideas are significant as a result of both politics and geography. The political divide between left and right-wing populist anti-system parties centers on their approaches to EU-related policies and the future of European integration. While the extremes on the left tend to focus on the economics, taking negative views of Eurozone policies but being more open toward "more Europe" (of an alternative kind), the extremes on the right emphasize the social, with negative views of migration as well as Eurozone policies, and in favor of "less Europe" (or even exit from the EU).[2] Such diverging approaches are only further complicated by national context, where history, economy, culture, and politics combine with the differential economic impact of the Eurozone crisis—in particular in North/South terms—to make for nationally specific anti-system parties and populisms.[3] Finally, the "supply side" of populism also matters, that is, the personality and skills of individual leaders and their ability to galvanize social movements and build political parties through their discursive strategies and (social) media presence.

This chapter discusses Europe's "politics *against* policy" by exploring the many different ways in which politicization "at the bottom" has taken hold. The first section examines the politicization of European citizens as a result of their rising Euroskepticism and declining trust in national and EU political institutions. The second section explores the economic and social sources of their discontent. The third section considers the factors contributing to the increasing political polarization that has produced differing patterns of party realignment in the EU's macro-regions, including the effects of the Eurozone crisis followed by the migration crisis against a background of different socioeconomic configurations and political institutions. The final section of the chapter explores the ways in which Euroskeptic parties have been able to build support, with a closer inspection of the populist parties' playbook.

Citizens' Rising Euroskepticism and Declining Political Trust

The Eurozone crisis led to a dramatic increase in anti-EU feelings and loss of political trust in political institutions. The most striking political response to the

---

[1] Hoeglinger 2016.   [2] Van Elsas et al. 2016; de Vries 2018.   [3] Hopkin 2020.

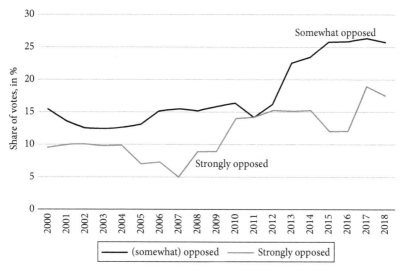

Figure 10.1. Share of vote for parties that oppose European integration in the EU-28, 2000–2018

Source: Dijkstra et al. 2018 (based on their own calculations, Chapel Hill Expert Survey data, and national sources)

Eurozone crisis was the increase in votes for anti-establishment Euroskeptic parties. Before the crisis, from 2000 to 2008, these parties' mean share of votes was 25 percent. In the aftermath of the crisis, between 2009 and 2016, and even before the sharper increases sparked by the victories of Brexit and Trump, anti-establishment parties climbed to 32 percent overall, with the strongest growth in the South, at close to 10 percent change; in the North, the change came to 6 percent.[4] The overall share of Eurosceptic parties, as defined by the Chapel Hill Expert Survey in terms of parties strongly opposed to European integration and somewhat opposed parties between 2000 and 2018, can be seen in Figure 10.1. Those strongly opposed to European integration—whether pledging to leave the EU, such as the British United Kingdom Independence Party (UKIP) the Dutch Party for Freedom (PVV) and the French National Front (FN--later RN for National Rally), or to scale it back significantly, such as Italy's League (Lega, formerly Northern League), the German Alternative for Germany (AfD), and Hungary's Jobbik—went from 10 percent to 18 percent. Those somewhat opposed to European integration, advocating significant change but not exit—such as Italy's Five Star Movement (MS5), Hungary's Fidesz, and the UK Conservative Party—grew from 15 percent to 26 percent.[5]

Underlying this increase in citizens' Euroskeptic politicization was a major loss of trust in political institutions. Eurobarometer polls show marked declines in trust in national governments and the EU (see Figure 10.2). Trust in the EU dropped from a high of 57 percent in 2007 to a low of 31 percent between 2011

---

[4] Algan et al. 2018.   [5] Dijkstra et al. 2018, p. 2.

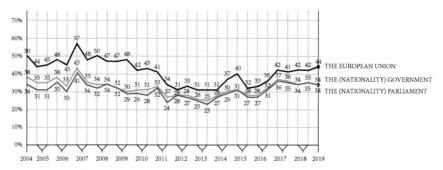

Figure 10.2. Trust in the European Union, national government, and national parliament

Note: The question (QA8a) is: 'I would like to ask you a question about how much trust you have in certain media and institutions. For each of the following media and institutions, please tell me if you tend to trust it or tend not to trust it. (%—EU—Tend to Trust)

Source: Eurobarometer (2004–2018)

and 2014, while trust in national governments started lower, at 43 percent in 2007, and dropped more, to 28 percent in 2012 and 25 percent in 2013. In both cases, after a brief recovery, trust dropped again in response to the migration crisis of 2015. Only in 2017, and continuing in 2018, did trust in the EU climb back up to 42 percent, and then to 44 percent in 2019—which nonetheless remained still way below the 2007 level. Trust in national governments did not show quite the same resilience: at 34 percent in 2019, it remained 9 points below the 2007 score.[6]

Much as with the rise of Euroscepticism, the loss of trust in institutions has been highly differentiated. The European Quality of Life Survey shows this quite dramatically for a sample of countries in Northern and Southern Europe that experienced the differential effects of the Eurozone crisis (see Figure 10.3). For almost all countries, 2012 was the nadir in terms of trust in government. Greece in particular suffered a precipitous drop at the time, recovering only slightly by 2017—a product of its ongoing economic problems under Troika supervision. Portugal instead, after a significant drop, rallied, with the largest margin of improvement among all the countries—reflecting its improved economic situation under a left-of-center government. Germany, perhaps not surprisingly, was the only country that went up in trust in government at the height of the crisis, and continued upward in 2017. In contrast, France was the only country that started at a high level but continued to slide downward. These differences can be explained by German citizens perceiving the country as largely succeeding in driving the EU agenda and doing well economically, whereas French citizens have long been dissatisfied with national government leaders' failures internally to solve the countries' economic problems and/or to drive the European agenda in a more pro-growth direction.[7]

---

[6] Eurobarometer surveys 2004–19.
[7] Note that the data were collected in 2016, prior to the election of Macron.

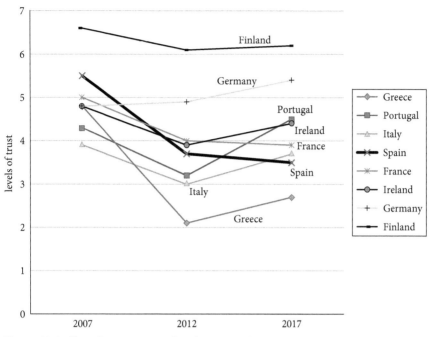

Figure 10.3. Trust in government in select countries, 2007, 2012, 2017

Source: European Quality of Life Survey 2016--Eurofound 2017 (Based on the question(s) *Q35e* from the European Quality of Life Survey 2016) https://www.eurofound.europa.eu/eqls2016

Other indicators are equally revealing of citizens' increasing dissatisfaction with their governing authorities. For example, Eurobarometer surveys chart the decline in the positive image of the EU, which went from 52 percent in 2007 to 30 percent in 2012, while the negative image went up from 15 percent in 2007 to 29 percent in 2012—neck and neck with the positive responses.[8] Although in 2019 the number of those with a positive image had come back up to 45 percent, it was still lower than in 2007. But again the results remained highly differentiated. Portugal registered 60 percent of respondents with a positive image, versus Greece at 33 percent.[9] The favorability of the EU at the height of the crisis also suffered. A Pew survey of 2013 found that the EU's favorability had dropped 15 points from a median of 60 percent in 2007 to 45 percent in 2013, with the percentage change most dramatic in Spain, down from 80 percent in 2007 to 46 percent in 2013; France, from 62 percent to 41 percent; and Italy, from 54 percent to 38 percent.[10]

Loss of trust in the EU, negative images of it, and its drop in favorability went hand in hand with the rise of Euroskepticism. A study by Dijkstra and colleagues demonstrates this clearly through correlations between the citizens' loss of trust

---

[8] Eurobarometer EB 78 (Dec. 2012).   [9] Eurobarometer Spring 2019.
[10] Pew 2013.

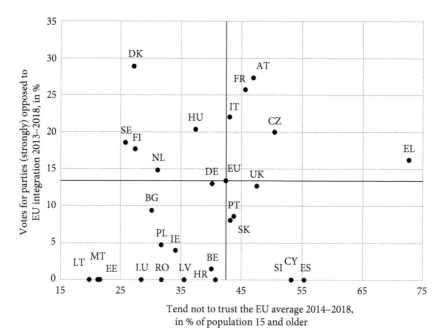

Figure 10.4. Votes for parties strongly opposed to EU integration and lack of trust in the EU, 2013–18, by citizens as percentage of the population (15 and older) *Source*: Dijkstra et al. 2018

in the EU and their support for strong Euroskeptic parties (see Figure 10.4). Greece is certainly the best case for showing that very high levels of distrust have correlated with votes for parties critical of EU integration (most notably the 2015 victory of the populist extreme left party Syriza). And other countries, such as Austria, France, and Italy, with a significant level of distrust also correlate with strong support for highly Euroskeptic parties.[11]

Sources of Citizen Discontent

In the literature on the rise of populist discontent, scholars often divide between those who argue that "it's the economy, stupid," related to rising unemployment and declining industries,[12] and those who prefer sociocultural explanations, focused on identity and anti-immigrant sentiment.[13] But posing an either/or question on whether the rise of populism is fueled by the economic grievances of those feeling threatened by globalization and Europeanization or by a cultural

---

[11] Dijkstra et al. 2018.   [12] Eg, Rodrik 2018; Algan et al. 2018.
[13] Inglehart and Norris 2017; Hochschild and Mollenkopt 2009; Berezin 2009; Kuhn 2015.

backlash focused on fears and prejudices makes little sense. Although the economics clearly took a front seat during the Eurozone crisis, the migration crisis
introduced its own separate issues while also building on discontent related to the
former. Moreover, citizens' responses often differ depending upon whether we are
considering electorates and parties of the right or the left, and whether we focus
on Northern or Southern European countries, let alone if we add in Central and
Eastern European countries. As a result, we are likely to see a multidimensional
set of reasons, in particular if, rather than simply correlating the economics with
the politics, we look more deeply into the multidimensional set of reasons people
have for voting.[14]

On the economic side of the debate, recent in-depth quantitative studies convincingly show a direct connection between the economics and the politics. Yann
Algan and collaborators, for example, find a strong relationship between increasing unemployment and voting for non-mainstream parties, in particular populist
challengers, as well as with a decline in trust in national and European political
institutions.[15] Dijkstra and collaborators add a geographical dimension to this
analysis, arguing that once such factors as long-term economic and industrial
decline combined with low levels of education and a lack of local employment
opportunities are taken into account, wealthier people in poor places are more
likely to vote for anti-EU parties than poorer people. So explaining the rise of
anti-establishment voting is more complicated than simply saying that it is about
those "left behind" by globalization, that is, about poor people living in poor
places, or older and less educated people living in rural areas subject to decline in
population and employment.[16] Instead, regional differences within countries,
along with urban/rural divides, matter greatly. There are "hot spots" for anti-EU
voting in Southern Denmark, Northern Italy, Southern Austria, Eastern Germany,
Eastern Hungary, and Southern Portugal. Moreover, rural areas and small towns
tend to be more Euroskeptic than bigger cities, whether we consider cities versus
their rural surroundings in Eastern France, such as Lille, Metz, Nancy, and
Strasbourg; in East Germany, such as Berlin, Dresden, and Leipzig; or in Northern
Italy, such as Milan and Turin.[17] More succinctly, then, in the words of Rodríguez-
Pose, it is the "revenge of the places that don't matter" rather than just the people,
with long-term economic and industrial declines having fueled discontent,
encouraging people—and in particular the relatively well off, with well-paid jobs
or pensions—to vent their anger.[18] Carlo Bastasin calls this "secular divergence,"
and explains it as a function of the ways in which globalization and Europeanization
have produced major regional divergences within European countries, dividing

---

[14] See De Vries 2018.   [15] Algan et al. 2018.   [16] Dijkstra et al. 2018.
[17] Dijkstra et al. 2018.
[18] Rodríguez-Pose 2018, p. 201; see also discussion in Dijkstra et al. 2018.

those moving up (or already there) in thriving urban agglomerations from those moving down (or fearing it) in declining peri-urban and rural locations.[19]

But if those most attracted to anti-system parties are people in declining places who are relatively more wealthy, with jobs, pensions, and savings, rather than the poorest anywhere without jobs or money, then this is also where the socioeconomic merges with the sociocultural, as worries about loss of jobs combine with fears of loss of status.[20] Such fears generally meld into concerns about migration, in particular for once predominant sectors of the population worried about what the "changing faces of the nation" will do to their status. These are the people—older, less educated, white, and male—whose worldview seems threatened by changing demographics resulting from rising immigrant populations. Often, these are the very same people who are equally troubled by intergenerational shifts to post-materialist values such as cosmopolitanism and multiculturalism.[21] They can be people who are well off financially but subscribe to socially conservative philosophies and/or oppose socially liberal policy programs. Alternatively, they may favor a generous welfare state, but only for "their own."[22]

A Pew study of July 2018 further confirms the finding that the economy is only one among a number of factors, in this case when it comes to support for nationalist populist parties on the extremes of the right.[23] The study sees such things as nostalgia for the past and ethnocentrism as more defining. For example, among those saying life is worse for people like them than it was fifty years ago, Pew found 44 percent with a favorable view of the German AfD (versus only 16 percent with an unfavorable view of the AfD), 43 percent favoring Sweden Democrats (versus 17 percent), 62 percent favoring the French National Front (versus 41 percent), and 34 percent favoring the Dutch PVV (versus 13 percent). This is not to say that attitudes toward the economy are unimportant. A separate Pew study from September 2019 also found that supporters of populist parties generally had more negative views of the state of the economy, including large percentages of those with favorable views of the AfD, the Sweden Democrats, the National Front, and the PVV.[24] Negativity, in sum, characterizes all aspects of supporters of populist parties, in particular on the extreme right of the political spectrum.

Citizen support for Euroskeptic parties cannot be explained solely by reference to people's socioeconomic conditions and sociocultural attitudes, however. Such support has multiple dimensions that, as Catherine de Vries argues, involve not just the socioeconomic and sociocultural but also the "kaleidoscope" of people's beliefs about the short-term benefits of EU policies for them, as well as about how

---

[19] Bastasin 2019.   [20] For more on this, see Gidron and Hall 2017; Hopkin 2020.
[21] Inglehart and Norris 2016.   [22] Afonso and Rennwald 2018; Hopkin 2020.
[23] Pew July 19, 2018 https://www.pewresearch.org/fact-tank/2018/07/19/populist-views-in-europe-its-not-just-the-economy/
[24] Pew Sept. 18, 2018 https://www.pewglobal.org/2018/09/18/a-decade-after-the-financial-crisis-economic-confidence-rebounds-in-many-countries/

the EU as a polity will deliver for them in the longer term.[25] Somewhat counterintuitively, she demonstrates that in countries in which citizens suffered economically from harsh austerity, support for the EU and the euro remain relatively high—such as in Ireland, Spain, or Cyprus, where exit from the euro was not seen as an option—although this is not the case in Italy. Such attitudes contrast with rising Euroskepticism in countries that have benefited enormously from the Single Market and the Eurozone and that did not experience significant economic spillovers from the Eurozone crisis, such as Germany or the Netherlands. These are countries where exit from the EU polity has seemed more of an option, and anti-migration policy more appealing.[26] But in all such countries, too, support for the euro remained high even at the height of the crisis.[27]

So how do we explain continued support for the euro, in particular in Southern Europe, despite the rise in Euroskeptic parties? Sara Hobolt and Christopher Wratil suggest that even as citizens continued to support the euro, their reasons had increasingly less to do with the euro's link to identity and increasingly more to do with self-interest. A utility-based logic rather than an identity-based one most likely explains why, despite the crisis, support remained strong—even though the public may have been increasingly unhappy about the euro's effects.[28]

Citizens' political preferences on a continuum from the left to the right also play an important role in their attitudes toward the EU, affecting whether their dissatisfaction comes out mainly in their views of its policies or in their positions on the strengthening of EU integration. As Erika van Elsas and collaborators note, while left-wing citizens tend to be more dissatisfied with the current EU, right-wing citizens have a greater tendency to oppose future strengthening. More specifically, whereas left-wing citizens' support for economic redistribution increases their dissatisfaction with the current EU, their egalitarian values have little effect on their view of future integration, which may favor deeper integration if culturally progressive. In contrast, right-wing citizens' opposition is purely cultural in terms of the current and future EU.[29] In short, ideological divides of the left and right remain of great importance, as a recent Pew study of citizens' support for populist versus mainstream parties of the left, right, and center also concludes.[30]

Political Polarization and Party Realignments
in the Shadow of Populism

Although public disenchantment with the EU in any form is mainly seen in the rise of populist Euroskeptic parties, especially on the radical right,[31] it can also be

---

[25] De Vries 2018, p. 4.   [26] De Vries 2018, p. 6.   [27] Pew Survey, May 2013.
[28] Hobolt and Wratil 2015.   [29] Van Elsas et al. 2016.   [30] Simmons et al. 2018.
[31] Gómez-Reino and Lamazares 2013.

found in the polarization of views across national European public spheres.[32] Parties in Eurozone and non-Eurozone countries alike display such polarization, but differently. Geography matters. But so do divisions based on the differing socioeconomic impact of the crisis, the political divergences between the left and right, and the cleavages among citizens between a more cosmopolitan open idea of Europe and a more xenophobic closed idea intensified in the wake of the Eurozone crisis.[33] The politics have played out differently, however, also as a result of institutional factors related to the electoral system, welfare state configuration, and variety of capitalism.[34] But whatever the country context, as mainstream parties struggled to manage the economic and social fallout of the crisis in an environment of increasing political volatility, political systems in country after country experienced major party realignments.

The Eurozone crisis divided the EU along geographical, class, and partisan party lines. Geographically, it largely pitted the South against the North, with the South voicing anger against "Northern" impositions of austerity, the North against further supra-national institutionalization and loan bailouts for the South. But there was also a cleavage between elites and the masses, with the arguments of political elites engaged in crisis management focused primarily on economic and political efficiency, in contrast to the mass public's greater engagement in the normative debates about who was to blame and who should pay.[35] As for mainstream political parties, both right and left tended to articulate a depoliticizing discourse on the economic issues, casting crisis responses as a matter of economic common sense and the result of external constraints.[36] But while center-right parties generally supported austerity, arguing that the country needed to rise to the challenge by tightening its belt, center-left parties often seemed to be missing in action on this particular issue.

For the most part, the center left felt compelled to be "responsible," meaning to implement austerity measures while in power or to support them while in opposition. This was frequently in contradiction with party platforms that had shifted to the left at the time of the crisis, by promising to protect the welfare state and fight neoliberal economic policies, including austerity. Such contradiction created internal tensions within center-left political parties, which only added to the ongoing identity crisis of parties that were in most cases now more skeptical of the neoliberal policies they had themselves espoused in the 1990s and early 2000s, when they had supported the Third Way.[37] It also helps explain why center-left parties in particular experienced a historic collapse in electoral support across Europe, even as radical left parties benefited from a marked increase in support, in particular in Southern Europe, where unemployment had increased significantly.[38]

---

[32] Kriesi and Grande 2015.   [33] Kriesi et al. 2008.
[34] Manow et al. 2018; Iversen and Soskice 2018.   [35] Kriesi et al. 2012, Kriesi 2014.
[36] Borriello 2017.   [37] Bremer 2018.   [38] Gomez and Ramiro 2017.

The center right was not spared the disruption. But it is easier to be a conservative establishment party imposing policies of economic austerity than a left-wing establishment party, which pays a much higher electoral price than the establishment right under the same circumstances.[39] That said, the center right was also increasingly embattled, losing to the anti-system populist extremes on the right which promised to defend the welfare state for "their" (country's) citizens while shifting the debate to migration, blaming refugees and migrants for the parlous state of the economy and mainstream parties for failing to protect the borders.[40]

Challenges to both center-right and center-left parties in government also came from the waves of protest triggered directly by the Eurozone crisis responses, in particular in Southern Europe. People took to the streets in Greece, Italy, Portugal, and Spain not only to attempt to prevent austerity policies but also to call for more democracy.[41] The protests were primarily focused on the socioeconomic sources of discontent, as unemployment and poverty increased exponentially. They lasted more or less two years, and were largely a rejection of mainstream governments. In Greece, the protests were often nightly, and very violent. But even Portugal, known for its weak civil society and protest scene, experienced a significant increase in protests.[42] These protests spurred social movements, such as the Spanish *indignados*, which managed to mobilize members for demonstrations that got them nothing other than, sometimes, news coverage,[43] and were met with widespread repression. The emergence of extreme left challenger parties such as Syriza in Greece and Podemos in Spain was a natural consequence of the lack of impact of the protest movements, as was the strengthening of existing social movement parties in other countries, such as the Five Star Movement in Italy and the far left in Portugal.[44]

Protest was also seen in Northern Europe, albeit later. In Germany, PEGIDA (Patriotic Europeans against the Islamization of the Occident), a vocal anti-immigrant, anti-Islam social movement, emerged in 2014, holding rallies with official estimates at up to 25,000, unofficial at 40,000. It then fed into the populist extreme right party Alternative for Germany (AfD), once AfD had added the issue of opposition to migration to its original identity as an anti-euro party.[45] Germany's troubles, which saw riots in the East German town of Chemnitz, with violent attacks on immigrants, have sources in the sense of abandonment felt by large parts of the citizenry located in particular in small towns and rural areas with declining populations and industries, in keeping with the general trends discussed earlier.

---

[39] Alonso and Ruiz-Rufino 2018.
[40] Afonso and Rennwald 2018; Hopkin 2020.
[41] Altiparmakis and Lorenzini 2018; Accornero and Ramos Pinto 2015.
[42] Accornero and Pinto 2015.   [43] Armingeon and Baccaro 2013.
[44] Della Porta et al. 2017.   [45] Arzheimer 2015.

In France, a similar protest phenomenon in terms of root sources, but not the anti-migration focus, began in October 2018. The "*gilets jaunes*" (yellow vests), the anti-government demonstrators wearing the yellow vests of drivers in distress, disrupted urban centers and rural roundabouts on successive Saturdays, garnering public sympathy and support especially initially (although this declined over time in direct relationship to the increase in violence). The yellow vests' multiple complaints centered on their sense of abandonment by the state and feelings of social isolation in the countryside. As one such yellow vest put it: "Our elites are talking about the end of the world when we are talking about the end of the month."[46] The protest has also been profoundly anti-political, with a rejection of any informal leaders who sought to form a political party for the 2019 EP elections.[47] Its lack of a clear political definition helps explain why both extreme right and extreme left party leaders sought to capture the yellow vests' support for their respective parties.

With all this political upheaval, party alignments changed profoundly, but varied according to Europe's macro-regions. Sven Hutter and Hans-Peter Kriesi describe such variation in a study that makes use of a relational content analysis of newspaper articles to show that the shift in party alignments across Europe's macro-regions—Northwestern, Southern, and Central-Eastern European—is in line with the differential impact of the two crises on these regions as well as on specific countries within regions. In Northwestern Europe, where a unified political left was pitted against the populist radical right, with the moderate right in between, the radical right has since the 1980s (beginning with the National Front in France) been the driving force of the reconfiguration of a cultural-identitarian axis. The "creditor vs debtor" nations experience of the Euro crisis, whatever the political preferences, simply gave it more steam, as did the anti-migration themes of the refugee crisis.[48]

In contrast, Southern Europe, which was much harder hit by the Euro crisis, experienced an electoral shift that was more on the political and economic side than the cultural-identitarian. The main focus in the South was a rejection of mainstream national elites due to internal dysfunctions (weak state capacity, clientelism, and corruption) and of European elites due to Eurozone conditionality, whether formal or informal.[49] This was epitomized by Greece, with the breakdown of the ruling social democratic party (PASOK) at the start of the crisis and the rise of the new extreme left challenger Syriza, which took power in 2015.[50] But already as of the 2012 Greek elections, European integration had become so important an issue that it had completely restructured the Greek political space.[51] The transformative impact of the crisis was equally in evidence in the case of Italy,

[46] *Financial Times* Dec. 28, 2018.   [47] See, eg, McAuley 2019.
[48] Hutter and Kriesi 2019.   [49] Hutter and Kriesi 2019.   [50] Vasilopoulou 2018.
[51] Katsanidou and Otjes 2016.

with the breakdown of the left and the increasing marginalization of right-wing mainstream parties, culminating in the double populist victory in 2018 of the League and the Five Star Movement. In fact, across Southern Europe, both the radical left and the radical right adopted Euroskeptic positions.[52]

Central and Eastern Europe is more mixed in terms of regional cases, since these countries were affected much more by the financial crisis than by the Eurozone crisis (none were members of the Eurozone at the onset of the crisis). Party systems are poorly institutionalized, unstable, and highly volatile. Conflict is mainly connected to cultural issues and the identification of enemies, whether internal (eg, ethnic minorities, Roma, and Jews) or external (eg, foreign companies or NGOs supported by foreign donors—Soros in Hungary being the most high-profile case). As a result, the refugee crisis was largely a political opportunity for populist governments, as opposed to an actual crisis for the countries.[53]

So how do we map these differing patterns of populist upheaval and party realignment onto the socioeconomic and sociocultural sources of discontent? Philip Manow and collaborators see the rise on the one hand of radical right challenger parties in Nordic Europe, focused on the sociocultural dimension, joined by socioeconomic welfare chauvinism; and the rise on the other hand of radical left challenger parties in Southern Europe, pushing more redistributive issues in a context of much more particularistic, less generous welfare states, with the salience of socioeconomics increased by the impact of the euro crisis. In between are the Continental European countries, where most follow the pattern of the Nordic countries, with radical right challenger parties, and France, which follows both North and South, with radical right and radical left challenger parties.[54]

Mainstream Party Politics and the Eurozone Crisis

Beginning in 2010, as a result of the Eurozone crisis, many sitting governments lost power, mainly to the mainstream opposition, in particular in countries that found themselves in trouble.[55] At the same time, non-mainstream challenger parties of various kinds began making impressive inroads across Europe: 2014 was a watershed year for gains by the non-mainstream in the EP elections and 2015 significant as the first time that a populist Euroskeptic coalition government took office, in Greece. But starting in 2016, the contagion effect of the British referendum on exit from the EU, together with the Trump election in the United States, opened the floodgates. Elections in country after country charted higher scores for Euroskeptic parties everywhere, with mainstream parties having increasing difficulty forming governments while populist challenger

---

[52] Hutter and Kriesi 2019; Morlino and Raniolo 2017.   [53] Hutter and Kriesi 2019.
[54] Manow et al. 2018.   [55] Giuliani and Massari 2019.

parties in some countries became partners in coalition governments with mainstream parties (such as in Austria) or even headed their own coalition governments (as in Italy).

Mainstream parties everywhere struggled to maintain power during the Eurozone crisis largely because they found themselves caught between their EU-related responsibilities and their discontented citizens' demands for responsiveness.[56] Social democratic parties in particular had a hard time of it, with many falling to historic lows, in particular in the periphery.[57] But even core countries like Germany and France were significantly affected—although Germany's mainstream parties largely survived the turmoil, in contrast to those in France.

Mainstream Parties' Political Fortunes in the Periphery

The Eurozone crisis hit countries in the periphery particularly hard. Predictably, the most dramatic case of party realignment occurred in Greece, where mainstream parties were constrained by MOUs (memoranda of understanding) imposing strict conditionality, to which they felt they had to agree in order to stop the country from crashing out of the Eurozone.[58] It is small wonder that after rapid turnovers in government—with the collapse of the center left followed by a short stint with an appointed technocrat and then a mainstream coalition headed by the center right—there came a radical left populist party, Syriza, winning a plurality of votes in the 2015 elections to form a governing coalition with a small nationalist ultra-right party. It is also perhaps not surprising that Italy, constrained by informal conditionality, saw a similarly dizzying succession of governments, including a technocratic one, which was followed by the 2018 electoral victory of the radical *Movimento Cinque Stelle* (M5S) or Five Star Movement, which then formed a double populist government with the extreme right League.

But with or without the rise of populist parties, many mainstream parties in power at the inception of the crisis have yet to recover. For example, the Irish conservative party Fianna Fáil, the dominant party in Ireland since Independence, suffered the worst defeat of a sitting government since the foundation of the Irish state, dropping from seventy-seven seats in 2007 to twenty in 2011. It was blamed for having failed to regulate the banks before the financial crisis and was responsible for the late-night decision in 2008 to bail out the banks without knowing how much it would cost, thereby saddling the country with the massive debts that would ultimately push it into the loan bailout program. Fianna Fáil has remained in opposition ever since.

---

[56] Clements et al. 2018.   [57] Morlino and Raniolo 2017.
[58] Gemenis and Nezi, 2015, p. 30; Katsanidou and Otjes 2016.

Similarly, the Greek center-left party PASOK (Panhellenic Socialist Movement) went from being the largest party in the Greek Parliament in the 2009 election, with 43.92 percent of the popular vote, to third place in 2012, with 13.18 percent of the vote, and then down to the smallest party in Parliament in the January 2015 election, at 4.7 percent of the popular vote. In the September 2015 election it retained this position, with 6.3 percent of the popular vote. Its fall was entirely due to the Greek debt crisis. Center-left Prime Minister George Papandreou had in 2009 revealed the real budgetary deficit hidden by the previous New Democracy center-right government, but, having been unable to persuade EU leaders to act until the costs of a bailout had risen astronomically, he then had to implement the first bailout program under the "diktats" of the Troika beginning in May 2010. A year later, he was confronted with massive protests organized by new social movements such as "True Democracy Now." By October 2011, with the country in dire straits, he called a referendum on the bailout program, only to quickly withdraw it in response to EU leaders' objections (as previously discussed), and then resigned.[59] A technocratic government headed by Luca Papademos was then appointed, supported by the parties of the center left and center right. This was followed nine months later by new elections in which neither mainstream party could form a new government, resulting in a coalition government led by the center-right New Democracy.

The 2015 elections gave the populist extreme left Syriza party 36.34 percent of the vote, with the center-right New Democracy in second place with 27.81 percent of the vote and the neo-fascist Golden Dawn at 6.28 percent, leaving PASOK in seventh place—and out of the running for the foreseeable future.[60] In the July 2019 elections it had essentially gone out of business, absorbed into the new centrist coalition party KINAL, which garnered only 8.10 percent of the vote. In contrast, New Democracy won a sweeping victory against the Syriza government, with Syriza taking PASOK's place as the party of opposition.

The Spanish social democratic party PSOE fared somewhat better than the Greek social democrats, having gone from 43.87 percent of the popular vote in 2008 to 28.76 percent in 2011, and down to 22 percent in 2015 and 22.63 percent in 2016. The problem for the Spanish social democratic government in May 2010 was that Prime Minister José Zapatero was forced to succumb to pressure from the European Central Bank (ECB) and Council leaders to push through a drastic austerity package which only just squeaked through the parliament, with a vote of 169 in favor and 168 against. But the government nonetheless largely managed to maintain its social democratic commitments, such that the "pillars of social cohesion" remained "untouchable."[61] It was left to the Conservative People's Party (PP), which won the elections in late 2011, to institute further austerity measures

---

[59] See discussion in Chapter 5 on the Council.   [60] Featherstone 2016; Siani-Davies 2017.
[61] Ban 2016, pp. 200–4.

and to fully deregulate the labor markets.[62] PSOE came back to head a minority government only in 2018 as a result of a corruption scandal involving the governing center-right Prime Minister from the People's Party (PP)—without, however, the kind of political legitimacy that would have come with winning an election. That test came in April 2019, and was successfully passed when PSOE received 28.7 percent of the vote, way ahead of the conservative PP at 16.7 percent—even though the party had difficulty forming a government because it did not get a majority in the election, and Podemos balked at supporting the party without being given substantial representation in the government. A new left of center coalition government was finally formed only after new elections in November 2019.

Among center-left parties, only the Portuguese Socialist Party (PS) seems to have fully recovered. Having lost power in 2011 to the conservatives, on the back of the bailout program, it returned to head a left-leaning government after the 2015 elections. Despite the fact that the conservatives had won a plurality in those elections, they lost the governing majority they had enjoyed since 2011, and within a month of establishing a minority government the center-left PS replaced them in a governing alliance with two radical left parties. The government's pledge to stay within the austerity limits while passing more redistributive policies seemed to have been a winning formula.[63] The government remains very popular, and has largely been credited with Portugal's economic recovery, which also helps explain the gains in citizens' trust in government charted above, and the fact that it was re-elected in October 2019.

Arguably the most dramatic story after that of Greece is the collapse in Italy of the two main centrist parties on the right and the left, entirely due to the economic crisis.[64] The story begins with the resignation of Prime Minister Berlusconi, pushed out through a combination of behind-the-scenes pressure from Sarkozy and Merkel and the markets pricing up the cost of refinancing the debt (as discussed in Chapter 5), and the designation of a technocratic government made up of academics, backed by a coalition of center-right and center-left parties.[65] At the time, there were debates about the possible democratic deficit of the executive in this "blocked" or "suspended" democracy.[66] But the government was generally considered politically legitimate, just as similar technical governments had been in the 1990s.

The new "technical" Prime Minister, Mario Monti, was mandated to carry out a program of "blood and tears" in order to restore market confidence while putting the country back on the road to economic recovery.[67] But Monti's double-headed program to "save Italy" through major budgetary cuts and then "grow Italy" through structural reforms failed to restart the economy and was highly contested, and

[62] Ban 2016, pp. 204–7.   [63] See discussion in Chapter 6.
[64] Morlino and Raniolo 2017.   [65] For a brief history, see Orsina 2019.
[66] Fusaro 2012; Ceccarini, Diamanti, and Lazar 2012; Gualmini and Schmidt 2013.
[67] Gualmini and Schmidt 2013, p. 357–9.

little over a year later elections were held.[68] The results of the February 2013 vote gave Beppe Grillo's populist Five Star Movement party a 25 percent share of the vote, making it impossible for the winning center-left Democratic Party (PD) to broker a coalition government. A two-month impasse was broken only once the octagenarian President Napolitano agreed to another mandate, and then named Enrico Letta as Prime Minister to head a grand coalition government with the support of the center right and center left.

But less than a year later, Matteo Renzi had pushed out Letta to become Prime Minister. In the 2014 EP elections that came soon thereafter, Renzi's win with 40 percent of the votes gave him the credibility to push flexibility at the EU level and a reform program at home. In exchange for maintaining the deficit at 2.9 percent, he proposed to engage in labor market reforms through the so-called Jobs Act.[69] The latter proved extremely unpopular, and contributed in no small way to the failure of his signature institutional initiative to reform the composition and powers of the Parliament as well as to alter the division of powers between the state and the regions. That initiative, generally seen as giv-ing too much power to the winning majority, went down to massive defeat in a 2016 constitutional referendum, leading to Renzi's resignation and replacement by yet another Prime Minister, Paolo Gentilone. Renzi's demise was due in no small measure not just to his unpopular reforms but also to his own incessant self-promotion and over-communication, which ensured that he "lost both the establishment and the people."[70]

The next round of elections in 2018 upended the traditional party system. The PD was demoted to second place with 19.14 per cent of the vote, behind the Five Star Movement's (M5S) 32.22 percent; meanwhile Berlusconi's center right fell to fourth place with 14.43 percent of the vote, behind its erstwhile junior partner, the extreme right League (formerly Northern League), in third place with 17.61 percent of the vote. Italian President Mattarella then asked M5S to form a new government—as speculation had it, on the assumption that it would fail and thereby make it necessary to appoint a new technocratic government. When the M5S's negotiations to form a coalition government with the PD failed, it negoti-ated a "contract" for governing with the League and made unknown law professor Giuseppe Conte Prime Minister; the leaders of the two parties became Deputy Prime Ministers, with the M5S's Luigi di Maio as Foreign Minister and the League's Matteo Salvini as Interior Minister. For the first time in Italy's demo-cratic history, neither the center right nor the center left was in power.

---

[68] Riera and Russo 2016; Della Porta et al. 2017; Orsina 2019.
[69] Picot and Tassinari 2017; see discussion in Chapter 6, in the section on the effects of austerity and structural reform in Southern Europe.
[70] Orsina 2019, p. 12.

Mainstream Parties' Political Fortunes in Core Countries

That mainstream parties in the periphery encountered major problems in maintaining their majorities in the face of rising Euroskepticism and citizen discontent was perhaps to be expected, given their difficulties as debtor nations that had to absorb the worst effects of the crisis. But how do we explain the fact that core countries such as Germany and France also experienced major political disruption? How do we account for the fact that Germany—a country seemingly inoculated against radical right politics, in marked contrast to Austria[71]—saw the rise of not only the anti-euro, anti-immigrant AfD party but also the racist PEGIDA social movement? And what do we make of France, where the center-right President Sarkozy was ejected after one term in office while his successor, President François Hollande, chose not to run again for fear of losing; and where no mainstream party appeared in the second round of the 2017 presidential elections, which pitted the anti-system but pro-European "critical center" party of Emmanuel Macron against the extreme right National Front of Marine Le Pen?

Even for those leaders who managed to maintain their incumbency, governing has not been easy. In Germany, although Chancellor Merkel stayed in office, she was increasingly challenged not only from the outside by the rise of a new anti-system party, the AfD, but also from the inside, by members of her own coalition government. Her coalition with the pro-austerity, strongly neoliberal Free Democrats (FPD), which had achieved historic gains in the 2009 elections, left her little room for maneuver when dealing with the Eurozone crisis. The FPD's equally historic defeat in the 2013 election, which left it without seats in Parliament, brought Merkel back into a new grand coalition with the SPD, and gave her more breathing space. But once the migration crisis hit, bringing with it her historic decision to open the borders to a million Syrian refugees, the backlash came not only from outside—with the rise of PEGIDA and the AfD—but also from within her own party coalition, from the CSU (Christian Social Union), which took an increasingly hard line on migration. Weakened in the 2017 elections, when the CDU/CSU lost a large portion of its vote share, it took many months before Merkel was able to forge a coalition with the SPD, following failed discussions with the FDP, now back in the Bundestag. And after losses in regional elections in 2018, Merkel stood down as party leader, although continuing in her mandate as Chancellor.

The travails of Merkel and the CDU were nothing compared to those of the other major German mainstream party, the Social Democrats (SPD). The party's Hartz IV labor market and welfare reforms in the mid 2000s—largely credited for the revival of the German economy but also for the dualization of the workforce and increased in-work poverty connected to low-paying service sector

---

[71] See Art 2006.

jobs, as discussed in Chapter 9—hit its own electorate hardest. The reforms were seen as a betrayal by many of the party's traditional voters, in particular in parts of Germany suffering from industrial decline and rural depopulation. Being part of coalition governments from 2009 to 2013, and again beginning in 2017 (despite opposition by the SPD's youth wing), also did not help the party develop a clear profile that sufficiently distinguished it from the CDU, in contrast to the Greens, with their alternative environmental message, or the extreme left *Die Linke*. Although the SPD did push for more expansionary fiscal and social policy, it also maintained ordoliberal orthodoxy when it came to macroeconomic policy—including when an SPD finance minister replaced Schäuble after the 2017 elections. In that election, the SPD, led by candidate Martin Schulz, scored only 20.5 percent of the vote—its worst result since the creation of the Federal Republic in 1949, and a "crushing" outcome, according to the SPD Secretary-General.[72] And in the May 2019 EP elections, it again scored a historic low, this time 15.8 percent of the vote.

Since the Eurozone crisis, France's mainstream parties have fared much worse than the German mainstream parties. In France, both the center right and the center left have become pale shadows of their former selves. The decline started with President Sarkozy, whose defeat in the 2012 election made him only the second President in the Fifth Republic not to have won a second term. His popularity was high during the financial crisis, when he actively sought to rally support for fiscal stimulus to save the world economy, and remained so at the inception of the Eurozone crisis, when he pushed for the rescue of Greece. But that popularity slowly faded with his turn to a discourse of stability and an emphasis on austerity for France and Europe more generally as part of the Merkozy couple. Sarkozy's economic policies, combined with growing resentment of his "bling-bling" lifestyle as President, contributed to his loss in the presidential elections to Socialist Party candidate François Hollande, who promised to end austerity and promote growth—but ended up doing neither.

A big part of Hollande's problem was that once elected, he shifted his discourse to one more in tune with that of his predecessor and Merkel, while passing an austerity package that went much farther than anything Sarkozy had implemented.[73] He did this largely on the assumption that France had to maintain its credibility with the markets and regain it with Germany by becoming more competitive while meeting the terms of the fiscal compact—an almost impossible task given France's more consumption-oriented growth model. But arguably worse than the decision to engage in austerity policies is that Hollande said little that served to legitimize his switch, other than to refer to his responsibility to honor

---

[72] *Financial Times* Oct. 17, 2018 https://www.ft.com/content/a1f88c3c-d154-11e8-a9f2-7574db66bcd5

[73] Glencross 2018.

pre-existing institutional requirements. This was in striking contrast to President Mitterrand's discourse at the time of his own famous U-turn on monetary policy in 1983, when he sought to legitimize abandoning his initial expansionist policies by expressing the bitter recognition that the constraints of globalization forced this upon him.[74] As a result, not only was Hollande the third French President not to have secured a second mandate, he was also noted for having had the lowest popularity rating of any President of the Fifth Republic up to that the time (12 percent in November 2014).

The 2017 election was something of a watershed for French politics,[75] and the result of what Bruno Cautrès and Anne Muxel describe as an "electoral revolution."[76] That revolution began with primaries that were held for the first time by both the center-right and center-left parties, with unexpected results.[77] Not only did the center-left Socialist Party (PS) find itself without a standard bearer once Hollande withdrew from the race, having realized he might go down to massive defeat (the first time a sitting President had not run for re-election).[78] The center-right party *Les Republicains* (LR) was also in trouble, with its leader, former Prime Minister François Fillon—who had been widely expected to win the presidential election— handicapped by a corruption scandal.[79] In the first round of the 2017 elections, Fillon's LR ended up in third place with 20.01 percent of the vote, behind the far right Marine Le Pen's FN at 21.30 percent, while the Socialist Party came in fifth place, at 6.36 percent, way behind the 19.58 percent polled by the far left *La France Insoumise* (France Unbowed) in fourth place. The winner, Emmanuel Macron, head of his newly created *La République en Marche* (LREM), came from nowhere to claim the self-described "critical center," taking votes from the center right and center left in the first round for his 24.01 percent score, and defeating Marine Le Pen in the second round by 66.1 percent against 33.9 percent. In the subsequent legislative elections in June 2017 Macron's LREM gained a majority, with 350 of the 577 seats in the National Assembly.

The emergence of Macron's *En Marche* was a dramatic illustration of French citizens' frustration with mainstream parties and leaders of both left and right. This was an anti-establishment candidate who rejected mainstream parties but was anti-populist and a pro-EU centrist. Initially, his positive discourse on the EU seemed to provide a resounding answer to the anti-EU populist extremes, while his electoral promises for economic reforms that would promote growth made it appear as if he would manage to be both responsive to citizens and responsible to Eurozone commitments. His election was greeted with great enthusiasm by lead-ers across Europe, as a strong rejection of the populism of both Trump in the United States and Brexit in the United Kingdom. And in France as well, his man-date was characterized by great public optimism.

---

[74] Karremans and Damhuis 2018.   [75] Kuhn 2017.   [76] Cautrès and Muxel 2019.
[77] Finchelstein 2019.   [78] Bréchon 2019.   [79] Teinturier and Lama 2019.

The honeymoon was not to last, either with EU leaders or the French public. Not only did Macron's proposals for EU-level reform not produce anything tangible, given Northern European resistance, but also his reform agenda at the national level only seemed to do more of what people had not liked about the policies of Hollande. Macron's large majority in the French National Assembly meant that he was able to impose what he had promised—often by decree with regard to labor market reforms and the abolition of the tax on wealth (the *ISF*). But while the parliamentary opposition was weak and fragmented, he was losing the hybrid bases of his electoral support.[80] And then came the *gilet jaunes*. Macron's response—to earmark 10 billion euros in extra spending to defuse the protests—meant that France was to breach the EU's 3 percent deficit limit in 2019, possibly causing him trouble in Brussels. But his decision to hold the "*grand débats*" (debates with citizens organized by local authorities across France) seemed to work in terms of bringing his popularity back up from a low of 20 percent, on the back of his multiple extended appearances in local debates to discuss the issues with all comers.

The question remains as to whether Macron will be able to satisfy an increasingly discontented French citizenry. But for the moment, Macron continues to command the center. In the 2019 EP elections, regardless of all the discontent, Macron's LREM (despite being handicapped by a poor lead candidate) came in a respectable second, with the LREM's 22.42 percent putting it only a hair behind the extreme right RN's 23.34 percent, with both winning twenty-three seats. The center right, in contrast, went down to a historic defeat with only 8.48 percent of the vote, albeit ahead of the socialists at 6.19 percent—putting the latter even behind the far left *France Insoumise* (FI), which garnered 6.31 percent of the vote.

Populist Parties and the Eurozone Crisis

For all populist challenger parties, Euroskepticism was a unifying theme, often with pledges to exit the euro and/or the EU if elected. But the Euroskeptic rhetoric softened by 2018 or 2019, in particular with the spectacle of Brexit, as many extremist parties especially on the right largely backpedaled on their pledges. Instead, they insisted that they would stay in to fight for a different EU, with more nationalist norms and more closed to migrants.

Populist Parties on the Extremes of the Right

Among all such populist parties, arguably the most remarkable changes have come on the extremes of the right. Although hard right parties had marked

---

[80] Strudel 2019.

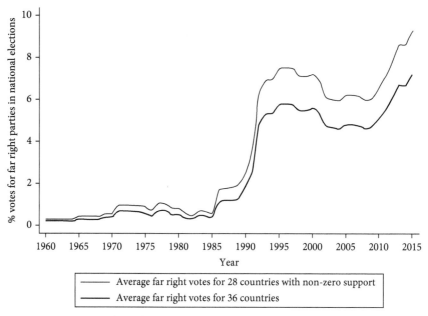

Figure 10.5. Average far-right vote 1960–2015

Note: Top line indicates average far right votes for 28 countries with non-zero support; bottom line indicates average far right votes for 36 countries

Source: Halikiopoulou 2018, based on Armingeon et al., 2017

significant gains from the 1980s on, peaking in the 1990s then declining slightly in the 2000s, the Eurozone crisis beginning in 2010 gave them a major new impetus. Figure 10.5 shows how far-right parties generally have increased over time in Europe between 1960 and 2015.

Populist anti-system parties on the extreme right can be found across Europe, but they have flourished in particular in Northern Europe, for all the reasons discussed earlier. In Denmark, the Danish Peoples Party, which had been a force to be reckoned with since the 1990s on anti-immigration issues, made historic gains in the June 2015 elections, enabling it to become the second largest party in the country and precipitating the collapse of the center-left government. In Finland, the True Finns broke through in the 2011 Finnish elections, and by the April 2019 elections the (renamed) Finns became the second largest party with 17.5 percent of the vote. In Sweden, the Sweden Democrats broke through with 5.7 percent of the vote in 2010, and more than doubled their support in the September 2014 elections, receiving 12.9 percent of the votes.

In Continental Europe in 2017, Austria saw the Freedom Party (FPÖ)—the party founded by the late Jörg Haider, which in the early 2000s had been in a coalition government with the conservative government to the great consternation of EU member-state leaders—again become a junior partner in a conservative government (which collapsed in spring 2019 due to a scandal involving the head of the FPÖ). New elections in September 2019 then led to an unprecedented coalition government of the conservatives and the greens as of January 2020. Additionally, in France the FN went to the second round of the presidential elections in 2017, with Marine Le Pen's 33.9 percent of the vote outdoing her father's 18 percent in the 2002 presidential elections. Even Germany, which had long seemed vaccinated against the extreme right, saw the meteoric rise of the AfD from 4.7 percent in the 2013 elections to 12.6 percent in 2017, although this was still modest compared to the 20+ percent seen by extreme right parties in elections in the Netherlands, Austria, and France.

Such parties can also be found in Southern Europe, most notably in the populist coalition government in Italy in power in 2018-2019. The League had become increasingly popular over the course of its time in office, polling 34.3 percent in the 2019 EP elections (up from its 17 percent in the 2018 election), while its Five Star Movement "radical center" coalition partner fell precipitously to 17.1 percent in the polls. Elsewhere in the South, however, extreme right populist parties have been small. In Greece, the ultra-nationalist party Independent Greeks (Anel), the government coalition partner of Syriza, got 3.7 percent of votes in the 2015 election, while much farther to the hard right, the neo-Nazi Golden Dawn party received approximately 7 percent of the vote in 2015. Both failed to make the threshold in the 2019 elections. In Spain, in contrast, the neo-fascist Vox party went from 0.2 percent of the vote in 2014 to 10.3 percent of the vote in 2019.

Trigger events such as the Eurozone crisis and the migration crisis alone cannot explain this enormous increase in support for the right-wing extremes. A lot also has to do with the ways in which successful extreme right parties have transformed themselves in order to expand their appeal to wider audiences, with more opportunistic as opposed to ideologically driven approaches to the issues. The transformations since the 1980s, when most hard right parties had fascist or neo-Nazi leanings and evinced nostalgia for an authoritarian past, are striking. The changes came about largely in the 2000s, as many such parties distanced themselves from ideologies based in fascism and racism, often with new leaders and new narratives that stressed the ideational as opposed to the biological bases of national belonging. Nationalism remained, but rather than identifying the out-group in terms of race or common descent, it was excluded on the basis of a lack of shared liberal values such as democracy, multiculturalism, and rule of law.[81] The buzzword for this was "tolerance", with a discourse clearly directed mainly at Muslims and their purported lack of tolerance for the key elements of liberal democracy.

One of the earliest examples of the use of such tolerance discourse was by Pym Fortyn in the Netherlands in the early 2000s, who excoriated Muslim

[81] Halikiopoulou 2018, pp. 69–71.

immigration on the grounds that, as a tolerant country, the Netherlands needed to be intolerant of the intolerant (ie, Muslims who were against homosexuals such as him and equality for women). But while Fortyn's was a flash party that split and quickly disappeared, Geert Wilders' Freedom Party (PVV) reclaimed Fortyn's electorate with a discourse that railed against "the Islamization of the Netherlands" as well as the EU and the euro. Although Wilders' 2012 campaign promise to withdraw the Netherlands from the EU and to return to the guilder turned out to be a bridge too far, losing him nine seats, by 2017 his party was back up to twenty.[82] Its vote share in 2017 was less than predicted, however, mainly because the conservative Dutch Prime Minister Mark Rutte moved closer to the populist extremes with a discourse that claimed that he was providing "his own, gentler version of anti-immigrant populism,"[83] stating that "if you don't like it here, you can leave."[84] In the 2019 EP elections, though, Wilders' party lost big, in this case to another extreme right party.

Another party for which anti-immigration and Islam became major issues was the German AfD. At its foundation in 2013 by economics professors and professionals, it was an anti-euro party with a "soft" Euroskepticism opposing the currency union and all bailouts but maintaining a commitment to the European project.[85] But it very quickly turned into a strongly nationalist extreme right political party with controversial leaders, and gained support from the PEGIDA movement. In addition to hardening Euroskepticism, such as the claim in its 2016 national election manifesto that the EU "has become an undemocratic construct" with "non-transparent uncontrolled bureaucracies," it focused on anti-immigration and identity issues such as opposition to state support for sexual diversity and gender mainstreaming.[86] It reiterated this same range of issues in its 2019 EP election manifesto,[87] while adding climate change skepticism to the grid by deriding the science behind clean-air policy as "particulate matter hysteria."[88]

Climate change skepticism has also been a recent vote-getter in Scandinavia. The extreme right Finns party came in second in the April 2019 national elections largely due to a discourse stating, for example, that aggressive climate change policies were an elitist approach that hurt the working class.[89] But the party's main message was primarily Euroskeptic, with its leap from obscurity to third party in

---

[82] *Financial Times* Nov. 13, 2011.   [83] *Reuters* March 16, 2017.
[84] *Wall Street Journal Online* March 12, 2017.   [85] Arzheimer 2015.
[86] Alternative für Deutschland (2016). *Manifesto for Germany. The political programme of the Alternative for Germany.* https://www.afd.de/wp-content/uploads/sites/111/2017/04/2017-04-12_afd-grundsatzprogramm-englisch
[87] Alternative für Deutschland (2019) EUROPAWAHLPROGRAMM Programm der Alternative für Deutschland für die Wahl zum 9. Europäischen Parlament: https://www.afd.de/wp-content/uploads/sites/111/2019/02/AfD_Europawahlprogramm_A5-hoch_RZ.pdf
[88] *New York Times* April 12, 2019.   [89] *New York Times* April 14, 2019.

2011 significant for having exerted strong pressure on the mainstream government to delay its approval of the second Greek bailout.[90]

Arguably the most successful transition from a longstanding hard right party
to populist extreme right is that of the National Front in France. From its founding
in the 1970s and its breakthrough in elections in the early 1980s up until the mid
2000s, the party led by Jean Marie Le Pen was strongly nationalist in its ideology,
anti-EU and anti-immigrant on policies, and neoliberal on economics. Le Pen's
discourse also evinced nostalgia for the "law and order" of the Vichy government
and Marshal Pétain, alongside anti-semitic allusions with frequent Holocaust
denials and other provocative statements that landed him foul of the law.[91] In his
classic study of the National Front as a "national-populist party," Pierre André
Taguieff cast Le Pen as the ideal-typical demagogic leader who purports to speak
for "the people" and to persuade through propagandistic formulas, such as those
equating foreigners to unemployment and threats to law and order, while claiming "legitimate anger" against the decadence of the country.[92]

The discourse changed with Le Pen's daughter, Marine Le Pen, who managed
to "de-demonize" the party, modernize its policy positions, and thereby enlarge
its electoral base by attracting younger voters while closing the gender gap.[93]
Her shift, as with many of the more successful extreme right parties, has been to
what Dominic Reynié calls "heritage populism," in which such parties present
themselves as the main protectors of liberty and accuse the elite and mainstream parties of failing to uphold the society's values and of being complacent
in the face of Islamisation.[94] While Le Pen stuck with the party's longstanding
anti-euro and anti-EU stance, she made a pragmatic shift away from her father's
hard right positions, including his anti-semitism and his conservative neoliberal condemnation of the welfare state. This was the formula for success, so
much so that by 2012 close to a third of the population saw her ideas as "banal,"
that is, ordinary and therefore acceptable, up from 22 percent only a year earlier.[95]
In the presidential elections of 2017 the party had therefore seemed ready for a
major breakthrough, but it fizzled out as a result of a range of problems, including
poor strategy and corruption charges.[96] Arguably most important in the relatively
poor showing was Marine Le Pen's disastrous performance in her televised
debate with Macron,[97] in particular when he ridiculed her idea of having a parallel currency to the euro. After the election defeat in 2017 the FN seemed to be
a spent force—only to rebound with the *gilets jaunes*, whose *ressentiment*, or
resentment, of the urban elites fit well with the kind of discourse Marine Le Pen
had long been articulating.

[90] Bergmann 2017.   [91] Perrineau 2014.   [92] Taguieff 1984.
[93] Ivaldi 2015; Stockemer and Amengay 2015; Mayer 2015.   [94] Reynié 2016, pp. 52–3.
[95] *Le Monde* Jan. 13, 2012.   [96] Perrineau 2019.   [97] Mercier 2019.

The transition of the Italian extreme right League is somewhat different. In this case, it went from a hard right regionalist party to a national populist party. In its first incarnation, led by Umberto Bossi as the Northern League, it sought to create "Padania," an imagined community stopping somewhere before Rome, while cutting Southern Italy loose.[98] But once Matteo Salvini took over in 2013, he slowly transformed the Northern League into the "League," a national party which, by the 2018 elections, focused mainly on protecting all of Italy from the "threats" coming from further south—that is, North Africa—related to migration. The party's vehement polemic against migration was matched with policies once Salvini entered the government as Deputy Prime Minister and Minister of the Interior, most dramatically in refusals to allow boats full of people rescued at sea to dock at Italian ports. The League's economic policies were a mix of neoliberalism, with its support of a flat tax, and ethno-socialism, with its defense of the welfare state. It also remained largely against the EU, which it described in its election manifesto as "a gigantic supranational body, devoid of true democratic legitimacy and structured through a sprawling bureaucratic structure that dictates the agenda to our governments." The League promised to remain in the EU only if all its treaties since Maastricht were revisited so as to return to "a form of free and peaceful cooperation among states of a mainly economic nature," at the same time identifying "the euro [as] the main cause of our economic decline, a currency designed for Germany and multinationals and contrary to the needs of Italy and the small businesses."[99]

By 2019, however, while the League did not officially rescind its threat to leave the EU, its statements and actions while in coalition government suggest it had indeed backed away from this position. Threatening to leave the EU and/or the euro was no longer in fashion, largely because of shifts in public opinion in response to the unfolding drama of Brexit. In Nordic Europe, for example, in February 2019 the Sweden Democrat leader made a U-turn on leaving the EU, deciding instead to push for changing the EU from within.[100] But even prior to this, Marine Le Pen had clearly stated, following her electoral defeat, that she was no longer calling for exit from the euro or the EU, and renamed the FN the RN (*Rassemblement National*—National Rally). In contrast, in Germany the AfD, in its 2019 EP election program, still promised "Dexit" as a last resort if its reform demands were not met.[101]

---

[98] McDonnell 2006.

[99] https://www.leganord.org/notizie/news-2018/16455-elezioni-2018-programma-di-governo-lega-salvini-premier

[100] *EU Observer*, Feb. 3 2019 https://euobserver.com/tickers/144063

[101] See EUROPAWAHLPROGRAMM Programm der Alternative für Deutschland für die Wahl zum 9. Europäischen Parlament: https://www.afd.de/wp-content/uploads/sites/111/2019/02/AfD_Europawahlprogramm_A5-hoch_RZ.pdf

Populist Parties on the Extremes of the Left

Populist parties on the extreme left have also grown in strength since the Eurozone crisis. This was a remarkable shift, given the precipitous decline, if not disappearance, of hard-left parties after 1989.[102] Generally speaking, they doubled their numbers in national elections between 2004 and 2016, going from 5 percent to 10 percent, although the extreme right had more impressive gains, going from 7 to 15 percent of total votes.[103] They also charted significant increases in the 2014 EP election, with the radical left's seats going up to fifty-two seats from thirty-five in the 2009 election, prior to the onset of the sovereign debt crisis. In Southern Europe in particular, the crisis contributed to the electoral success of extreme left parties such as the Progressive Party of Working People (AKEL) in Cyprus, a formally Marxist-Leninist party that had been electorally successful since the island's independence from the United Kingdom in the 1960s; Syriza as well as other even harder left parties in Greece; Podemos in Spain; FI in France; and more. In Northern Europe, extreme left parties also made significant gains, including the Socialist Party in the Netherlands, *Die Linke* (The Left) in Germany, or the Left Alliance in Finland.[104]

All such parties tend to share three main characteristics: they are ideologically to the left of social democratic and green parties; they reject contemporary capitalism and the neoliberal project while advocating for alternative economic and political power structures; and they put great importance on economic and social inequalities, with radical redistributive policies for remedies.[105] As for attitudes toward the EU, theirs is a "soft" Euroskepticism[106] in which, as discussed earlier, the main concerns are the socioeconomic rather than the sociocultural impact, with emphasis on creating a better EU rather than leaving. That said, parties vary a great deal in their positions, with some opposed to almost everything that the EU stands for and others hoping to change it from within.[107]

If we take the EP 2014 manifesto of the radical left parties as a metric for the compromise position on the EU, we find a call for a "re-foundation" of the EU, with criticism of the "ultraliberalism" imposed by European "technocrats" and of a euro that is "at the exclusive service of the financial markets."[108] In the buildup to the 2019 EP elections, a number of extreme-left populist parties reiterated the call for a refounding of Europe along with complaints about a technocratic Europe with neoliberal austerity policies. Others went even further. The program of Jean-Luc Mélenchon's *La France Insoumise* struck a "sovereignist" note not far from that of the extreme right, complaining about the EU undermining national

[102] March and Mudde 2005.   [103] Hix 2018.   [104] Beaudonnet and Gomez 2017.
[105] March 2011; Beaudonnet and Gomez 2017; Gomez et al. 2016.
[106] Szczerbiak and Taggart 2008.   [107] Charalambous 2011.
[108] PEL (2014) "Manifesto for the 2014 European Elections. Escaping Austerity, Rebuilding Europe," available at http://dnpprepo.ub.rug.nl/618/

sovereignty and democracy. Among its proposals, the party called for a Plan A to renegotiate the treaties so as to promote social solidarity and ecological sustainability and a Plan B, if Plan A failed, which would "construct new European cooperations liberated from the austerity treaties with all countries willing to share in the project"[109]—which was vague on whether it meant exit from the euro. In contrast, other extreme left parties were not at all vague in their decisions as a result of Brexit negotiations to abandon calls to leave the EU, including Sweden's Left Party, which gave up on "Swexit" ahead of the EP elections.[110]

Among left populist parties, arguably the most significant in terms of gains in political power have been those in Southern Europe, where the Eurozone crisis hit hardest. In Spain, support for *Podemos* ("We Can"), the challenger party on the extreme left—but also for *Ciudadanos* (Citizens) in the critical center—came from disapproval of the two mainstream parties' economic policies of austerity combined with concerns about corruption. In 2014, citizen disapproval of the government was at an extraordinary high of 70 percent, matched by a 70 percent disapproval rating for the opposition.[111] With the EP elections of 2014, that disapproval was concretized by a 40 percent point decline in traditional party support. *Podemos*—founded that same year, building its constituency on the "15M/*Indignados*" protest movement and its ideas on Latin American left populism and the work of Ernesto Laclau—gained 8 percent of the vote, making for five seats in the EP. In the national elections of 2015 it received 21 percent of the vote, and it gained a similar number in the 2016 election. It thus constituted the third largest party in Spain—although its drop in the 2019 election to only 14.3 percent put it in fourth place, behind the resurgent PSOE, the PP, and *Ciudadanos*.

Among extreme left parties, only Syriza in Greece has played a leading role in government. Its trajectory since 2015, when it won in a surprise defeat of the mainstream parties, has been something of an object lesson for the left in Europe. While starting on the far left, with major promises to upend Eurozone policy, it ended up implementing everything it had railed against in its campaign. But nonetheless, four years later, it looks to be the new social democratic force on the Greek political landscape, displacing PASOK.

Syriza began far to the left in its electoral program published in 2014, when it promised a clear choice between European negotiation by a Syriza government or acceptance of the creditor's terms by the Samaras government. Its campaign slogan proclaimed that "Hope is coming; Greece goes forward; Europe is changing," as the party promised to end austerity while staying in the euro—on the assumption that Greece's creditors would not risk "Grexit."[112] The party campaigned on

---

[109] LFI (2019) "L'Avenir en commun, en Europe aussi!" Programme de la France Insoumise pour les Elections Européennes 2019 https://lafranceinsoumise.fr/app/uploads/2019/02/ProgrammeEurope-A5.pdf
[110] *The Local* Feb. 18, 2019.   [111] Bosch and Durán 2017.   [112] Featherstone 2016, p. 4.

demands for significant debt relief, a "growth clause" for debt financing, a grace period for debt servicing, and greater flexibility in the SGP.[113] Once in government, in spring 2015, Syriza added red lines on further pension cuts while proposing higher minimum wages and collective bargaining, although at the same time it sought compromise with creditors in a range of areas. The Troika institutions would have none of this, and for the new bailout they insisted on further spending cuts, lower pensions, and a wider VAT base while refusing any debt relief outright. When the government refused, the ECB pulled the plug on its emergency financing, precipitating a crisis during which Syriza first introduced capital controls (on June 29) and then defaulted on an International Monetary Fund (IMF) loan. Prime Minister Tsipras then called a referendum on whether Greece should accept the creditors' bailout conditions, stating in a televised address that his government had tried to find "a viable agreement that respects democracy" but that effort had failed and "the people must decide free of any blackmail."[114] He then campaigned for the *oxi* (no) and won, with 61 percent of votes opposing the bailout conditions. But as discussed earlier, faced with the likelihood that Greece would be excluded from the Eurozone if he honored the vote, he interpreted the no vote as a "yes" to stay in the euro, and accepted the even more punitive package. He then called for new elections in September 2015 which brought back to power a Syriza stripped of some of its most radical elements, which gave Tsipras a mandate to implement the program.

Tsipras' victory suggests that in the Greek context, his inability to deliver on his campaign promises in the first election or in the referendum was not disqualifying. This was due in large measure to his discourse, in which he constructed an inclusive Greek identity made up of "the ordinary people," for whom he promised to "restore their dignity and represent their interests against the Greek and European establishment,"[115] with an "us vs. them" opposition between the powerful wealthy elite and the non-privileged suffering the brunt of years of mismanagement and austerity imposed by previous governments, the EU, and Germany.[116] But although Tsipras' invective against Greek political elites and the EU helped solidify domestic support, it certainly did nothing to help in his relations with EU member-state leaders in loan bailout negotiations, as we have already seen. Moreover, policies that continued with the austerity and structural reforms demanded by the Troika, and that increased taxes on the middle classes (now defined as anyone earning over 2,000 euros a month) even as it reduced them for the poorest, proved extremely unpopular. This helps explain Syriza's bad results in the EP elections of May 2019 and in the snap elections of the Greek Parliament in July 2019, when New Democracy won a majority of 40 percent of the popular

---

[113] Syriza, 2014.   [114] Cited in Mody 2018, p. 418.   [115] Stavrakakis 2015.
[116] Stavrakakis 2015; Stavrakakis and Katsambekis 2014; see discussion in Van Esch 2017, pp. 232–3.

vote. That said, Syriza did not do all that badly—it became the main left-wing party of opposition, replacing PASOK, with a respectable score of 32 percent.

Populist Parties in the Radical Center

Populist challenger parties appear not only on the extremes of the right and the left but also in what I think of as the "radical center."[117] The radical center consists of political parties that draw citizens' votes and support from both extremes of the political spectrum, with a mix of positions that appeal to both. Andrea Pirro's term for this phenomenon is "polyvalent populism," where the populist frame succeeds in incorporating ideas from the "new politics" of the libertarian left as much as the "new populism" of the radical right.[118]

For the moment, there is only one party that is readily classifiable here: the Five Star Movement. This may be not so much because the M5S is unique but rather because the radical center is itself unstable. Parties that start there may quickly move farther to the extremes of either the right or the left. The AfD is one such example, since it initially drew support from citizens on the extremes of right and left, with its radical stance against the euro, but soon became clearly right-wing extremist when it took up the anti-immigrant issue, among others. UKIP is arguably another example, in particular in its early years when it campaigned mainly on its opposition to the EU and migration, without the racist overtones of the Brexit campaign, and pushed for direct democracy. In further support for this category of "radical center" we could add that all three parties were initially part of the same European Parliament grouping, the Europe of Freedom and Democracy (EFDD)—although the AfD quickly left to join the extreme right grouping and UKIP imploded following its success in the British referendum (although it continued to sit in the EP), and came back briefly as the Brexit party to sit in the same grouping.

The Five Star Movement differs from populist parties clearly identifiable on the extremes of the right or the left by its ideas as well as its organization, although it shares certain basic traits with all other such parties. It is a hybrid between the old-style political party and a social movement, providing online voting for the leadership and for policy initiatives.[119] Much like other populist movements and parties, its discourse is anti-establishment, anti-elite, and anti-party, with a charismatic leader, Beppe Grillo, a comedian, who used a populist style of speaking to "the people" through everyday language, often slanderous.[120] His successor, Luigi di Maio, has sought to follow the same playbook, albeit with somewhat less success.

---

[117] Schmidt and Luke 2019.   [118] Pirro 2018.
[119] Morlino and Raniolo 2017; Passarelli and Tuorto 2018.
[120] Ceccarini and Bordignon, 2016.

Moreover, like many populist parties on the extremes of the right or the left, in particular in Southern Europe, the party was built on the conviction that the country's elites were deeply corrupt, in contrast with the fundamentally honest ordinary people.[121] But beyond this, M5S differs with regard to the range of ideas and potential constituencies to which it appeals. Importantly, this is not just a protest party for citizens dissatisfied with the system; it is also a party that appeals because of its political ideas.[122] At the beginning of the movement in particular, those ideas emphasized post-materialist and environmentalist values, with a focus on urban quality of life and ethical consumerism.[123] This stance translated into longstanding opposition to the high-speed train between Turin and Lyon— which was a point of contention for the coalition government between the League, which supports it, and the M5S, which continues to oppose it. These environmental ideas, which would generally appeal to supporters of "green" parties, also combined with "left libertarian" values associated with citizen empowerment through direct democracy.[124]

But while green and left libertarian ideas seemed to categorize the party on the extreme left, the discourse of Grillo and Di Maio also articulated a range of ideas more often associated with the extreme right. Grillo's political discourse in particular repeatedly claimed that Italian citizens were oppressed by politicians, mass media, and large businesses, and that decision-making power had to be returned to the common people,[125] while his economic discourse promoted the interests of small and medium businesses, described as oppressed by public bureaucracy, taxation, and unfair competition from multinational companies.[126] As Fabio Franchino and Fedra Negri argue, the right-leaning aspects of the M5S also come out in their focus on fiscal moderation, along with lukewarm attachment to the euro—although the party's push for the *"reddito di cittadinanza"* (guaranteed citizen income) may be a break with this. But even more defining with regard to its extreme right leanings were the party's opposition to adoption by same-sex couples, to mandatory vaccinations for children, and to the repeal of a law making illegal immigration a crime.[127]

Finally, the M5S resembles other populist parties on the extremes of the right in terms of its virulent critiques of the EU and the euro, including UKIP and the AfD, the other two parties that were initially members of its EP party group, the EFDD. That said, when Grillo called an online referendum to abandon the EFDD for the Alliance of Liberals and Democrats for Europe (ALDE) (an initiative ultimately rejected by ALDE), 79 percent of M5S supporters agreed, suggesting again that the party and its supporters are more radical center than extreme right.[128]

---

[121] Orsina 2019, p. 11.   [122] Passarelli and Tuorto 2018.
[123] Tronconi 2015, p. 3.   [124] Tronchino 2015.
[125] Bordignon and Ceccarini 2013; Corbetta and Gualmini 2013.   [126] Caruso 2016.
[127] Franchino and Negri 2018.   [128] Franchino and Negri 2018.

Conclusion

The upsurge of populist anti-system parties has altered the political landscape, challenging mainstream parties' hold on government and power. The reasons for citizens' disenchantment are many, but major contributing factors are the failures of Eurozone governance with regard to both the output performance and the throughput procedures, as discussed in previous chapters. The disenchantment can be seen in the eroded trust in the EU and national governments, along with increasing Euroskepticism. The ways in which the resulting political turmoil has played out differ according to the EU's macro-regions, and is highly dependent upon the institutional contexts of welfare democracies. This said, we cannot fully understand why or how mainstream parties declined, or populist parties on the extreme right, extreme left, or in the radical center prospered, without taking seriously the country-specific failures of mainstream parties to respond to citizen discontent or the country-specific successes of populist parties' political ideas and discourse.

The decline of mainstream parties along with the rise of populist parties has not only made for more problematic politics "at the bottom," having replaced the longstanding national-level "politics *without* policy" with a new "politics *against* policy". It also had significant consequences for the EU, making for increasingly disruptive bottom-up politics, which has also had serious knock-on effects for politics at the top, as discussed in Part II. The question for the EU today is how to regain citizen trust and support while reducing the dissatisfaction that has contributed to their voting for the political extremes. This takes us back to issues of output legitimacy, to ensure better economic performance, and to throughput legitimacy, to change governance procedures in ways that enable citizens to feel that they have sufficient political voice in and control over the decisions that affect them the most. In the conclusion, we provide some preliminary suggestions.

Conclusion
How to (Re-)Envision Eurozone Governance
Beyond Governing by Rules and Ruling by Numbers

Three final questions regarding the EU's (euro) crisis of legitimacy still need to be addressed. First, how can we understand Eurozone crisis governance from the more general perspective of international organization and supranational governance? Second, how could we re-envision a more legitimate Eurozone governance, with better throughput processes, political input, and policy output? Third, how would any such re-envisioned Eurozone governance fit into the future of EU governance as a whole?

In response to the first question, this chapter argues that Eurozone governance has gone much farther in undermining national sovereignty and democracy than any other EU policy domain, let alone any other regional or international organization, without providing the expected benefits from the shared supranational authority and control. Yes, the Euro was indeed saved, but at what cost to generalized economic growth and political stability?

In response to the second question, the chapter suggests that a re-envisioned Eurozone governance could benefit from retaining the elaborate architecture of coordination while deepening risk-sharing, but only if it were democratized and decentralized, with much greater differentiated implementation. Macroeconomic policymaking requires more differentiated country-specific targets developed via more transparent debates among major EU actors, while the European Semester needs to be governed by more bottom-up rather than top-down processes. Only with differentiated policies better adapted to the differences in national political economies that are generated and debated by national political parties is there any chance for better economic performance. This is also the best foil against populism.

Finally, in response to the third question, the chapter rethinks EU governance as requiring more differentiated integration as well. Such differentiation takes the form of a *soft-core* Europe, characterized by multiple clusters of member states with overlapping participation in the EU's many policy communities, in contrast to the *hard core* often proposed for the Eurozone. But such differentiation is not without its problems, given EU decision rules and the need for deeper integration

Europe's Crisis of Legitimacy: Governing by Rules and Ruling by Numbers in the Eurozone. Vivien A. Schmidt, Oxford University Press (2020). © Vivien A. Schmidt.
DOI: 10.1093/oso/9780198797050.001.0001

in some policy areas (eg, migration or security and defense), more highly differentiated integration in others (ie, the Eurozone). Institutional reforms would also be necessary to ensure a positive future for differentiated integration. While the EU would continue to require a single set of institutions, it would need modified decision rules to allow for more (and less) differentiation depending upon the area.

EU and Eurozone Governance in International Perspective

Our analysis of Europe's crisis of legitimacy is not only applicable to the Eurozone crisis and is not limited to the EU. It serves equally as a more general primer on the dilemmas facing supranational governance institutions and the nation states that take part in them. Ensuring the legitimacy of international organizations (IOs) has gained increasing importance in recent years, as nation states have given up more and more national autonomy and control in exchange for shared authority and joint control in international and regional governance organizations.[1] Concerns about legitimacy in supranational governance mirror those for the EU, including political considerations regarding IOs' authority and activities,[2] performance issues related to IOs' ability to solve problems for the common good,[3] and procedural matters concerning the quality of IOs' governance processes.[4] The vast literature on "good governance" has often been another way into such questions of legitimacy.[5] Equally relevant are critiques of IOs' use of emergency powers to engage in "crisis exploitation," as in the case of the Eurogroup's actions under cover of the Troika,[6] or of IOs falling into a "hypocrisy trap," as in the Commission's reinterpretation of the rules by stealth.[7]

Changes in the international political economy have added to the challenges facing supranational governance bodies and national democracies alike. Forty years ago, when national economies were still largely controlled by national governments, the spheres of capitalism and democracy were seemingly co-terminus. Today, capitalism has become global while democracy remains local. And capitalism itself has been transformed as a result of ever-increasing globalization, moving from the embedded liberalism of the postwar years, in which free markets were balanced by state autonomy and welfare-based domestic policies,[8] to the dis-embedded neoliberalism of the current era, in which freer markets have undermined both state autonomy and welfare-based policies. These changes, as Dani Rodrik argues, have meant that whereas during the moderate globalization

---

[1] Schmidt 2002; Tallberg and Zürn 2019; Rittberger and Schroeder 2016.
[2] Buchanan and Keohane 2006, 407; Archibugi et al. 2012.
[3] Pogge 2002; Dellmuth and Tallberg 2015.
[4] March and Olsen 1995; Grigorescu 2007; Olsen 2015.   [5] Eg, Fukuyama 2016.
[6] Kreuder-Sonnen 2019b; see also White 2015.   [7] Weaver 2008.
[8] Ruggie 1982.

of the postwar Bretton Woods settlement, nation states were able to retain their sovereignty and democracy, today they face a trilemma in which under conditions of hyperglobalization they must choose between abandoning either national sovereignty or democracy.[9] In the EU, under the hyper-Europeanization of Eurozone governance, member states risk giving up national democracy and sovereignty.

Complicating matters even further is the fact that the nation state is no longer the central focus of democracy. It has become denationalized and dispersed, as decision-making has moved upwards to international and (supranational) regional bodies; downwards to (subnational) regional governments, corporate actors, and non-governmental organizations (NGOs); and sideways to regulatory agencies, public/private partnerships, and self-regulatory bodies.[10] This is a challenge to traditional views of democracy and legitimacy as situated at the level of the nation state, in particular when decision-making moves upwards, outside the confines of the nation state. For European member states, that democratic challenge is compounded by the presence of the EU as an intermediary layer between them and the global.[11]

Nowhere have these multiple issues—the dispersion of governing competence, the pressures of globalization and regionalization, and the dilemmas of supranational governance—been as salient as for the European Union. The EU has deepened regional integration among its nation-state members more than any other supranational organization as it moved responsibility for decision-making up from the national level to the supranational in policy area after policy area, including areas at the heart of national sovereignty, such as money, borders, and security.[12] Where the policies have been effective and the processes efficient, deeper integration has not posed significant problems for member-state democracies. But with the recent series of crises, beginning with the Eurozone crisis, the shortcomings of the policies and processes have had a deleterious impact on member-state politics. In the Eurozone crisis in particular, the EU, until recently regarded as one of the most innovative experiments in governance beyond the nation state,[13] may very well have gone too far too fast. The rules-based, numbers-targeting governance processes imposed by intergovernmental actors and overseen by supranational officials have undermined both member-state governments' "sovereign" autonomy and their democratic legitimacy. Even though the rules-based governance has softened since 2015, such governance remains contested while the politics continue to be problematic. National governments still find themselves obligated to follow the rules, however flexibly applied, while citizens see themselves as having no direct political say over the policies, like them or not. Moreover, the policies did not work!

---

[9] Rodrik 2011.　　[10] Bieling 2007.
[11] See discussion in Schmidt 2009a.　　[12] Keohane and Hoffmann 1991; Bickerton 2012.
[13] Zürn 2000.

How or whether the EU resolves its crisis of legitimacy will tell us a lot about the future of regional and global governance more generally. For the moment, despite the incremental changes that have ameliorated the situation, Eurozone governance appears stuck in limbo, with rules that it cannot or will not formally change, and without the tools to stabilize the Eurozone while fostering the conditions for economic growth for all of its members, not just some.

Re-Envisioning Eurozone Governance

So what could the EU do to resolve the Eurozone crisis, and help to defuse at least some of the major problems of legitimacy generated by that crisis? Any answer has to come to grips with the realities of member states' divided preferences, in particular between North and South; the institutional constraints imposed by the unanimity rule on treaties; the split-level legitimacy where output policies and throughput processes are generated at the EU level and input at the national; and the triple politicization of the EU—with increasing political contestation at the bottom, from the bottom up, and at the top.

The only Eurozone reform capable of responding to all such problems is one that provides for greater differentiation and decentralization in Eurozone governance. It is certainly the case that common rules and goals are necessary. But when we are considering the complexities of capitalism, where heterogeneity provides comparative advantage and there are so many different paths to growth, the one-size approach to economic policy via austerity and structural reform is—and has proven to be—a dangerous experiment. Better would be to decentralize the exercise of control as much as possible, and thereby to rebuild trust in the EU level by trusting the national level more.

More Coordination and Decentralization for Differentiated Eurozone Governance

One way to rethink Eurozone governance would be to change the ways in which the European Central Bank (ECB) deals with monetary policy and the Commission implements the European Semester. With regard to monetary policy, for example, in place of the ECB's fixed numerical targets, the Eurozone should allow greater differentiation in rates of deficit and debt, with differential country-specific targets. This would entail using the SGP criteria as general guidelines for variable yearly targets, depending upon the Eurozone's employment as well as inflation prospects, but with differentiated targets for individual euro members depending on where they are in their economic cycle, with the differentiated targets taken together adding up in the end to the overall target.[14]

This more fine-tuned approach to macroeconomic governance could begin with the ECB announcing an overall set of target numbers, followed by the Commission, in consultation with member states and experts, coming up with differentiated recommendations for member-state macroeconomic targets. Such recommendations could then be debated in the Eurogroup as well as the Commission, the European Parliament (EP), and the Council. This would ensure not only better working macroeconomic policies but also greater political legitimacy as a result of the public debates and deliberations, especially if national parliaments were also consulted. This process is not so very different in spirit from the kind of macroeconomic coordination provided by the Bundesbank in the 1960s and early 1970s in tandem with the social partners, when it signaled its targeted inflation rate ahead of the start of Germany's patterned wage-bargaining system, leaving management and labor to reach different bargains according to region and industrial sector. The alternative is of course simply to get rid of the rules altogether, and allow member states to go bankrupt, which is Martin Sandbu's preferred solution.[15] But there is little appetite for this, and not only because of the countries too big to fail with banks too big to bail, in particular in the absence of a European Monetary Fund and significant financial backstop for the Single Resolution Fund. It is also because the member states have bought into the SGP criteria as their macroeconomic *modus vivendi*. It is with this in mind that I propose transforming the criteria from rigid numbers into loose guidelines.

As for the Commission, rather than continuing with the seemingly top-down policies of the European Semester—however flexibly interpreted through derogations of the rules and recalibrations of the numbers—the whole exercise should become more bottom-up. The Semester already has an extraordinarily elaborate architecture of economic coordination, reaching into all the Eurozone ministries of finance and country economic experts. Such governance appears highly centralized and top-down with its seemingly restrictive rules and sanction-triggering numbers (even though the reality as we have already seen is more horizontal and consultative than the appearances). Worse, it has not been particularly effective, and has added to the problematic politicization at the bottom.

In order to make the European Semester more politically input-legitimate as well as more output-effective, why not decentralize Semester governance by

---

[14] The European Fiscal Board's recommendation in its September 2019 report to get rid of the deficit rule and instead rely on a simpler medium-term debt ceiling and a ceiling on the net primary expenditure growth for a period of three years, with an escape clause triggered on the basis of independent judgment, is a different variant on this kind of recommendation. See: https://ec.europa.eu/info/publications/2019-annual-report-european-fiscal-board_en

[15] Sandbu 2015.

making it more bottom-up than top-down? Why not use the existing coordination system to ensure that countries consult on their plans while themselves determining what works for their very specific economic growth models and varieties of capitalism? These could again be debated with the other member states in the Eurogroup as well as the Commission. But the decisions would be those of the countries, assuming that they can make good cases for why their policies would produce growth and prosperity for their country. Moreover, why not have the national productivity or fiscal councils act more as industrial policy councils rather than structural adjustment hawks? They could become the equivalent of consultative bodies providing recommendations to the government about how to move forward in terms of investment and growth while providing vital information to business and labor through widespread consultation, much as the French "Plan" did at its height in the 1950s and early 1960s. This would ensure greater member-state ownership of the European Semester because they would truly own their national plans. But they would additionally benefit from a coordination process in which they would learn from the examples of other countries' plans as well as from Commission recommendations and Council debates on their own plans.

Such changes in macroeconomic policy and the European Semester are likely to promote not only better economic performance but also much more political legitimacy at the national level. This is because they would put responsibility for the country's economics back in national governments' hands. This could in turn help counter the populist drift in many countries, as political parties of the mainstream right and left could begin again to differentiate their policies from one another, with proposals for different pathways to economic health and the public good. Portugal since 2015 is the demonstration case for this.

None of this will work, however, if member states continue to have to contend with excessive debt loads that weigh on their economies (Greece and Italy), or are left without significant investment funds to stimulate growth (Portugal, Spain, Italy, France). Some countries continue to have massive surpluses while failing to invest sufficiently (Germany and other smaller Northern European countries). At a minimum, banking union needs to be completed by a serious financial backstop and individual deposit insurance. Furthermore, some extra form of solidarity is necessary, with the European Stability Mechanism turned into a real European Monetary Fund (EMF), some form of mutualized debt instruments such as Eurobonds or safe assets,[16] EU investment resources that dwarf the Juncker Plan (as called for by Macron), and more. In other words, differentiated decentralization with continuing coordination for the Eurozone would also benefit from being accompanied by deeper fiscal integration. But in its absence, at the very least member states should be allowed to invest their own

---

[16] Claessens et al. 2012.

resources in infrastructure, education, and training, incurring long-term debt at low interest rates that do not count toward the deficit. This was actually what Juncker was expected to have proposed in his 2016 State of the Union speech to the EP, but then didn't![17]

More Solidarity Mechanisms across Crisis Areas and More Resources

If the EU is to win back hearts and minds, it also needs to add carrots to the sticks. For the Eurozone, many have already proposed some sort of unemployment risk sharing or reinsurance fund for all countries to pay into to use when their unemployment rises above a certain threshold, or a cyclical adjustment fund,[18] which has also been endorsed by the new President of the European Commission, Ursula von der Leyen. But the EU as a whole would equally benefit from an intra-European "EU mobility adjustment fund" to support the extra costs for social services and the retraining needs of workers in countries with greater than usual EU migrant worker inflows. This might have worked for the UK, with a mobility fund addressing Brexit supporters' fears about the impact of EU freedom of movement on the National Health Service. But even more significantly, it could benefit other member states with other kinds of out-migration as opposed to in-migration concerns. Such a fund, for example, could compensate Greece for the costs of educating the thousands of medical doctors who have gone to practice in Germany, or the Central and Eastern European countries such as Latvia or Romania suffering from massive brain drain.

More integration through new solidarity mechanisms has great advantages, especially if a EU mobility adjustment fund were accompanied by a European fund for refugee support. Different countries would benefit at different times from the funds, which could be triggered when any one country finds itself overburdened by the extra costs it incurs because of its openness to refugees as much as because of the asymmetric functioning of the Single Market and the Single Currency.

Different funding mechanisms are possible, including from member-state contributions, but the best would be from the EU's own resources, based on the monetary gains of the Single Market and Single Currency. This could involve using a proportion of VAT collected in trans-border transactions or of the (stalled) Financial Transactions Tax. And what about a EU "solidarity tax" levied on all

---

[17] It is also recommended by the 2019 European Fiscal Board report, as part of the 'golden rule' for public investment exempting expenditures in infrastructure, research, and education. See: https://ec.europa.eu/info/publications/2019-annual-report-european-fiscal-board_en, p. 77.

[18] Dullien 2014; Enderlein et al. 2013.

citizens and residents of the EU, which would have the added advantage of building a sense of citizen-to-citizen solidarity?[19] This might ensure that no one could claim any longer that the EU was a "transfer union" in which one or more member states paid for the rest. That said, if these are not on the cards for the moment, at least distributing the money the EU does have would help, by actually disbursing the structural funds to the regions most in need—which often receive less than 10 percent of that to which they are entitled.

Rethinking EU Governance as a "Soft Core" Europe

Our last question concerns how this re-envisioned Eurozone governance might fit with EU governance, and what the future of such EU governance might be. The EU was never going to become the United States of Europe. But is it going to become a *two-speed* Europe?[20] A Europe of concentric circles surrounding a compact core?[21] A Europe with a *hard core* centered on the Eurozone (as former French President Hollande first proposed and French President Macron then re-launched)? A Europe of different "Unions"?[22] A Europe of different "clubs" beyond the Single Market?[23] Or, failing these, a Europe completely à la carte, with "club governance," as many fear?[24]

Here, we steer a middle course through such debates, arguing that the future is likely to consist of a *soft-core* Europe made up of the multiple clusters of member states that overlap in their participation in the EU's many policy communities. In any such soft core, a large majority of member states will continue to belong to a plurality of policy communities, including the Eurozone, security and defense, and Schengen, in addition to more specialized cooperative arrangements. Such overlapping memberships should make for a more cohesive European Union in which all members feel some sense of belonging, even though countries will not all belong to all policy communities beyond the Single Market. For this to work, however, a single set of institutions remains a key requirement.

More Differentiated EU Integration through a "Soft Core" Europe

Differentiated integration is generally taken to mean that, beyond the Single Market to which all member states naturally belong, and assuming the non-negotiable requirements that members be democracies that respect the rule of law and accept the *acquis communautaires*, member states need not all proceed together at

---

[19] Schmidt 2009a.   [20] Piris 2012.
[21] Eg, Glienicker group 2013; Eiffel group 2014; Future of Europe Group 2012.
[22] Fabbrini 2015.   [23] Demertzis et al. 2018.   [24] Majone 2014; see also Fabbrini 2019.

the same rate to converge on the same single array of policies. Alongside the ideal of uniformity of the early years, in which all member states were expected to deepen integration in the same ways at the same speed, has long been the practice of differentiated integration, in which member states' differing needs and preferences have largely been accommodated.[25] EU leaders themselves implicitly acknowledged both the reality and the continued necessity of differentiated integration in the "Rome declaration" of March 25, 2017, when they stated: "We will act together, at different paces and intensity where necessary, while moving in the same direction, as we have done in the past, in line with the Treaties and keeping the door open to those who want to join later."[26]

The question is therefore not whether but *how* that differentiation will develop, since the EU is already highly differentiated. While all member states are part of the Single Market, which is the "community of communities," membership in other policy areas is highly variable. Such variable geometry includes Schengen borders, the Common Security and Defense Policy (CSDP), and the Charter of Fundamental Rights, in addition to "outside insiders" such as Norway, Iceland, and Switzerland, which participate in the Single Market, Schengen, and CSDP but do not have a vote. And then there is European Monetary Union, which, despite representing an area of deepest integration, also displays significant differentiation among EU member states. The Eurozone includes nineteen out of twenty-seven member states, but with differentiated integration through other member states' participation. All EU member states signed up to the Stability and Growth Pact, the European Semester, and the Six Pack; all EU member states except the United Kingdom and the Czech Republic agreed to abide by the "Golden Rule" of low deficits and debt of the Fiscal Compact; and all nineteen Eurozone members plus Bulgaria, Denmark, Poland, and Romania joined the Euro Plus Pact (focused on improving competitiveness, employment, and fiscal consolidation). But only Eurozone members are part of the Two-Pack and have access to the European Stability Mechanism (ESM), whereas banking union remains open to any other member states interested in joining but currently includes only Eurozone members.[27]

Given all this differentiation, the only realistic way to think about the EU's future organization is in terms of a *soft-core* Europe, in which some policy areas—such as security and defense policy and migration and refugee policy— still require deeper integration, while others such as the Eurozone arguably require less. The problem with a *two-speed* Europe is that it does not reflect the realities of what is already a *multi-speed* Europe, with different member states

[25] Schmidt 2009a, 2019b.
[26] "The Rome Declaration: Declaration of the leaders of 27 member states and of the European Council, the European Parliament and the European Commission," http://www.consilium.europa.eu/en/press/press-releases/2017/03/25-romedeclaration/
[27] For more detail see Schmidt 2019b.

participating in different policy communities. But a *hard-core* Europe coalesced around a small group of Eurozone countries is equally unworkable, given diverging ideas and interests among the main countries expected to coalesce.

Most importantly, a hard-core Europe assumes that France and Germany will be able to reach productive agreement on a wide range of future policies. This is open to question. The two countries remain far apart even on Eurozone policy, as we have already seen. Germany stands for restrictive budgetary policy to maintain stability, France for more expansionary policy to promote growth. Were such a hard core to be established, it would most likely be dominated by Germany. And for the moment at least, French President Macron's ambitious proposals for institutional reforms (such as a Eurozone Finance Minister) and fiscal capacity (worth several percentage points of GDP) have not borne fruit, receiving lukewarm responses at best from German leaders.

The creation of a smaller hard core around Germany and France seems unrealistic not only because of difficulties of agreement between the two key players but also because it could create a deep rift between the smaller core and the rest.[28] Furthermore, why assume that a cluster of member states that takes the lead in one policy area (ie, the Eurozone) would have the ability, let alone the will or imagination, to lead in the others (eg, in security or migration)? In fact, deeper integration in one area could instead produce an even higher degree of differentiation in other policy areas.[29]

The EU could retain its appeal for all, however, if the Eurozone were to be seen as just one of the EU's many policy "communities," and if the EU as a whole were seen as consisting of a *soft* core of multiple clusters of member states, in which any duo or trio of member states would take leadership in any given policy community. Different "leadership constellations," in other words, would allow for forward movement in different policy communities without the existence of a hard core, most notably in the Eurozone but also in CSDP.[30] As for migration policy, given the problems of reaching a common policy during the migrant crisis, this might be an area where deeper integration involving EU-wide agreement on principles of treatment could be accompanied by more differentiated integration regarding the modalities of implementation—with, for example, positive incentives in place of imposed quotas.[31] Such a "soft-core" vision of the EU is not far from the conceptualization of the EU as made up of "clubs" beyond a bare-bones common base largely co-terminus with the Single Market, with common rules regarding respect for democracy and social rights, and a common set of institutions including the legal system.[32] The main difference is that the soft-core vision sees members of all such policy communities involved in ongoing processes of interaction, as participants in the same sets of institutions and forums of debate.

---

[28] Emmanouilidis 2017.   [29] Tocci 2014.   [30] Balfour and Kirch 2017.
[31] Chebel d'Appolonia 2019.   [32] Demertzis et al. 2018.

Reforming the Institutional Rules

Seeing the future of EU integration as a differentiated process of member-state participation in different policy communities beyond the Single Market would thus allow for each "community" to develop further while constituting its own special system of governance. But for such differentiated integration to work effectively and legitimately, and for all member states to feel part of this *soft-core* EU, whatever their level of involvement, they need to have institutional voice and vote in the sectors in which they participate. This contradicts Prodi's earlier promise to the EU's neighborhood of "everything but institutions," since policy participation needs to come with institutional engagement. All member states should be able to exercise voice in all areas, but vote only in those areas in which they participate. Since all are members of the most significant policy community, the Single Market, this ensures that they will be voting a lot. But in areas of deepened differentiated integration such as the Eurozone, were member states to pledge their own resources to a EU budget, their representatives would be the only ones to vote on the budget, although everyone could discuss it. This means that there would not be a separate Eurozone Parliament or even more ambitious "European Assembly," as called for by Thomas Piketty and colleagues,[33] but rather a separate grouping of MEPs of contributing Eurozone members brought together to vote on such matters.

To make EU governance truly workable, the institutional decision-making rules also require revision. The unanimity rule for intergovernmental decision-making needs to be abandoned in many areas. In its place, supermajorities and opt-outs should become the main *modus operandi*. The most sensible replacement would be one setting up "constitutional" treaties amendable by two-thirds or four-fifths majorities. At the same time, many of the current treaty-based laws should become ordinary legislation, amendable by simple majority through the Community Method—as detailed by Dieter Grimm.[34] Thus, for example, while the Lisbon Treaty would remain a constitutional treaty, amendable however by two-thirds or four-fifths majorities, the various treaties involving the Eurozone should become ordinary legislation. This means that they would be open to amendment through political debates and compromise, and subject to the co-decision method—all of which would enhance EU political legitimacy. In other instances, such as the Fiscal Compact Treaty, rather than becoming ordinary legislation (unnecessary since its substance is largely contained in the Six Pack and Two Pack), it should be abolished altogether. But that would require intergovernmental decision. In the case of new legislation, moreover, whether ordinary or constitutional, opt-outs for individual member states should be allowed for exceptional

---

[33] See http://tdem.eu/le-traite/   [34] Grimm 2015.

reasons, such as where a member state's government, citizens, and/or parliament reject the initiative.[35]

The knotty problem remains the question of politics at the bottom. There can be no differentiation in the EU's core commitments to the rule of law and democratic principles guaranteeing free and fair elections, independence of the judiciary, and freedom of the press.[36] And representative institutions need to be reinforced. At the moment, the EU serves the purpose of the populists by hollowing out national representative institutions, enabling populists to claim that they are the true representatives of the people. To change this, the EU needs to do more to reinforce citizen representation and participation. For the Eurozone in particular, this at the very least demands more involvement of the European Parliament in decision-making, through a return to the Community Method. Turning Eurozone treaties into ordinary legislation, moreover, would help break the stalemate that makes it impossible to change such legislation (given the unanimity rule), and make them subject to political debate. And the EU as a whole must devise new means of encouraging citizen participation.

Conclusion

The future of EU governance remains open. Different options are on the table but the most workable possibility is a future as a *soft core* of multiple overlapping clusters of member states in the EU's many policy communities. In this context, increasing flexibility in the EU's governance processes along with decentralization to the benefit of the member states, where appropriate, is the best response to national level anti-EU politicization. But *soft-core* differentiation also has certain common institutional requirements, including one set of laws overseen by the Court of Justice of the European Union (CJEU) and ensured by national courts,[37] with one set of central, overarching institutions, including the Commission, Council, and European Parliament. That said, any number of specialized "made-to-purpose" institutions may be established to deepen integration in any given policy community, just as in the Eurozone the ECB is in charge of monetary policy and the ESM of providing bailout funds, with banking union having its own further set of institutions.

But this still leaves the question of how to construct a more legitimate EU, in particular given the problematic politicization of EU-related issues at the national level. Deeper integration must at the same time allow for greater national differentiation and decentralization. In this context, the consultative process at the national level would feed into EU-level recommendations, more in tune with

---

[35] Scharpf 2014.   [36] Kelemen 2019.   [37] See Kelemen 2019.

the changing realities in national and EU economies and responsive to the heterogeneous needs of member states' economies.

A final question: What hope can we have that any of these many suggestions for a more differentiated Eurozone governance within a more differentiated EU governance system will be carried out, and thereby build toward greater legitimacy in the policies, politics, and procedures? In the Eurozone's immediate future, little is likely to change radically, since we cannot expect EU institutional actors to reverse stability rules and numerical targets that have become embedded in their practices as well as touted in their discourses—even in the unlikely event that there were to be a shift in the political orientation of the EP and the Council. But this does not rule out the incremental alteration of the rules and recalculation of the numbers over the medium term. Such incremental change would depend upon whether the decision-making system as a whole had reached a new "democratic settlement" in which the co-decision method were the main *modus operandi*, with the EP brought into Eurozone governance alongside the Council, while the ECB returned to its more limited original responsibility for monetary and banking policy alone and the Commission acted more as enabler rather than enforcer in the European Semester.

As for the political economic ideas embodied in the evolving rules, although one cannot expect a paradigm shift back to neo-Keynesian expansionism, we could posit the emergence of a new set of ideas to replace such discredited concepts as "expansionary fiscal contraction."[38] In place of "contractionary expansionism" could come a new paradigm of "expansionary stability" or "stable expansionism" in which the stability rules are made compatible with growth-enhancing policies. If this were the outcome, then the Eurozone crisis would have done what past crises have been touted to do: after an initial period of delayed or failed responses, the EU muddles through to a more positive set of results while deepening its own integration. If this were to be the case, looking back thirty years hence, analysts might very well situate the beginning of the new political economic paradigm of "expansionary stability" at the current moment of incremental decentralized implementation of the rules and differentiated macroeconomic coordination. But this demands leadership from the EU's institutional actors, and vision. And for the moment at least, these remain in short supply while populism threatens.

---

[38] The concept was originally developed by Giavazzi and Pagano 1990.

Bibliography

Accornero, Guya and Ramos Pinto, Pedro (2015) "'Mild Mannered' Protest and Mobilization in Portugal under Austerity, 2010–2013," *West European Politics* 38 (3): 491–515

Afonso, Alexandre and Rennwald, Line (2018) "Social Class and the Changing Welfare State Agenda of Radical Right Parties in Europe" in *Welfare Democracies and Party Politics*, eds Philip Manow, Bruno Palier, and Hanna Schwander. Oxford: Oxford University Press

Agamben, Giorgio (1998) *Homo Sacer: Sovereign Power and Bare Life* Stanford: Stanford University Press

Alcidi, Cinzia A., Giovannini, Alessandro, and Piedrafita, Sonia (2014) *Enhancing the Legitimacy of EMU Governance* CEPS Special Report No. 98. Brussels (December)

Albertazzi, Daniele and Mueller, Sean (2017) "Populism and Liberal Democracy" in *The Populist Radical Right: A Reader*, ed. Cas Mudde. London: Routledge

Alesina, Alberto, Carloni, Dorian, and Lecce, Giampaolo (2012) "The Electoral Consequences of Large Fiscal Adjustments" in *Fiscal Policy after The Financial Crisis*, eds Alberto Alesina and Francesco Giavazzi. Chicago, IL: University of Chicago Press

Algan, Yann, Papaioannou, Elias, Passari, Evgenia, and Guriev, Sergei M. (2018) The European Trust Crisis and the Rise of Populism (February 22). EBRD Working Paper No. 208.

Alonso, Sonia and Ruiz-Rufino, Rubén (2018) "The Costs of Responsibility for the Political Establishment of the Eurozone (1999–2015)," *Party Politics* DOI: 10.1177/1354068818766182

Altiparmakis, Argyrios and Lorenzini, Jasmine (2018) "Disclaiming National Representatives: Protest Waves in Southern Europe during the Crisis," *Party Politics* 24 (1): 78–89

Andeweg, Rudy and Aarts, Kees (2017) "Studying Political Legitimacy," in *Myth and Reality of the Legitimacy Crisis*, eds Carolien van Ham, Jacques Thomassen, Kees Aarts, and Rudy Andeweg. Oxford: Oxford University Press

Apeldoorn, Bastiaan van (2013) "The European Capitalist Class and the Crisis of Its Hegemonic Project," in *Socialist Register 2014*. Pontypool: Merlin

Archibugi, Daniele, Mathias Koenig-Archibugi, and Raffaele Marchetti, eds (2012) *Global Democracy: Normative and Empirical Perspectives*. Cambridge: Cambridge University Press

Armingeon, Klaus and Baccaro, Lucio (2013) "The Sorrows of the Young Euro: Policy Responses to the Sovereign Debt Crisis," in *Coping with Crisis*, eds Nancy Bermeo and Jonas Pontusson. New York: Russell Sage Foundation

Art, David (2006) *The Politics of the Nazi Past in Germany and Austria*. New York: Cambridge University Press

Arzheimer, K. (2015) "The AfD: Finally a Successful Right-Wing Populist Eurosceptic Party for Germany?" *West European Politics* 38 (3): 535–56

Asmussen, Jörg (2012) "Building Trust in a World of Unknown Unknowns: Central Bank Communication between Markets and Politics in the Crisis." Speech at the European Communication Summit 2012, Brussels (July 6)

Auel, Katrin (2007) "Democratic Accountability and National Parliaments—Redefining the Impact of Parliamentary Scrutiny," *European Law Journal* 13 (4): 487–504

Auel, Katrin and Höing, Oliver (2014) "Parliaments in the Euro Crisis: Can the Losers of Integration Still Fight Back?" *Journal of Common Market Studies* 52 (6): 1184–93

Baccaro, Lucio and Pontusson, Jonas (2016) "Rethinking Comparative Political Economy: The Growth Model Perspective," *Politics and Society* 44 (2): 175–207

Bach, Stefan, Thiemann, Andreas and Zucco, Aline (2018) "Looking for the Missing Rich: Tracing the Top Tail of the Wealth Distribution." DIW (German Institute for Economic Research) Berlin Discussion Papers 1717 (January 23)

Baker, Andrew (2018) "Macroprudential Regimes and the Politics of Social Purpose," *Review of International Political Economy*, DOI: 10.1080/09692290.2018.1459780

Balfour, Rosa and Kirch, Anna-Lena (2017) "Can Core Europe Move Forward Without a Core?" *German Marshall Fund* Policy Brief no. 005

Ballesteros, Marta, Canetta, Emanuella, and Zaciu, Alexandru (2014) "European Citizens' Initiative—First Lessons of Implementation." Study for the Constitutional Affairs Committee, European Parliament. PE 509.982

Ban, Cornel (2016) *Ruling Ideas: How Global Neoliberalism Goes Local* New York: Oxford University Press

Ban, Cornel (2020) "The European Monetary Union: How Did the Euro Area Get a Lender of Last Resort?" in *Governance and Politics in the Post-Crisis European Union*, eds Ramona Coman, Amandine Crespy, and Vivien A. Schmidt. Cambridge: Cambridge University Press

Ban, Cornel and Patenaude, Brian (2019) "The Professional Politics of the Austerity Debate: A Comparative Field Analysis of the European Central Bank and the International Monetary Fund," *Public Administration* early view online: https://doi.org/10.1111/padm.12561

Ban, Cornel and Seabrooke, Leonard (2017) "From Crisis to Stability: How to Make the European Stability Mechanism Transparent and Accountable." Report for Transparency International EU, Brussels

Banchoff, Thomas (1999) "National Identity and EU Legitimacy in France and Germany" in *Legitimacy and the European Union: The Contested Polity*, eds T. Banchoff and M. P. Smith. London and New York: Routledge

Barbier, Cécile (2012) "La prise d'autorité de la Banque centrale européenne et les dangers démocratiques de la nouvelle gouvernance économique dans l'Union européenne." Research Paper for the *Observatoire Social Européen* no. 9 (November)

Barnett, Michael and Duvall, Raymond (2005) "Power in International Politics," *International Organization* 59 (4): 39–75

Basham, James and Roland, Aanor (2014) "Policy-Making of the European Central Bank during the Crisis: Do Personalities Matter?" Institute for International Political Economy Berlin. Working Paper no. 38/2014

Bastasin, Carlo (2015) *Saving Europe* 2nd edition. Washington DC: Brookings

Bastasin, Carlo (2019) *Secular Divergence* Washington DC: Brookings Brief

Batory, Agnes (2016) "Defying the Commission: Creative Compliance and Respect for the Rule of Law," *Public Administration* 94 (3): 685–99

Bauer, Michael and Becker, Stephan (2014) "The Unexpected Winner of the Crisis: The European Commission's Strengthened Role in Economic Governance," *Journal of European Integration* 36 (3): 213–29

Beaudonnet, Laurie and Gomez, Raul (2017) "Red Europe versus No Europe?" *West European Politics* 40 (2): 316–35

BBC (2019) "Inside Europe, Episode 2: Ten Years of Turmoil—Going for Broke (on the Eurozone Crisis)" Feb. 4, 2019 https://www.youtube.com/watch?v=Wl5vynTpYtg&t=3s

Beck, Ulrich (2013) *German Europe* Cambridge: Polity

Becker, Stefan, Bauer, Michael W., Connolly, Sara and Kassim, Hussein (2016) "The Commission: Boxed In and Constrained, but Still an Engine of Integration," *West European Politics* 39 (5): 1011–31

Beetham, David (1991) *The Legitimation of Power* London: Macmillan

Beetham, David (2013) "Revisiting Legitimacy, Twenty Years On" in *Legitimacy and Criminal Justice*, eds Justin Tankebee and Alison Liebling. Oxford: Oxford University Press

Beetham, David and Lord, Christopher (1998) *Legitimacy and the European Union* London: Longman

Bekkers, Victor and Edwards, Arthur (2007) "Legitimacy and Democracy" in *Governance and the Democratic Deficit*, eds V. J. J. M. Bekkers, Geske Dijkstra, Arthur Edwards, and Menno Fener. Aldershot: Ashgate

Bellamy, Richard (2010) "Democracy Without Democracy? Can the EU's Democratic 'Outputs' Be Separated from the Democratic 'Inputs' Provided by Competitive Parties and Majority Rule?" *Journal of European Public Policy* 17(1): 2–19

Bellamy, Richard and Weale, Albert (2015) "Political Legitimacy and European Monetary Union: Contracts, Constitutionalism and the Normative Logic of Two-Level Games," *Journal of European Public Policy* 22 (2): 257–74

Benz, Arthur and Papadopoulos, Yannis (2006) *Governance and Democracy: Comparing National, European and International Experience* London: Routledge

Beramendi, Pablo, Häusermann, Silja, Kitschelt Herbert, and Kriesi, Hanspeter, eds (2015) *The Politics of Advanced Capitalism* Cambridge: Cambridge University Press

Berezin, Mabel (2009) *Illiberal Politics in Neoliberal Times* New York: Cambridge University Press

Bergmann, Eirikur (2017) *Nordic Nationalism and Right Wing Populist Politics* London: Palgrave Macmillan

Bes, Bart Joachim (2016) "Europe's Executive in Stormy Weather: How Does Politicization Affect Commission Officials' Attitudes?" *Comparative European Politics* 15 (4): 533–56

Bianculli, Andrea C., Fernández-i-Marín, Xavier and Jordana, Jacint, eds (2014) *Accountability and Regulatory Governance: Audiences, Control, and the Politics of Regulation* Basingstoke: Palgrave

Bickerton, Christopher (2012) *European Integration: From Nation States to Member States* Oxford: Oxford University Press

Bickerton, Christopher J., Hodson, Dermot, Puetter Uwe (2015) "The New Intergovernmentalism and the Study of European Integration" in *The New Intergovernmentalism*, eds Christopher J. Bickerton, Dermot Hodson, and Puetter Uwe. Oxford: Oxford University Press

Biegón, D. (2013) "Specifying the Arena of Possibilities: Post-Structuralist Narrative Analysis and the European Commission's Legitimation Strategies," *Journal of Common Market Studies* 51 (2): 194–211

Bieling, Hans-Jürgen (2007) "The Other Side of the Coin: Conceptualizing the Relationship between Business and the State in the Age of Globalisation," *Business and Politics* 9 (3): 1–20

Blyth, Mark (2013) *Austerity: The History of a Dangerous Idea* Oxford: Oxford University Press

Bobba, Giuliano (2019) "Social Media Populism: Features and 'Likeability' of Lega Nord Communication on Facebook," *European Political Science* 18 (1): 11–23

Bohman, J. (1996) *Public Deliberation—Pluralism, Complexity and Democracy* Cambridge, MA: MIT Press

Bokhorst, David J. (2019) *Governing Imbalances in the Economic and Monetary Union. A Political Economy Analysis of the Macroeconomic Imbalance Procedure* PhD Dissertation, University of Amsterdam

Bonikowski, B. (2017) "Ethno-Nationalist Populism and the Mobilization of Collective Resentment," *The British Journal of Sociology* 68 (1): 181–213

Boomgaarden, H. G. and de Vreese, C. H. (2016) "Do European Elections Create a European Public Sphere?" in *(Un)intended Consequences of European Parliamentary Elections*, eds W. van der Brug and C. H. de Vreese. Oxford: Oxford University Press

Bordignon, F. and Ceccarini, L. (2013) "Five Stars and a Cricket: Beppe Grillo Shakes Italian Politics," *South European Society and Politics* 18 (4): 427–49

Bornschier, S. (2010) *Cleavage Politics and the Populist Right*. Philadelphia: Temple University Press

Borowiak, Craig (2011) *Accountability and Democracy: The Pitfalls and Promise of Popular Control* New York: Oxford University Press

Borriello, Arthur (2017) "'There is no alternative': How Italian and Spanish Leaders' Discourse Obscured the Political Nature of Austerity," *Discourse & Society* 28 (3): 241–61

Börzel, Tanja (2001) "Non-Compliance in the European Union. Pathology or Statistical Artefact?" *Journal of European Public Policy* 8 (5): 803–24

Börzel, Tanja A. and Risse, Thomas (2018) "From the Euro to the Schengen Crises: European Integration Theories, Politicization, and Identity Politics," *Journal of European Public Policy* 25 (1): 83–108

Bosch, Agustí and Durán, Iván M. (2017) "How Does Economic Crisis Impel Emerging Parties on the Road to Elections? The Case of the Spanish Podemos and Ciudadanos," *Party Politics* https://doi.org/10.1177/1354068817710223

Bosco, Anna, and Verney, Susannah (2012) "Electoral Epidemic: The Political Cost of Economic Crisis in Southern Europe, 2010–11," *South European Society and Politics* 17 (2): 129–54

Boswell, Christina (2018) *Manufacturing Political Trust: Targets and Performance Management in Public Policy* Cambridge: Cambridge University Press

Bovens, Mark (2007) "Analysing and Assessing Accountability: A Conceptual Framework," *European Law Journal* 13 (4): 447–68

Bovens, Mark (2010) "Two Concepts of Accountability: Accountability as a Virtue and as a Mechanism," *West European Politics* 33 (5): 946–67

Bovens, M. Curtin, D, and t'Hart, P., eds (2010) *The Real World of EU Accountability* Oxford: Oxford University Press

Bovens, Mark, Goodin, Robert E., and Schillemans, Thomas, eds (2014a) *The Oxford Handbook of Public Accountability* Oxford: Oxford University Press

Bovens, Mark, Schillemans, Thomas, and Goodin, Robert E. (2014b) "Public Accountability" in *The Oxford Handbook of Public Accountability*, eds Mark Bovens, Robert E. Goodin, and Thomas Schillemans. Oxford: Oxford University Press

Bovens, Mark and Curtin, Dierdre (2016) "An Unholy Trinity of EU Presidents? Political Accountability of EU Executive Power" in *The End of the Eurocrats' Dream: Adjusting to European Diversity*, eds Damian Chalmers, Markus Jachtenfuchs, and Christian Joerges. Cambridge: Cambridge University Press

Bozzini, Emanuela and Smismans, Stijn (2016) "More Inclusive European Governance through Impact Assessments" *Comparative European Politics* 14 (1): 89–106

Braun, Benjamin (2013) "Preparedness, Crisis Management and Policy Change: The Euro Area at the Critical Juncture of 2008–2013," *British Journal of Political and International Relations* 17 (3): 419–41

Braun, Benjamin (2017) "Two Sides of the Same Coin? Independence and Accountability of the European Central Bank." Report for Transparency International EU (Brussels)

Braun, Benjamin and Hübner, Martina (2018) "Fiscal Fault, Financial Fix? Capital Markets Union and the Quest for Macroeconomic Stabilization in the Euro Area," *Competition & Change*, early view online at DOI: 10.1177/1024529417753555

Braun, Daniela, Hutter, Swen, and Kerscher, Alena (2016) "What Type of Europe? The Salience of Polity and Policy Issues in European Parliament Elections," *European Union Politics* 17 (4): 570–92

Braun, Daniela and Schmitt, Hermann (2018) "Different Emphases, Same Positions? The Election Manifestos of Political Parties in the EU Multilevel Electoral System Compared," *Party Politics* https://doi.org/10.1177/1354068818805248

Brazys, Samuel and Regan, Aidan (2017) "The Politics of Capitalist Diversity in Europe: Explaining Ireland's Divergent Recovery from the Euro Crisis," *Perspectives on Politics* 15 (2): 411–27

Bréchon, Pierre (2019) "Les naufragés du Parti socialiste" in *Histoire d'une Révolution Électorale (2015–2018)*, eds Bruno Cautrès and Anne Muxel. Paris: Classiques Garnier

Bremer, Björn (2018) "The Missing Left? Economic Crisis and the Programmatic Response of Social Democratic Parties in Europe," *Party Politics* 24 (1): 23–38

Browning, Christopher R. (2004) *The Origins of the Final Solution: The Evolution of Nazi Jewish Policy, September 1939–March 1942.* London: Random House/William Heinemann

Brunnermeier, Markus K., James, Harold, and Landau, Jean-Pierre (2016) *The Euro and the Battle of Ideas.* Princeton: Princeton University Press

Buchanan, Allen, and Keohane, Robert O. (2006) The Legitimacy of Global Governance Institutions. *Ethics & International Affairs* 20 (4): 405–37

Buiter, Willem H., Corsetti, Giancarlo, and Pesenti, Paolo A. (1998) *Financial Markets and European Monetary Cooperation: The Lessons of the 1992–3 Exchange Rate Mechanism Crisis* Cambridge: Cambridge University Press

Buiter, W. and Rahbari, E. (2012) "The European Central Bank as Lender of Last Resort for Sovereigns in the Eurozone," *Journal of Common Market Studies* Annual Review 50: 6–35

Bulmer, Simon and Paterson, William (2013) "Germany as the EU's Reluctant Hegemon? Of Economic Strength and Political Constraints," *Journal of European Public Policy* 20 (10): 1387–405

Bürgin, Alexander (2018) "Intra- and Inter-Institutional Leadership of the European Commission President: An Assessment of Juncker's Organizational Reforms," *Journal of Common Market Studies* 56 (4): 837–53

Buti, Marco (2017) "Europe, ten years after the crisis: out of the tunnel?" https://ec.europa.eu/info/sites/info/files/2017.10.10_columbia_the_response_to_the_crisis_marco_buti.pdf

Buti, Marco, and A. Turrini (2017) "Overcoming Eurozone wage inertia," VoxEU.org (6 October)

Caiani, Manuela, Della Porta, Donatella, and Wageman, Claudius (2012) *Mobilizing on the Extreme Right: Germany, Italy, and the United States* Oxford: Oxford University Press

Caporaso, James (2018) "Europe's Triple Crisis and the Uneven Role of Institutions: the Euro, Refugees, and Brexit," *Journal of Common Market Studies* online at https://doi.org/10.1111/jcms.12746

Caporaso, J. and Tarrow, S. (2008) "Polanyi in Brussels: European Institutions and the Embedding of Markets in Society." RECON Online Working Paper 2008/01. www.reconproject.eu/projectweb/portalproject/RECONWorkingPapers.html

Caramani, Daniele (2017) "Will vs. Reason: Populist and Technocratic Challenges to Representative Democracy," *American Political Science Review* 111 (1): 54–67

Caritas Europe (2015) see: https://www.caritas.eu/poverty-inequalities-rise/

Carstensen, Martin B. (2011) "Paradigm Man vs. the Bricoleur: An Alternative Vision of Agency in Ideational Change," *European Political Science Review* 3 (1): 147–67

Carstensen, Martin B. and Schmidt, Vivien A. (2016) "Power Through, Over and In Ideas: Conceptualizing Ideational Power in Discursive Institutionalism," *Journal of European Public Policy* 23 (3): 318–37

Carstensen, Martin B. and Schmidt, Vivien A. (2018a) "Power and Changing Modes of Governance in the Euro Crisis" *Governance* 31 (4): 609–24

Carstensen, Martin B. and Schmidt, Vivien A. (2018b) "Ideational Power and Pathways to Legitimation in the Euro Crisis," *Review of International Political Economy* 2 (6): 753–78

Cashore, Benjamin (2002) "Legitimacy and the Privatization of Environmental Governance," *Governance* 15 (4): 503–29

Cautrès, Bruno and Muxel, Anne, eds (2019) *Histoire d'une Révolution Électorale (2015–2018)*. Paris: Classiques Garnier

CEC (2006) The EU Economy 2006 Review, *European Economy* No.6, Brussels

Ceccarini, Luigi, Diamanti, Ilvo, and Lazar, Marc (2012) "Fine di un ciclo: la destrutturazione del sistema partitico italiano" in *Politica in Italia*, eds A. Bosco and D. McDonnell. Bologna: Il Mulino

Ceccarini, Luigi and Bordignon, Fabio (2016) "The Five Stars Continue to Shine: The Consolidation of Grillo's 'Movement Party' in Italy," *Contemporary Italian Politics* 8 (2): 131–59

Centeno, Mario (2018) "Portugal's Economic Recovery: From Sick Man to Poster Boy" Center for European Studies, Harvard University (April 18) See video at: https://ces.fas.harvard.edu/recordings/portugals-economic-recovery-from-sick-man-to-poster-boy

Cerutti, Furio (2008) "Why Legitimacy and Political Identity Matter in the European Union" in *The Search for a European Identity*, eds F. Cerutti and S. Lucarelli. London: Routledge

Chalmers, Damian (2013) "Democratic Self-Government in Europe: Domestic Solutions to the EU Legitimacy Crisis," *Policy Network Paper* (May), p. 10

Chalmers, Damian, Davies, Gareth, and Monti, Giorgio (2014) *European Union Law*, 3rd ed. Cambridge: Cambridge University Press

Champeau, Serge, Closa, Carlos, Innerarity, Danile, and Maduro, Miguel P. (2015) *The Future of Europe* London: Rowman and Littlefield

Charalambous, Giorgos (2011) "All the Shades of Red: Examining the Radical Left's Euroscepticism," *Contemporary Politics* 17 (3): 299–320

Chebel d'Appolonia, Ariane (2019) "EU Migration Policy and Border Controls: From Chaotic to Cohesive Differentiation," *Comparative Political Economy* 17 (2): 192–208

Cheneval, Francis and Frank Schimmelfennig (2013) "The Case for Demoicracy in the European Union," *Journal of Common Market Studies* 51 (2): 334–50

Chwieroth, Jeffrey M. (2010) *Capital Ideas: The IMF and the Rise of Financial Liberalization* Princeton, NJ: Princeton University Press

Cini, Michelle (2013) "EU Decision-Making on Inter-Institutional Agreements: Defining (Common) Rules of Conduct for European Lobbyists and Public Servants," *West European Politics* 36 (6): 1143–58

Claessens, Stijn, Mody, Ashoka, and Vallee, Shahin (2012) "Paths to Eurobonds," Bruegel Working Paper 2012/10. http://www.bruegel.org/publications/publication-detail/publication/733-paths-to-eurobonds/

Clements, Ben, Nanou, Kyriaki, and Real-Dato, José (2018) "Economic Crisis and Party Responsiveness on the Left–Right Dimension in the European Union," *Party Politics* 24 (1): 52–64

Clift, Ben (2018) *The IMF and the Politics of Austerity in the Wake of the Global Financial Crisis* Oxford: Oxford University Press

Clift, Ben (2012) "French Responses to the Global Economic Crisis: The Political Economy of 'Post-Dirigisme' and New State Activism" in *The Consequences of the Global Financial Crisis: The Rhetoric of Reform and Regulation*, eds Wyn Grant and Graham Wilson. Oxford: Oxford University Press

Coen, David, ed. (2007) *EU Lobbying: Empirical and Theoretical Studies* London: Routledge

Coen, David and Katsaitis, Alexander (2015) "Institutional and Constitutional Aspects of Special Interest Representation," Study for the AFCO Committee of the European Parliament PE 519.229 http://www.europarl.europa.eu/committees/en/supporting/analyses/search.html

Coen, David and Katsaitis, Alexander (2019) "Between Cheap Talk and Epistography: The Logic of Interest Group Access in the European Parliament's Committee Hearings," *Public Administration* 97 (4) 754–9

Coen, David and Richardson, Jeremy (2009) *Lobbying in the European Union: Institutions, Actors, and Issues* Oxford: Oxford University Press

Cohen, J. and Rogers, J. (1992) "Secondary Associations and Democratic Governance," *Politics and Society* 20 (4): 391–472

Coman, Ramona (2018) "How Have EU 'Fire-Fighters' Sought to Douse the Flames of the Eurozone's Fast- and Slow-Burning Crises? The 2013 Structural Funds Reform," *The British Journal of Politics and International Relations* 20 (3): 540–54

Coman, Ramona (2019a) "Why and How Do Think Tanks Expand Their Networks in Times of Crisis: The case of Bruegel and the Centre for European Policy Studies," *Journal of European Public Policy* 26 (2): 286–301

Coman, Ramona (2019b) "The Coordination of Macroeconomic Policies in the Aftermath of the Eurozone Crisis: Shaping Policies through Executive Politics" in *Rethinking the European Union and its Global Role from the 20th to the 21st Century. Liber Amicorum Mario Telo*, eds J. M. De Waele, G. Grevi, F. Ponjaert, and A. Weyembergh. Brussels: Editions de l'Université Libre de Bruxelles

Coman, Ramona, Crespy, Amandine, and Schmidt, Vivien A., eds (2020) *Governance and Politics in the Post-Crisis European Union* Cambridge: Cambridge University Press

Coman, Ramona and Sbaraglia, F. (2018) "Gouverner par la conditionnalité ou la flexibilité? La réforme de la politique de cohésion de l'Union européenne (2014–2020)," *Gouvernement et action publique* 2018/3: 35–55. DOI 10.3917/gap.183.0035

Constânci, Vítor (2013) Speech by Vice President of the ECB at the Bank of Greece in Athens, May 23, 2013

Copeland, Paul and Daly, Mary (2018) "The European Semester and EU Social Policy," *Journal of Common Market Studies* 56 (5): 1001–1018

Copelovitch, M., Frieden, J., and Walter, S. (2016) "The Political Economy of the Euro Crisis," *Comparative Political Studies* 49 (7): 811–40

Corbetta, P. and Gualmini, E. (2013) *Il Partito di Grillo* Bologna: Il Mulino

Costa, Olivier (2009) "Comment évaluer le parlement européen et ses membres?" in *Que Fait l'Europe*, eds Renaud Dehousse, Florence Deloche, and Sophie Jacquot. Paris: Presses de Sciences Po

Costa, Olivier, and Magnette, Paul (2003) "Idéologies et changement institutionnel dans l'Union européenne: Pourquoi les gouvernements ont-ils constamment renforcé le Parlement européen?" *Politique Européenne* 9: 49–7

Council of Europe (2013) "Safeguarding Human Rights in Times of Economic Crisis," Issue Paper, November

Cramme, Olaf and Hobolt, Sara B., eds (2015) *Democratic Politics in a European Union under Stress* Oxford: Oxford University Press

Crespy, Amandine (2012) *Qui a peur de Bolkestein?* Paris: Economica

Crespy, Amandine (2013) "Deliberative Democracy and the European Union: A Reappraisal of Conflict," *Political Studies* 62 (S1): 81–98

Crespy, Amandine (2016) *Welfare Markets in Europe* Basingstoke: Palgrave Macmillan

Crespy, Amandine (2018) "Relance de l'Europe: le double échec d'Emmanuel Macron" *Le Vif* (26 April) https://www.levif.be/actualite/international/relance-de-l-europe-le-double-echec-d-emmanuel-macron/article-opinion-832233.html

Crespy, Amandine and Menz, George (2015) "Commission Entrepreneurship and the Debasing of Social Europe Before and After the Eurocrisis," *Journal of Common Market Studies* 53 (4): 753–68

Crespy, Amandine and Parks, Louisa (2017) "The Connection between Parliamentary and Extra-Parliamentary Opposition in the EU: From ACTA to the Financial Crisis," *Journal of European Integration* 39 (4): 453–67

Crespy, Amandine and Schmidt, Vivien A. (2014) "The Clash of Titans: France, Germany and the Discursive Double Game of EMU Reform," *Journal of European Public Policy* 21 (8): 1085–101

Crespy, Amandine and Schmidt, Vivien A. (2017) "The EU's Economic Governance in 2016: Beyond Austerity?" in *Social Policy in the European Union: State of Play 2017*, eds B. Vanhercke, S. Sabato, and D. Bouget. Bruxelles/ETUI

Crespy, Amandine and Vanheuverzwijn, Pierre (2017) "What 'Brussels' Means by Structural Reforms: Empty Signifier or Constructive Ambiguity?" *Comparative European Politics* 7 (1): 92–111

Crouch, Colin (2004) *Post-Democracy* Cambridge: Polity Press

Crum, Ben (2012) *Learning from the EU Constitutional Treaty* London: Routledge

Crum, Ben (2013) "Saving the Euro at the Cost of Democracy?" *Journal of Common Market Studies* 51 (4): 614–30

Crum, Ben (2017) "National Parliaments and Constitutional Transformation in the EU," *European Constitutional Law Review* 13 (4): 817–35

Crum, Ben (2018) "Parliamentary Accountability in Multilevel Governance: What Role for Parliaments in Post-Crisis EU Economic Governance?" *Journal of European Public Policy* 25 (2): 268–86

Crum, Ben and Curtin, Deirdre (2015) "The Challenge of Making European Union Executive Power Accountable" in *The European Union: Democratic Principles and Institutional Architectures in Times of Crisis*, ed. Simona Piattoni. Oxford: Oxford University Press

Dahl, Robert A. (1965) "Reflections on Opposition in Western Democracies," *Government & Opposition*, 1(1): 7–24

Dahl, Robert A. (1968) "Power" in *International Encyclopedia of the Social Sciences*, vol 12, New York: Free Press

Darvas, Szolt and Leandro Alvaro (2015) "The Limitations of Policy Coordination in the Euro Area under the European Semester," *Bruegel Policy Contribution* 2015/19 (November)

Darvas, Szolt and Alvaro, Leandro (2016) "Implementation of European Semester Recommendations Worsens Further," Bruegel blog post, June 15, 2016, www.bruegel. org

De Bruycker, Iskander (2019) "Democratically Efficient, yet Responsive? How Politicization Facilitates Responsiveness in the European Union," *Journal of European Public Policy*, early view online at https://doi.org/10.1080/13501763.2019.1622587

De Grauwe, Paul (2006) "What Have We Learnt about Monetary Integration since the Maastricht Treaty?" *Journal of Common Market Studies* 44 (4): 711–30

De Grauwe, Paul (2013) "The Political Economy of the Euro," *Annual Review of Political Science* 16: 153–70

De Grauwe, Paul (2016) "Monetary Policy and Public Investment" *CEPS Comment*, Jan. 14 https://www.ceps.eu/publications/monetary-policy-and-public-investment

De Grauwe, Paul and Ji, Y. (2012) "Mispricing of Sovereign Risk and Macroeconomic Stability in the Eurozone," *Journal of Common Market Studies* 50 (6): 866–80

De Grauwe, Paul and Ji, Yuemei (2013) "Are Germans Really Poorer than Greeks, Italians, and Spaniards?" *Vox* (April 16) https://voxeu.org/article/are-germans-really-poorer-spaniards-italians-and-greeks

De la Porte, Caroline, and Heins, Elke (2015) "A New Era of European Integration? Governance of Labour Market and Social Policy Since the Sovereign Debt Crisis," *Comparative European Politics* 13 (1): 8–28

De Rynck, Stefaan (2016) "Banking on a Union: The Politics of Changing Eurozone Banking Supervision," *Journal of European Public Policy* 23 (1): 119–35

De Vries, Catherine (2017) "The Cosmopolitan-Parochial Divide: Changing Patterns of Party and Electoral Competition in the Netherlands and Beyond," *Journal of European Public Policy* OnlineFirst, doi.org/10.1080/13501763.2017.1339730

De Vries, Catherine (2018) *Euroskepticism and the Future of European Integration* Oxford: Oxford University Press

De Wilde, P. and Zürn, M. (2012) "Can the Politicisation of European Integration Be Reversed?" *Journal of Common Market Studies* 50 (1): 137–53

Debomey, D. (2016) *The EU, Despite Everything? European Public Opinion in the Age of the Crisis (2005–2015)* Paris: Notre Europe

Degner, Hanno and Leuffen, Dirk (2018) "Franco-German Cooperation and the Rescuing of the Eurozone," *European Union Politics* early view, DOI: 10.1177/1465116518811076

Dehousse, Renaud (2011a) "Référendum grec: une irresponsabilité choquante," *Telos* (Nov. 2) http://www.telos-eu.com/fr/article/referendum-grec-une-irresponsabilite-choquante

Dehousse, Renaud (2011b) "Are EU Legislative Procedures Truly Democratic?" Paper presented at the Harvard University Center for European Studies. Boston, March 2

Dehousse, Renaud (2016) "Why Has EU Macroeconomic Governance Become More Supranational?" *Journal of European Integration* 38 (5): 617–31

Della Porta, Donatella, ed. (2009) *Democracy in Social Movements* Basingstoke: Palgrave Macmillan

Della Porta, D., Fernandez, Joseba, Kouki, Hara and Mosca, Lorenzo (2017) *Movement Parties against Austerity* Cambridge: Polity Press

Dellmuth, Lisa M., and Tallberg, Jonas (2015) "The Social Legitimacy of International Organisations: Interest Representation, Institutional Performance, and Confidence Extrapolation in the United Nations," *Review of International Studies* 41 (3): 451–75

Delors, Jacques (1989) *Report on Economic and Monetary Union in the European Community* (Delors Report), April 17, http://aei.pitt.edu/1007

Delpla, Jacques, and Von Weizsäcker, Jakob (2011) "Eurobonds: The Blue Bond Concept and Its Implications," Bruegel Policy Contribution, Issue 2011/02, (March) http://bruegel.org/2011/03/eurobonds-the-blue-bond-concept-and-its-implications/

Demertizis, Maria, Pisani-Ferry, Jean, Sapir, André, Wieser, Thomas, and Wolff, Guntram (2018) "One Size Does Not Fit All: European Integration by Differentiation," *Bruegel Policy Brief*, issue 3 (September)

Diamond, Larry and Morlino, Leonardo (2016) "The Quality of Democracy" in *In Search of Democracy*, ed. Larry Diamond. London: Routledge

Dijkstra, Lewis, Poelman, Hugo, and Rodríguez-Pose, Andrés (2018) "The Geography of EU Discontent," Working Paper, Directorate-General for Regional and Urban Policy, European Commission. WP 12/2018

Dinan, Desmond (2014) "Governance and Institutions: The Unrelenting Rise of the European Parliament," *Journal of Common Market Studies* Annual Review 52: 109–24

Dinan, Desmond (2015) "Governance and Institutions: The Year of the *Spitzenkandidaten*," *Journal of Common Market Studies* Annual Review 53: 93–107

Dingwerth, Klaus (2007) *The New Transnationalism: Transnational Governance and Democratic Legitimacy* New York: Palgrave Macmillan

Draghi, Mario (2011) "Introductory Statement to the Press Conference (with Q&A)." Frankfurt: ECB (November 3). http://www.ecb.int/press/pressconf/2011/html/is111103.en.htm

Draghi, Mario (2012) Speech by Mario Draghi, President of the European Central Bank at the Global Investment Conference in London (July 26) https://www.ecb.europa.eu/press/key/date/2012/html/sp120726.en.html

Draghi, Mario (2015a) Introductory speech by Mario Draghi, President of the ECB, "Structural Reforms, Inflation and Monetary Policy," ECB Forum on Central Banking Sintra (May 22) https://www.ecb.europa.eu/press/key/date/2015/html/sp150522.en.html

Draghi, Mario (2015b) "Introductory statement by Mario Draghi, President of the ECB," Hearing at the European Parliament's Economic and Monetary Affairs Committee Brussels (November 12) https://www.ecb.europa.eu/press/key/date/2015/html/sp151112.en.html

Drahokoupil, J. and Myant, M. (2011) *Transition Economies: Political Economy in Russia, Eastern Europe, and Central Asia* Hoboken, NJ: John Wiley & Sons

Drudi, Francesco, Alain Durré, and Mogelli, Francesco Paolo (2012) "The Interplay of Economic Reforms and Monetary Policy: The Case of the Eurozone," *Journal of Common Market Studies* 50 (6): 881–98

Dryzek, J. and Niemeyer, S. (2008) "Discursive Representation," *American Political Science Review* 102 (4): 481–92

Dullien, Sebastian (2014) "The Macroeconomic Stabilisation Impact of a European Basic Unemployment Insurance Scheme," *Intereconomics* 49 (4): 189–93

Dullien, Sebastian and Guérot, Ulrike (2012) "The Long Shadow of Ordoliberalism: Germany's Approach to the Euro Crisis," *European Council on Foreign Relations*, Policy Brief 49

Dunphy, Richard (2004) *Contesting Capitalism? Left Parties and European Integration* Manchester: Manchester University Press

Dür, Andreas, and Mateo, Gemma. (2012) "Who Lobbies the European Union? National Interest Groups in a Multilevel Polity," *Journal of European Public Policy* 19: 969–87

Dür, Andreas, Marshall, David, and Bernhagen, Patrick (2019) *The Political Influence of Business in the European Union* Ann Arbor: University of Michigan Press

Dyson, Kenneth, ed. (2002) *European States and the Euro* Oxford: Oxford University Press

Dyson, Kenneth and Featherstone, Kevin (1996) "Italy and EMU as a '*Vincolo Esterno*': Empowering the Technocrats, Transforming the State," *Southern European Society and Politics* 1 (2): 272–99

Dyson, Kenneth and Featherstone, Kevin (1999) *The Road to Maastricht: Negotiating Economic and Monetary Union* Oxford: Oxford University Press

Easton, David (1965) *A Systems Analysis of Political Life* New York: Wiley

Efstathiou, Konstantino and Wolff, Guntram B. (2019a) "What Drives National Implementation of EU Policy Recommendations?" *Bruegel Working Paper* Issue 4 (April 25) https://bruegel.org/2019/04/what-drives-national-implementation-of-eu-policy-recommendations/

Efstathiou, Konstantino and Wolff, Guntram B. (2019b) "EU Policy Recommendations: A Stronger Legal Framework is not enough to foster National Compliance," *Vox Blog Post* https://voxeu.org/article/stronger-eu-legal-framework-not-enough-foster-national-compliance

Eichengreen, Barry (1991) "Is Europe an Optimum Currency Area?" National Bureau of Economic Research NBER Working Paper 3579 http://www.nber.org/papers/w3579.pdf

Eichengreen, Barry (2012) "European Monetary Integration with the Benefit of Hindsight," *Journal of Common Market Studies* 50 (1): 123–36

Eiffel Group (2014) *For a Euro Community*, February 14, 2014, http://www.bruegel.org/about/person/view/389-the-eiffel-group

Emmanouilidis, Janis A. (2017) "The Future of a More Differentiated E(M)U," Paper prepared for the "EU60: Refounding Europe" initiative *Istituto Affari Internazionali* Rome (February 14)

Emmeneger, Patrick, Häusermann, Silja, Palier, Bruno, and Seeleib-Kaiser, Martin (2012) *The Age of Dualization: The Changing Face of Inequality in Deindustrializing Societies* Oxford: Oxford University Press

Enderlein, H., coordinator (2012) Completing the Euro—A Road Map towards Fiscal Union in Europe. Report of the "Tommaso Padoa-Schioppa Group." Notre Europe Study No. 92. http://renesmits.eu/CompletingTheEuro_ReportPadoa-SchioppaGroup_NE_June2012_011.pdf

Enderlein, Henrik, Guttenberg, Lucas, and Spiess, Jann (2013) "Blueprint for a Cyclical Shock Insurance in the Euro Area," Notre Europe/Jacques Delor Institute Studies and Reports (September). http://www.institutdelors.eu/wp-content/uploads/2018/01/blueprintforacyclicalshockinsurancene-jdisept2013.pdf?pdf=ok

Epstein, Rachel and Rhodes, Martin (2016) "The Political Dynamics behind Europe's New Banking Union," *West European Politics* 39 (3): 415–37

Eriksen, E. O., ed. (2006) *Making the European Polity—Reflexive Integration in Europe* London: Routledge

Erne, Roland (2015) "A Supranational Regime that Nationalizes Social Conflict: Explaining European Trade Unions' Difficulties in Politicizing European Economic Governance," *Labor History* 56 (3): 345–68

Eurofound (2017) *Occupational Change and Wage Inequality: European Jobs Monitor 2017* Publications Office of the European Union, Luxembourg

European Commission (2015) "New guidelines to the European Parliament, the EU Council, the ECB, the EIB, the Economic and Social Committee, and the Committee of the Regions for making the best use of the flexibility within the existing rules of the Stability and Growth Pact" COM(2015)12 final, January 13, 2015

European Commission (2016) Communication: "Towards a positive fiscal stance for the Euro area" COM(2016)727 (November 16)

European Commission (2019) "2019 European Semester: country-specific recommendations" COM(2019) 500 final (June 5, 2019)

European Parliament (2015) "The Impact of the Crisis on Fundamental Rights across Member States of the EU: Comparative Analysis. Study prepared for the Committee on Civil Liberties, Justice and Home Affairs of the EP, PE 510.021 2015 http://statewatch.org/news/2015/mar/ep-study-cris-fr.pdf

Eurostat (2013) *Manual on Government Deficit and Debt: Implementation of ESA95*, Luxembourg: Eurostat

Eurostat (2015) "Unemployment Statistics" http://ec.europa.eu/eurostat/statistics-explained/index.php?title=Unemployment_statistics&oldid=232726

Fabbrini, Federico (2014) "The Euro-Crisis and the Courts," *Berkeley Journal of International Law* 32 (1): 64–123

Fabbrini, Sergio (2013) "Intergovernmentalism and Its Limits: Assessing the European Union's Answer to the Euro Crisis," *Comparative Political Studies* 46 (9): 1003–29

Fabbrini, Sergio (2015) *Which European Union? Europe after the Euro Crisis* Cambridge: Cambridge University Press

Fabbrini, Sergio (2016) "From Consensus to Domination: The Intergovernmental Union in a Crisis Situation," *Journal of European Integration* 38 (5): 587–99

Fabbrini, Sergio (2019) "Alternative Governance Models: 'Hard Core' in a Differentiated Europe," *Comparative Political Economy* 17 (2): 278–93

Falkner, Gerda, ed. (2011) *The EU's Decision Traps: Comparing Policies* Oxford: Oxford University Press

Falkner, Gerda (2017) *EU Policies in Times of Crisis* London: Routledge

Falkner, Gerda, Treib, Oliver, Harlapp, Miriam, and Leiber, S. (2005) *Complying with Europe: EU Harmonisation and Soft Law in the Member-States* Cambridge: Cambridge University Press

Fasone, Cristina (2014) "European Economic Governance and Parliamentary Representation. What Place for the European Parliament?" *European Law Journal* 20 (2): 164–85

Fawcett, P. and Marsh, D. (2014) "Depoliticisation, Governance and Political Participation," *Policy & Politics* Special Issue 42 (2): 171–88

Featherstone, Kevin (2011) "The Greek Sovereign Debt Crisis and EMU: A Failing State in a Skewed Regime," *Journal of Common Market Studies* 49 (2): 193–211

Featherstone, Kevin (2016) "Conditionality, Democracy, and Institutional Weakness: The Euro-Crisis Trilemma," *Journal of Common Market Studies* Annual Review 1–17

Feldstein, Martin (1997) "The Political Economy of the European Economic and Monetary Union: Political Sources of an Economic Liability," National Bureau of Economic Research NBER Working Paper 6150. Available at http://www.nber.org/papers/w6150.pdf

Ferguson, James (1990) *The Anti-Politics Machine: "Development," Depoliticization, and Bureaucratic Power in Lesotho* Cambridge: Cambridge University Press

Ferrera, Maurizio. (2017) "The Stein Rokkan Lecture 2016, Mission Impossible? Reconciling Economic and Social Europe after the Euro Crisis and Brexit," *European Journal of Political Research* 5 (6): 3–22

Finchelstein, Gilles (2019) "Primaires, là où tout commence...et où beaucoup s'explique" in *Histoire d'une Révolution Électorale (2015–2018)* eds Bruno Cautrès and Anne Muxel. Paris: Classiques Garnier

Fischer-Lescano, A. (2014) *Human Rights in Times of Austerity Policy: The EU Institutions and the Conclusion of Memoranda of Understanding* Baden-Baden: Nomos

Flinders, Matthew (2008) *Delegated Governance and the British State* Oxford: Oxford University Press

Follesdal, Andreas (2006) "The Legitimacy Deficits of the European Union," *Journal of Political Philosophy* 14 (4): 441–68

Follesdal, Andreas and Hix, Simon (2006) "Why There Is a Democratic Deficit in the EU: A Response to Majone and Moravcsik," *Journal of Common Market Studies* 44 (3): 533–62

Fossum, John-Erik (2016) "Reflections on EU Legitimacy and Governing," *European Papers* 1 (1): 1033–40

Fraccaroli, Nicolò, Giovannini, Alessandro, and Jamet, Jean-François (2018) "The Evolution of the ECB's Accountability Practices during the Crisis," *ECB Economic Bulletin* issue 5 (August 9): 47–71. https://www.ecb.europa.eu/pub/economic-bulletin/articles/2018/html/ecb.ebart201805_01.en.html#toc1

Franchino, Fabio and Negri, Fedra (2018) "The Fiscally Moderate Italian Populist Voter," *Party Politics* DOI: 10.1177/1354068818761180

Franck, Thomas (1995) *Fairness in International Law and Institutions* New York: Oxford University Press

Franklin, Mark, Marsh, Michael, and McLaren, Lauren (1994) "Uncorking the Bottle: Popular Opposition to European Unification in the Wake of Maastricht," *Journal of Common Market Studies* 32 (4): 101–17

Franklin, Mark and van der Eijk, Cees (2007) "The Sleeping Giant" in *European Elections and Domestic Politics*, eds Wouter Van der Brug and Cees Van der Eijk. Notre Dame: University of Notre Dame Press

Freund, Daniel (2017) "Who to Blame When You Can't Blame Brussels?" *EU Observer* (July 12). https://euobserver.com/opinion/138474

Frieden, Jeffry, and Stefanie Walter (2017) "Understanding the Political Economy of the Eurozone Crisis: A Political Scientist's Guide." *Annual Review of Political Science* 20 (1): 371–90

Fromage, Diane. (2018) "The European Parliament in the Post-Crisis Era: An Institution Empowered on Paper Only?" *Journal of European Integration* 40 (3): 281–94

Fukuyama, F. (2016) "Governance: What Do We Know, and How Do We Know It?" *Annual Review of Political Science* 19: 89–105

Fusaro, Carlo (2012) "La formazione del governo Monti e il ruolo del presidente della Repubblica" in *Politica in Italia. I fatti dell'anno e le interpretazioni*, eds A. Bosco and D. McDonnell. Bologna: Il Mulino

Future of Europe Group (2012) *Final Report of the Future of Europe Group*, September 17, 2012, http://www.auswaertiges-amt.de/EN/Europa/Aktuell/120918-Zukunftsgruppe_Warschau_node.html

Gabor, Daniela and Ban, Cornel (2016) "Europe's Toxic Twins: Government Debt in Financialized Times" in *The Routledge Companion to Banking Regulation and Reform*, eds Ismail Ertürk and Daniela Gabor. London: Routledge

Gemenis, K. and Nezi, R. (2015) "Government-Opposition Dynamics during the Economic Crisis in Greece," *Journal of Legislative Studies* 21 (1): 14–34

Genschel, Philip and Jachtenfuchs, Marcus, eds. (2014) *Beyond the Regulatory Polity? The European Integration of Core State Powers* Oxford: Oxford University Press

Gianviti, François, Krueger, Anne O., Pisani-Ferry, Jean, Sapir, André, and Von Hage, Jürgen (2010) "A European Mechanism for Sovereign Debt Crisis Resolution: A Proposal," *Bruegel Blueprint Series* (November 9)

Giavazzi, Francesco and Pagano, Marco (1990) "Can Severe Fiscal Contractions be Expansionary?" *NBER Macroeconomics Annual*. 5: 75–111

Giddens, Anthony (2014) *Turbulent and Mighty Continent: What Future for Europe?* Cambridge: Polity

Gidron, Noam and Hall, Peter A. (2017) "The Politics of Social Status: Economic and Cultural Roots of the Populist Right," *The British Journal of Sociology* 68 (1): 57–68

Giuliani, Marco and Massari, Sergio Alberto (2019) "The Economic Vote at the Party Level: Electoral Behaviour during the Great Recession," *Party Politics* 25 (3): 461–73

Glencross, A. (2018) "Post-Democracy and Institutionalized Austerity in France: Budgetary Politics during François Hollande's Presidency," *French Politics* 16 (2): 119–34

Glienicker Group (2013) *Towards a Euro Union* (October 18, 2013) http://www.bruegel. org/about/person/view/373-the-glienicker-group

Glynn, Irial (2015) "Just One of the 'PIIGS' or a European Outlier? Studying Irish Emigration from a Comparative Perspective," *Irish Journal of Sociology* 23 (2): 93–113

Gocaj, Ledina and Meunier, Sophie (2013) "Time Will Tell: The EFSF, the ESM, and the Euro Crisis," *Journal of European Integration* 35 (3): 239–53

Gomez, Raul, Morales, Laura, and Ramiro, Luis (2016) "Varieties of Radicalism: Examining the Diversity of Radical Left Parties and Voters in Western Europe," *West European Politics* 39 (2): 351–79

Gomez, Raul and Ramiro, Luis (2017) "Beyond the 2008 Great Recession: Economic Factors and Electoral Support for the Radical Left in Europe," *Party Politics* https://doi. org/10.1177/1354068817718949

Gómez-Reino, Margarita and Llamazares, Iván (2013) "The Populist Radical Right and European Integration: A Comparative Analysis of Party-Voter Links," *West European Politics* 36 (4): 789–816

Goodin, Robert E. and Dryzek, John S. (2006) "Deliberative Impacts: The Macro-Political Uptake of Mini-Publics," *Politics and Society* 34 (2): 219–44

Grande, Edgar (1996) "The State and Interest Groups in a Framework of Multi-Level Decision-Making: The Case of the European Union," *Journal of European Public Policy* 3 (3): 318–38

Greenwood, Justin (2007) "Organized Civil Society and Democratic Legitimacy in the European Union," *British Journal of Political Science* 37 (2): 333–57

Grigorescu, Alexandru (2007) "Transparency of Intergovernmental Organizations," *International Studies Quarterly* 51 (3): 625–48

Grimm, Dieter (1995) "Does Europe Need a Constitution?" *European Law Journal* 1 (3): 282–302

Grimm, Dieter (1997) "Does Europe Need a Constitution?" in *The Question of Europe*, eds P. Gowan and P. Anderson. London: Verso

Grimm, Dieter (2015) "The Democratic Costs of Europeanization: The European Case," *European Law Journal* 21 (4): 460–73

Gualmini, Elizabetta and Schmidt, Vivien A. (2013) "The Political Sources of Italy's Economic Problems," *Comparative European Politics* 11 (3): 360–82

Haas, Ernst (1958) *The Uniting of Europe* Stanford, CA: Stanford University Press

Haas, P. M. (1992) "Introduction: Epistemic Communities and International Policy Coordination," *International Organization* 46: 1–35

Habermas, Jürgen (1996) *Between Facts and Norms: Contributions to a Discourse Theory of Law and Democracy* Cambridge, MA: MIT Press

Habermas, Jürgen (2001) *The Postnational Constellation* Cambridge, MA: MIT Press

Hagemann, Sara and Franchino, Fabio (2016) "Transparency vs Efficiency? A Study of Negotiations in the Council of the European Union," *European Union Politics* 17 (3): 408–28

Hajer, Maarten (2012) "A Media Storm in the World Risk Society," *Critical Policy Studies* 6 (4): 452–64

Halikiopoulou, Daphne (2018) "A Right-Wing Populist Momentum? A Review of 2017 Elections across Europe," *Journal of Common Market Studies* 56 Annual Review: 63–73

Halikiopoulou, Daphne and Vasilopoulou, S. (2014) "Support for the Far Right in the 2014 European Parliament Elections: A Comparative Perspective," *The Political Quarterly* 85 (3): 285–8

Hall, Peter A. (2012) "The Economics and Politics of the Euro Crisis," *German Politics* 21 (4): 355–71

Hall, Peter A. (2018) "Varieties of Capitalism in Light of the Euro Crisis," *Journal of European Public Policy* 25 (1): 7–30

Hall, Peter and Soskice, David (2001) *Varieties of Capitalism: The Institutional Foundations of Comparative Advantage* Oxford: Oxford University Press

Hallerberg, Mark, Marzinotto, Benedicta, and Wolff, Guntram (2012) "On the Effectiveness and Legitimacy of EU Economic Policies," *Bruegel Policy Brief* 4 (November)

Hallerberg, Mark, Marzinotto, Benedicta, and Wolff, Guntram (2018) "Explaining the Evolving Role of the National Parliaments under the European Semester," *Journal of European Public Policy* 25 (2): 250–267

Ham, Carolien van, Thomassen, Jacques, Aarts, Kees, and Andeweg, Rudy (2017) *Myth and Reality of the Legitimacy Crisis* Oxford: Oxford University Press

Hancké, Bob (2013) *Unions, Central Banks, and EMU: Labour Market Institutions and Monetary Integration in Europe* Oxford: Oxford University Press

Harlow, Carol (2016) "The Limping Legitimacy of European Lawmaking: A Barrier to Integration," *European Papers* 1(1): 29–54

Harlow, Carol. and Rawlings, Richard (2007) "Promoting Accountability in Multi-Level Governance," *European Law Journal* 13 (4): 542–62

Hartlapp, M., Metz, J., and Rauh, C. (2014) *Which Policy for Europe? Power and Conflict inside the European Commission* Oxford: Oxford University Press.

Hassel, Anke (2011) "The Paradox of Liberalization: Understanding Dualism and the Recovery of the German Political Economy," LEQS Paper No. 42/2011 (September)

Hay, Colin (2007) *Why We Hate Politics* Cambridge: Polity Press

Heipertz, Martin and Verdun, Amy (2010) *Ruling Europe: The Politics of the Stability and Growth Pact* New York: Cambridge University Press

Helgadottir, Oddný (2016) "The Bocconi Boys Go to Brussels: Italian Economic Ideas, Professional Networks and European Austerity," *Journal of European Public Policy* 23 (3): 392–409

Hennessey, Alexandra (2013) 'Informal Governance and the Eurozone Crisis', *Journal of Contemporary European Studies* 21 (3): 430–47

Héritier, Adrienne (1999) "Elements of Democratic Legitimation in Europe: An Alternative Perspective," *Journal of European Public Policy* 6 (2): 269–82

Héritier, Adrienne (2003) "Composite Democracy in Europe: The Role of Transparency and Access to Information," *Journal of European Public Policy* 10 (5): 814–33

Héritier, Adrienne and Reh, Christine (2012) "Codecision and Its Discontents: Intra-Organisational Politics and Institutional Reform in the European Parliament," *West European Politics* 35 (5): 1134–1157

Héritier, Adrienne and Lehmkuhl, Dirk (2011) "New Modes of Governance and Democratic Accountability," *Government and Opposition* 46 (1): 126–44

Héritier, Adrienne, Moury, Catherine, Schoeller, Magnus G., Meissner, Katharina L., and Mota, Isabel (2016) "The European Parliament as a Driving Force of Constitutionalisation." Report for the Constitutional Affairs Committee of the European Parliament. PE 536.467

Hillebrandt, Maarten, Curtin, Deirdre, and Meijer, Albert. "Transparency in the EU Council of Ministers: An Institutional Analysis," *European Law Journal* 20 (1) (2014): 1–20

Hirst, Paul (1994) *Associative Democracy* Cambridge: Polity Press

Hix, Simon (2008) *What's Wrong with the European Union and How to Fix It* Cambridge: Polity Press

Hix, Simon (2018) "When Optimism Fails: Liberal Intergovernmentalism and Citizen Representation," *Journal of Common Market Studies* 56 (7): 1595–613

Hix, Simon and Høyland, B. (2013) "Empowerment of the European Parliament," *Annual Review of Political Science* 16: 171–89

Hobolt, Sara B. (2014) "A Vote for the President? The Role of Spitzenkandidaten in the 2014 European Parliament Elections," *Journal of European Public Policy* 21(10): 1528–40

Hobolt, Sara B. (2015) "Public Attitudes toward the Eurozone Crisis" in *Democratic Politics in a European Union under Stress*, eds Olaf Cramme and Sara B. Hobolt. Oxford: Oxford University Press

Hobolt, Sara B. and Wratil, Christopher (2015) "Public Opinion and the Crisis: The Dynamics of Support for the Euro," *Journal of European Public Policy* 22 (2): 238–56

Hochschild, Jennifer and Mollenkopt, John H. (2009) *Bringing Outsiders In: Transatlantic Perspectives on Immigrant Political Incorporation* Ithaca: Cornell University Press

Hodson, Dermot (2015) "*De Novo* Bodies and the New Intergovernmentalism: The Case of the European Central Bank," in *The New Intergovernmentalism*, eds Christopher Bickerton, Dermot Hodson, and Uwe Puetter. Oxford: Oxford University Press

Hodson, Dermot and Puetter, Uwe (2019) "The European Union in Disequilibrium: New Intergovernmentalism, Postfunctionalism, and Integration Theory in the Post-Maastricht Period," *Journal of European Public Policy* early access https://doi.org/10.108 0/13501763.2019.1569712

Hoeglinger, Dominic (2016) "The Politicisation of European Integration in Domestic Election Campaigns," *West European Politics* 39 (1): 44–63

Hodson, Dermot and Puetter, Uwe (2018) "Studying Europe after the Fall: Four Thoughts on Post-EU Studies," *Journal of European Public Policy* 25 (3): 465–74

Hoffmann, Stanley (1966) "Obstinate or Obsolete? The Fate of the Nation State and the Case of Western Europe," *Daedalus*, 95, 890–2

Holzhacker, Ronald (2007) "Democratic Legitimacy and the European Union," *Journal of European Integration* 29 (3): 257–69

Hood, Christopher (2010) "Accountability and Transparency," *West European Politics* 33 (5): 989–1009

Hooghe, Liesbet (2001) *The European Commission and the Integration of Europe* Cambridge: Cambridge University Press

Hooghe, Liesbet (2005) "Several Roads Lead to International Norms, but Few via International Socialization: A Case Study of the European Commission," *International Organization* 59(4): 861–98

Hooghe, Liesbet (2012) "Images of Europe: How Commission Officials Conceive Their Institution's Role," *Journal of Common Market Studies* 50(1): 87–111

Hooghe, Liesbet and Marks, Gary (2009) "A Postfunctionalist Theory of European Integration: From Permissive Consensus to Constraining Dissensus," *British Journal of Political Science* 39 (1): 1–23

Hooghe, Liesbet and Marks, Gary (2018) "Cleavage Theory Meets Europe's Crises: Lipset, Rokkan, and the Transnational Cleavage," *Journal of European Public Policy* 25 (1): 109–35

Hooghe, Liesbet and Marks, Gary (2019) "Grand Theories of European Integration in the Twenty-First Century," *Journal of European Public Policy*. Available at: https://doi.org/10.1080/13501763.2019.156971

Hooghe, Liesbet, Marks, Gary, and Wilson, Carole J. (2002) "Does Left/Right Structure Party Positions on European Integration?" *Comparative Political Studies* 35 (8): 965–89

Hopkin, Jonathan (2020) *Anti-System Politics: The Crisis of Market Liberalism in Rich Democracies* New York: Oxford University Press

Hopkin, Jonathan (2015), "The Troubled South: The Euro Experience in Italy and Spain" in *The Future of the Euro*, eds Matthias Matthijs and Mark Blyth. Oxford: Oxford University Press

Höpner, Martin, and Schäfer, Armin (2007) "A New Phase of European Integration: Organized Capitalisms in Post-Ricardian Europe," *MOIFG Discussion Paper* No. 2007/4. Available at http://ssrn.com/abstract=976162

Howarth, David (2007) "Making and Breaking the Rules: French Policy on EU 'Gouvernement Economique'," *Journal of European Public Policy* 14 (7): 1061–78

Howarth, David and Loedel, Peter (2003) *The European Central Bank: The New European Leviathan?* Basingstoke: Palgrave Macmillan

Howarth, David and Rommerskirchen, Charlotte (2013) "A Panacea for All Times? The German Stability Culture as Strategic Political Resource," *West European Politics* 36 (4): 750–70

Howell, Chris (2009) "The Transformation of French Industrial Relations: Labor Representation and the State in a Post-Dirigiste Era," *Politics & Society* 37 (2): 229–56

Hurd, Ian (2007) *After Anarchy: Legitimacy and Power in the United Nations Security Council*. Princeton, NJ: Princeton University Press

Hurrelmann, Achim, Gora, Anna, and Wagner, Andrea (2015) "The Politicization of European Integration: More than an Elite Affair?" *Political Affairs* 63 (1): 43–59

Hutter, Swen and Grande, Edgar (2019) "Politicizing Europe in Times of Crisis," *Journal of European Public Policy* 26 (7): 996–1017

Hutter, Swen, Grande, Edgar, and Kriesi, Hanspeter (eds) (2016) *Politicising Europe: Integration and Mass Politics* Cambridge: Cambridge University Press

Hutter, Swen and Kriesi, Hanspeter (2019) "The Politicization of European Integration in National Politics since the Great Recession," *Journal of European Public Policy* (forthcoming)

IMF (International Monetary Fund) (2013) "Greece: Ex Post Evaluation of Exceptional Access under the 2010 Stand-By Arrangement," IMF Country Report No. 13/156 (June) Washington DC: International Monetary Fund

IMF (International Monetary Fund) (2014) "Is It Time for an Infrastructure Push? The Macroeconomic Effects of Public Investment," *World Economic Outlook*, Chapter 3, October, 76–114

Imig, Doug and Tarrow, Sidney (eds) (2001) *Contentious Europeans*. Lanham, MD: Rowman & Littlefield

Inglehart, Ronald and Norris, Pippa (2017) "Trump and the Populist Authoritarian Parties: *The Silent Revolution* in Reverse," *Perspectives on Politics* 15 (2): 443–54

Ioannou, Demosthenes, Leblond, Patrick and Niemann, Arne (2015) "European Integration and the Crisis," *Journal of European Public Policy* 22 (2): 155–76

Ivaldi, Gilles (2015) "Towards the Median Economic Crisis Voter? The New Leftist Economic Agenda of the Front National in France," *French Politics* 13 (4): 346–69

Iversen, Torben, Soskice, David, and Hope, David (2016) "The Eurozone and Political Economic Institutions," *Annual Review of Political Science* 19 (1): 163–8

Iversen, Torben and Soskice, David (2018) "A Structural-Institutional Explanation of the Eurozone Crisis" in *Welfare Democracies and Party Politics: Explaining Electoral Dynamics in Times of Changing Welfare Capitalism*, eds Philip Manow, Bruno Palier, and Hanna Schwander. Oxford: Oxford University Press

Jabko, Nicolas (2006) *Playing the Market: A Political Strategy for United Europe, 1985–2005* Ithaca, NY: Cornell University Press

Jabko, Nicolas (2015) "The Crisis of EU Institutions and the Weakness of Economic Governance" in *The Future of the Euro*, eds Matthias Matthijs and Mark Blyth. New York: Oxford University Press.

Jacoby, Wade (2015) "The Timing of Politics and the Politics of Timing" in *The Future of the Euro*, eds Matthias Matthijs and Mark Blyth. New York: Oxford University Press

Joerges, Christian and Neyer, Jürgen (1997) "Transforming Strategic Interaction into Deliberative Problem-Solving," *Journal of European Public Policy* 4 (4): 609–25

Joerges, Christian (2014) "Three Transformations of Europe and the Search for a Way Out of Its Crisis" in *The European Crisis and the Transformation of Transnational Governance: Authoritarian Managerialism Versus Democratic Governance*, eds Christian Joerges and Carola Glinski. Oxford: Hart Publishing

Johnston, Alison (2016) *From Convergence to Crisis: Labor Markets and the Instability of the Euro* Ithaca, NY: Cornell University Press

Johnston, Alison and Regan, Aidan (2018) "Introduction: Is the European Union Capable of Integrating Diverse Models of Capitalism?" *New Political Economy* 23 (2): 145–59

Jones, Erik (2009) "Output Legitimacy and the Global Financial Crisis: Perceptions Matter," *Journal of Common Market Studies* 47 (5): 1085–105

Jones, Erik (2010) "Merkel's Folly," *Survival* 52 (3): 21–38

Jones, Erik (2013a) "Getting to Greece: Uncertainty, Misfortune, and the Origins of Political Disorder," *European Political Science* 12 (3): 294–304

Jones, Erik (2013b) "The Collapse of the Brussels-Frankfurt Consensus and the Future of the Euro" in *Resilient Liberalism: European Political Economy through Boom and Bust*, eds V. Schmidt and M. Thatcher. Cambridge: Cambridge University Press

Jones, Erik (2015a) "Forgotten Financial Union: How You Can Have a Euro Crisis without a Euro" in *The Future of the Euro*, eds Matthias Matthijs and Mark Blyth. New York: Oxford University Press

Jones, Erik (2015b) "Getting the Story Right: How You Should Choose between Different Interpretations of the European Crisis (and Why You Should Care)," *Journal of European Integration* 37 (7): 817–32

Jones, Erik, Kelemen, Daniel, and Meunier, Sophie (2015) "Failing Forward? The Euro Crisis and the Incomplete Nature of European Integration," *Comparative Political Studies* 49 (7): 1010–34

Judis, John B. (2016) *The Populist Explosion: How the Great Recession Transformed American and European Politics* New York: Columbia Global Report

Juncker, Jean-Claude in close cooperation with D. Tusk, J. Dijsselbloom, M. Draghi, and M. Schulz (2015) "Completing Europe's Economic and Monetary Union" [also known as the Five Presidents' Report] European Commission https://ec.europa.eu/commission/sites/beta-political/files/5-presidents-report_en.pdf

Kalionatis, Kostas (2019) "Redefining Austerity: A Lesson from Greece," *Social Europe Journal* (June 5) https://www.socialeurope.eu/redefining-austerity-greece

Kamlage, Jan-Hendrik and Patrizia Nanz (2017) "Crisis and Participation in the European Union," *Global Society* 31 (1): 65–82

Karremans, Johannes and Damhuis, Koen (2018) "The Changing Face of Responsibility: A Cross-Time Comparison of French Social Democratic Governments," *Party Politics* https://doi.org/10.1177/1354068818761197

Kassim, Hussein, Peterson, John, Bauer, Michael W., Connolly, Sara, Dehousse, Renaud, Hooghe, Liesbet, and Thompson, Andrew (2013) *The European Commission of the Twenty-First Century* Oxford: Oxford University Press

Katsanidou, Alexia and Otjes, Simon (2016) "How the European Debt Crisis Reshaped National Political Space: The Case of Greece," *European Union Politics* 17 (2): 262–84

Katz, Richard S. and Mair, Peter (1995) "Changing Models of Party Organization and Party Democracy: The Emergence of the Cartel Party," *Party Politics* 1 (4): 5–28

Katz, Richard S. and Wessels, Bernhard (1999) *The European Parliament, the National Parliaments, and European Integration* Oxford: Oxford University Press

Kelemen, R. Daniel (2019) "Is Differentiation Possible in Rule of Law?" *Comparative Political Economy* 17 (2): 246–60

Keohane, Robert, and Grant, Ruth (2005) "Accountability and Abuses of Power in World Politics," *American Political Science Review* 99 (1): 29–43

Keohane, R. and Hoffmann, S. (1991) *The New European Community* Boulder: Westview Press

Kiersey, Nicholas (2018) "Narrating Crisis in Ireland's Great Recession" in *Crisis in the Eurozone Periphery*, eds Owen Parker and Dimitris Tsarouhas. Basingstoke: Palgrave Macmillan

Kindleberger, Charles (1973) *The World in Depression, 1929–1939* Berkeley: University of California Press

Kingdon, John (1984) *Agendas, Alternatives, and Public Policies* New York: Longman

Kleine, Marieke (2013) *Informal Governance in the European Union* Ithaca: Cornell University Press

Kneip, Sascha and Merkel, Wolfgang (2018) "The Idea of Democratic Legitimacy." WZB Discussion Paper 2018. Berlin: WZB

Kohler-Koch, Beate. (2007) "The Organization of Interests and Democracy in the EU" in *Debating the Democratic Legitimacy of the European Union*, eds B. Kohler-Koch and B. Ritberger. Lanham, MD: Rowman and Littlefield

Kohler-Koch, Beate (2010) "Civil Society and EU Democracy: 'Astroturf' Representation?"' *Journal of European Public Policy* 17 (1): 100–16

Kohler-Koch, Beate and Quittkat, Christine (2013) *De-Mystification of Participatory Democracy: EU Governance and Civil Society* Oxford: Oxford University Press

Koopmans, Ruud (2004) "The Transformation of Political Mobilisation and Communication in European Public Spheres," 5th Framework Programme of the European Commission. Available from: http://europub.wz-berlin.de

Koopmans, Ruud and Statham, Paul, eds (2010) *The Making of a European Public Sphere* Cambridge: Cambridge University Press

Kosack, Stephen and Fung, Archon (2014) "Does Transparency Improve Governance?" *Annual Review of Political Science* 17: 65–87

Kreilinger, Valentin (2019) *National Parliaments in Europe's Post-Crisis Economic Governance*. Doctoral dissertation submitted to the Hertie School of Governance (Berlin)

Kreppel, Amie (1999) "The European Parliament's Influence over EU Policy Outcomes," *Journal of Common Market Studies* 37 (3): 521–38

Kreuder-Sonnen, Christian (2016) "Beyond Integration Theory: The (Anti-) Constitutional Dimension of European Crisis Governance," *Journal of Common Market Studies* 54 (6): 1350–66

Kreuder-Sonnen, Christian (2018a) "An Authoritarian Turn in Europe and European Studies?" *Journal of European Public Policy* 25 (3), 452–64 https://doi.org/10.1080/13501 763.2017.1411383

Kreuder-Sonnen, Christian (2018b) "Political Secrecy in Europe: Crisis Management and Crisis Exploitation," *West European Politics* 41 (4): 958–80

Kreuder-Sonnen, Christian (2019a) "International Authority and the Emergency Problematique: IO Empowerment through Crises," *International Theory* early view online https://doi.org/10.1017/S1752971919000010

Kreuder-Sonnen, Christian (2019b) *Emergency Powers of International Organizations: Between Normalization and Contestation* Oxford: Oxford University Press

Kriesi, Hanspeter (2014) "The Populist Challenge," *West European Politics* 37 (2): 379–99

Kriesi, Hanspeter (2016) "The Politicization of European Integration," *Journal of Common Market Studies* 54 Annual Review 32–47

Kriesi, Hanspeter and Grande, Edgar (2015) "Political Debate in a Polarizing Union" in *Democratic Politics in a European Union under Stress*, eds O. Cramme and S. Hobolt. Oxford: Oxford University Press

Kriesi, Hanspeter, Grande, Edgar, and Lachat, Robert (2008) *West European Politics in the Age of Globalization* Cambridge: Cambridge University Press

Kriesi, Hanspeter, Grande, Edgar, Dolezal, Martin, Helbling, Marc, Höglinger, Dominic, Hutter, Swen, and Wueest, Bruno (2012) *Political Conflict in Western Europe.* Cambridge: Cambridge University Press

Kröger, Sandra (2008) "Nothing but Consultation: The Place of Organized Civil Society in EU Policy-Making across Policies," *European Governance Papers* (EUROGOV) No. C-08-03 https://core.ac.uk/download/pdf/71735076.pdf

Kröger, Sandra (2019) "How Limited Representativeness Weakens Throughput Legitimacy in the EU: The Example of Interest Groups," *Public Administration* 97 (4) 770–83

Kuhn, Theresa (2015) *Experiencing European Integration: Transnational Lives and European Identity.* Oxford: Oxford University Press

Kuhn, Raymond (2017) "Expect the Unexpected: The 2017 French Presidential and Parliamentary Elections," *Modern & Contemporary France* 25 (4): 359–75

Kuo, Ming-Sung. (2014) "The Moment of Schmittian Truth: Conceiving of the State of Exception in the Wake of the Financial Crisis" in *The European Crisis and the Transformation of Transnational Governance: Authoritarian Managerialism Versus Democratic Governance*, eds Christian Joerges and Carola Glinski. Oxford: Hart Publishing

Laclau, Ernesto and Mouffe, Chantal (1985) *Hegemony and Socialist Strategy: Towards a Radical Democratic Politics.* Oxford: Blackwell

Laffan, Brigid (2014) "Testing Times: The Growing Primacy of Responsibility in the Euro Area," *West European Politics* 37 (2): 270–87

Lake, David A. (2007) "Escape from the State of Nature: Authority and Hierarchy in World Politics," *International Security* 32 (1): 47–79

Larch, Martin, van den Noord, Paul., and Jonung, Lars (2010) "The Stability and Growth Pact: Lessons from the Great Recession," *European Economy - Economic Papers* 429

Leeuwen, Theodore van (2007) "Legitimation in Discourse and Communication," *Discourse and Communication* 1 (1): 91–112

Leeuwen, Theodore van, and Wodak, Ruth (1999) "Legitimizing Immigration Control: A Discourse-Historical Analysis," *Discourse Studies* 1 (1): 83–118

Legrain, Philippe (2014) *European Spring: Why Our Economies and Politics Are in a Mess and How to Put them Right* London: Curtis Brown

Levi, Margaret (1998) "A State of Trust" in *Trust and Governance*, eds Valerie Braithwaite and Margaret Levi. New York: Russell Sage Foundation

Liebert, Ulrike and Trenz, Hans-Jörg (eds) (2009) *Civil Society and the Reconstitution of Democracy in Europe* Special Issue of *Policy and Society* 20 (1): 1–98

Lindberg, Leon and Scheingold, Stuart (1970) *Europe's Would-Be Polity: Patterns of Change in the European Community* New York: Prentice-Hall

Lindner, Fabian (2014) "How Social Europe Is Destroyed," *Social Europe Journal*, Nov. 4, 2014. http://www.social-europe.eu/2014/11/social-europe-destroyed-can-rebuild/

Lonergan, Eric (2019) "Draghi's Law of Conditional Safety," *Philosophy of Money* (blog) https://www.philosophyofmoney.net/draghis-law-conditional-safety/

Lord, Christopher (2004) *A Democratic Audit of the European Union.* Basingstoke: Palgrave Macmillan

Lord, Christopher and Beetham, David (2001) "Legitimizing the EU: Is There a 'Postparliamentary Basis' for Its Legitimation?" *Journal of Common Market Studies* 39 (3): 443–62

Lord, Christopher and Pollak, Johannes (2010) "Representation and Accountability: Communicating Tubes?" *West European Politics* 33 (5): 968–88

Lucarelli, Sonia, Cerutti, Furio, and Schmidt, Vivien A. (eds) (2010) *Debating Political Identity and Legitimacy in the European Union.* London: Routledge

Lundgren, Magnus, Bailer, Stefanie, Dellmuth, Lisa M., Tallberg, Jonas, and Târlea, Silvana (2019) "Bargaining Success in the Reform of the Eurozone," *European Union Politics* 20 (1): 65–88

Lütz, Susanne, Schneider, Sebastien, and Hilgers, Sven (2019) "Games Borrower Governments Play: The Implementation of Economic Adjustment Programmes in Cyprus and Portugal," *West European Politics* early view online DOI: 10.1080/01402382.2019.1583482

Lütz, Susanne and Kranke, Matthias (2014) "The European Rescue of the Washington Consensus? IMF and EU Lending to Eastern European Countries," *Review of International Political Economy* 21 (2): 310–38

Mabbett, Deborah and Schelkle, Waltraud (2014) "Searching under the Lamp-Post: The Evolution of Fiscal Surveillance," LEQS Paper No. 75/2014 (May)

MacDougall, Donald (1977) "Report of the Study Group on the Role of Public Finance in European Integration" (MacDougall Report), *Economic and Financial Series*, No. A 13 (April), http://aei.pitt.edu/36433

Maggetti, Martino (2012) "The Media Accountability of Independent Regulatory Agencies," *European Political Science Review* 4 (3): 385–408

Magnette, Paul (2003) "European Governance and Civic Participation: Beyond Elitist Citizenship?" *Political Studies* 51: 144–60

Magone, José M. (2014) "Portugal Is Not Greece: Policy Responses to the Sovereign Debt Crisis and the Consequences for the Portuguese Political Economy," *Perspectives on European Politics and Society*, 15 (3): 346–60

Mair, Peter (2006) "Political Parties and Party Systems" in *Europeanization*, eds P. Graziano and M. Vink. Basingstoke: Palgrave Macmillan

Mair, Peter (2013) *Ruling the Void: The Hollowing of Western Democracy* London: Verso

Mair, Peter and Thomassen, J. (2010) "Political Representation and Government in the European Union," *European Journal of Public Policy* 17: 20–35

Majone, Giandomenico (1993) "The European Community: An 'Independent Fourth Branch of Government'?" Working Paper, European University Institute. EUI SPS, 1993/09

Majone, Giandomenico (ed.) (1996) *Regulating Europe* London/New York: Routledge

Majone, Giandomenico (1998) "Europe's Democratic Deficit," *European Law Journal* 4 (1): 5–28

Majone, Gianomenico (2001) "Non-Majoritarian Institutions and the Limits of Democratic Governance," *Journal of Institutional and Theoretical Economics* 157 (1): 57–78

Majone, Giandomenico (2009) *Dilemmas of European Integration* Oxford: Oxford University Press

Majone, Giandomenico (2014) *Rethinking the Union of Europe Post-Crisis: Has Integration Gone Too Far?* Cambridge: Cambridge University Press

Manners, Ian (2002) "Normative Power Europe: A Contradiction in Terms?" *Journal of Common Market Studies* 40 (2): 235–58

Manow, Philip, Schwander, Hanna, and Palier, Bruno (2018) "Conclusions: Electoral Dynamics in Times of Changing Welfare Capitalism" in *Welfare Democracies and Party Politics*, eds Philip Manow, Bruno Palier, and Hanna Schwander. Oxford: Oxford University Press

Mansbridge, Jane (2015) 'A minimalist definition of deliberation' in *Development: Rethinking the Role of Voice and Collective Action in Unequal Societies,* eds Patrick Heller and Vijayendra Rao. Washington DC: World Bank Group

Mansbridge, Jane (1983) *Beyond Adversary Democracy*. Chicago: Chicago University Press

March, James and Olsen, Johan (1995) *Democratic Governance*. New York: Free Press

March, Luke (2011). *Radical Left Parties in Europe*. Abingdon: Routledge

March, Luke and Mudde, C. (2005) "What's Left of the Radical Left? The European Radical Left after 1989," *Comparative European Politics* 3: 23–49

March, Luke and Charlotte Rommerskirchen (2012) "Out of Left Field? Explaining the Variable Electoral Success of European Radical Left Parties," *Party Politics* 21 (1): 40–53

Maricut-Akbik, Adina and Puetter, Uwe (2018) "Deciding on the European Semester: the European Council, the Council and the Enduring Asymmetry between Economic and Social Policy Issues," *Journal of European Public Policy* 25 (19): 1–19

Matthijs, Matthias (2016) "Powerful Rules Governing the Euro: The Perverse Logic of German Ideas," *Journal of European Public Policy* 23 (3): 375–91

Matthijs, Matthias (2017a) "The Euro's 'Winner-Take-All' Political Economy: Institutional Choices, Policy Drift, and Diverging Patterns of Inequality," *Politics & Society* 44 (3): 393–422

Matthijs, Matthias (2017b) "Integration at What Price? The Erosion of National Democracy in the Euro Periphery," *Government and Opposition* 52 (2): 266–94

Matthijs, Matthias and Blyth, Mark (2011) "Why Only Germany Can Fix the Euro: Reading Kindleberger in Berlin," *Foreign Affairs* (Nov. 17) http://www.foreignaffairs.com/print/133968

Matthijs, Matthias and Blyth, Mark, eds (2015) *The Future of the Euro* New York: Oxford University Press

Matthijs, Matthias and McNamara, Kathleen (2015) "The Euro Crisis' Theory Effect: Northern Saints, Southern Sinners, and the Demise of the Eurobond," *Journal of European Integration* 37 (2): 229–45

Mayer, Nonna (2015) "The Closing of the Radical Right Gender Gap in France?" *French Politics* 13 (4): 391–414

McAuley, James (2019) "Low Visibility," *New York Review of Books* 66 (5): 58–62

McDonnell, Duncan (2006) "A Weekend in Padania: Regionalist Populism and the Lega Nord," *Politics* 26 (2): 126–32

McEvoy, Caroline (2016) "The Role of Political Efficacy on Public Opinion in the European Union," *Journal of Common Market Studies* 54 (5): 1159–74

McGowan, Müge, Adalet, Andrews, Dan and Mill, Valentine (2017) "The Walking Dead? Zombie Firms and Productivity Performance in OECD Countries," OECD, Economics Department Working Papers, no. 1372 https://www.oecd.org/eco/The-Walking-Dead-Zombie-Firms-and-Productivity-Performance-in-OECD-Countries.pdf

McNamara, Kathleen R. (1998) *The Currency of Ideas: Monetary Politics in the European Union*. Ithaca, NY: Cornell University Press

McNamara, Kathleen R. (2015a) *The Politics of Everyday Europe: Constructing Authority in the European Union* Oxford: Oxford University Press

McNamara, Kathleen R. (2015b) "The Forgotten Problem of Embeddedness: History Lessons for the Euro" in *The Future of the Euro*, eds Matthias Matthijs and Mark Blyth. New York: Oxford University Press

Meissner, Katharina and Schoeller, Magnus (2019) "Politicization by Stealth? The European Parliament between Integration and Disintegration," *Journal of Public Policy* (forthcoming)

Menon, Anand and Weatherill, Stephen (2008) "Transnational Legitimacy in a Globalising World," *West European Politics* 31 (3): 397–416

Mercier, Arnaud (2019) "Des débats télévisés enfin décisifs sur le vote" in *Histoire d'une Révolution Électorale (2015–2018)*, eds Bruno Cautrès and Anne Muxel. Paris: Classiques Garnier

Merkel, Wolfgang (2019) "Challenge or Crisis of Democracy" in *Democracy and Crisis*, eds Wolfgang Merkel and Sasha Kneip. London: Springer

Minenna, Marcello (2018) "A Look Back: What Eurozone Risksharing Really Meant," *Financial Times* (Oct. 10) https://ftalphaville.ft.com/2018/10/10/1539147600000/A-look-back--what-Eurozone--risk-sharing--actually-meant/

Mody, Ashoka (2015) "Living Dangerously without a Fiscal Union" *Bruegel Working Paper* 2015/03 (March). http://www.bruegel.org/download/parent/875-living-dangerously-without-a-fiscal-union/file/1788-living-dangerously-without-a-fiscal-union/

Mody, Ashoka (2018) *Eurotragedy: A Drama in Nine Acts* Oxford: Oxford University Press

Molina, Oscar and Rhodes, Martin (2007) "Conflict, Complementarities and Institutional Change in Mixed Market Economies" in *Beyond Varieties of Capitalism: Contradictions, Complementarities and Change*, eds B. Hancké, M. Rhodes, and M. Thatcher. Oxford: Oxford University Press

Moravcsik, Andrew (1993) "Preferences and Power in the European Community: A Liberal Intergovernmentalist Approach," *Journal of Common Market Studies* 31 (4): 611–28

Moravcsik, Andrew (1998) *The Choice for Europe: Social Purpose and State Power from Messina to Maastricht* Ithaca, NY: Cornell University Press

Moravcsik, Andrew (2002) "In Defence of the Democratic Deficit: Reassessing Legitimacy in the European Union," *Journal of Common Market Studies* 40 (4): 603–24

Morlino, Leonardo and Raniolo, F. (2017) *The Impact of the Economic Crisis on South European Democracies* New York: Springer

Moro, Giovanni (2011) *La Moneta della Discordia* Roma: Cooper Editore

Mortati, Costantino (1940) *La costituzione in senso materiale* Milano: Giuffré

Moschella, Manuela (2014) "Monitoring Macroeconomic Imbalances: Is EU Surveillance More Effective than IMF Surveillance?" *Journal of Common Market Studies* 52 (6): 1273–89

Moschella, Manuela (2017a) "Italy and the Fiscal Compact: Why Does a Country Commit to Permanent Austerity?" *Italian Review of Political Science* 47 (2): 205–25

Moschella, Manuela (2017b) "When Some Are More Equal than Others: National Parliaments and Intergovernmental Bailout Negotiations in the Eurozone," *Government and Opposition* 52 (2): 239–65

Moscovici, Pierre (2015) "After the Greek Psychodrama, What Improvements for the EMU?" *Notre Europe Tribune* (September 30)

Mouffe, Chantal (2005) *On The Political: Thinking in Action* London: Routledge

Mudde, Cas, ed. (2017a) *The Populist Radical Right: A Reader* London: Routledge

Mudde, Cas (2017b) "Conclusion: Studying Populist Radical Right Parties *and* Politics in the Twenty-First Century" in *The Populist Radical Right: A Reader*, ed. Cas Mudde. London: Routledge

Mudde, Cas and Kaltwasser, Cristobal Rovira (2012) *Populism in Europe and the Americas: Threat or Corrective to Democracy* Cambridge: Cambridge University Press

Mügge, Daniel K. and Stellinga, Bart (2015) "The Unstable Core of Global Finance: Contingent Valuation and Governance of International Accounting Standards," *Regulation and Governance* 9 (1): 47–62

Müller, Jan-Werner (2016) *What Is Populism?* Philadelphia: University of Pennsylvania Press

Munta, Mario (2020) "Building National Ownership of the European Semester: The Role of European Semester Officers, *European Politics and Society* 21 (1): 36–52

Myant, Martin, Theodoropoulou, Sotiria, and Piasna, Agnieszka (2016) *Unemployment, Internal Devaluation and Labour Market Deregulation in Europe*. Brussels: ETUI

Naurin, Daniel (2007) *Deliberation behind Closed Doors: Transparency and Lobbying in the European Union*. Colchester: ECPR Press

Newman, Abe (2015) "The Reluctant Leader: Germany's Euro Experience and the Long Shadow of Reunification" in *The Future of the Euro*, eds Matthias Matthijs and Mark Blyth. New York: Oxford University Press

Newton, Kenneth, and Norris, Pippa (2000) "Confidence in Public Institutions: Faith, Culture or Performance?" In *Disaffected Democracies*, eds Susan J. Pharr and Robert D. Putnam. Princeton: Princeton University Press

Nicolaïdis, Kalypso and Max Watson (2016) "Sharing the Eurocrats' Dream: A Demoi-cratic Approach to EMU Governance in the Post-Crisis Era" in Chalmers, Damian, Jachtenfuchs, Markus and Joerges, Christian (eds.) *The End of the EUrocrat's Dream*, Cambridge: Cambridge

Nicolaïdis, Kalypso (2003) "Our European Demoi-cracy: Is This Constitution a Third Way for Europe?" in *Whose Europe? National Models and the Constitution of the European Union*, eds K. Nicolaïdis and S. Weatherill. Oxford: Oxford University Press

Nicolaïdis, Kalypso (2013) "European Demoi-cracy and Its Crisis," *Journal of Common Market Studies* 51 (2): 351–69

Nicolaï, J.-P. and Valla, N., eds (2014) "Quelle France dans Dix Ans?" *France Stratégie* (June) www.strategie.gouv.fr

Nicoli, Francesco (2017) Democratic Legitimacy in the Era of Fiscal Integration," *Journal of European Integration* 39 (4): 389–404

Nielsen, Bodil and Smeets, Sandrino (2018) "The Role of the EU Institutions in Establishing the Banking Union: Collaborative Leadership in the EMU Reform Process," *Journal of European Public Policy* 25 (9): 1233–56

Novak, Stéphanie (2010) "Decision Rules, Social Norms and the Expression of Disagreement," *Social Science Information* 49 (1): 83–97

Novak, Stéphanie (2013) "The Silence of Ministers: Consensus and Blame Avoidance in the Council of the European Union," *Journal of Common Market Studies* 51 (6): 1091–107

OECD (2016) "Using the Fiscal Levers to Escape the Low-Growth Trap," in *OECD Economic Outlook*, Issue 2

Offe, Claus (1999) "How Can We Trust Our Fellow Citizens?" in *Democracy and Trust*, ed. Mark Warren. Cambridge: Cambridge University Press

Offe, Claus (2013) "Europe Entrapped: Does the EU Have the Political Capacity to Overcome Its Current Crisis?" *European Law Journal* 19 (5): 595–611

Olsen, Johan (2015) "Democratic Order, Autonomy, and Accountability," *Governance* 28 (4): 425–40

O'Reilly, Emily (2018) "How Transparent Are the EU Institutions?" CEPS Commentary (May 23)

Orphanides, Athanasios (2017) "ECB Monetary Policy and Euro Area Governance: Collateral Eligibility Criteria for Sovereign Debt." MIT Sloan School Working Paper 5258-17 (Nov. 20) https://papers.ssrn.com/sol3/papers.cfm?abstract_id=3076184

Orsina, Giovanni (2019) "Geneaology of a Populist Uprising: Italy, 1979–2019," *The International Spectator* online early view https://doi.org/10.1080/03932729.2019.1603896

Palier, Bruno and Thelen, Kathleen (2010) "Institutionalizing Dualism: Complementarities and Change in France and Germany," *Politics and Society* 38 (1): 119–48

Pansardi, Pamela and Battegazzorre, Francesco (2018) "The Discursive Legitimation Strategy of the President of the Commission: A Qualitative Content Analysis of the State of the Union Addresses (SOTEU)," *Journal of European Integration* (online June 18): https://www.tandfonline.com/doi/full/10.1080/07036337.2018.1482286

Papadimitriou, Dimistris, Pegasiou, Adonis, and Zartaloudis, Sotirios (2019) "European Elites and the Narrative of the Greek Crisis: A Discursive Institutionalist Analysis," *European Journal of Political Research* 58 (2): 435–64

Papadopoulos, Yannis (2010) "Accountability and Multi-Level Governance: More Accountability, Less Democracy?" *West European Politics* 33 (5): 1030–49

Pappas, Takis S. (2019) *Populism and Liberal Democracy*

Parker, Owen (2018) "A Genealogy of EU Discourses and Practices of Deliberative Governance: Beyond States and Markets?" *Public Administration* 97 (4): 741–53

Parker, Owen and Tsarouhas, Dimitris, eds (2018) *Crisis in the Eurozone Periphery: The Political Economies of Greece, Spain, Ireland and Portugal* Basingstoke: Palgrave Macmillan

Parkinson, John and Mansbridge, Jane (2012) *Deliberative Systems: Deliberative Democracy at the Large Scale* New York: Cambridge University Press

Parsons, Craig and Matthijs, Matthias (2015) "European Integration Past, Present and Future: Moving Forward through Crisis?" in *The Future of the Euro*, eds Matthias Matthijs and Mark Blyth. New York: Oxford University Press

Passarelli, G. and Tuorto, D. (2018) "The Five Star Movement: Purely a Matter of Protest?" *Party Politics* 24 (2): 129–40

Pavolini, Emmanuele, León, Margarita, Guillén, Ana, and Ascoli, Ugo (2015) "From Austerity to Permanent Strain? The EU and Welfare State Reform in Italy and Spain," *Comparative European Politics* 13 (1): 56–76

Peet, John and Laguardia, Anton (2014) *Unhappy Union: How the Euro Crisis—And Europe—Can Be Fixed* London: The Economist and Profile Books

Perez, Sofia and Matsaganis, Manos (2018) "The Political Economy of Austerity in Southern Europe," *New Political Economy* 23 (2): 192–207

Perez, Sophia and Rhodes, Martin (2015) "The Evolution and Crises of Social Models in Italy and Spain" in *European Social Models from Crisis to Crisis: Employment and Inequality in the Era of Monetary Integration*, eds J. E. Dolvik and A. Martin. Oxford: Oxford University Press

Perrineau, Pascal (2019) "Marine Le Pen. Les panélistes y croient puis doutent…" in Bruno Cautrès and Anne Muxel, eds, *Histoire d'une Révolution Électorale (2015–2018)* Paris: Classiques Garnier

Perrineau, Pascal (2014) *La France face au Front* Paris: Fayard

Peterson, John (2015) "The Commission and the New Intergovernmentalism" in *The New Intergovernmentalism*, eds C. Bickerton, Dermot Hodson, and Uwe Puetter. Oxford: Oxford University Press

Pew Research Center (2013) "The New Sick Man of Europe: The European Union," *Pew Survey Research* (May 13) https://www.pewresearch.org/global/2013/05/13/the-new-sick-man-of-europe-the-european-union/

Pianta, Mario (2013) "Democracy Lost: The Financial Crisis in Europe and the Role of Civil Society," *Journal of Civil Society* 9 (2): 148–61

Picot, Georg and Tassinari, Arianna (2017) "All of One Kind? Labour Market Reforms under Austerity in Italy and Spain," *SocioEconomic Review* 15 (2): 461–82

Piketty, Thomas (2014) *Capital in the Twenty-First Century* Cambridge, MA: Belknap Press of Harvard University

Piris, Jean-Claude (2012) *The Future of Europe: Toward a Two-Speed EU?* Cambridge: Cambridge University Press

Pirro, Andrea (2018) "The Polyvalent Populism of the 5 Star Movement," *Journal of Contemporary European Studies* 26 (4): 443–58

Pisani-Ferry, Jean (2006) "Only One Bed for Two Dreams: A Critical Retrospective on the Debate over the Economic Governance of the Euro Area," *Journal of Common Market Studies* 44 (4): 823–44

Pitkin, Hannah (1967) *The Concept of Representation* Berkeley, CA: University of California Press

Pochet, Philippe (2010) *What's Wrong with EU2020?* European Trade Union Institute Policy Brief, European Social Policy 2

Pogge, Thomas (2002) *World Poverty and Human Rights: Cosmopolitan Responsibilities and Reforms.* Cambridge, MA: Polity Press

Pollitt, Christopher, and Bouckaert, Geert (2011) *Public Management Reform: A Comparative Analysis of New Public Management, Governance, and the Neo-Weberian State* Oxford: Oxford University Press

Prodi, Romano (2001) "Italy, Europe," *Daedalus* 130 (2): 7–12

Prosser, Thomas (2017) "Insiders and Outsiders on a European Scale," *European Journal of Industrial Relations* 23 (2): 135–50

Ptak, R. (2009) "Neoliberalism in Germany," in *The Mont Pèlerin Society*, eds P. Mirowski and D. Plehwe. Cambridge, MA: Harvard University Press

Puetter, Uwe (2012) "Europe's Deliberative Intergovernmentalism," *Journal of European Public Policy* 19 (2): 161–78

Puetter, Uwe (2014) *The European Council and the Council: New Intergovernmentalism and Institutional Change* Oxford: Oxford University Press

Quatremer, Jean (2016) *Liberation* (June 12) http://www.liberation.fr/auteur/1876-jean-quatremer

Quatremer, Jean (2019) *Il Faut Achever l'Euro* Paris: Calmann-Lévy

Radaelli, Claudio (2002) "The Italian State and the Euro" in *The European State and the Euro*, ed. K. Dyson. Oxford: Oxford University Press

Rasmussen, Maja Kluger (2015) "The Battle for Influence: The Politics of Business Lobbying in the European Parliament," *Journal of Common Market Studies* 53 (2): 365–82

Raudla, Ringa, Cepilovs, Aleksandrs, Kattel, Rainer, and Sutt, Linda (2018) "The European Union as a Trigger of Discursive Change: The Impact of the Structural Deficit in Estonia and Latvia," *Central European Journal of Public Policy* 12 (2): 1–15

Rauh, Christian (2016) *A Responsive Technocracy: EU Politicisation and the Consumer Politics of the European Commission* Colchester, UK: ECPR Press

Regan, Aidan and Brazys, Samuel (2018) "Celtic Phoenix or Leprechaun Economics? The Politics of an FDI-led Growth Model in Europe," *New Political Economy* 28 (3): 223–38

Rehn, Olli (2013) "Recovery Is Within Reach," August 13, 2013 http://blogs.ec.europa.eu/rehn/recovery-is-within-reach/

Reynié, Dominique (2016) "'Heritage Populism' and France's National Front," *Journal of Democracy* 27 (4): 47–57

Riera, Pedro and Russo, Luana (2016) "Breaking the Cartel: The Geography of the Electoral Support of New Parties in Italy and Spain," *Italian Political Science Review/Rivista Italiana di Scienza Politica* 46 (2): 219–41

Risse, Thomas (2010) *A Community of Europeans?* Ithaca, NY: Cornell University Press

Risse, Thomas, ed. (2015) *European Public Spheres* Oxford: Oxford University Press

Risse, Thomas and Kleine, Marieke (2007) "Assessing the Legitimacy of the EU's Treaty Revision Methods," *Journal of Common Market Studies* 45 (1): 69–80

Rittberger, B. (2003) "The Creation and Empowerment of the European Parliament," *Journal of Common Market Studies* 41 (2): 203–25

Rittberger, Berthold (2005) *Building Europe's Parliament: Democratic Representation beyond the Nation State* Oxford: Oxford University Press

Rittberger, Berthold (2014) "Integration without Representation? The European Parliament and the Reform of Economic Governance in the EU," *Journal of Common Market Studies* 52 (6): 1174–83

Rittberger, Berthold and Schroeder, Philipp (2016) "The Legitimacy of Regional Institutions" in *The Oxford Handbook of Comparative Regionalism*, eds Tanja A. Boerzel and Thomas Risse. Oxford: Oxford University Press

Rodríguez-Pose, A. (2018) "The Revenge of the Places that Don't Matter (and What to Do About It)," *Cambridge Journal of Regions, Economy and Society* 11 (1): 189–209

Rodrik, Dani (2011) *The Globalization Paradox: Democracy and the Future of the World Economy* New York: Norton

Rodrik, Dani (2018) "Populism and the Economics of Globalization," *Journal of International Business Policy* 1: 12–33

Roederer-Rynning, Christine and Greenwood, Justin (2015) "The Culture of Trilogues," *Journal of European Public Policy* 22 (8): 1148–65

Rosanvallon, Pierre (2011) *Democratic Legitimacy: Impartiality, Reflexivity, Proximity* Princeton: Princeton University Press

Roseman, Mark (2002) *The Villa, The Lake, The Meeting: Wannsee and the Final Solution* London: Allen Lane

Roth, Alexander and Wolff, Guntram (2018) "Understanding (the Lack of) German Public Investment," Bruegel blog post, June 19

Rubio, Eulalia (2015) "Federalizing the Eurozone: Towards a True European Budget?" *Istituto Affari Internazionali*, Working Paper 15/50 (Dec. 28) iaiwp1550.pdf

Ruggie, John (1982) "International Regimes, Transactions, and Change: Embedded Liberalism in the Postwar Economic Order," *International Organization* 36: 379–415

Ruzza, Carlo and Della Sala, Vincent, eds (2007) *Governance and Civil Society* Manchester: Manchester University Press

Sabatier, Paul (1993) "Policy Change over a Decade or More" in H. C. Jenkins-Smith and P. Sabatier, *Policy Change and Learning: An Advocacy Coalition Approach* Boulder, CO: Westview

Sabel, Charles F. and Zeitlin, Jonathan (2010) *Experimentalist Governance in the European Union: Towards a New Architecture.* Oxford: Oxford University Press

Sacchi, Stefano (2015) "Conditionality by Other Means: EU Involvement in Italy's Structural Reforms in the Sovereign Debt Crisis," *Comparative European Politics* 13 (1): 77–92

Sacchi, Stefano (2018) "The Italian Welfare State in the Crisis: Learning to Adjust?" *South European Society and Politics* 23 (1): 29–46

Salines, Marion, Glöckler, Gabriel, and Truchiewski, Zbigniew (2012) "Existential Crisis, Incremental Response: The Eurozone's Dual Institutional Evolution 2007–2011," *Journal of European Public Policy* 19 (5): 665–81

Sanchez Salgado, Rosa (2014) "Rebalancing EU Interest Representation? Associative Democracy and EU Funding of Civil Society Organizations," *Journal of Common Market Studies* 52 (2): 337–353

Sandbu, Martin (2015) *Europe's Orphan: The Future of the Euro and the Politics of Debt* Princeton, NJ: Princeton University Press

Sandholtz, Wayne, and Stone Sweet, Alec, eds (1998) *European Integration and Supranational Governance* Oxford: Oxford University Press

Sapir, André Wolff, Guntram de Sousa, Carlos, and Terzi, Alessio (2014) "The Troika and Financial Assistance in the Euro Area: Successes and Failures." Report for the European Parliament's Economic and Monetary Affairs Committee. http://bruegel.org/2014/02/the-troika-and-financial-assistance-in-the-euro-area-successes-and-failures/

Sauerbrey, Anna (2015) "European Political Poker," *International New York Times* (August 10) http://www.nytimes.com/2015/08/10/opinion/anna-sauerbrey-european-political-poker.html?_r=0

Savage, James and Verdun, Amy (2016) "Strengthening the European Commission's Budgetary and Economic Surveillance Capacity Since Greece and the Euro Area Crisis," *Journal of European Public Policy* 23 (1): 101–18

Scharpf, Fritz W. (1970) *Demokratietheorie zwischen Utopie und Anpassung* Konstanz: Universitätsverlag

Scharpf, Fritz W. (1988) "The Joint Decision Trap," *Public Administration* 66 (3), 239–78

Scharpf, Fritz W. (1999) *Governing in Europe* Oxford: Oxford University Press

Scharpf, Fritz W. (2010) "The Asymmetry of European Integration, or Why the EU Cannot Be a Social Market Economy," *Socio-Economic Review* 8 (2): 211–50

Scharpf, Fritz W. (2012a) "Monetary Union, Fiscal Crisis and the Pre-emption of Democracy," in Joachim Jens Hesse, ed., *Zeitschrift für Staats- und Europawissenschaften* 9 (2): 163–98 http://www.zse.nomos.de/fileadmin/zse/doc/Aufsatz_ZSE_11_02.pdf

Scharpf, Fritz W. (2012b) "Legitimacy Intermediation in the Multilevel European Polity and Its Collapse in the Eurocrisis," MPIfG Discussion Paper 12/6 http://www.mpifg.de/pu/mpifg_dp/dp12-6.pdf

Scharpf, Fritz W. (2013) "Monetary Union, Fiscal Crisis and the Disabling of Democratic Accountability" in *Politics in the Age of Austerity*, eds A. Schäfer and W. Streeck. Cambridge: Polity

Scharpf, Fritz W. (2014) "After the Crash: A Perspective on Multilevel European Democracy," *MPIfG Discussion Paper 14/21*, Cologne: Max Planck Institute for the Study of Societies

Scharpf, Fritz W. (2015) "Political Legitimacy in a Non-Optimal Currency Area" in *Democratic Politics in a European Union under Stress*, eds Olaf Cramme and Sara B. Hobolt. Oxford: Oxford University Press

Scharpf, Fritz W. and Schmidt, Vivien A. (2000) *Welfare and Work in the Open Economy* Vol I: *From Vulnerability to Competitiveness* Oxford: Oxford University Press

Schelkle, Waltraud (2009) "The Contentious Creation of the Regulatory State in Fiscal Surveillance," *West European Politics* 32 (4): 829–46

Schelkle, Waltraud (2015) "The Insurance Potential of a Non-Optimum Currency Area" in *Democratic Politics in a European Union under Stress*, eds O. Cramme and S. Hobolt. Oxford: Oxford University Press

Schelkle, Waltraud (2017) *The Political Economy of Monetary Solidarity: Understanding the Euro Experiment* Oxford: Oxford University Press

Scheoller, Magnus G. (2018) "The Rise and Fall of Merkozy: Franco-German Bilateralism as a Negotiation Strategy in Eurozone Crisis Management," *Journal of Common Market Studies* 56 (5): 1019–35

Schild, Joachim (2013) "Leadership in Hard Times: Germany, France, and the Management of the Eurozone Crisis," *German Politics and Society* 31 (1): 24–47

Schillemans, Thomas (2011) "Does Horizontal Accountability Work?" *Administration & Society* 43 (4): 387–416

Schimmelfennig, Frank (2014) "European Integration in the Euro Crisis: The Limits of Postfunctionalism," *Journal of European Integration* 36 (3): 321–37

Schimmelfennig, Frank (2015a) "Liberal Intergovernmentalism and the Euro Area Crisis," *Journal of European Public Policy* 22 (2): 177–95

Schimmelfennig, Frank (2015b) "What's the News in 'New Intergovernmentalism'? A Critique of Bickerton, Hodson and Puetter," *Journal of Common Market Studies* 53: 723–30

Schimmelfennig, Frank (2018) "European Integration (Theory) in Times of Crisis: A Comparison of the Euro and Schengen Crises," *Journal of European Public Policy* 25 (7): 969–89

Schimmelfennig, Frank (2019) "Getting around No: How Governments React to Negative EU Referendums," *Journal of European Public Policy* 26 (7): 1056–74

Schmidt, Susanne K. (2018) *The European Court of Justice and the Policy Process: The Shadow of Case Law* Oxford: Oxford University Press

Schmidt, Vivien A. (2002) *The Futures of European Capitalism* Oxford: Oxford University Press

Schmidt, Vivien A. (2006) *Democracy in Europe* Oxford: Oxford University Press

Schmidt, Vivien A. (2008) "Discursive Institutionalism: The Explanatory Power of Ideas and Discourse," *Annual Review of Political Science* 11: 303–26

Schmidt, Vivien A. (2009a) "Re-Envisioning the European Union: Identity, Democracy, Economy," *Journal of Common Market Studies* 47 Annual Review 17–42

Schmidt, Vivien A. (2009b) "Putting the Political Back into Political Economy by Bringing the State Back Yet Again," *World Politics* 61 (3): 516–48

Schmidt, Vivien A. (2010a) "Taking Ideas and Discourse Seriously: Explaining Change through Discursive Institutionalism as the Fourth 'New Institutionalism'" *European Political Science Review* 2 (1): 1–25

Schmidt, Vivien A. (2010b) "The European Union's Eurozone Crisis and What (not) to do about it," *Brown Journal of World Affairs* 17 (1): 199–214

Schmidt, Vivien A. (2011) "Can Technocratic Government Be Democratic?" *Telos* (Nov. 23) http://www.telos-eu.com/en/article/can-technocratic-government-be-democratic

Schmidt, Vivien A. (2012a) "Discursive Institutionalism: Scope, Dynamics, and Philosophical Underpinnings" in *The Argumentative Turn Revised: Public Policy as Communicative Practice*, eds Frank Fischer and Herbert Gottweis. Durham, NC: Duke University Press

Schmidt, Vivien A. (2012b) "What Happened to the State-Influenced Market Economies? France, Italy, and Spain Confront the Crisis as the Good, the Bad, and the Ugly" in *The Consequences of the Global Financial Crisis: The Rhetoric of Reform and Regulation*, eds Wyn Grant and Graham Wilson. Oxford: Oxford University Press

Schmidt, Vivien A. (2013) "Democracy and Legitimacy in the European Union Revisited: Input, Output *and* 'Throughput'," *Political Studies* 61 (1): 2–22

Schmidt, Vivien A. (2014) "Speaking to the Markets or to the People? A Discursive Institutionalist Analysis of EU Leaders' Discourse during the Eurozone Crisis," *British Journal of Politics and International Relations* 16 (1): 188–209

Schmidt, Vivien A. (2015a) "Forgotten Democratic Legitimacy: 'Governing by the Rules' and 'Ruling by the Numbers'" in *The Future of the Euro*, eds Matthias Matthijs and Mark Blyth. New York: Oxford University Press

Schmidt, Vivien A. (2015b) "Changing the Policies, Politics, and Processes of the Eurozone in Crisis: Will This Time Be Different?" in *Social Developments in the EU 2015*, eds David Natali and Bart Vanhercke. Brussels: European Social Observatory (OSE) and European Trade Union Institute (ETUI)

Schmidt, Vivien A. (2015c) "The Eurozone's Crisis of Democratic Legitimacy: Can the EU Rebuild Public Trust and Support for European Economic Integration?" Report prepared for the Commission, Directorate General for Economic and Financial Affairs (DG ECFIN), in partial completion of the DG ECFIN Fellowship Initiative 2014–2015 (June 22, 2015). DG ECFIN Discussion Paper 15 (Sept. 2015): https://ec.europa.eu/info/publications/economy-finance/eurozones-crisis-democratic-legitimacy-can-eu-rebuild-public-trust-and-support-european-economic-integration_en

Schmidt, Vivien A. (2016a) "Reinterpreting the Rules 'by Stealth' in Times of Crisis: The European Central Bank and the European Commission," *West European Politics* 39 (5): 1032–52

Schmidt, Vivien A. (2016c) "The Roots of Neo-Liberal Resilience: Explaining Continuity and Change in Background Ideas in Europe's Political Economy," *British Journal of Politics and International Relations* 18 (2): 318–34

Schmidt, Vivien A. (2017a) "Britain-Out and Trump-In: A Discursive Institutionalist Analysis of the British Referendum on the EU and the US Presidential Election," *Review of International Political Economy* 24 (2): 248–69

Schmidt, Vivien A. (2017b) "Theorizing Ideas and Discourse in Political Science: Intersubjectivity, Neo-Institutionalisms, and the Power of Ideas," *Critical Review* 29 (2): 248–26

Schmidt, Vivien A. (2017c) "Where Is the European Union Today? Will It Survive? Can it Revive? A Review Essay," *Perspectives on Politics* 15 (2): 495–502

Schmidt, Vivien A. (2018a) "Rethinking EU Governance: From 'Old' to 'New' Approaches," *Journal of Common Market Studies* 57 (7): 1544–61

Schmidt, Vivien A. (2018b) "The Past Decade and the Future of Governance and Democracy: Populist Challenges to Liberal Democracy" in *A Transcendent Decade: Toward a New Enlightenment?* BBVA Foundation, Madrid: Turner Publishing

Schmidt, Vivien A. (2019a) "Politicization in the EU: Between National Politics and EU Political Dynamics," *Journal of European Public Policy* 26 (7): 1018–36

Schmidt, Vivien A. (2019b) "The Future of Differentiated Integration: A 'Soft-Core' Multi-Clustered Europe of Overlapping Policy Communities," *Comparative European Politics* 17 (2): 294–315

Schmidt, Vivien A. and Luke, Michael (2019) "The Radical Center: An Empirical Analysis of New Party Families in Europe." Paper prepared for presentation at the Midwestern Political Science Association meetings (Chicago, IL, April 4–7)

Schmidt, Vivien A. and Thatcher, M. (2013) "The Resilience of Neo-Liberal Ideas" in *Resilient Liberalism: European Political Economy through Boom and Bust*, eds V. Schmidt and M. Thatcher. Cambridge: Cambridge University Press

Schmidt, Vivien A. and Wood, Matthew (2019) "Conceptualizing Throughput Legitimacy: Procedural Mechanisms of Accountability, Transparency, Inclusiveness and Openness in EU Governance," *Public Administration* 97 (4: 727–40)

Schmitt, Hermann and Thomassen, Jacques (1999) *Political Representation and Legitimacy in the European Union* Oxford: Oxford University Press

Schoenmaker, Dirk and Gros, Daniel (2012) "A European Deposit Insurance and Resolution Fund." DSF Policy Paper n. 21 (May)

Schön-Quinlivan, Emmanuelle and Scipioni, Marco (2017) "An Exploratory Analysis of the Politicization of the European Commission Macroeconomic Policy Positioning, 2010–2017." Paper prepared for presentation at the Council for European Studies Conference (Glasgow, July 12–14)

Scipioni, Marco (2018) "*De Novo* Bodies and EU Integration: What Is the Story behind EU Agencies' Expansion?" *Journal of Common Market Studies* 56 (4): 768–78

Seabrooke, Leonard and Eleni Tsingou (2016) "Bodies of Knowledge in Reproduction: Epistemic Boundaries in the Political Economy of Fertility," *New Political Economy* 21 (1): 69–89

Seabrooke, Leonard and Eleni Tsingou (2018) "Europe's Fast and Slow Burning Crises," *Journal of European Public Policy* 26 (3): 468–81

Siani-Davies, Peter (2017) *Crisis in Greece* London: C. Hurst & Co.

Simmons, Katie, Silver, Laura, Johnson, Courtney, Taylor, Kyle and Wike, Richard (2018) "In Western Europe, Populist Parties Tap Anti-Establishment Frustration but Have Little Appeal across Ideological Divide," Pew Research Center (July 12) http://assets. pewresearch.org/wp-content/uploads/sites/2/2018/07/12092128/Pew-Research-Center_Western-Europe-Political-Ideology-Report_2018-07–12.pdf

Skidelsky, Robert. (2013) "Austere Illusions," *Social Europe* (May 22) http://www.social-europe.eu/2013/05/austere-illusions/

Smismans, Stijn (2003) "European Civil Society: Shaped by Discourses and Institutional Interests," *European Law Journal* 9 (4): 473–95

Smith, Melanie (2012) "Developing Administrative Principles in the EU: A Foundational Model of Legitimacy?" *European Law Journal* 18 (2): 269–88

Spiegel, Peter (2014) "If the Euro Falls, Europe Falls," *Financial Times* (May 14, 15, 17)

Standring, Adam (2018) "Depoliticising Austerity: Narratives of the Portuguese Debt Crisis 2011–15," *Policy and Politics* 46 (1): 149–64

Stasavage, David (2004) "Open-Door or Closed-Door? Transparency in Domestic and International Bargaining," *International Organization* 58(4): 667–703

Stavrakakis, Yannis (2015) "Populism in Power: Syriza's Challenge to Europe," *Juncture* 21 (4): 273–80

Stavrakakis, Yannis. and Katsambekis, Giorgios (2014) "Left-Wing Populism in the European Periphery: The Case of SYRIZA," *Journal of Political Ideologies* 19 (2): 119–42

Steffek, Jens (2015) "The Output Legitimacy of International Organizations and the Global Public Interest," *International Theory* 7 (2): 263–93

Steffek, Jens (2019) "The Limits of Proceduralism: Critical Remarks on the Rise of 'Throughput Legitimacy'," *Public Administration* 97 (4): 784–96s

Sternberg, Claudia S. (2015) "Political Legitimacy between Democracy and Effectiveness," *European Political Science Review* 7 (4): 615–38

Sternberg, Claudia S., Gartzou-Katsouyanni, Kira, and Nicholaidis, Kalypso (2018) *The Greco-German Affair in the Euro Crisis: Mutual Recognition Lost?* London: Palgrave Macmillan

Stockemer, D. and Amengay, A. (2015) "The Voters of the FN under Jean-Marie Le Pen and Marine Le Pen: Continuity or Change?" *French Politics* 13 (4): 370–90

Stone Sweet, Alec, Sandholtz, Wayne and Fligstein, Neil, eds (2001) *The Institutionalization of Europe* Oxford: Oxford University Press

Storm, S. and Naastepad, C. W. M. (2015) "NAIRU Economics and the Eurozone Crisis," *International Review of Applied Economics* 29 (6): 843–77

Streeck, Wolfgang (2013) *Buying Time: The Delayed Crisis of Democratic Capitalism* London: Verso

Streeck, Wolfgang and Elsässer, Lea, (2017) Monetary Disunion: The Domestic Politics of Euroland, MPIfG Discussion Paper 14/ 17 http://www.mpifg.de/pu/mpifg_dp/dp14-17.pdf

Strudel, Sylvie (2019) "Quand le premier de cordée dévisse" in *Histoire d'une Révolution Électorale (2015–2018)*, eds Bruno Cautrès and Anne Muxel. Paris: Classiques Garnier

Syriza (2014) The Thessaloniki Programme (September 13) https://www.syriza.gr/article/ id/59907/SYRIZA---THE-THESSALONIKI-PROGRAMME.html

Szczerbiak, Aleks and Taggart, Paul (2008) *Opposing Europe? The Comparative Party Politics of Euroscepticism* Vol. 2. Oxford: Oxford University Press

Taggart, Paul (2000) *Populism* Buckingham: Open University Press

Taggart, Paul and Szczerbiak, Aleks. (2013) "Coming in from the Cold? Euroscepticism, Government Participation and Party Positions on Europe," *Journal of Common Market Studies* 51 (1): 17–37

Taguieff, Pierre André (1984) "La Rhétorique du national-populisme," *Mots* 9: 113–38

Tallberg, Jonas and Zürn, Michael (2019) "The Legitimacy and Legitimation of International Organisations: Introduction and Framework," *Review of International Organizations* 14: 581–606

Teague, Paul and Donaghey, James (2004) "The Irish Experiment in Social Partnership," in H. Katz, W. Lee, and J. Lee (eds), *The New Structure of Labour Relations*. Ithaca, NY: Cornell University Press

Teinturier, Brice and Lama, Amandine (2019) "La stupéfaction face à l'incroyable chute de François Fillon" in *Histoire d'une Révolution Électorale (2015–2018)*, eds Bruno Cautrès and Anne Muxel. Paris: Classiques Garnier

Thatcher, Mark (2013) "Supranational Neo-Liberalization: The EU's Regulatory Model of Economic Markets" in *Resilient Liberalism: European Political Economy through Boom and Bust*, eds Vivien A. Schmidt and Mark Thatcher. Cambridge: Cambridge University Press

Thelen, Kathleen (2004) *How Institutions Evolve: The Political Economy of Skills in Germany, Britain, the United States, and Japan*. New York: Cambridge University Press

Thompson, Dennis F. (2008) 'Deliberative democratic theory and empirical political science', *Annual Review of Political Science* 11: 497–520

Thompson, Helen (2015) "Germany and the Eurozone Crisis," *New Political Economy* 20 (6): 851–70

Tilford, Simon and Springford, John (2013) *New York Times* (Dec. 2) http://www.nytimes. com/2013/12/03/opinion/deflating-german-excuses.html

Tocci, Natalie (2014) "Imagining Post-Crisis Europe," *Imagining Europe* Istituto Affari Internazionali Working Paper no. 10 (June)

Todd, Emanuel (1998) *L'Illusion Économique* Paris: Gallimard

Tooze, Adam (2018) *Crashed: How a Decade of Financial Crises Changed the World* New York: Viking

Torres, Francisco (2006) "On the Efficiency-Legitimacy Trade-off in EMU" in *EMU Rules: The Political and Economic Consequences of European Monetary Integration*, eds Francisco Torres, Amy Verdun and Hans Zimmerman. Baden-Baden: Nomos

Tortola, Piero (2019) "The Politicisation of the European Central Bank: What Is It, and How to Study It," *Journal of Common Market Studies* early view: https://doi.org/10.1111/ jcms.12973

Tortola, Piero and Pansardi, Pamela (2018) "The Charismatic Leadership of the ECB Presidency: A Language-Based Analysis" *European Journal of Political Research* 58 (1): 96–116

Toulmin, Stephen (1958) *The Uses of Argument* Cambridge: Cambridge University Press

Treib, Oliver (2014) "The Voter Says No but Nobody Listens: Causes and Consequences of the Eurosceptic vote in the 2014 European Elections," *Journal of European Public Policy* 21 (10): 1541–54

Trenz, Hans-Jörg and Eder, Klaus (2004) "The Democratizing Dynamics of a European Public Sphere," *European Journal of Social Theory* 7 (1): 5–25

Trichet, Jean-Claude (2009) "Introductory Comments with Q and A," European Central Bank, Press Conference (May 7). http://www.ecb.europa.eu/press/pressconf/2009/html/is090507.en.html)

Tronconi, F, ed. (2015) *Beppe Grillo's Five Star Movement: Organisation, Communication and Ideology* Farnham: Ashgate Publishing

Tsebelis, George (1994) "The Power of the European Parliament as a Conditional Agenda Setter," *American Political Science Review* 88 (1): 128–42

Tsebelis, George (2016) "Lessons from the Greek Crisis," *Journal of European Public Policy* 23 (1): 25–41

Tsingou, E. (2014) "Club Governance and the Making of Global Financial Rules," *Review of International Political Economy* 22 (2): 225–56

Tsoukalis, Loukas (2016) *In Defense of Europe* Oxford: Oxford University Press

Tucker, Paul (2018) *Unelected Power: The Quest for Legitimacy in Central Banking and the Regulatory State* Princeton: Princeton University Press

Urbinati, Nadia (2006) *Representative Democracy: Principles and Genealogy* Chicago: University of Chicago Press

Usherwood, Simon and Startin, Nick (2013) "Euroscepticism as a Persistent Phenomenon," *Journal of Common Market Studies* 51(1): 1–16

Vail, Mark I. (2018) *Liberalism in Illiberal States: Ideas and Economic Adjustment in Contemporary Europe* Oxford: Oxford University Press

Van der Brug, W. and de Vreese, C. H., eds (2016) *(Un)intended Consequences of European Parliamentary Elections* Oxford: Oxford University Press

Van der Eijk, Cees and Franklin, Mark (2007) "The Sleeping Giant," in Wouter Van der Brug and Cees Van der Eijk, eds. *European Elections and Domestic Politics*. Notre Dame: University of Notre Dame Press

Van Esch, Femke A. W. J. (2017) "The Paradoxes of Legitimate EU Leadership," *Journal of European Integration* 39 (2): 223–37

Van Elsas, Erika J., Hakhverdian, Armen and van der Brug, Wouter (2016) "United against a Common Foe? The Nature and Origins of Euroscepticism among Left-Wing and Right-Wing Citizens," *West European Politics* 39 (6): 1181–204

Van Middelaar, Luuk (2013) *The Passage to Europe: How a Continent Became a Union* London: Yale University Press

Van Middelaar, Luuk (2019) *Alarums & Excursions: Improvising Politics on the European Stage* Newcastle upon Tyne: Agenda Publishing

Van Rompuy, Herman et al. (2012) "Towards a Genuine Economic and Monetary Union" (5 Dec.)

Vanheuverzwijn, Pierre and Crespy, Amandine (2018) "Macro-Economic Coordination and Elusive Ownership in the European Union," *Public Administration* 96 (3): 578–93

Varoufakis, Yanis (2016) *And the Weak Suffer What They Must? Europe, Austerity and the Threat to Global Stability* London: The Bodley Head (Vintage)

Varoufakis, Yanis (2017) *Adults in the Room: My Battle with Europe's Deep Establishment* London: The Bodley Head (Vintage)

Vasileva-Dienes, Alexandra and Schmidt, Vivien (2018) "Conceptualizing Capitalism in the 21st Century: The BRICs and the European Periphery" *Contemporary Politics* 25 (3): 255–75

Vasilopoulou, S. (2018) "The Party Politics of Euroscepticism in Times of Crisis: The Case of Greece," *Politics*. Online First http://eprints.whiterose.ac.uk/128036/

Vauchez, Antoine (2015) *Democratizing Europe* Basingstoke: Palgrave

Verdun, Amy (1999) "The Role of the Delors Committee in the Creation of EMU: An Epistemic Community?" *Journal of European Public Policy* 6 (2): 308–28

Verdun, Amy (2015) "A Historical Institutionalist Explanation of the EU's Responses to the Euro Area Financial Crisis" *Journal of European Public Policy* 22 (2): 219–37

Verdun, Amy and Zeitlin, Jonathan (2018) "Introduction: the European Semester as a new architecture of EU socioeconomic governance in theory and practice", *Journal of European Public Policy*, 25 (2): 137–148

Vesan, Patrik and Corti, Francesco (2019) "New tensions over Social Europe? The European Pillar of Social Rights and the Debate within the European Parliament," *Journal Common Market Studies* 57(5): 977–994

Warren, Thomas (2018) "The European Parliament and the Eurozone Crisis: An Exceptional Actor?" *British Journal of Politics and International Relations* 16 (1): 188–209

Warren, Thomas, Holden, Patrick, and Howell, Kerry E. (2017) "The European Commission and Fiscal Governance Reform: A Strategic Actor?" *West European Politics* 40 (6): 1310–30

Weaver, Catherine (2008) *Hypocrisy Trap: The World Bank and the Poverty of Reform* Princeton University Press

Weber, Max (1946) "Politics as a Vocation" in *Max Weber: Essays in Sociology* translated and edited by H. H. Gerth and C. Wright Mills. New York: Oxford University Press

Weber, Max (1978) *Economy and Society*, edited by Guenther Roth and Claus Wittich. Berkeley: University of California Press

Webber, Douglas, ed. (1999) *The Franco-German Relationship in the European Union* London: Routledge

Webber, Douglas (2019) "Trends in European Political (Dis)integration: An Analysis of Postfunctionalist and Other Explanations," *Journal of European Public Policy* 26 (8): 1134–52

Weiler, Joseph H. H. (1995) "The State 'Uber Alles': Demos, Telos and the German Maastricht Decision," Jean Monnet Working Paper Series 6/95, Cambridge: Harvard Law School

Weiler, Joseph H. H. (1996) "European Neo-Constitutionalism: In Search of Foundations for the European Constitutional Order," *Political Studies* 44 (3): 517–33

Weiler, Joseph H. H. (1999) *The Constitution of Europe*. Cambridge: Cambridge University Press

Werner, Pierre (1970) *Report to the Council and the Commission on the Realisation by Stages of Economic and Monetary Union in the Community* (Werner Report), Supplement to Bulletin No. 11, http://aei.pitt.edu/1002

Wessels, Wolfgang and Rozenberg, Olivier (2013) "Democratic Control in the Member States of the European Council and the Euro Zone Summits". *Study PE 474.392.* http://www.europarl.europa.eu/RegData/etudes/etudes/join/2013/474392/IPOLAFCO_ET(2013)474392_EN.pdf

White, Jonathan (2015) "Emergency Europe," *Political Studies* 63 (2): 300–318

Wille, Anchrit (2010) "The European Commission's Accountability Paradox" in *The Real World of EU Accountability*, eds M. Bovens, D. Curtin, and P. t'Hart. Oxford: Oxford University Press

Williams, Shirley (1991) "Sovereignty and Accountability in the European Community" in *The New European Community*, eds R. Keohand and S. Hoffmann. Boulder, CO: Westview Press

Wilson, James Q. (1980) *The Politics of Regulation* New York: Basic Books

Wimmel, Andreas (2009) "Theorizing the Democratic Legitimacy of European Governance: A Labyrinth with No Exit?" *European Integration* 31 (2): 181–99

Wodak, Ruth (2015) *The Politics of Fear: What Right Wing Populist Discourses Mean* London: Sage

Wolf, Martin (2013) *Financial Times* (September 24)

Wonka, Arndt (2007) "Technocratic and Independent? The Appointment of European Commissioners and Its Policy Implications," *Journal of European Public Policy* 14 (2): 169–89

Wood, Matthew (2015) "Beyond Accountability: Political Legitimacy and Delegated Water Governance in Australia," *Public Administration* 93 (4): 1012–30

Wren, Anne (2013) "Introduction: The Political Economy of Post-Industrial Societies" in *The Political Economy of the Service Transition*, ed. A. Wren. Oxford: Oxford University Press

Zaller, John R. (1992) *The Nature and Origins of Mass Opinion* New York: Cambridge University Press

Zapatero, José Luis Rodriguez (2013) *El Dilema: 600 Días de Vértigo* Barcelona: Editorial Planeta

Zeitlin, Jonathan and Vanhercke, Bart (2014) "Socializing the European Semester? Economic Governance and Social Policy Coordination in Europe 2020." Report prepared for the Swedish Institute of European Studies (SIEPS)

Zeitlin, Jonathan and Vanhercke, Bart (2018) "Socializing the European Semester: EU Social and Economic Policy Coordination in Crisis and Beyond," *Journal of European Public Policy* 25 (2): 149–74

Zürn, Michael (2000) "Democratic Governance beyond the Nation-State," *European Journal of International Relations* 6 (2): 183–221

Zürn, Michael (2016) "Opening Up Europe: Next Steps in Politicisation Research," *West European Politics* 39 (1): 164–82

Zürn, Michael (2019) "Politicization Compared: At National, European, and Global Levels," *Journal of European Public Policy* 26 (7): 977–55

Zürn, Michael, Binder, Martin, and Ecker-Ehrhardt, Matthias (2012) "International Authority and Its Politicisation," *International Theory* 4 (1): 60–106

Index

For the benefit of digital users, indexed terms that span two pages (e.g., 52–53) may, on occasion, appear on only one of those pages.